MW01233783

Sydney, Australia, 1899

Ellen G. White

LIFE SKETCHES
OF ELLEN G. WHITE

BEING A NARRATIVE OF HER EXPERIENCE TO 1881 AS WRITTEN BY HERSELF WITH A SKETCH OF HER SUBSEQUENT LABORS AND OF HER LAST SICKNESS COMPILED FROM ORIGINAL SOURCES

Pacific Press® Publishing Association
Nampa, Idaho
Oshawa, Ontario, Canada
www.pacificpress.com

PACIFIC
PRESS
PUB.
ASSN.
LITHO
IN
U.S.A.

PREFACE

The story of the early Christian experience and public labors of Mrs. Ellen G. White was first printed in the year 1860, in a little volume of three hundred pages, entitled, "My Christian Experience, Views, and Labors, in Connection with the Rise and Progress of the Third Angel's Message."

This narrative of her life and labors to 1860, was amplified by her, and was republished in 1880 as a part of a larger work, entitled, "Life Sketches of James White and Ellen G. White." This, as well as the earlier autobiography, has long been out of print.

In the present volume will be found, as told in her own language, a brief story of her childhood days, her conversion, and her early Christian experiences in connection with the great second advent movement of 1840 to 1844. In a vivid way she tells of the sorrows and joys of her youthful ministry in the years that followed. She pictures the trials, the struggles, and the successes that attended the labors of a few earnest souls from whose endeavors sprang the churches that afterward united to form the Seventh-day Adventist denomination.

The story of her more extended travels and labors in connection with her husband, Elder James White, she briefly relates from the time of their marriage in 1846 to his death in 1881.

With chapter forty-two, on page 255, her life-story is continued by C. C. Crisler, who, with the assistance of her son, W. C. White, and D. E. Robinson, has completed the sketch.

In the closing chapters many interesting incidents regarding travels and labors have been passed over briefly, in order that place might be found for the quotation of some of her most inspiring and instructive utterances regarding the development of Christian experience, and the duty laid upon every follower of Christ to be a true disciple of Him who gave His life for the salvation of the world. The final pages give an account of her last sickness, and of the funeral services.

Of Mrs. White it may assuredly be said, "She hath done what she could." Hers was a life filled with inspiration for all engaged in soul-winning service.

PUBLISHERS.

CONTENTS

I. CHILDHOOD 17-19
Misfortune
Education

II. CONVERSION 20-25
Early Impressions
A Spiritual Revival
Righteousness by Faith
The Burden Lifted
"In Newness of Life"
Uniting with the Methodist Church

III. STRIVINGS AGAINST DOUBT . . . 26-31
The Advent Cause in Portland
In Perplexity over Sanctification
The Doctrine of Eternal Punishment

IV. BEGINNING OF PUBLIC LABORS . 32-42
Dream of Temple and Lamb
Dream of Seeing Jesus
Friendly Sympathy and Counsel
My First Public Prayer
A View of the Father's Love
Bearing Testimony
Laboring for Young Friends

V. SEPARATION FROM THE CHURCH . 43-53
Doctrinal Differences
The Hope of the Second Advent
Last Testimony in Class Meeting
Spreading the Advent Message
The Immortality Question
The Pastor's Visit
The Church Trial

VI. The Disappointment of 1843-44 . 54-63
Meetings in Beethoven Hall
An Exhortation by Elder Brown
Joyous Expectancy
Days of Perplexity
An Error in Reckoning
Hope Renewed
A Trial of Faith
A Period of Preparation
The Passing of the Time

VII. My First Vision 64-68

VIII. Call to Travel 69-73
Encouragement from the Brethren
Fear of Self-Exaltation
Among the Believers in Maine

IX. Answers to Prayer . . . 74-76

X. Labors in New Hampshire . . 77-84
Encouragement for Elder Morse
A Lack of True Godliness
Spiritual Magnetism
Meeting at Brother Collier's
The "Cannot-Sin" Theory
True Sanctification

XI. Meeting Fanaticism . . . 85-94
A False Humility
Fruits of the "No-Work" Doctrine
The Dignity of Labor
A Severe Trial
Exhortations to Faithfulness
The Seal of Divine Approval
Lessons from the Past

XII. THE SABBATH OF THE LORD . . 95, 96

XIII. MARRIAGE AND UNITED LABORS . 97-104
In Confirmation of Faith
Fervent, Effectual Prayer
Labors in Massachusetts
A View of the Heavenly Sanctuary

XIV. STRUGGLES WITH POVERTY . . 105-109
First Visit to Connecticut
Conference at Rocky Hill
Earning Means to Visit Western New York

XV. LABORS IN WESTERN NEW YORK IN 1848 110-115
Conference at Volney
Visit to Brother Snow's — Hannibal
Meeting at Port Gibson
Visit to Brother Harris's — Centerport
Visit to Brother Abbey's — Brookfield

XVI. A VIEW OF THE SEALING . . 116-119

XVII. ENCOURAGING PROVIDENCES . . 120-124
Healing of Gilbert Collins
Healing of Sister Temple
The Family of Leonard Hastings
Moving to Connecticut in 1849
Living Waters — A Dream

XVIII. BEGINNING TO PUBLISH . . . 125-128
"The Present Truth"
Visit to Maine
Advancing by Faith
Residence in Oswego

XIX. Visiting the Scattered Flock . 129-135
At Camden, N. Y.
In Vermont
Rising above Despondency
In Canada East
The Meeting at Johnson, Vt.
Return to New York

XX. Publishing Again . . . 136-141
Satan's Efforts to Hinder
Triumphing Through Faith
The *Review and Herald*
Removal to Saratoga Springs

XXI. In Rochester, New York . . 142-147
Death of Robert Harmon
Pressing On
Conversion of the Office Foreman
Nathaniel and Anna White

XXII. Advancing under Difficulties . 148-156
First Visit to Michigan
Writing and Traveling
Deliverance from Disease
Visit to Michigan and Wisconsin — 1854
Return to Rochester
Death of Anna White

XXIII. Removal to Michigan . . . 157-159
Comforting Assurances
Captivity Turned

XXIV. Labors in the Middle West — 1856-58 160-163
A Victory at Waukon, Iowa
View at Lovett's Grove, Ohio
Writing "Spiritual Gifts," Vol. 1

XXV. Personal Trials 164-166
Efforts to Establish the Publishing Work
Parental Cares
Loss of Children

XXVI. Battling Against Disease . 167-172
The Sickness of Elder James White
Sojourn at Dansville, N. Y.
Seasons of Prayer and Blessing

XXVII. Conflicts and Victory . . 173-177
Labors at Wright, Mich.
At Greenville, Mich.
Visit to Battle Creek — March, 1867
Laying Hold on God

XXVIII. Among the Churches in New England 178-182
In Maine
Revival Services at Washington, N. H.
In Vermont and New York
Return to Michigan

XXIX. Reclaiming the Lost . . 183-189
An Encouraging Dream
Visiting Churches in Michigan
Caring for the Sick
Revival Meetings at Greenville
The Lost Sheep
En Route to Battle Creek
The General Conference of May, 1868

XXX. Traveling the Narrow Way . 190-193

XXXI. Burden Bearers . . . 194-196

XXXII. A Solemn Dream . . . 197-202

XXXIII. Missionary Work . . . 203-207

XXXIV. Broader Plans . . . 208-210

XXXV. Into All the World . . . 211-215
Special Preparation
Opening Providences
Sowing Beside All Waters
Publications in Many Languages
A Harvest of Precious Souls

XXXVI. Circulating the Printed Page 216-218

XXXVII. Public Labors in 1877 . . 219-228
Special Services for College Students
Temperance Meetings
On the Indiana Camp Ground
Walking Out by Faith
The Eastern Camp Meetings
Return to Michigan and California

XXXVIII. Visit to Oregon . . . 229-234
The Voyage
Meetings of Special Interest
A Prison Service
The Return Journey

XXXIX. From State to State . . 235-240
In Colorado
The New England Conference
Meeting in Maine
At Battle Creek
Kansas Camp Meetings
Visit to Texas

XL. A View of the Judgment . 241-246
Times of Test and Trial
A Call for Burden Bearers

XLI. The Death of Elder James White 247-254

XLII. Fortitude under Affliction . 255-260
Personal Reflections
Finding Rest in Labor for Souls
Special Efforts for the Youth

XLIII. Restoration of Health . . 261-266

XLIV. Writing and Speaking . . 267-280
Visit to Battle Creek
The Path of Obedience
Ripening for the Harvest
Lay Members as Missionaries for God
An Example of Self-Sacrifice
Filling Up the Ranks of Workers
Establishing Faith in Bible Truth
The General Conference of 1883
Closing Labors in the East

XLV. Labors in Central Europe . 281-290
The "Imprimerie Polyglotte"
Publishing Houses in Many Lands
The Sale of Literature
The Training of Colporteurs
Development Through Faithful Service
Visits to Italy

XLVI. LABORS IN GREAT BRITAIN AND SCANDINAVIA . . . 291-308
Consecration, Courage, Confidence
Dispelling the Darkness
First Visit to Scandinavia
Second Visit to Scandinavia
Fifth European Missionary Council
Efficiency in Missionary Service
"Go Forward!"
A Remarkable Development
Messages of Hope and Courage

XLVII. IN CONFIRMATION OF CONFIDENCE 309-318
Proposals Regarding Centralization
Suggested Changes in Policy
Formal Consideration of Proposed Changes
A Special Committee Council
The Sabbath Service

XLVIII. DANGER IN ADOPTING WORLDLY POLICY IN THE WORK OF GOD . 319-330

XLIX. ACROSS THE PACIFIC . . . 331-343
The Voyage
The Australian Conference Meeting
Consideration of School Interests
Sickness, and Change of Plans
The Opening of the Australasian Bible School
Encompassed by Infirmities
A Review of Experience
The Australian Conference of January, 1893
Labors in New Zealand

L. THE FIRST AUSTRALIAN CAMP MEETING 344-348

LI. THE AVONDALE SCHOOL . . . 349-378
Work and Education
Looking for a Suitable Property
An Industrial Experiment
A Beautiful Dream
Help from Friends in Africa
Putting Up the First Buildings
Another Test of Faith
Aims and Objects
Missionary Labor the Highest Training
Fields White unto the Harvest
A Training Ground for Mission Fields
After Many Years

LII. THROUGH THE SOUTH TO THE CONFERENCE OF 1901 . . . 379-387
Centers of Influence and of Training
Special Opportunities in the South
Institutional Training in Many Lands
Self-Supporting Missionaries
Reorganization

LIII. AT THE NATION'S CAPITAL . . 388-398
From Battle Creek to the East
In Search of a Site
Favorable Conditions at Takoma Park, D. C.
An Advance Step
Words of Encouragement
"Arise, and Build"

LIV. In Southern California . . 399-406

LV. The San Francisco Earthquake . 407-415
Retributive Judgments
Working the Cities from Outpost Centers
Scenes of Destruction
Warnings and Exhortations
Calls to Repentance

LVI. At the 1909 General Conference . 416-424
A Representative Gathering
The Work in the Cities
Special Efforts in New England
Delegations from Abroad
Strife among the Nations
Important Counsels

LVII. Closing Labors 425-439
Personal Activities
The Pioneers of the Message
Giving the Trumpet a Certain Sound
Book Manuscript Work
A Solemn Charge

LVIII. Last Sickness 440-449

LIX. The "Elmshaven" Funeral Service 450-455

LX. The Memorial Service at Richmond 456-461

LXI. The Funeral Services at Battle Creek 462-480
In the Tabernacle
Address by Elder Daniells
Discourse by Elder Haskell
At the Grave

LIFE SKETCHES

I

CHILDHOOD

I was born at Gorham, Maine, Nov. 26, 1827. My parents, Robert and Eunice Harmon, were for many years residents of this State. In early life they became earnest and devoted members of the Methodist Episcopal Church. In that church they held prominent connection, and labored for the conversion of sinners, and to build up the cause of God, for a period of forty years. During this time they had the joy of seeing their children, eight in number, all converted and gathered into the fold of Christ.

MISFORTUNE

While I was but a child, my parents removed from Gorham to Portland, Maine. Here, at the age of nine years, an accident happened to me which was to affect my whole life. In company with my twin sister and one of our schoolmates, I was crossing a common in the city of Portland, when a girl about thirteen years of age, becoming angry at some trifle, threw a stone that hit me on the nose. I was stunned by the blow, and fell senseless to the ground.

When consciousness returned, I found myself in a merchant's store. A kind stranger offered to take me home in his carriage, but I, not realizing my weakness, told him that I preferred to walk. Those present were not aware that my injury was so serious, and allowed me to go; but after walking only a few rods, I grew faint and dizzy. My twin sister and my schoolmate carried me home.

I have no recollection of anything further for some time after the accident. My mother said that I noticed nothing, but lay in a stupor for three weeks. No one but herself thought it possible for me to recover, but for some reason she felt that I would live.

When I again aroused to consciousness, it seemed to me that I had been asleep. I did not remember the accident, and was ignorant of the cause of my illness. A great cradle had been made for me, and in it I lay for many weeks. I was reduced almost to a skeleton.

At this time I began to pray the Lord to prepare me for death. When Christian friends visited the family, they would ask my mother if she had talked with me about dying. I overheard this, and it roused me. I desired to become a Christian, and prayed earnestly for the forgiveness of my sins. I felt a peace of mind resulting, and loved every one, feeling desirous that all should have their sins forgiven, and love Jesus as I did.

I gained strength very slowly. As I became able to join in play with my young friends, I was forced to learn the bitter lesson that our personal appearance often makes a difference in the treatment we receive from our companions.

EDUCATION

My health seemed to be hopelessly impaired. For two years I could not breathe through my nose, and was able to attend school but little. It seemed impossible for me to study and to retain what I learned. The same girl who was the cause of my misfortune, was appointed monitor by our teacher, and it was among her duties to assist me in my writing and other lessons. She always seemed sincerely sorry for the great injury she had done me, although I was careful not to remind her of it. She was tender and patient with me, and seemed sad and thoughtful as she saw me laboring under serious disadvantages to get an education.

My nervous system was prostrated, and my hand trembled so that I made but little progress in writing, and could get no farther than the simple copies in coarse hand. As I endeavored to bend my mind to my studies, the letters in the page would run together, great drops of perspiration would stand upon my brow, and a faintness and dizziness would seize me. I had a bad cough, and my whole system seemed debilitated.

My teachers advised me to leave school, and not pursue my studies further till my health should improve. It was the hardest struggle of my young life to yield to my feebleness, and decide that I must leave my studies, and give up the hope of gaining an education.

II

CONVERSION

In March, 1840, William Miller visited Portland, Maine, and gave a course of lectures on the second coming of Christ. These lectures produced a great sensation, and the Christian church on Casco Street, where the discourses were given, was crowded day and night. No wild excitement attended the meetings, but a deep solemnity pervaded the minds of those who heard. Not only was a great interest manifested in the city, but the country people flocked in day after day, bringing their lunch baskets, and remaining from morning until the close of the evening meeting.

In company with my friends, I attended these meetings. Mr. Miller traced down the prophecies with an exactness that struck conviction to the hearts of his hearers. He dwelt upon the prophetic periods, and brought many proofs to strengthen his position. Then his solemn and powerful appeals and admonitions to those who were unprepared, held the crowds as if spellbound.

EARLY IMPRESSIONS

Four years previous to this, on my way to school, I had picked up a scrap of paper containing an account of a man in England who was preaching that the earth would be consumed in about thirty years from that time. I took this paper home and read it to the family. In contemplating the event predicted, I was seized with terror; the time seemed so short for the conversion and salvation of the world. Such a deep impression was made upon my mind by the little paragraph on the scrap of paper, that I could scarcely sleep for several nights, and prayed continually to be ready when Jesus came.

I had been taught that a temporal millennium would take place prior to the coming of Christ in the clouds of heaven; but now I was listening to the startling announcement that Christ was coming in 1843, only a few short years in the future.

A SPIRITUAL REVIVAL

Special meetings were appointed where sinners might have an opportunity to seek their Saviour and prepare for the fearful events soon to take place. Terror and conviction spread through the entire city. Prayer meetings were established, and there was a general awakening among the various denominations; for they all felt more or less the influence that proceeded from the teaching of the near coming of Christ.

When sinners were invited forward to the anxious seat, hundreds responded to the call; and I, among the rest, pressed through the crowd and took my place with the seekers. But there was in my heart a feeling that I could never become worthy to be called a child of God. I had often sought for the peace there is in Christ, but I could not seem to find the freedom I desired. A terrible sadness rested on my heart. I could not think of anything I had done to cause me to feel sad; but it seemed to me that I was not good enough to enter heaven, that such a thing would be altogether too much for me to expect.

A lack of confidence in myself, and a conviction that it would be impossible to make any one understand my feelings, prevented me from seeking advice and aid from my Christian friends. Thus I wandered needlessly in darkness and despair, while they, not penetrating my reserve, were entirely ignorant of my true state.

RIGHTEOUSNESS BY FAITH

The following summer my parents went to the Methodist camp meeting at Buxton, Maine, taking me with them. I was fully resolved to seek the Lord in earnest there, and obtain, if possible, the pardon of my sins. There was a great longing in my heart for the Christian's hope and the peace that comes of believing.

I was much encouraged while listening to a discourse from the words, "I will go in unto the king, . . . and if I perish, I perish." Esther 4:16. In his remarks the speaker referred to those who were wavering between hope and fear, longing to be saved from their sins and receive the pardoning love of Christ, yet held in doubt and bondage by timidity and fear of failure. He counseled such ones to surrender themselves to God, and venture upon His mercy without delay. They would find a gracious Saviour ready to present to them the scepter of mercy, even as Ahasuerus offered to Esther the signal of his favor. All that was required of the sinner, trembling in the presence of his Lord, was to put forth the hand of faith and touch the scepter of His grace. That touch insured pardon and peace.

Those who were waiting to make themselves more worthy of divine favor before they ventured to claim the promises of God, were making a fatal mistake. Jesus alone cleanses from sin; He only can forgive our transgressions. He has pledged Himself to listen to the petition and grant the prayer of those who come to Him in faith. Many have a vague idea that they must make some wonderful effort in order to gain the favor of God. But all self-dependence is vain.

It is only by connecting with Jesus through faith that the sinner becomes a hopeful, believing child of God.

These words comforted me, and gave me a view of what I must do to be saved.

I now began to see my way more clearly, and the darkness began to pass away. I earnestly sought the pardon of my sins, and strove to give myself entirely to the Lord. But my mind was often in great distress, because I did not experience the spiritual ecstasy that I considered would be the evidence of my acceptance with God, and I dared not believe myself converted without it. How much I needed instruction concerning the simplicity of faith!

THE BURDEN LIFTED

While bowed at the altar with others who were seeking the Lord, all the language of my heart was: "Help, Jesus; save me, or I perish! I will never cease to entreat till my prayer is heard and my sins are forgiven." I felt my needy, helpless condition as never before.

As I knelt and prayed, suddenly my burden left me, and my heart was light. At first a feeling of alarm came over me, and I tried to resume my load of distress. It seemed to me that I had no right to feel joyous and happy. But Jesus seemed very near to me; I felt able to come to Him with all my griefs, misfortunes, and trials, even as the needy ones came to Him for relief when He was upon earth. There was a surety in my heart that He understood my peculiar trials, and sympathized with me. I can never forget this precious assurance of the pitying tenderness of Jesus toward one so unworthy of His notice. I learned more of the divine character of Christ in that short period, when bowed among the praying ones, than ever before.

One of the mothers in Israel came to me and said, "Dear child, have you found Jesus?" I was about to answer, "Yes," when she exclaimed, "Indeed you have; His peace is with you, I see it in your face!"

Again and again I said to myself: "Can this be religion? Am I not mistaken?" It seemed too much for me to claim, too exalted a privilege. Though too timid to confess it openly, I felt that the Saviour had blessed me and pardoned my sins.

"IN NEWNESS OF LIFE"

Soon after this the camp meeting closed, and we started for home. My mind was full of the sermons, exhortations, and prayers we had heard. Everything in nature seemed changed. During the meeting, clouds and rain had prevailed a greater part of the time, and my feelings had been in harmony with the weather. Now the sun shone bright and clear, and flooded the earth with light and warmth. The trees and grass were a fresher green, the sky a deeper blue. The earth seemed to smile under the peace of God. So the rays of the Sun of Righteousness had penetrated the clouds and darkness of my mind, and dispelled its gloom.

It seemed to me that every one must be at peace with God, and animated by His Spirit. Everything that my eyes rested upon seemed to have undergone a change. The trees were more beautiful, and the birds sang more sweetly than ever before; they seemed to be praising the Creator in their songs. I did not care to talk, for fear this happiness might pass away, and I should lose the precious evidence of Jesus' love for me.

My life appeared to me in a different light. The affliction that had darkened my childhood seemed to have been dealt me in mercy, for my good, to turn my heart away from the world and its unsatisfying pleasures, and incline it toward the enduring attractions of heaven.

UNITING WITH THE METHODIST CHURCH

Soon after our return from the camp meeting, I, with several others, was taken into the church on probation. My mind was very much exercised on the subject of baptism. Young as I was, I could see but one mode of baptism authorized by the Scriptures, and that was immersion. Some of my Methodist sisters tried in vain to convince me that sprinkling was Bible baptism. The Methodist minister consented to immerse the candidates if they conscientiously preferred that method, although he intimated that sprinkling would be equally acceptable with God.

Finally the time was appointed for us to receive this solemn ordinance. It was a windy day when we, twelve in number, went down into the sea to be baptized. The waves ran high and dashed upon the shore, but as I took up this heavy cross, my peace was like a river. When I arose from the water, my strength was nearly gone, for the power of the Lord rested upon me. I felt that henceforth I was not of this world, but had risen from the watery grave into a newness of life.

The same day in the afternoon I was received into the church in full membership.

III

STRIVINGS AGAINST DOUBT

I again became very anxious to attend school and make another trial to obtain an education, and I entered a ladies' seminary in Portland. But upon attempting to resume my studies, my health rapidly failed, and it became apparent that if I persisted in attending school, it would be at the expense of my life. With great sadness I returned to my home.

I had found it difficult to enjoy religion in the seminary, surrounded by influences calculated to attract the mind and lead it from God. For some time I felt a constant dissatisfaction with myself and my Christian attainments, and did not continually realize a lively sense of the mercy and love of God. Feelings of discouragement would come over me, and this caused me great anxiety of mind.

THE ADVENT CAUSE IN PORTLAND

In June, 1842, Mr. Miller gave his second course of lectures at the Casco Street church in Portland. I felt it a great privilege to attend these lectures; for I had fallen under discouragements, and did not feel prepared to meet my Saviour. This second course created much more excitement in the city than the first. With few exceptions, the different denominations closed the doors of their churches against Mr. Miller. Many discourses from the various pulpits sought to expose the alleged fanatical errors of the lecturer; but crowds of anxious listeners attended his meetings, and many were unable to enter the house. The congregations were unusually quiet and attentive.

Mr. Miller's manner of preaching was not flowery or oratorical, but he dealt in plain and startling facts, that roused his hearers from their careless indifference. He supported his statements and theories by Scripture proof as he progressed. A convincing power attended his words, that seemed to stamp them as the language of truth.

He was courteous and sympathetic. When every seat in the house was full, and the platform and places about the pulpit seemed overcrowded, I have seen him leave the desk, and walk down the aisle, and take some feeble old man or woman by the hand and find a seat for them, then return and resume his discourse. He was indeed rightly called "Father Miller," for he had a watchful care over those who came under his ministrations, was affectionate in his manner, of a genial disposition and tender heart.

He was an interesting speaker, and his exhortations, both to professed Christians and the impenitent, were appropriate and powerful. Sometimes a solemnity so marked as to be painful, pervaded his meetings. A sense of the impending crisis of human events impressed the minds of the listening crowds. Many yielded to the conviction of the Spirit of God. Gray-haired men and aged women with trembling steps sought the anxious seats; those in the strength of maturity, the youth and children, were deeply stirred. Groans and the voice of weeping and of praise to God were mingled at the altar of prayer.

I believed the solemn words spoken by the servant of God, and my heart was pained when they were opposed or made the subject of jest. I frequently attended the meetings, and believed that Jesus was soon to come in the clouds of heaven; but my great anxiety was to be ready to meet Him. My mind constantly dwelt upon the subject of holiness of heart. I longed above all things to obtain this great blessing, and feel that I was entirely accepted of God.

IN PERPLEXITY OVER SANCTIFICATION

Among the Methodists I had heard much in regard to sanctification, but had no definite idea in regard to it. This blessing seemed away beyond my reach, a state of purity my heart could never know. I had seen persons lose their physical strength under the influence of strong mental excitement, and had heard this pronounced to be the evidence of sanctification. But I could not comprehend what was necessary in order to be fully consecrated to God. My Christian friends said to me: "Believe in Jesus *now!* Believe that He accepts you *now!*" This I tried to do, but found it impossible to believe that I had received a blessing which, it seemed to me, should electrify my whole being. I wondered at my own hardness of heart in being unable to experience the exaltation of spirit that others manifested. It seemed to me that I was different from them, and forever shut out from the perfect joy of holiness of heart.

My ideas concerning justification and sanctification were confused. These two states were presented to my mind as separate and distinct from each other; yet I failed to comprehend the difference or understand the meaning of the terms, and all the explanations of the preachers increased my difficulties. I was unable to claim the blessing for myself, and wondered if it was to be found only among the Methodists, and if, in attending the advent meetings, I was not shutting my self away from that which I desired above all else,—the sanctifying Spirit of God.

Still I observed that some of those who claimed to be sanctified, manifested a bitter spirit when the subject of the soon coming of Christ was introduced. This did not seem to me a manifestation of the holiness which they professed. I could not understand why ministers from the pulpit should so oppose the doctrine that Christ's second coming was near. Reformation had followed the preaching of this belief, and many of the most devoted ministers and laymen had received it as the truth. It seemed to me that those who sincerely loved Jesus would be ready to accept the tidings of His coming, and rejoice that it was at hand.

I felt that I could claim only what they called justification. In the word of God I read that without holiness no man should see God. Then there was some higher attainment that I must reach before I could be sure of eternal life. I studied over the subject continually; for I believed that Christ was soon to come, and feared He would find me unprepared to meet Him. Words of condemnation rang in my ears day and night, and my constant cry to God was, "What shall I do to be saved?"

THE DOCTRINE OF ETERNAL PUNISHMENT

In my mind the justice of God eclipsed His mercy and love. The mental anguish I passed through at this time was very great. I had been taught to believe in an eternally burning hell; and as I thought of the wretched state of the sinner without God, without hope, I was in deep despair. I feared that I should be lost, and that I should live throughout eternity suffering a living death. The horrifying thought was ever before me, that my sins were too great to be forgiven, and that I should be forever lost.

The frightful descriptions that I had heard of souls in perdition sank deep into my mind. Ministers in the pulpit drew vivid pictures of the condition of the lost. They taught that God proposed to save none but the sanctified; that the eye of God was upon us always; that God Himself was keeping the books with the exactness of infinite wisdom; and that every sin we committed was faithfully registered against us, and would meet its just punishment.

Satan was represented as eager to seize upon his prey, and bear us to the lowest depths of anguish, there to exult over our sufferings in the horrors of an eternally burning hell, where, after the tortures of thousands upon thousands of years, the fiery billows would roll to the surface the writhing victims, who would shriek, "How long, O Lord, how long?" Then the answer would thunder down the abyss, "Through all eternity!" Again the molten waves would engulf the lost, carrying them down into the depths of an ever restless sea of fire.

While listening to these terrible descriptions, my imagination would be so wrought upon that the perspiration would start, and it was difficult to suppress a cry of anguish, for I seemed already to feel the pains of perdition. Then the minister would dwell upon the uncertainty of life: one moment we might be here, and the next in hell; or one moment on earth, and the next in heaven. Would we choose the lake of fire and the company of demons, or the bliss of heaven with angels for our companions? Would we hear the voice of wailing and the cursing of lost souls through all eternity, or sing the songs of Jesus before the throne?

Our heavenly Father was presented before my mind as a tyrant, who delighted in the agonies of the condemned; not as the tender, pitying Friend of sinners, who loves His creatures with a love past all understanding, and desires them to be saved in His kingdom.

When the thought took possession of my mind that God delighted in the torture of His creatures, who were formed in His image, a wall of darkness seemed to separate me from Him. When I reflected that the Creator of the universe would plunge the wicked into hell, there to burn through the ceaseless rounds of eternity, my heart sank with fear, and I despaired that so cruel and tyrannical a being would ever condescend to save me from the doom of sin.

I thought that the fate of the condemned sinner would be mine,—to endure the flames of hell forever, even as long as God Himself existed. Almost total darkness settled upon me, and there seemed no way out of the shadows. Could the truth have been presented to me as I now understand it, much perplexity and sorrow would have been spared me. If the love of God had been dwelt upon more, and His stern justice less, the beauty and glory of His character would have inspired me with a deep and earnest love for my Creator.

IV

BEGINNING OF PUBLIC LABORS

Up to this time I had never prayed in public, and had only spoken a few timid words in prayer meeting. It was now impressed upon me that I should seek God in prayer at our small social meetings. This I dared not do, fearful of becoming confused and failing to express my thoughts. But the duty was impressed upon my mind so forcibly that when I attempted to pray in secret, I seemed to be mocking God, because I had failed to obey His will. Despair overwhelmed me, and for three long weeks no ray of light pierced the gloom that encompassed me.

My sufferings of mind were intense. Sometimes for a whole night I would not dare to close my eyes, but would wait until my twin sister was fast asleep, then quietly leave my bed and kneel upon the floor, praying silently, with a dumb agony that cannot be described. The horrors of an eternally burning hell were ever before me. I knew that it was impossible for me to live long in this state, and I dared not die and meet the terrible fate of the sinner. With what envy did I regard those who realized their acceptance with God! How precious did the Christian's hope seem to my agonized soul!

I frequently remained bowed in prayer nearly all night, groaning and trembling with inexpressible anguish, and a hopelessness that passes all description. "Lord, have mercy!" was my plea, and like the poor publican I dared not lift my eyes to heaven, but bowed my face upon the floor. I became very much reduced in flesh and strength, yet kept my suffering and despair to myself.

DREAM OF TEMPLE AND LAMB

While in this state of despondency, I had a dream that made a deep impression upon my mind. I dreamed of seeing a temple, to which many persons were flocking. Only those who took refuge in that temple would be saved when time should close; all who remained outside would be forever lost. The multitudes without who were going about their various ways, derided and ridiculed those who were entering the temple, and told them that this plan of safety was a cunning deception, that in fact there was no danger whatever to avoid. They even laid hold of some to prevent them from hastening within the walls.

Fearful of being ridiculed, I thought best to wait until the multitude dispersed, or until I could enter unobserved by them. But the numbers increased instead of diminishing, and fearful of being too late, I hastily left my home and pressed through the crowd. In my anxiety to reach the temple I did not notice or care for the throng that surrounded me.

On entering the building, I saw that the vast temple was supported by one immense pillar, and to this was tied a lamb all mangled and bleeding. We who were present seemed to know that this lamb had been torn and bruised on our account. All who entered the temple must come before it and confess their sins. Just before the lamb were elevated seats, upon which sat a company looking very happy. The light of heaven seemed to shine upon their faces, and they praised God and sang songs of glad thanksgiving that seemed like the music of the angels. These were they who had come before the lamb, confessed their sins, received pardon, and were now waiting in glad expectation of some joyful event.

Even after I had entered the building, a fear came over me, and a sense of shame that I must humble myself before these people; but I seemed compelled to move forward, and was slowly making my way around the pillar in order to face the lamb, when a trumpet sounded, the temple shook, shouts of triumph arose from the assembled saints, an awful brightness illuminated the building, then all was intense darkness. The happy people had all disappeared with the brightness, and I was left alone in the silent horror of night.

I awoke in agony of mind, and could hardly convince myself that I had been dreaming. It seemed to me that my doom was fixed; that the Spirit of the Lord had left me, never to return.

DREAM OF SEEING JESUS

Soon after this I had another dream. I seemed to be sitting in abject despair, with my face in my hands, reflecting like this: If Jesus were upon earth, I would go to Him, throw myself at His feet, and tell Him all my sufferings. He would not turn away from me; He would have mercy upon me, and I would love and serve Him always.

Just then the door opened, and a person of beautiful form and countenance entered. He looked upon me pitifully, and said: "Do you wish to see Jesus? He is here, and you can see Him if you desire it. Take everything you possess, and follow me."

I heard this with unspeakable joy, and gladly gathered up all my little possessions, every treasured trinket, and followed my guide. He led me to a steep and apparently frail stairway. As I began to ascend the steps, he cautioned me to keep my eyes fixed upward, lest I should grow dizzy and fall. Many others who were climbing the steep ascent fell before gaining the top.

Finally we reached the last step, and stood before a door. Here my guide directed me to leave all the things that I had brought with me. I cheerfully laid them down. He then opened the door, and bade me enter. In a moment I stood before Jesus. There was no mistaking that beautiful countenance; that expression of benevolence and majesty could belong to no other. As His gaze rested upon me, I knew at once that He was acquainted with every circumstance of my life and all my inner thoughts and feelings.

I tried to shield myself from His gaze, feeling unable to endure His searching eyes; but He drew near with a smile, and laying His hand upon my head, said, "Fear not." The sound of His sweet voice thrilled my heart with a happiness it had never before experienced. I was too joyful to utter a word, but, overcome with emotion, sank prostrate at His feet. While I was lying helpless there, scenes of beauty and glory passed before me, and I seemed to have reached the safety and peace of heaven. At length my strength returned, and I arose. The loving eyes of Jesus were still upon me, and His smile filled my soul with gladness. His presence awoke in me a holy reverence and an inexpressible love.

My guide now opened the door, and we both passed out. He bade me take up again all the things I had left without. This done, he handed me a green cord coiled up closely. This he directed me to place next my heart, and when I wished to see Jesus, take it from my bosom, and stretch it to the utmost. He cautioned me not to let it remain coiled for any length of time, lest it should become knotted and difficult to straighten. I placed the cord near my heart, and joyfully descended the narrow stairs, praising the Lord, and telling all whom I met where they could find Jesus.

This dream gave me hope. The green cord represented faith to my mind, and the beauty and simplicity of trusting in God began to dawn upon my soul.

FRIENDLY SYMPATHY AND COUNSEL

I now confided all my sorrows and perplexities to my mother. She tenderly sympathized with and encouraged me, advising me to go for counsel to Elder Stockman, who then preached the advent doctrine in Portland. I had great confidence in him, for he was a devoted servant of Christ. Upon hearing my story, he placed his hand affectionately upon my head, saying with tears in his eyes: "Ellen, you are only a child. Yours is a most singular experience for one of your tender age. Jesus must be preparing you for some special work."

He then told me that even if I were a person of mature years and thus harassed by doubt and despair, he would tell me that he *knew* there was hope for me through the love of Jesus. The very agony of mind I had suffered was positive evidence that the Spirit of the Lord was striving with me. He said that when the sinner becomes hardened in guilt, he does not realize the enormity of his transgression, but flatters himself that he is about right, and in no particular danger. The Spirit of the Lord leaves him, and he becomes careless and indifferent or recklessly defiant. This good man told me of the love of God for His erring children; that instead of rejoicing in their destruction, He longed to draw them to Himself in simple faith and trust. He dwelt upon the great love of Christ and the plan of redemption.

Elder Stockman spoke of my early misfortune, and said it was indeed a grievous affliction, but he bade me believe that the hand of a loving Father had not been withdrawn from me; that in the future life, when the mist that then darkened my mind had vanished, I would discern the wisdom of the providence which had seemed so cruel and mysterious. Jesus said to His disciples, "What I do thou knowest not now; but thou shalt know hereafter." John 13:7. In the great future we should no longer see as through a glass darkly, but come face to face with the mysteries of divine love.

"Go free, Ellen," said he; "return to your home trusting in Jesus, for He will not withhold His love from any true seeker." He then prayed earnestly for me, and it seemed that God would certainly regard the prayer of His saint, even if my humble petitions were unheard. My mind was much relieved, and the wretched slavery of doubt and fear departed as I listened to the wise and tender counsel of this teacher in Israel. I left his presence comforted and encouraged.

During the few minutes in which I received instruction from Elder Stockman, I had obtained more knowledge on the subject of God's love and pitying tenderness, than from all the sermons and exhortations to which I had ever listened.

MY FIRST PUBLIC PRAYER

I returned home, and again went before the Lord, promising to do and suffer anything He might require of me, if only the smiles of Jesus might cheer my heart. The same duty was again presented to me that had troubled my mind before,— to take up my cross among the assembled people of God. An opportunity was not long wanting; there was a prayer meeting that evening at my uncle's, which I attended.

As the others knelt for prayer, I bowed with them, trembling, and after a few had prayed, my voice arose in prayer before I was aware of it. In that moment the promises of God appeared to me like so many precious pearls that were to be received only for the asking. As I prayed, the burden and agony of soul that I had so long endured, left me, and the blessing of the Lord descended upon me like the gentle dew. I praised God from the depths of my heart. Everything seemed shut out from me but Jesus and His glory, and I lost consciousness of what was passing around me.

The Spirit of God rested upon me with such power that I was unable to go home that night. When I awakened to realization, I found myself cared for in the house of my uncle, where we had assembled for the prayer meeting. Neither my uncle nor my aunt enjoyed religion, although the former had once made a profession, but had since backslidden. I was told that he had been greatly disturbed while the power of God rested upon me in so special a manner, and had walked the floor, sorely troubled and distressed in his mind.

When I was first struck down, some of those present were greatly alarmed, and were about to run for a physician, thinking that some sudden and dangerous indisposition had attacked me; but my mother bade them let me alone, for it was plain to her, and to the other experienced Christians, that it was the wondrous power of God that had prostrated me. When I did return home, on the following day, a great change had taken place in my mind. It seemed to me that I could hardly be the same person that left my father's house the previous evening. This passage was continually in my thoughts: "The Lord is my shepherd; I shall not want." Ps. 23:1. My heart was full of happiness as I softly repeated these words.

A VIEW OF THE FATHER'S LOVE

Faith now took possession of my heart. I felt an inexpressible love for God, and had the witness of His Spirit that my sins were pardoned. My views of the Father were changed. I now looked upon Him as a kind and tender parent, rather than a stern tyrant compelling men to a blind obedience. My heart went out toward Him in a deep and fervent love. Obedience to His will seemed a joy; it was a pleasure to be in His service. No shadow clouded the light that revealed to me the perfect will of God. I felt the assurance of an indwelling Saviour, and realized the truth of what Christ had said: "He that followeth Me shall not walk in darkness, but shall have the light of life." John 8:12.

My peace and happiness were in such marked contrast with my former gloom and anguish that it seemed to me as if I had been rescued from hell and transported to heaven. I could even praise God for the misfortune that had been the trial of my life, for it had been the means of fixing my thoughts upon eternity. Naturally proud and ambitious, I might not have been inclined to give my heart to Jesus had it not been for the sore affliction that had cut me off, in a manner, from the triumphs and vanities of the world.

For six months not a shadow clouded my mind, nor did I neglect one known duty. My whole endeavor was to do the will of God, and keep Jesus and heaven continually in mind. I was surprised and enraptured with the clear views now presented to me of the atonement and the work of Christ. I will not attempt to further explain the exercises of my mind; suffice it to say that old things had passed away, all things had become new. There was not a cloud to mar my perfect bliss. I longed to tell the story of Jesus' love, but felt no disposition to engage in common conversation with any one. My heart was so filled with love to God and the peace that passeth understanding, that I loved to meditate and pray.

BEARING TESTIMONY

The night after receiving so great a blessing, I attended the advent meeting. When the time came for the followers of Christ to speak in His favor, I could not remain silent, but rose and related my experience. Not a thought had entered my mind of what I should say; but the simple story of Jesus' love to me fell from my lips with perfect freedom, and my heart was so happy to be liberated from its bondage of dark despair, that I lost sight of the people about me, and seemed to be alone with God. I found no difficulty in expressing my peace and happiness, except for the tears of gratitude that choked my utterance.

Elder Stockman was present. He had recently seen me in deep despair, and as he now saw my captivity turned, he wept aloud, rejoicing with me, and praising God for this proof of His tender mercy and loving kindness.

Not long after receiving this great blessing, I attended a conference meeting at the Christian church, where Elder Brown was pastor. I was invited to relate my experience, and felt not only great freedom of expression, but happiness, in telling my simple story of the love of Jesus and the joy of being accepted of God. As I spoke, with subdued heart and tearful eyes, my soul seemed drawn toward heaven in thanksgiving. The melting power of the Lord came upon the assembled people. Many were weeping and others praising God.

Sinners were invited to arise for prayers, and many responded to the call. My heart was so thankful to God for the blessing He had given me, that I longed to have others participate in this sacred joy. My mind was deeply interested for those who might be suffering under a sense of the Lord's displeasure and the burden of sin. While relating my experience, I felt that no one could resist the evidence of God's pardoning love that had wrought so wonderful a change in me. The reality of true conversion seemed so plain to me that I felt like helping my young friends into the light, and at every opportunity exerted my influence toward this end.

LABORING FOR YOUNG FRIENDS

I arranged meetings with my young friends, some of whom were considerably older than myself, and a few were married persons. A number of them were vain and thoughtless; my experience sounded to them like an idle tale, and they did not heed my entreaties. But I determined that my efforts should never cease till these dear souls, for whom I had so great an interest, yielded to God. Several entire nights were spent by me in earnest prayer for those whom I had sought out and brought together for the purpose of laboring and praying with them.

Some of these had met with us from curiosity to hear what I had to say; others thought me beside myself to be so persistent in my efforts, especially when they manifested no concern on their own part.

But at every one of our little meetings I continued to exhort and pray for each one separately, until every one had yielded to Jesus, acknowledging the merits of His pardoning love. Every one was converted to God.

Night after night in my dreams I seemed to be laboring for the salvation of souls. At such times special cases were presented to my mind; these I afterward sought out and prayed with. In every instance but one these persons yielded themselves to the Lord. Some of our more formal brethren feared that I was too zealous for the conversion of souls; but time seemed to me so short that it behooved all who had a hope of a blessed immortality and looked for the soon coming of Christ, to labor without ceasing for those who were still in their sins and standing on the awful brink of ruin.

Though I was very young, the plan of salvation was so clear to my mind, and my personal experience had been so marked, that, upon considering the matter, I knew it was my duty to continue my efforts for the salvation of precious souls, and to pray and confess Christ at every opportunity. My entire being was offered to the service of my Master. Let come what would, I determined to please God, and live as one who expected the Saviour to come and reward the faithful. I felt like a little child coming to God as to my father, and asking Him what He would have me to do. Then as my duty was made plain to me, it was my greatest happiness to perform it. Peculiar trials sometimes beset me. Those older in experience than myself endeavored to hold me back and cool the ardor of my faith; but with the smiles of Jesus brightening my life, and the love of God in my heart, I went on my way with a joyful spirit.

V

SEPARATION FROM THE CHURCH

My father's family still occasionally attended the Methodist church, and also the class meetings held in private houses.

One evening my brother Robert and myself went to class meeting. The presiding elder was present. When it came my brother's turn to bear testimony, he spoke with great humility, yet with clearness, of the necessity for a complete fitness to meet our Saviour when He should come in the clouds of heaven with power and great glory. While my brother was speaking, a heavenly light glowed upon his usually pale countenance. He seemed to be carried in spirit above present surroundings, and spoke as if in the presence of Jesus.

When I was called upon to speak, I arose, free in spirit, with a heart full of love and peace. I told the story of my great suffering under the conviction of sin, how I had at length received the blessing so long sought,— an entire conformity to the will of God,— and expressed my joy in the tidings of the soon coming of my Redeemer to take His children home.

DOCTRINAL DIFFERENCES

In my simplicity I expected that my Methodist brethren and sisters would understand my feelings and rejoice with me, but I was disappointed; several sisters groaned and moved their chairs noisily, turning their backs upon me. I could not think what had been said to offend them, and spoke very briefly, feeling the chilling influence of their disapprobation.

When I had ceased speaking, the presiding elder

asked me if it would not be more pleasant to live a long life of usefulness, doing others good, than to have Jesus come speedily and destroy poor sinners. I replied that I longed for the coming of Jesus. Then sin would have an end, and we would enjoy sanctification forever, with no devil to tempt and lead us astray.

When the presiding elder addressed others in the class, he expressed great joy in anticipating the temporal millennium, when the earth should be filled with the knowledge of the Lord as the waters cover the sea. He longed to see this glorious period ushered in.

After the meeting closed, I was conscious of being treated with marked coldness by those who had formerly been kind and friendly to me. My brother and I returned home feeling sad that we should be so misunderstood by our brethren, and that the subject of the near coming of Jesus should awaken such bitter opposition in their breasts.

THE HOPE OF THE SECOND ADVENT

On the way home we talked seriously concerning the evidences of our new faith and hope. "Ellen," said Robert, "are we deceived? Is this hope of Christ's soon appearing upon the earth a heresy, that ministers and professors of religion oppose it so bitterly? They say that Jesus will not come for thousands and thousands of years. If they even approach the truth, then the world cannot come to an end in our day."

I dared not give unbelief a moment's encouragement, but quickly replied: "I have not a doubt but that the doctrine preached by Mr. Miller is the truth. What power attends his words! what conviction is carried home to the sinner's heart!"

We talked the matter over candidly as we walked along, and decided that it was our duty and privilege to look for our Saviour's coming, and that it would be safest to make ready for His appearing, and be prepared to meet Him with joy. If He did come, what would be the prospect of those who were now saying, "My Lord delayeth His coming," and had no desire to see Him? We wondered how ministers dared to quiet the fears of sinners and backsliders by saying, "Peace, peace!" while the message of warning was being given all over the land. The period seemed very solemn to us; we felt that we had no time to lose.

"'A tree is known by its fruits,'" remarked Robert. "What has this belief done for us? It has convinced us that we were not ready for the coming of the Lord; that we must become pure in heart, or we cannot meet our Saviour in peace. It has aroused us to seek for new strength and grace from God.

"What has it done for you, Ellen? Would you be what you are now if you had never heard the doctrine of Christ's soon coming? What hope has it inspired in your heart; what peace, joy, and love has it given you? And for me it has done everything. I love Jesus, and all Christians. I love the prayer meeting. I find great joy in reading my Bible and in prayer."

We both felt strengthened by this conversation, and resolved that we would not be turned from our honest convictions of truth, and the blessed hope of Christ's soon coming in the clouds of heaven. We were thankful that we could discern the precious light, and rejoice in looking for the coming of the Lord.

LAST TESTIMONY IN CLASS MEETING

Not long after this, we again attended the class meeting. We wanted an opportunity to speak of the precious love of God that animated our souls. I particularly wished to tell of the Lord's goodness and mercy to me. So great a change had been wrought in me that it seemed my duty to improve every opportunity of testifying to the love of my Saviour.

When my turn came to speak, I stated the evidences I enjoyed of Jesus' love, and that I looked forward with the glad expectation of meeting my Redeemer soon. The belief that Christ's coming was near had stirred my soul to seek more earnestly for the sanctification of the Spirit of God.

Here the class leader interrupted me, saying, "You received sanctification through Methodism, through *Methodism,* sister, not through an erroneous theory."

I felt compelled to confess the truth, that it was not through Methodism that my heart had received its new blessing, but by the stirring truths concerning the personal appearing of Jesus. Through them I had found peace, joy, and perfect love. Thus my testimony closed, the last that I was to bear in class with my Methodist brethren.

Robert then spoke in his meek way, yet in so clear and touching a manner that some wept and were much moved; but others coughed dissentingly, and seemed quite uneasy.

After leaving the classroom, we again talked over our faith, and marveled that our Christian brethren and sisters could so ill endure to have a word spoken in reference to our Saviour's coming. We were convinced that we ought no longer to attend the class meeting. The hope of the glorious appearing of Christ filled our souls, and would find expression when we rose to speak. It was evident that we could have no freedom in the class meeting; for our testimony provoked sneers and taunts that reached our ears at the close of the meeting, from brethren and sisters whom we had respected and loved.

SPREADING THE ADVENT MESSAGE

The Adventists held meetings at this time in Beethoven Hall. My father, with his family, attended them quite regularly. The period of the second advent was thought to be in the year 1843. The time seemed so short in which souls could be saved that I resolved to do all that was in my power to lead sinners into the light of truth.

I had two sisters at home,— Sarah, who was several years older than myself, and my twin sister Elizabeth. We talked the matter over among ourselves, and decided to earn what money we could, and spend it in buying books and tracts to be distributed gratuitously. This was the best we could do, and we did this little gladly.

Our father was a hatter, and it was my allotted task to make the crowns of the hats, that being the easiest part of the work. I also knit stockings at twenty-five cents a pair. My heart was so weak that I was obliged to sit propped up in bed to do this work; but day after day I sat there, happy that my trembling fingers could do something to bring in a little pittance for the cause I loved so dearly. Twenty-five cents a day was all I could earn. How carefully would I lay aside the precious bits of silver taken in return, which were to be expended for reading matter to enlighten and arouse those who were in darkness!

I had no temptation to spend my earnings for my own personal gratification. My dress was plain; nothing was spent for needless ornaments, for vain display appeared sinful in my eyes. So I had ever a little fund in store with which to purchase suitable books. These were placed in the hands of experienced persons to send abroad.

Every leaf of this printed matter seemed precious in my eyes; for it was as a messenger of light to the world, bidding them prepare for the great event near at hand. The salvation of souls was the burden of my mind, and my heart ached for those who flattered themselves that they were living in security, while the message of warning was being given to the world.

THE IMMORTALITY QUESTION

One day I listened to a conversation between my mother and a sister, in reference to a discourse which they had recently heard, to the effect that the soul had not natural immortality. Some of the minister's proof texts were repeated. Among them I remember these impressed me very forcibly: "The soul that sinneth, it shall die." Eze. 18:4. "The living know that they shall die: but the dead know not anything." Eccl. 9:5. "Which in His times He shall show, who is the blessed and only Potentate, the King of kings, and Lord of lords; who *only* hath immortality." 1 Tim. 6:15, 16. "To them who by patient continuance in well-doing seek for glory and honor and immortality, eternal life." Rom. 2:7.

"Why," said my mother, after quoting the foregoing passage, "should they seek for what they already have?"

I listened to these new ideas with an intense and painful interest. When alone with my mother, I inquired if she really believed that the soul was not immortal. Her reply was, that she feared we had been in error on that subject, as well as upon some others.

"But, mother," said I, "do you really believe that the soul sleeps in the grave until the resurrection? Do you think that the Christian, when he dies, does not go immediately to heaven, nor the sinner to hell?"

She answered: "The Bible gives us no proof that there is an eternally burning hell. If there is such a place, it should be mentioned in the Sacred Book."

"Why, mother!" cried I, in astonishment, "this is strange talk for you! If you believe this strange theory, do not let any one know of it; for I fear that sinners would gather security from this belief, and never desire to seek the Lord."

"If this is sound Bible truth," she replied, "instead of preventing the salvation of sinners, it will be the means of winning them to Christ. If the love of God will not induce the rebel to yield, the terrors of an eternal hell will not drive him to repentance. Besides, it does not seem a proper way to win souls to Jesus by appealing to one of the lowest attributes of the mind,—abject fear. The love of Jesus attracts; it will subdue the hardest heart."

It was some months after this conversation before I heard anything further concerning this doctrine; but during this time my mind had been much exercised upon the subject. When I heard it preached, I believed it to be the truth. From the time that light in regard to the sleep of the dead dawned upon my mind, the mystery that had enshrouded the resurrection vanished, and the great event itself assumed a new and sublime importance. My mind had often been disturbed by its efforts to reconcile the immediate reward or punishment of the dead with the undoubted fact of a future resurrection and judgment. If at death the soul entered upon eternal happiness or misery, where was the need of a resurrection of the poor moldering body?

But this new and beautiful faith taught me the reason why inspired writers had dwelt so much upon the resurrection of the body; it was because the entire being was slumbering in the grave. I could now clearly perceive the fallacy of our former position on this question.

THE PASTOR'S VISIT

Our family were all deeply interested in the doctrine of the Lord's soon coming. My father had stood as one of the pillars of the Methodist church. He had acted as exhorter, and as leader of meetings held in homes at a distance from the city. However, the Methodist minister made us a special visit, and took the occasion to inform us that our faith and Methodism could not agree. He did not inquire our reasons for believing as we did, nor make any reference to the Bible in order to convince us of our error; but he stated that we had adopted a new and strange belief that the Methodist church could not accept.

My father replied that he must be mistaken in calling this a new and strange doctrine; that Christ Himself, in His teachings to His disciples, had preached His second advent. He had said: "In My Father's house are many mansions: if it were not so, I would have told you. I go to prepare a place for you. And if I go and prepare a place for you, I will come again, and receive you unto Myself; that where I am, there ye may be also." John 14: 2, 3. When He was taken up to heaven, as His faithful followers stood gazing after their vanishing Lord, "behold, two men stood by them in white apparel; which also said, Ye men of Galilee, why stand ye gazing up into heaven? this same Jesus, which is taken up from you into heaven, shall so come in like manner as ye have seen Him go into heaven.'' Acts 1:10, 11.

''And,'' said my father, warming with his subject, ''the inspired Paul wrote a letter to encourage his brethren in Thessalonica, saying: 'To you who are troubled rest with us, when the Lord Jesus shall be revealed from heaven with His mighty angels, in flaming fire taking vengeance on them that know not God, and that obey not the gospel of our Lord Jesus Christ: who shall be punished with everlasting destruction from the presence of the Lord, and from the glory of His power; when He shall come to be glorified in His saints, and to be admired in all them that believe . . . in that day.' 2 Thess. 1:7-10. 'For the Lord Himself shall descend from heaven with a shout, with the voice of the Archangel, and with the trump of God: and the dead in Christ shall rise first: then we which are alive and remain shall be caught up together with them in the clouds, to meet the Lord in the air: and so shall we ever be with the Lord. Wherefore comfort one another with these words.' 1 Thess. 4:16-18.

''This is high authority for our faith. Jesus and His apostles dwell upon the event of the second advent with joy and triumph; and the holy angels proclaim that Christ, who ascended to heaven, shall come again. This is our offense,— believing the word of Jesus and His disciples. This is a very old doctrine, and bears no taint of heresy.''

The minister did not attempt to refer to a single text that would prove us in error, but excused himself on the plea of a want of time. He advised us to quietly withdraw from the church, and avoid the publicity of a trial. We were aware that others of our brethren were meeting with similar treatment for a like cause, and we did not wish it understood that we were ashamed to acknowledge our faith, or were unable to sustain it by Scripture; so my parents insisted that they should be acquainted with the reasons for this request.

The only answer to this was an evasive declaration that we had walked contrary to the rules of the church. and the best course would be to voluntarily withdraw from it to save a trial. We answered that we preferred a regular trial, and demanded to know what sin was charged to us, as we were conscious of no wrong in looking for and loving the appearing of the Saviour.

THE CHURCH TRIAL

Not long after, we were notified to be present at a meeting to be held in the vestry of the church. There were but few present. The influence of my father and his family was such that our opposers had no desire to present our cases before a larger number of the congregation. The single charge preferred was that we had walked contrary to their rules. Upon asking what rules we had violated, it was stated, after a little hesitation, that we had attended other meetings, and had neglected to meet regularly with our class.

We stated that a portion of the family had been in the country for some time past, that none who remained in the city had been absent from class meeting more than a few weeks, and they were morally compelled to remain away because the testimonies they bore met with such marked disapprobation. We also reminded them that certain persons who had not attended class meeting for a year were yet held in good standing.

It was asked if we would confess that we had departed from their rules, and if we would also agree to conform to them in the future. We answered that we dared not yield our faith or deny the sacred truth of God; that we could not forego the hope of the soon coming of our Redeemer; that after the manner which they called heresy we must continue to worship the Lord.

My father in his defense received the blessing of God, and we all left the vestry with free spirits, happy in the consciousness of the approving smile of Jesus.

The next Sunday, at the commencement of the love feast, the presiding elder read off our names, seven in number, as discontinued from the church. He stated that we were not expelled on account of any wrong or immoral conduct, that we were of unblemished character and enviable reputation; but we had been guilty of walking contrary to the rules of the Methodist church. He also declared that a door was now open, and all who were guilty of a similar breach of the rules would be dealt with in like manner.

There were many in the church who waited for the appearing of the Saviour, and this threat was made for the purpose of frightening them into subjection. In some cases this policy brought about the desired result, and the favor of God was sold for a place in the church. Many believed, but dared not confess their faith, lest they should be turned out of the synagogue. But some left soon afterward, and joined the company of those who were looking for the Saviour.

At this time the words of the prophet were exceedingly precious: "Your brethren that hated you, that cast you out for My name's sake, said, Let the Lord be glorified: but He shall appear to your joy, and they shall be ashamed." Isa. 66:5.

VI

THE DISAPPOINTMENT OF 1843-44

With carefulness and trembling we approached the time when our Saviour was expected to appear. With solemn earnestness we sought, as a people, to purify our lives, that we might be ready to meet Him at His coming. Meetings were still held at private houses in different parts of the city, with the best results. Believers were encouraged to work for their friends and relatives, and conversions were multiplying day by day.

MEETINGS IN BEETHOVEN HALL

Notwithstanding the opposition of ministers and churches, Beethoven Hall, in the city of Portland, was nightly crowded; especially was there a large congregation on Sundays. All classes flocked to these meetings. Rich and poor, high and low, ministers and laymen, were all, from various causes, anxious to hear for themselves the doctrine of the second advent. Many came who, finding no room to stand, went away disappointed.

The order of the meetings was simple. A short and pointed discourse was usually given, then liberty was granted for general exhortation. There was, as a rule, the most perfect stillness possible for so large a crowd. The Lord held the spirit of opposition in check while His servants explained the reasons of their faith. Sometimes the instrument was feeble, but the Spirit of God gave weight and power to His truth. The presence of the holy angels was felt in the assembly, and numbers were daily added to the little band of believers.

AN EXHORTATION BY ELDER BROWN

On one occasion, while Elder Stockman was preaching, Elder Brown, a Christian Baptist minister, whose name has been mentioned before in this narrative, was sitting in the desk listening to the sermon with intense interest. He became deeply moved, and suddenly his face grew pale as the dead, he reeled in his chair, and Elder Stockman caught him in his arms just as he was falling to the floor, and laid him on the sofa back of the desk, where he lay powerless until the discourse was finished.

He then arose, his face still pale, but shining with light from the Sun of Righteousness, and gave a very impressive testimony. He seemed to receive holy unction from above. He was usually slow of speech, with an earnest manner, entirely free from excitement. On this occasion his solemn, measured words carried with them a new power.

He related his experience with such simplicity and candor that many who had been greatly prejudiced were affected to tears. The Spirit of God was felt in his words and seen upon his countenance. With a holy exaltation he boldly declared that he had taken the word of God as his counselor; that his doubts had been swept away and his faith confirmed. With earnestness he invited his brother ministers, church members, sinners, and infidels to examine the Bible for themselves, and charged them to let no man turn them from the purpose of ascertaining what was the truth.

When he had finished speaking, those who desired the prayers of the people of God were invited to rise. Hundreds responded to the call. The Holy Spirit rested upon the assembly. Heaven and earth seemed to approach each other. The meeting lasted until a late hour of the night. The power of the Lord was felt upon young, old, and middle-aged.

Elder Brown did not either then or afterward sever his connection with the Christian church, but he was looked upon with great respect by his people.

JOYOUS EXPECTANCY

As we returned to our homes by various ways, a voice praising God would reach us from one direction, and as if in response, voices from another and still another quarter shouted, "Glory to God, the Lord reigneth!" Men sought their homes with praises upon their lips, and the glad sound rang out upon the still night air. No one who attended these meetings can ever forget those scenes of deepest interest.

Those who sincerely love Jesus can appreciate the feelings of those who watched with the most intense longing for the coming of their Saviour. The point of expectation was nearing. The time when we hoped to meet Him was close at hand. We approached this hour with a calm solemnity. The true believers rested in a sweet communion with God,— an earnest of the peace that was to be theirs in the bright hereafter. None who experienced this hope and trust can ever forget those precious hours of waiting.

Worldly business was for the most part laid aside for a few weeks. We carefully examined every thought and emotion of our hearts, as if upon our deathbeds, and in a few hours to close our eyes forever upon earthly scenes. There was no making of "ascension robes" for the great event; we felt the need of internal evidence that we were prepared to meet Christ, and our white robes were purity of soul, character cleansed from sin by the atoning blood of our Saviour.

DAYS OF PERPLEXITY

But the time of expectation passed. This was the first close test brought to bear upon those who believed and hoped that Jesus would come in the clouds of heaven. The disappointment of God's waiting people was great. The scoffers were triumphant, and won the weak and cowardly to their ranks. Some who had appeared to possess true faith seemed to have been influenced only by fear; and now their courage returned with the passing of the time, and they boldly united with the scoffers, declaring that they had never been duped to really believe the doctrine of Miller, who was a mad fanatic. Others, naturally yielding or vacillating, quietly deserted the cause.

We were perplexed and disappointed, yet did not renounce our faith. Many still clung to the hope that Jesus would not long delay His coming; the word of the Lord was sure, it could not fail. We felt that we had done our duty, we had lived up to our precious faith; we were disappointed, but not discouraged. The signs of the times denoted that the end of all things was at hand; we must watch and hold ourselves in readiness for the coming of the Master at any time. We must wait with hope and trust, not neglecting the assembling of ourselves together for instruction, encouragement, and comfort, that our light might shine forth into the darkness of the world.

AN ERROR IN RECKONING

Our calculation of the prophetic time was so simple and plain that even children could understand it. From the date of the decree of the king of Persia, found in Ezra 7, which was given in 457 before Christ, the 2300 years of Daniel 8:14 were supposed to terminate with 1843. Accordingly we looked to the end of this year for the coming of the Lord. We were sadly disappointed when the year entirely passed away, and the Saviour had not come.

It was not at first perceived that if the decree did not go forth at the beginning of the year 457 B. C., the 2300 years would not be completed at the close of 1843. But it was ascertained that the decree was given near the close of the year 457 B. C., and therefore the prophetic period must reach to the fall of the year 1844. Therefore the vision of time did not tarry, though it had seemed to do so. We learned to rest upon the language of the prophet: "The vision is yet for an appointed time, but at the end it shall speak, and not lie: though it tarry, wait for it; because it will surely come, it will not tarry." Hab. 2:3.

God tested and proved His people by the passing of the time in 1843. The mistake made in reckoning the prophetic periods was not at once discovered, even by learned men who opposed the views of those who were looking for Christ's coming. Scholars declared that Mr. Miller was right in his calculation of the time, though they disputed him in regard to the event that would crown that period. But they, and the waiting people of God, were in a common error on the question of time.

Those who had been disappointed were not long left in darkness; for in searching the prophetic periods with earnest prayer the error was discovered, and the tracing of the prophetic pencil down through the tarrying time. In the joyful expectation of the coming of Christ, the apparent tarrying of the vision had not been taken into account, and was a sad and unlooked-for surprise. Yet this very trial was necessary to develop and strengthen the sincere believers in the truth.

HOPE RENEWED

Our hopes now centered on the coming of the Lord in 1844. This was also the time for the message of the second angel, who, flying through the midst of heaven, cried, "Babylon is fallen, is fallen, that great city." Rev. 14:8. That message was first proclaimed by the servants of God in the summer of 1844. As a result, many left the fallen churches. In connection with this message the "midnight cry"[1] was given: "Behold, the Bridegroom cometh; go ye out to meet Him." In every part of the land light was given concerning this message, and the cry aroused thousands. It went from city to city, from village to village, and into the remote country regions. It reached the learned and talented, as well as the obscure and humble.

This was the happiest year of my life. My heart was full of glad expectation; but I felt great pity and anxiety for those who were in discouragement and had no hope in Jesus. We united, as a people, in earnest prayer for a true experience and the unmistakable evidence of our acceptance with God.

A TRIAL OF FAITH

We needed great patience, for the scoffers were many. We were frequently greeted by scornful references to our former disappointment. The orthodox churches used every means to prevent the belief in Christ's soon coming from spreading. No liberty

[1] See Matt. 25:1-13.

was granted in their meetings to those who dared mention a hope of the soon coming of Christ. Professed lovers of Jesus scornfully rejected the tidings that He whom they claimed as their best Friend was soon to visit them. They were excited and angered against those who proclaimed the news of His coming, and who rejoiced that they should speedily behold Him in His glory.

A PERIOD OF PREPARATION

Every moment seemed to me of the utmost importance. I felt that we were doing work for eternity, and that the careless and uninterested were in the greatest peril. My faith was unclouded, and I appropriated to myself the precious promises of Jesus. He had said to His disciples, "Ask, and ye shall receive." I firmly believed that whatever I asked in accordance with the will of God, would certainly be granted to me. I sank in humility at the feet of Jesus, with my heart in harmony with His will.

I often visited families, and engaged in earnest prayer with those who were oppressed by fears and despondency. My faith was so strong that I never doubted for a moment that God would answer my prayers. Without a single exception, the blessing and peace of Jesus rested upon us in answer to our humble petitions, and the hearts of the despairing ones were made joyful by light and hope.

With diligent searching of heart and humble confessions, we came prayerfully up to the time of expectation. Every morning we felt that it was our first work to secure the evidence that our lives were right before God. We realized that if we were not advancing in holiness, we were sure to retrograde. Our interest for one another increased; we prayed much with and for one another. We assembled in the orchards and groves to commune with God and to offer up our petitions to Him, feeling more fully in His presence when surrounded by His natural works. The joys of salvation were more necessary to us than our food and drink. If clouds obscured our minds, we dared not rest or sleep till they were swept away by the consciousness of our acceptance with the Lord.

THE PASSING OF THE TIME

The waiting people of God approached the hour when they fondly hoped their joys would be complete in the coming of the Saviour. But the time again passed unmarked by the advent of Jesus. It was a bitter disappointment that fell upon the little flock whose faith had been so strong and whose hope had been so high. But we were surprised that we felt so free in the Lord, and were so strongly sustained by His strength and grace.

The experience of the former year was, however, repeated to a greater extent. A large class renounced their faith. Some who had been very confident, were so deeply wounded in their pride that they felt like fleeing from the world. Like Jonah, they complained of God, and chose death rather than life. Those who had built their faith upon the evidence of others, and not upon the word of God, were now as ready to again change their views. This second great test revealed a mass of worthless drift that had been drawn into the strong current of the advent faith, and been borne along for a time with the true believers and earnest workers.

We were disappointed, but not disheartened. We resolved to refrain from murmuring at the trying ordeal by which the Lord was purging us from the dross and refining us like gold in the furnace; to submit patiently to the process of purifying that God deemed needful for us; and to wait with patient hope for the Saviour to redeem His tried and faithful ones.

We were firm in the belief that the preaching of definite time was of God. It was this that led men to search the Bible diligently, discovering truths they had not before perceived. Jonah was sent of God to proclaim in the streets of Nineveh that within forty days the city would be overthrown; but God accepted the humiliation of the Ninevites, and extended their period of probation. Yet the message that Jonah brought was sent of God, and Nineveh was tested according to His will. The world looked upon our hope as a delusion, and our disappointment as its consequent failure; but though we were mistaken in the event that was to occur at that period, there was no failure in reality of the vision that seemed to tarry.

Those who had looked for the coming of the Lord were not without comfort. They had obtained valuable knowledge in the searching of the Word. The plan of salvation was plainer to their understanding. Every day they discovered new beauties in the sacred pages, and a wonderful harmony running through all, one scripture explaining another, and no word used in vain.

Our disappointment was not so great as that of the disciples. When the Son of man rode triumphantly into Jerusalem, they expected Him to be crowned king. The people flocked from all the region about, and cried, "Hosanna to the Son of David." Matt. 21:9. And when the priests and elders besought Jesus to still the multitude, He declared that if they should hold their peace, even the stones would cry out, for prophecy must be fulfilled. Yet in a few days these very disciples saw their beloved Master, whom they believed would reign on David's throne, stretched upon the cruel cross above the mocking, taunting Pharisees. Their high hopes were disappointed, and the darkness of death closed about them. Yet Christ was true to His promises. Sweet was the consolation He gave His people, rich the reward of the true and faithful.

Mr. Miller and those who were in union with him supposed that the cleansing of the sanctuary spoken of in Daniel 8:14 meant the purifying of the earth by fire prior to its becoming the abode of the saints. This was to take place at the second advent of Christ; therefore we looked for that event at the end of the 2300 days, or years. But after our disappointment the Scriptures were carefully searched, with prayer and earnest thought; and after a period of suspense, light poured in upon our darkness; doubt and uncertainty were swept away.

Instead of the prophecy of Daniel 8:14 referring to the purifying of the earth, it was now plain that it pointed to the closing work of our High Priest in heaven, the finishing of the atonement, and the preparing of the people to abide the day of His coming.

VII

MY FIRST VISION

It was not long after the passing of the time in 1844, that my first vision was given me. I was visiting Mrs. Haines at Portland, a dear sister in Christ, whose heart was knit with mine; five of us, all women, were kneeling quietly at the family altar. While we were praying, the power of God came upon me as I had never felt it before.

I seemed to be surrounded with light, and to be rising higher and higher from the earth. I turned to look for the advent people in the world, but could not find them, when a voice said to me, "Look again, and look a little higher." At this I raised my eyes, and saw a straight and narrow path, cast up high above the world. On this path the advent people were traveling to the city which was at the farther end of the path. They had a bright light set up behind them at the beginning of the path, which an angel told me was the "midnight cry." This light shone all along the path, and gave light for their feet, so that they might not stumble.

If they kept their eyes fixed on Jesus, who was just before them, leading them to the city, they were safe. But soon some grew weary, and said the city was a great way off, and they expected to have entered it before. Then Jesus would encourage them by raising His glorious right arm, and from His arm came a light which waved over the advent band, and they shouted "Alleluia!" Others rashly denied the light behind them, and said that it was not God that had led them out so far. The light behind them went out, leaving their feet in perfect darkness, and they stumbled and lost sight of the mark and of Jesus, and fell off the path down into the dark and wicked world below.

Soon we heard the voice of God like many waters, which gave us the day and hour of Jesus' coming. The living saints, 144,000 in number, knew and understood the voice, while the wicked thought it was thunder and an earthquake. When God spoke the time, He poured upon us the Holy Ghost, and our faces began to light up and shine with the glory of God, as Moses' did when he came down from Mount Sinai.

The 144,000 were all sealed and perfectly united. On their foreheads was written, "God, New Jerusalem," and a glorious star containing Jesus' new name. At our happy, holy state the wicked were enraged, and would rush violently up to lay hands on us to thrust us into prison, when we would stretch forth the hand in the name of the Lord, and they would fall helpless to the ground. Then it was that the synagogue of Satan knew that God had loved us who could wash one another's feet, and salute the brethren with a holy kiss, and they worshiped at our feet.

Soon our eyes were drawn to the east, for a small black cloud had appeared, about half as large as a man's hand, which we all knew was the sign of the Son of man. We all in solemn silence gazed on the cloud as it drew nearer, and became lighter, glorious, and still more glorious, till it was a great white cloud. The bottom appeared like fire; a rainbow was over the cloud, while around it were ten thousand angels, singing a most lovely song; and upon it sat the Son of man. His hair was white and curly, and lay on His shoulders; and upon His head were many crowns. His feet had the appearance of fire; in His right hand was a sharp sickle; in His left, a silver trumpet. His eyes were as a flame of fire, which searched His children through and through. Then all faces gathered paleness, and those that God had rejected gathered blackness. Then we all cried out: "Who shall be able to stand? Is my robe spotless?" Then the angels ceased to sing, and there was some time of awful silence, when Jesus spoke: "Those who have clean hands and pure hearts shall be able to stand; My grace is sufficient for you." At this our faces lighted up, and joy filled every heart. And the angels struck a note higher and sang again, while the cloud drew still nearer the earth.

Then Jesus' silver trumpet sounded, as He descended on the cloud, wrapped in flames of fire. He gazed on the graves of the sleeping saints, then raised His eyes and hands to heaven, and cried, "Awake! awake! awake! ye that sleep in the dust, and arise." Then there was a mighty earthquake. The graves opened, and the dead came up clothed with immortality. The 144,000 shouted "Alleluia!" as they recognized their friends who had been torn from them by death, and in the same moment we were changed and caught up together with them to meet the Lord in the air.

We all entered the cloud together, and were seven days ascending to the sea of glass, when Jesus brought the crowns, and with His own right hand placed them on our heads. He gave us harps of gold and palms of victory. Here on the sea of glass the 144,000 stood in a perfect square. Some of them had very bright crowns, others not so bright. Some crowns appeared heavy with stars, while others had but few. All were perfectly satisfied with their crowns. And they were all clothed with a glorious white mantle from their shoulders to their feet. Angels were all about us as we marched over the sea of glass to the gate of the city. Jesus raised His mighty, glorious arm, laid hold of the pearly gate, swung it back on its glittering hinges, and said to us, "You have washed your robes in My blood, stood stiffly for My truth, enter in." We all marched in and felt that we had a perfect right in the city.

Here we saw the tree of life and the throne of God. Out of the throne came a pure river of water, and on either side of the river was the tree of life. On one side of the river was a trunk of a tree, and a trunk on the other side of the river, both of pure, transparent gold. At first I thought I saw two trees. I looked again, and saw that they were united at the top in one tree. So it was the tree of life on either side of the river of life. Its branches bowed to the place where we stood, and the fruit was glorious; it looked like gold mixed with silver.

We all went under the tree, and sat down to look at the glory of the place, when Brethren Fitch and Stockman, who had preached the gospel of the kingdom, and whom God had laid in the grave to save them, came up to us and asked us what we had passed through while they were sleeping. We tried to call up our greatest trials, but they looked so small compared with the far more exceeding and eternal weight of glory that surrounded us, that we could not speak them out, and we all cried out, "Alleluia! heaven is cheap enough!" and we touched our glorious harps and made heaven's arches ring.

After I came out of vision, everything seemed changed; a gloom was spread over all that I beheld. Oh, how dark this world looked to me! I wept when

I found myself here, and felt homesick. I had seen a better world, and it had spoiled this for me.

I related this vision to the believers in Portland, who had full confidence that it was from God. They all believed that God had chosen this way, after the great disappointment in October, to comfort and strengthen His people. The Spirit of the Lord attended the testimony, and the solemnity of eternity rested upon us. An unspeakable awe filled me, that I, so young and feeble, should be chosen as the instrument by which God would give light to His people. While under the power of the Lord, I was filled with joy, seeming to be surrounded by holy angels in the glorious courts of heaven, where all is peace and gladness; and it was a sad and bitter change to wake up to the realities of mortal life.

VIII

CALL TO TRAVEL

In my second vision, about a week after the first, the Lord gave me a view of the trials through which I must pass, and told me that I must go and relate to others what He had revealed to me. It was shown me that my labors would meet with great opposition, and that my heart would be rent with anguish; but that the grace of God would be sufficient to sustain me through all.

After I came out of this vision I was exceedingly troubled, for it pointed out my duty to go out among the people and present the truth. My health was so poor that I was in constant bodily suffering, and to all appearance had but a short time to live. I was only seventeen years of age, small and frail, unused to society, and naturally so timid and retiring that it was painful for me to meet strangers.

For several days, and far into the night, I prayed that this burden might be removed from me, and laid upon some one more capable of bearing it. But the light of duty did not change, and the words of the angel sounded continually in my ears, "Make known to others what I have revealed to you."

Hitherto when the Spirit of God had urged me to duty, I had risen above myself, forgetting all fear and timidity in the thought of Jesus' love and the wonderful work He had done for me.

But it seemed impossible for me to perform this work that was presented before me; to attempt it seemed certain failure. The trials attending it appeared more than I could endure. How could I, a child in years, go forth from place to place, unfolding to the people the holy truths of God? My heart shrank in terror from the thought. My brother Robert, but two years older than myself, could not accompany me, for he was feeble in health, and his timidity was greater than mine; nothing could have induced him to take such a step. My father had a family to support, and could not leave his business; but he repeatedly assured me that if God had called me to labor in other places, He would not fail to open the way for me. But these words of encouragement brought little comfort to my desponding heart; the path before me seemed hedged in with difficulties that I was unable to overcome.

I coveted death as a release from the responsibilities that were crowding upon me. At length the sweet peace I had so long enjoyed left me, and despair again pressed upon my soul.

ENCOURAGEMENT FROM THE BRETHREN

The company of believers in Portland were ignorant concerning the exercises of my mind that had brought me into this state of despondency; but they knew that for some reason my mind had become depressed, and they felt that this was sinful on my part, considering the gracious manner in which the Lord had manifested Himself to me. Meetings were held at my father's house, but my distress of mind was so great that I did not attend them for some time. My burden grew heavier until the agony of my spirit seemed more than I could bear.

At length I was induced to be present at one of the meetings in my own home. The church made my case a special subject of prayer. Father Pearson, who in my earlier experience had opposed the manifestations of the power of God upon me, now prayed earnestly for me, and counseled me to surrender my will to the will of the Lord. Like a tender father he tried to encourage and comfort me, bidding me believe I was not forsaken by the Friend of sinners.

I felt too weak and despondent to make any special effort for myself, but my heart united with the petitions of my friends. I cared little now for the opposition of the world, and felt willing to make every sacrifice if only the favor of God might be restored to me.

While prayer was offered for me, that the Lord would give me strength and courage to bear the message, the thick darkness that had encompassed me rolled back, and a sudden light came upon me. Something that seemed to me like a ball of fire struck me right over the heart. My strength was taken away, and I fell to the floor. I seemed to be in the presence of the angels. One of these holy beings again repeated the words, "Make known to others what I have revealed to you."

Father Pearson, who could not kneel on account of his rheumatism, witnessed this occurrence. When I revived sufficiently to see and hear, he rose from his chair, and said: "I have seen a sight such as I never expected to see. A ball of fire came down from heaven, and struck Sister Ellen Harmon right on the heart. *I saw it! I saw it!* I can never forget it. It has changed my whole being. Sister Ellen, have courage in the Lord. After this night I will never doubt again. We will help you henceforth, and not discourage you."

FEAR OF SELF-EXALTATION

One great fear that had oppressed me was that if I obeyed the call of duty, and went out declaring myself to be one favored of the Most High with visions and revelations for the people, I might yield to sinful exaltation, and be lifted above the station that was right for me to occupy, bring upon myself the displeasure of God, and lose my own soul. I had known of such cases, and my heart shrank from the trying ordeal.

I now entreated that if I must go and relate what the Lord had shown me, I should be preserved from undue exaltation. Said the angel: "Your prayers are heard, and shall be answered. If this evil that you dread threatens you, the hand of God will be stretched out to save you; by affliction He will draw you to Himself, and preserve your humility. Deliver the message faithfully; endure unto the end, and you shall eat the fruit of the tree of life and drink of the water of life."

After recovering consciousness of earthly things, I committed myself to the Lord, ready to do His bidding, whatever that might be.

AMONG THE BELIEVERS IN MAINE

It was not long before the Lord opened the way for me to go with my brother-in-law to my sisters in Poland, thirty miles from my home, and while there I had an opportunity to bear my testimony. For three months my throat and lungs had been so diseased that I could talk but little, and that in a low and husky tone. On this occasion I stood up in meeting and commenced to speak in a whisper. I continued thus for about five minutes, when the soreness and obstruction left me, my voice became clear and strong, and I spoke with perfect ease and freedom for nearly two hours. When my message was ended, my voice was gone until I again stood before the people, when the same singular restoration was repeated. I felt a constant assurance that I was doing the will of God, and saw marked results attending my efforts.

The way providentially opened for me to go to the eastern part of Maine. Brother Wm. Jordan was going on business to Orrington, accompanied by his sister, and I was urged to go with them. As I had promised the Lord to walk in the path He opened before me, I dared not refuse. The Spirit of God attended the message I bore at this place; hearts were made glad in the truth, and the desponding ones were cheered and encouraged to renew their faith.

At Orrington I met Elder James White. He was acquainted with my friends, and was himself engaged in work for the salvation of souls.

I also visited Garland, where a large number collected from different quarters to hear my message.

Soon after this I went to Exeter, a small village not far from Garland. Here a heavy burden rested upon me, from which I could not be free until I had related what had been shown me in regard to some fanatical persons who were present. I declared that they were deceived in thinking that they were actuated by the Spirit of God. My testimony was very displeasing to these persons and their sympathizers.

Soon after this I returned to Portland, having borne the testimony that God had given me, and experiencing His approbation at every step.

IX

ANSWERS TO PRAYER

In the spring of 1845 I made a visit to Topsham, Maine. On one occasion quite a number of us were assembled at the house of Brother Stockbridge Howland. His eldest daughter, Miss Frances Howland, a very dear friend of mine, was sick with the rheumatic fever, and under the doctor's care. Her hands were so badly swollen that the joints could not be distinguished. As we sat together speaking of her case, Brother Howland was asked if he had faith that his daughter could be healed in answer to prayer. He answered that he would try to believe that she might, and presently declared that he did believe it possible.

We all knelt in earnest prayer to God in her behalf. We claimed the promise, "Ask, and ye shall receive." John 16:24. The blessing of God attended our prayers, and we had the assurance that God was willing to heal the afflicted one. One of the brethren present cried out, "Is there a sister here who has the faith to go and take her by the hand, and bid her arise in the name of the Lord?"

Sister Frances was lying in the chamber above, and before he ceased speaking Sister Curtis was on her way to the stairs. She entered the sickroom with the Spirit of God upon her, and taking the invalid by the hand, said, "Sister Frances, in the name of the Lord arise, and be whole." New life shot through the veins of the sick girl, a holy faith took possession of her, and obeying its impulse, she rose from her bed, stood upon her feet, and walked the room, praising God for her recovery. She was soon dressed, and came down into the room where we were assembled, her countenance lighted up with unspeakable joy and gratitude.

The next morning she took breakfast with us. Soon after, as Elder White was reading from the fifth chapter of James for family worship, the doctor came into the hall, and, as usual, went upstairs to visit his patient. Not finding her there, he hurried down, and with a look of alarm opened the door of the large kitchen where we were all sitting, his patient with us. He gazed upon her with astonishment, and at length ejaculated, "So Frances is better!"

Brother Howland answered, "The Lord has healed her," and the reader resumed his chapter where he had been interrupted: "Is any sick among you? let him call for the elders of the church; and let them pray over him." James 5:14. The doctor listened with a curious expression of mingled wonder and incredulity upon his face, nodded, and hastily left the room.

The same day Sister Frances rode three miles, returning home in the evening, and although it was rainy, she sustained no injury, and continued to improve rapidly in health. In a few days, at her request, she was led down into the water and baptized. Although the weather and the water were very cold, she received no injury, but from that time was free from the disease, and in the enjoyment of her usual health.

At this time Brother Wm. H. Hyde was very sick with dysentery. His symptoms were alarming, and the physician pronounced his case almost hopeless. We visited him and prayed with him, but he had come under the influence of certain fanatical persons, who were bringing dishonor upon our cause. We wished to remove him from among them, and petitioned the

Lord to give him strength to leave that place. He was strengthened and blessed in answer to our prayers, and rode four miles to the house of Brother Patten, but after arriving there he seemed to be rapidly sinking.

The fanaticism and errors into which he had fallen through an evil influence seemed to hinder the exercise of his faith, but he gratefully received the plain testimony borne him, made humble confession of his fault, and took his position firmly for the truth.

Only a few who were strong in faith were permitted to enter the sickroom. The fanatics whose influence over him had been so injurious, and who had persistently followed him to Brother Patten's, were positively forbidden to come into his presence, while we prayed fervently for his restoration to health. I have seldom known such a reaching out to claim the promises of God. The salvation of the Holy Spirit was revealed, and power from on high rested upon our sick brother and upon all present.

Brother Hyde immediately dressed and walked out of the room, praising God, and with the light of heaven shining upon his countenance. A farmer's dinner was ready upon the table. Said he, "If I were well, I should partake of this food; and as I believe God has healed me, I shall carry out my faith." He sat down to dinner with the rest, and ate heartily without injury. His recovery was complete and permanent.

X

LABORS IN NEW HAMPSHIRE

About this time I was shown that it was my duty to visit our people in New Hampshire. My constant and faithful companion at this time was Louisa Foss, a sister of Samuel Foss, the husband of my sister Mary. I can never forget her kind and sisterly attention to me in my journeyings. We were also accompanied by Elder Files and his wife, who were old and valued friends of my family, and by Brother Ralph Haskins and Elder James White.

We were cordially received by our friends in New Hampshire, but there were wrongs existing in that field which burdened me much. We had to meet a spirit of self-righteousness that was very depressing.

ENCOURAGEMENT FOR ELDER MORSE

While visiting at the house of Elder Washington Morse, I was very ill. Prayer was offered in my behalf, and the Spirit of God rested upon me. I was taken off in vision, and some things were shown me concerning the case of Elder Morse in connection with the disappointment of 1844.

Elder Morse had been firm and consistent in the belief that the Lord would come at that time; but when the period passed without bringing the event expected, he was perplexed and unable to explain the delay. Although bitterly disappointed, he did not renounce his faith, as some did, calling it a fanatical delusion; but he was bewildered, and could not understand the position of God's people on prophetic time. He had been so earnest in declaring that the coming of the Lord was near, that when the time passed, he was despondent, and did nothing to encourage the disappointed people, who were like sheep without a shepherd, left to be devoured of wolves.

The case of Jonah was presented before me. Elder Morse was in a condition similar to that of the disappointed prophet. He had proclaimed that the Lord would come in 1844. The time had passed. The check of fear that had partially held the people was removed, and they indulged in derision of those who had looked in vain for Jesus. Elder Morse felt that he was a byword among his neighbors, an object of jest, and he could not be reconciled to his position. He did not think of the mercy of God in granting the world a longer time in which to prepare for His coming, that the warning of the judgment might be heard more widely, and the people tested with greater light. He thought only of the humiliation of God's servants.

Instead of being discouraged at his disappointment, as was Jonah, Elder Morse should have cast aside his selfish sorrow, and gathered up the rays of precious light that God had given His people. He should have rejoiced that the world was granted a reprieve; and he should have been ready to aid in carrying forward the great work yet to be done upon the earth, in bringing sinners to repentance and salvation.

A LACK OF TRUE GODLINESS

It was difficult to accomplish much good in New Hampshire. We found little spirituality there. Many pronounced their experience in the movement of 1844 a delusion. It was hard to reach this class, for we could not accept the position they ventured to take. A number who had been active preachers and exhorters in 1844, now seemed to have lost their moorings and did not know where we were in prophetic time; they were fast uniting with the spirit of the world.

SPIRITUAL MAGNETISM

In New Hampshire we had to contend with a species of spiritual magnetism, of a similar character with mesmerism. It was our first experience of this kind, and happened thus: Arriving at Claremont, we were told that there were two parties of Adventists, one party denying their former faith, and another a small number who believed that in their past experience they had been led by the providence of God. We were directed to two men especially as holding views similar to our own. We found that there was much prejudice against these men, but supposed that they were persecuted for righteousness' sake. We called on them, and were kindly received and courteously treated. We soon learned that they claimed perfect sanctification, declaring that they were above the possibility of sin.

These men wore excellent clothes, and had an air of ease and comfort. While we were talking with them, a little boy, about eight years old, and literally clad in dirty rags, entered the room in which we were sitting. We were surprised to find that this child was the son of one of these men. The mother looked exceedingly ashamed and annoyed; but the father, utterly unconcerned, continued to talk about his high spiritual attainments, without the slightest recognition of his little son.

His sanctification had suddenly lost its charm in my eyes. Wrapped in prayer and meditation, throwing off all the toil and responsibilities of life, this man had failed to provide for the actual wants of his family or to give his children fatherly attention. He seemed to forget that the greater our love for God, the stronger should be our love and care for those whom He has given us. The Saviour never taught idleness and abstract devotion, to the neglect of the duties lying directly in our pathway.

This husband and father declared that the attainment of true holiness carried the mind above all earthly thoughts. Still he sat at the table and ate temporal food. He was not fed by a miracle. Some one had to provide the food that he ate, although about this matter he troubled himself little, his time being so entirely devoted to spiritual things. Not so his wife, upon whom rested the burden of the family. She toiled unremittingly in every department of household labor to keep up the home. Her husband declared that she was not sanctified, that she allowed worldly things to draw her mind away from religious subjects.

I thought of our Saviour, who labored so untiringly for the good of others. "My Father worketh hitherto, and I work" (John 5:17), He declared. The sanctification that He taught was shown by deeds of kindness and mercy, and the love that leads men and women to regard others better than themselves.

In speaking of faith, one of them said, "All that we have to do is to believe, and whatever we ask of God will be given us."

Elder White suggested that there were conditions attached to this promise. " 'If ye abide in Me,' Christ said, 'and My words abide in you, ye shall ask what ye will, and it shall be done unto you.' John 15:7. Your theory of faith," he continued, "must have a foundation."

A sister of one of these men requested a private interview with me. She had much to say concerning entire consecration to God, and endeavored to draw out my views in regard to this subject. While talking, she held my hand in hers, and with the other softly stroked my hair. I prayed that angels of God might protect me from the unholy influences which this attractive young woman was seeking to exercise over me with her fair speeches and gentle caresses. She had much to say in regard to the spiritual attainments and great faith of her brother. Her mind seemed to be very much occupied with him and his experience. I felt that I must be guarded in what I said, and was glad when the interview was ended.

These persons who made such lofty professions, were deceiving the unwary. They had much to say about charity covering a multitude of sins. I could not agree with their views and feelings, and felt that they were wielding a terrible power for evil, and was glad to get away from their presence.

As soon as the views of these people were crossed, they manifested a stubborn, self-righteous spirit that rejected all instruction. Though professing great humility, they were boastful in their sophistry of sanctification, and resisted all appeals to reason. We felt that all our efforts to convince them of their error were useless, as they took the position that they were not learners, but teachers.

MEETING AT BROTHER COLLIER'S

In the afternoon we went to the house of Brother Collier, where we proposed to hold a meeting that evening. We asked Brother Collier some questions regarding these men, but he gave us no information.

"If the Lord sent you here," he said, "you will ascertain what spirit governs them, and will solve the mystery for us."

Both of these men attended the meeting at Brother Collier's. While I was earnestly praying for light and the presence of God, they began to groan and to cry "Amen!" apparently throwing their sympathy with my prayer. But my heart was immediately oppressed with a great weight. The words died upon my lips, and darkness overshadowed the whole meeting.

Elder White arose, and said: "I am distressed. The Spirit of God is grieved. I resist this influence in the name of the Lord. O God, rebuke this foul spirit."

I was immediately relieved, and rose above the shadows. But again, while I was speaking words of encouragement and faith to those present, their groanings and amens chilled me. Once more Elder White rebuked the spirit of darkness, and again the power of God rested upon me while I spoke to the people. These agents of the enemy were then so bound as to be unable to exert their baleful influence again that night.

After the meeting, Elder White said to Brother Collier: "Now I can tell you concerning these two men. They are acting under a satanic influence, yet attributing all to the Spirit of the Lord."

"I believe God sent you to encourage us," he replied. "We call their influence mesmerism. They affect the minds of others in a remarkable way, and have controlled some to their great damage. We seldom hold meetings here; for they intrude their presence, and we can have no union with them. They manifest deep feeling, as you observed to-night, but they crush the very life from our prayers, and leave an influence blacker than Egyptian darkness. I have never seen them tied up before to-night."

THE "CANNOT-SIN" THEORY

During family prayer that night, the Spirit of the Lord rested upon me, and I was shown many things in vision. These men were presented to me as doing great injury to the cause of God. While professing sanctification, they were transgressing the sacred law. They were corrupt at heart, and those in union with them were under a satanic delusion, obeying their carnal instincts instead of the word of God.

They held that those who are sanctified cannot sin. And this naturally led to the belief that the affections and desires of the sanctified ones were always right, and never in danger of leading them into sin. In harmony with these sophistries, they were practising the worst sins under the garb of sanctification, and through their deceptive, mesmeric influence were gaining a strange power over some of their associates, who did not see the evil of these apparently beautiful but seductive theories.

Terrible was their power over the people, for while holding their attention and winning their confidence through a mesmeric influence, they led the innocent and unsuspecting to believe that this influence was the Spirit of God. Therefore those who followed their teachings were deceived into the belief that they and their associates who claimed to be wholly sanctified, could fulfill all the desires of their hearts without sin.

Clearly the deceptions of these false teachers were laid open before me, and I saw the fearful account that stood against them in the book of records, and the terrible guilt that rested upon them for professing complete holiness while their daily acts were offensive in the sight of God.

Some time after this, the characters of these persons were developed before the people, and the vision given in reference to them was fully vindicated.

TRUE SANCTIFICATION

"Believe in Christ," was the cry of these claimants of sanctification. "Only believe; this is all that is required of you. Only have faith in Jesus."

The words of John came forcibly to my mind, "If we say that we have no sin, we deceive ourselves, and the truth is not in us." 1 John 1:8. I was shown that those who triumphantly claim to be sinless, show by their very boasting that they are far from being without taint of sin. The more clearly fallen man comprehends the character of Christ, the more distrustful will he be of himself, and the more imperfect will his works appear to him, in contrast with those which marked the life of the spotless Redeemer. But those who are far from Jesus, those whose spiritual perceptions are so clouded by error that they cannot comprehend the character of the great Exemplar, conceive of Him as altogether such a one as themselves, and dare to talk of their own perfection of holiness. But they are far from God; they know little of themselves, and less of Christ.

XI

MEETING FANATICISM

As I returned to Portland, there were increasing evidences of the desolating effects of fanaticism. Some seemed to think that religion consisted in great excitement and noise. They would talk in a manner that would irritate unbelievers, and have an influence to arouse hatred against themselves and the doctrines they taught. Then they would rejoice that they suffered persecution. Unbelievers could see no consistency in such a course. The brethren in some places were prevented from assembling for meetings. The innocent suffered with the guilty.

I carried a sad and heavy heart much of the time. It seemed so cruel that the cause of Christ should be injured by the course of these injudicious men. They were not only ruining their own souls, but placing upon the cause a stigma not easily removed. And Satan loved to have it so. It suited him well to see the truth handled by unsanctified men; to have it mixed with error, and then all together trampled in the dust. He looked with triumph upon the confused, scattered state of God's children.

We trembled for the churches that were to be subjected to this spirit of fanaticism. My heart ached for God's people. Must they be deceived and led away by this false enthusiasm? I faithfully pronounced the warnings given me of the Lord; but they seemed to have little effect, except to make these persons of extreme views jealous of me.

A FALSE HUMILITY

There were some who professed great humility, and advocated creeping on the floor like children, as an evidence of their humility. They claimed that the words of Christ in Matthew 18:1-6 must have a literal fulfillment at this period, when they were looking for their Saviour to return. They would creep around their houses, on the street, over bridges, and in the church itself.

I told them plainly that this was not required; that the humility which God looked for in His people was to be shown by a Christlike life, not by creeping on the floor. All spiritual things are to be treated with sacred dignity. Humility and meekness are in accordance with the life of Christ, but they are to be shown in a dignified way.

A Christian reveals true humility by showing the gentleness of Christ, by being always ready to help others, by speaking kind words and performing unselfish acts, which elevate and ennoble the most sacred message that has come to our world.

FRUITS OF THE "NO-WORK" DOCTRINE

There were some in Paris, Maine, who believed that it was sin to work. The Lord gave me a reproof for the leader in this error, declaring that he was going contrary to the word of God in abstaining from labor, in urging his errors upon others, and in denouncing all who did not receive them. He rejected every evidence which the Lord gave to convince him of his error, and was determined to make no change in his course. He took weary journeys, walking great distances to places where he would receive only abuse, and thought that in so doing he was suffering for Christ's sake. Impressions were followed, and reason and judgment were laid aside.

I saw that God would work for the salvation of His people: that this misguided man would soon manifest himself, so that all the honest in heart would see that he was not actuated by a right spirit, and that his career would soon close. Soon afterward the snare was broken, and he had but little more influence over the brethren. He denounced the visions as being of the devil, and continued to follow his impressions, until his mind was deranged and his friends were obliged to confine him. At last he made a rope of some of his bed clothing, with which he hanged himself, and his followers were brought to realize the fallacy of his teachings.

THE DIGNITY OF LABOR

God ordained that the beings He created should work. Upon this their happiness depends. No one in the Lord's great domain of creation was made to be a drone. Our happiness increases and our powers develop as we engage in useful employment.

Action gives power. Entire harmony pervades the universe of God. All the heavenly beings are in constant activity; and the Lord Jesus, in His life work, has given an example for every one. He went about "doing good." God has established the law of obedient action. Silent but ceaseless, the objects of His creation do their appointed work. The ocean is in constant motion. The springing grass, which to-day is and to-morrow is cast into the oven, does its errand, clothing the fields with beauty. The leaves are stirred to motion, and yet no hand is seen to touch them. The sun, moon, and stars are useful and glorious in fulfilling their mission.

At all times the machinery of the body continues its work. Day by day the heart throbs, doing its regular, appointed task, unceasingly forcing its crimson current to all parts of the body. Action, action, is seen pervading the whole living machinery. And man, his mind and body created in God's similitude, must be active in order to fill his appointed place. He is not to be idle. Idleness is sin.

A SEVERE TRIAL

In the midst of my experiences in meeting fanaticism, I was subjected to a severe trial. If the Spirit of God rested upon any one in meeting, and he glorified God by praising Him, some raised the cry of mesmerism; and if it pleased the Lord to give me a vision in meeting, some would say that it was the effect of excitement and mesmerism.

Grieved and desponding, I often went alone to some retired place to pour out my soul before Him who invites the weary and heavy-laden to come and find rest. As my faith claimed the promises, Jesus would seem very near. The sweet light of heaven would shine around me, and I would seem to be encircled by the arms of my Saviour, and would there be taken off in vision. But when I would relate what God had revealed to me alone, where no earthly influence could affect me, I was grieved and astonished to hear some intimate that those who lived nearest to God were most liable to be deceived by Satan.

Some would have had me believe that there was no Holy Spirit, and that all the exercises that holy men of God experienced, were only the effect of mesmerism or the deception of Satan.

Those who had taken extreme views of certain texts of Scripture, refraining wholly from labor, and rejecting all who would not receive their ideas on this and other points pertaining to religious duty, charged me with conforming to the world. On the other hand, the nominal Adventists charged me with fanaticism, and I was falsely represented as the leader of the fanaticism which I was laboring constantly to arrest.

Different times were set for the Lord to come, and were urged upon the brethren. But the Lord showed me that they would pass by, for the time of trouble must take place before the coming of Christ; and that every time a date was set, and passed, it would weaken the faith of God's people. For this I was charged with being the evil servant that said, "My Lord delayeth His coming." Matt. 24:48.

All these things weighed heavily upon my spirits, and in the confusion I was sometimes tempted to doubt my own experience.

While at family prayers one morning, the power of God began to rest upon me, and the thought rushed into my mind that it was mesmerism, and I resisted it. Immediately I was struck dumb, and for a few moments was lost to everything around me. I then saw my sin in doubting the power of God, and that for so doing I was struck dumb, but that my tongue should be loosed in less than twenty-four hours. A card was held up before me, on which were written in letters of gold the chapter and verse of fifty texts of Scripture.

After I came out of vision, I beckoned for the slate, and wrote upon it that I was dumb, also what I had seen, and that I wished the large Bible. I took the Bible, and readily turned to all the texts that I had seen upon the card.[1]

I was unable to speak all day. Early the next morning my soul was filled with joy, and my tongue was loosed to shout the high praises of God. After that I dared not doubt, or for a moment resist the power of God, however others might think of me.

---

[1] NOTE.—For these texts, see "Early Writings," pp. 24-31, new edition.

Up to this time I could not write; my trembling hand was unable to hold a pen steadily. While in vision, I was commanded by an angel to write the vision. I obeyed, and wrote readily. My nerves were strengthened, and from that day to this my hand has been steady.

EXHORTATIONS TO FAITHFULNESS

It was a great cross for me to relate to the erring what had been shown me concerning them. It caused me great distress to see others troubled or grieved. And when obliged to declare the messages, I would often soften them down, and make them appear as favorable for the individual as I could, and then would go by myself and weep in agony of spirit. I looked upon those who seemed to have only their own souls to care for, and thought if I were in their condition I would not murmur. It was hard to relate the plain, cutting testimonies given me of God. I anxiously watched the result, and if the persons reproved rose up against the reproof, and afterward opposed the truth, these queries would arise in my mind: Did I deliver the message just as I should? Could there not have been some way to save them? And then such distress pressed upon my soul that I often felt that death would be a welcome messenger, and the grave a sweet resting place.

I did not realize that I was unfaithful in thus questioning and doubting, and did not see the danger and sin of such a course, until in vision I was taken into the presence of Jesus. He looked upon me with a frown, and turned His face from me. It is not possible to describe the terror and agony I then felt. I fell upon my face before Him, but had no power to utter a word. Oh, how I longed to be covered and hid from that dreadful frown! Then could I realize, in some degree, what the feelings of the lost will be when they cry to the mountains and rocks, "Fall on us, and hide us from the face of Him that sitteth on the throne, and from the wrath of the Lamb." Rev. 6:16.

Presently an angel bade me rise, and the sight that met my eyes can hardly be described. Before me was a company whose hair and garments were torn, and whose countenances were the very picture of despair and horror. They came close to me, and rubbed their garments upon mine. As I looked at my garments, I saw that they were stained with blood. Again I fell like one dead, at the feet of my accompanying angel. I could not plead one excuse, and longed to be away from that holy place.

The angel raised me to my feet, and said: "This is not your case now, but this scene has passed before you to let you know what your situation must be if you neglect to declare to others what the Lord has revealed to you. But if you are faithful to the end, you shall eat of the tree of life, and shall drink of the river of the water of life. You will have to suffer much, but the grace of God is sufficient."

I then felt willing to do all that the Lord might require me to do, that I might have His approbation, and not feel His dreadful frown.

THE SEAL OF DIVINE APPROVAL

Those were troublous times. If we had not stood firmly then, we should have made shipwreck of our faith. Some said we were stubborn; but we were obliged to set our faces as a flint, and turn not to the right hand nor to the left.

For years we labored to beat back the prejudice and subdue the opposition that at times threatened to overwhelm the faithful standard bearers of truth—the heroes and heroines of faith. But we found that those who were seeking God in humility and contrition of soul, were able to discern between the true and the false. "The meek will He guide in judgment: and the meek will He teach His way." Ps. 25:9.

God gave us a precious experience in those days. When brought in close conflict with the powers of darkness, as we frequently were, we laid the whole matter before the mighty Helper. Again and again we prayed for strength and wisdom. We would not yield the point; we felt that help must come. And through faith in God, the enemy's artillery was turned against himself, glorious victories were gained to the cause of truth, and we were made to realize that God gave not His Spirit by measure unto us. Had it not been for these special evidences of God's love, had He not thus, by the manifestation of His Spirit, set His seal to the truth, we might have become discouraged; but these proofs of divine guidance, these living experiences in the things of God, strengthened us to fight manfully the battles of the Lord. The believing ones could more clearly discern how God had mapped out their course, guiding them amid trials, disappointments, and fierce conflicts. They grew stronger as they met and overcame obstacles, and gained a rich experience at every step they advanced.

LESSONS FROM THE PAST

In later years I have been shown that the false theories advanced in the past have by no means been given up. As favorable opportunities come, they will have a resurrection. Let us not forget that everything is to be shaken that can be shaken. The enemy will be successful in overthrowing the faith of some, but those who are true to principle will not be shaken. They will stand firm amid trial and temptation. The Lord has pointed out these errors; and those who do not discern where Satan has come in, will continue to be led in false paths. Jesus bids us be watchful, and strengthen the things that remain, which are ready to die.

We are not called upon to enter into controversy with those who hold false theories. Controversy is unprofitable. Christ never entered into it. "It is written" is the weapon used by the world's Redeemer. Let us keep close to the Word. Let us allow the Lord Jesus and His messengers to testify. We know that their testimony is true.

Christ is over all the works of His creation. In the pillar of fire, He guided the children of Israel, His eyes seeing past, present, and future. He is to be recognized and honored by all who love God. His commandments are to be the controlling power in the lives of His people.

The tempter comes with the supposition that Christ has removed His seat of honor and power into some unknown region, and that men need no longer be inconvenienced by exalting His character and obeying His law. Human beings are to be a law unto themselves, he declares. These sophistries exalt self and make nothing of God. Restraint and moral control in the human family are destroyed. Restraint upon vice grows more and more feeble. The world loves not, fears not God. And those who do not love or fear God soon lose all sense of obligation to one another. They are without God and without hope in the world.

Those teachers who do not daily bring the word of God into their life work, are in great peril. They have not a saving knowledge of God or of Christ. It is those who do not live the truth who are most inclined to invent sophistries to occupy the time and absorb the attention that ought to be given to the study of God's word. It is a fearful mistake for us to neglect the study of the Bible to investigate theories that are misleading, diverting minds from the words of Christ to fallacies of human production.

We need no fanciful teaching regarding the personality of God. What God desires us to know of Him is revealed in His word and His works. The beautiful things of nature reveal His character and His power as Creator. They are His gift to the race, to show His power, and to show that He is a God of love. But no one is authorized to say that God Himself in person is in flower or leaf or tree. These things are God's handiwork, revealing His love for mankind.

Christ is the perfect revelation of God. Let those who desire to know God, study the work and teaching of Christ. To those who receive Him and believe on Him, He gives power to become the sons of God.

XII

THE SABBATH OF THE LORD

While on a visit to New Bedford, Mass., in 1846, I became acquainted with Elder Joseph Bates. He had early embraced the advent faith, and was an active laborer in the cause. I found him to be a true Christian gentleman, courteous and kind.

The first time he heard me speak, he manifested deep interest. After I had ceased speaking, he arose and said: "I am a doubting Thomas. I do not believe in visions. But if I could believe that the testimony the sister has related to-night was indeed the voice of God to us, I should be the happiest man alive. My heart is deeply moved. I believe the speaker to be sincere, but cannot explain in regard to her being shown the wonderful things she has related to us."

Elder Bates was resting upon Saturday, the seventh day of the week, and he urged it upon our attention as the true Sabbath. I did not feel its importance, and thought that he erred in dwelling upon the fourth commandment more than upon the other nine.

But the Lord gave me a view of the heavenly sanctuary. The temple of God was open in heaven, and I was shown the ark of God covered with the mercy seat. Two angels stood one at either end of the ark, with their wings spread over the mercy seat, and their faces turned toward it. This, my accompanying angel informed me, represented all the heavenly host looking with reverential awe toward the law of God, which had been written by the finger of God.

Jesus raised the cover of the ark, and I beheld the tables of stone on which the ten commandments were written. I was amazed as I saw the fourth commandment in the very center of the ten precepts, with a soft halo of light encircling it. Said the angel, "It is the only one of the ten which defines the living God who created the heavens and the earth and all things that are therein."

When the foundations of the earth were laid, then was also laid the foundation of the Sabbath. I was shown that if the true Sabbath had been kept, there would never have been an infidel or an atheist. The observance of the Sabbath would have preserved the world from idolatry.

The fourth commandment has been trampled upon, therefore we are called upon to repair the breach in the law and plead for the desecrated Sabbath. The man of sin, who exalted himself above God, and thought to change times and laws, brought about the change of the Sabbath from the seventh to the first day of the week. In doing this he made a breach in the law of God. Just prior to the great day of God, a message is sent forth to warn the people to come back to their allegiance to the law of God, which antichrist has broken down. Attention must be called to the breach in the law, by precept and example.

I was shown that the precious promises of Isaiah 58:12-14 apply to those who labor for the restoration of the true Sabbath.

I was shown that the third angel proclaiming the commandments of God and the faith of Jesus, represents the people who receive this message, and raise the voice of warning to the world to keep the commandments of God and His law as the apple of the eye; and that in response to this warning, many would embrace the Sabbath of the Lord.

XIII

MARRIAGE AND UNITED LABORS

Aug. 30, 1846, I was united in marriage to Elder James White. Elder White had enjoyed a deep experience in the advent movement, and his labors in proclaiming the truth had been blessed of God. Our hearts were united in the great work, and together we traveled and labored for the salvation of souls.

IN CONFIRMATION OF FAITH

In November, 1846, I attended, with my husband, a meeting at Topsham, Maine, at which Elder Joseph Bates was present. He did not then fully believe that my visions were of God. That meeting was a season of much interest. The Spirit of God rested upon me; I was wrapped in a vision of God's glory, and for the first time had a view of other planets. After I came out of vision, I related what I had seen. Elder Bates then asked if I had studied astronomy. I told him I had no recollection of ever looking into an astronomy. Then he said, "This is of the Lord." His countenance shone with the light of heaven, and he exhorted the church with power.

Regarding his attitude toward the visions, Elder Bates made the following statement:

"Although I could see nothing in them that militated against the Word, yet I felt alarmed and tried exceedingly, and for a long time unwilling to believe that it was anything more than what was produced by a protracted debilitated state of her body.

"I therefore sought opportunities in the presence of others, when her mind seemed freed from excitement (out of meeting), to question and cross-question her, and her friends which accompanied her, especially her elder sister, to get if possible at the truth. During the number of visits she has made to New Bedford and Fairhaven since, while at our meetings, I have seen her in vision a number of times, and also in Topsham, Maine; and those who were present during some of those exciting scenes know well with what interest and intensity I listened to every word, and watched every move to detect deception or mesmeric influence. And I thank God for the opportunity I have had with others to witness these things. I can now confidently speak for myself. I believe the work is of God, and is given to comfort and strengthen His 'scattered, torn, and peeled people,' since the closing up of our work for the world in October, 1844."[1]

FERVENT, EFFECTUAL PRAYER

During the meeting at Topsham, I was shown that I would be much afflicted, and that we would have a trial of our faith after our return to Gorham, where my parents were then living.

On our return, I was taken very sick, and suffered extremely. My parents, husband, and sisters united in prayer for me, but I suffered on for three weeks. I often fainted like one dead, but in answer to prayer revived again. My agony was so great that I pleaded with those around me not to pray for me; for I thought their prayers were protracting my sufferings. Our neighbors gave me up to die. For a time it pleased the Lord to try our faith.

Brother and Sister Nichols, of Dorchester, Mass., had heard of my affliction, and their son Henry came to Gorham, bringing things for my comfort. During

[1] From a broadside, entitled, "A Vision," published in April, 1847 (press of Benjamin Lindsey, New Bedford), and reprinted by Elder James White in "A Word to the Little Flock," page 21, May, 1847.

his visit, my friends again united in prayer for my recovery. After others had prayed, Brother Henry Nichols began to pray most fervently; and with the power of God resting upon him, he arose from his knees, came across the room, and laid his hands upon my head, saying, "Sister Ellen, Jesus Christ maketh thee whole," and fell back, prostrated by the power of God. I believed that the work was of God, and the pain left me. My soul was filled with gratitude and peace. The language of my heart was: "There is no help for us but in God. We can be in peace only as we rest in Him and wait for His salvation."

LABORS IN MASSACHUSETTS

A few weeks after this, on our way to Boston, we took the steamer at Portland. A violent storm came up, and we were in great peril. But through the mercy of God we were all landed safe.

Of our labors in Massachusetts during February and the first week in March, my husband wrote from Gorham, Maine, March 14, 1847, shortly after our return home:

"While we have been from our friends here near seven weeks, God has been merciful to us. He has been our strength on the sea and land. Ellen has enjoyed the best state of health for six weeks past that she has for so long a time for six years. We are both enjoying good health. . . .

"Since we left Topsham, we have had some trying times. We have also had many glorious, heavenly, refreshing seasons. On the whole, it has been one of the best visits we ever had to Massachusetts. Our brethren at New Bedford and Fairhaven were mightily strengthened and confirmed in the truth and power of God. Brethren in other places were also much blessed."

A VIEW OF THE HEAVENLY SANCTUARY [2]

At a meeting held on Sabbath day, April 3, 1847, at the home of Brother Stockbridge Howland, we felt an unusual spirit of prayer. And as we prayed, the Holy Ghost fell upon us. We were very happy. Soon I was lost to earthly things, and was wrapped in a vision of God's glory.

I saw an angel flying swiftly to me. He quickly carried me from the earth to the holy city. In the city I saw a temple, which I entered. I passed through a door before I came to the first veil. This veil was raised, and I passed into the holy place. Here I saw the altar of incense, the candlestick with seven lamps, and the table on which was the showbread. After viewing the glory of the holy, Jesus raised the second veil, and I passed into the holy of holies.

In the holiest I saw an ark; on the top and sides of it was purest gold. On each end of the ark was a lovely cherub, with its wings spread out over it. Their faces were turned toward each other, and they looked downward. Between the angels was a golden censer. Above the ark, where the angels stood, was an exceeding bright glory, that appeared like a throne where God dwelt. Jesus stood by the ark, and as the saints' prayers came up to Him, the incense in the censer would smoke, and He would offer up their prayers with the smoke of the incense to His Father.

In the ark was the golden pot of manna, Aaron's rod that budded, and the tables of stone, which folded together like a book. Jesus opened them, and I saw the ten commandments written on them with the finger

---

[2] See "Early Writings," new edition, pp. 32-35.

of God. On one table were four, and on the other six. The four on the first table shone brighter than the other six. But the fourth, the Sabbath commandment, shone above them all; for the Sabbath was set apart to be kept in honor of God's holy name. The holy Sabbath looked glorious—a halo of glory was all around it. I saw that the Sabbath commandment was not nailed to the cross. If it was, the other nine commandments were; and we are at liberty to break them all, as well as to break the fourth. I saw that God had not changed the Sabbath, for He never changes. But the pope had changed it from the seventh to the first day of the week; for he was to change times and laws.

And I saw that if God had changed the Sabbath from the seventh to the first day, He would have changed the writing of the Sabbath commandment, written on the tables of stone, which are now in the ark in the most holy place of the temple in heaven; and it would read thus: The first day is the Sabbath of the Lord thy God. But I saw that it read the same as when written on the tables of stone by the finger of God, and delivered to Moses on Sinai, "But the seventh day is the Sabbath of the Lord thy God." I saw that the holy Sabbath is, and will be, the separating wall between the true Israel of God and unbelievers; and that the Sabbath is the great question to unite the hearts of God's dear, waiting saints.

I saw that God had children who do not see and keep the Sabbath. They have not rejected the light upon it. And at the commencement of the time of trouble, we were filled with the Holy Ghost as we went forth and proclaimed the Sabbath more fully. This enraged the churches and nominal Adventists, as they could not refute the Sabbath truth. And at this time God's chosen all saw clearly that we had the truth, and they came out and endured the persecution with us. I saw the sword, famine, pestilence, and great confusion in the land. The wicked thought that we had brought the judgments upon them, and they rose up and took counsel to rid the earth of us, thinking that then the evil would be stayed.

In the time of trouble we all fled from the cities and villages, but were pursued by the wicked, who entered the houses of the saints with a sword. They raised the sword to kill us, but it broke, and fell as powerless as a straw. Then we all cried day and night for deliverance, and the cry came up before God.

The sun came up, and the moon stood still. The streams ceased to flow. Dark, heavy clouds came up, and clashed against each other. But there was one clear place of settled glory, whence came the voice of God like many waters, which shook the heavens and the earth. The sky opened and shut, and was in commotion. The mountains shook like a reed in the wind, and cast out ragged rocks all around. The sea boiled like a pot, and cast out stones upon the land.

And as God spoke the day and the hour of Jesus' coming, and delivered the everlasting covenant to His people, He spoke one sentence, and then paused, while the words were rolling through the earth. The Israel of God stood with their eyes fixed upward, listening to the words as they came from the mouth of Jehovah, and rolled through the earth like peals of loudest thunder. It was awfully solemn. And at the end of every sentence the saints shouted, "Glory! Alleluia!" Their countenances were lighted up with the glory of God; and they shone with the glory, as did the face of Moses when he came down from Sinai.

The wicked could not look on them for the glory. And when the never ending blessing was pronounced on those who had honored God in keeping His Sabbath holy, there was a mighty shout of victory over the beast and over his image.

Then commenced the jubilee, when the land should rest. I saw the pious slave rise in triumph and victory, and shake off the chains that bound him, while his wicked master was in confusion, and knew not what to do; for the wicked could not understand the words of the voice of God.

Soon appeared the great white cloud. It looked more lovely than ever before. On it sat the Son of man. At first we did not see Jesus on the cloud, but as it drew near the earth we could behold His lovely person. This cloud, when it first appeared, was the sign of the Son of man in heaven.

The voice of the Son of God called forth the sleeping saints, clothed with glorious immortality. The living saints were changed in a moment, and were caught up with them into the cloudy chariot. It looked all over glorious as it rolled upward. On either side of the chariot were wings, and beneath it wheels. And as the chariot rolled upward, the wheels cried, "Holy," and the wings, as they moved, cried, "Holy," and the retinue of holy angels around the cloud cried, "Holy, holy holy, Lord God Almighty!" And the saints in the cloud cried, "Glory! Alleluia!" And the chariot rolled upward to the holy city. Jesus threw open the gates of the golden city, and led us in. Here we were made welcome, for we had kept "the commandments of God," and had a "right to the tree of life." Rev. 14:12; 22:14.

Gorham, Maine July 13th 47.

Dear Brother Bates

As James is at work & sisters are from home thought I would employ my self in writing a line to you my helth is quite good for me my faith is still strong that that very same Jesus that assended up into heaven will so come in like manner as he went up, & that very very soon. I have had many trials of late discouragement at times has laid fast hold upon me it semed impossable to shake it off but thank God satan has not got the victory over me yet & by the grace of God he never shall. I know & feel my weakness but I have laid hold upon the strong arm of Jehovah & I can say today I know that my redeemer liveth & if he lives I shall live also O how good it would be to meet with a few of like precious faith to exort & comfort one another with words of holy cheer from the word of God. the sheep are now scattered but thank God they are about to be gathered to a good pasture o how sweet it will be to meet all the blood washed throng in the city of our God tis then well sing the song of moses & the lamb as we march through the gates into the City bearing the palms of victory & wearing the Crowns of glory Bro Bates you write in a letter to James something about the bridegrooms coming as stated in the first published visions by the letter you would like to know wether I had light on the bridegrooms coming before I saw it in vision I can readily answer no: The Lord shew me the travil of the advent band & midnight cry in december but he did not shew me the bridegrooms coming untill February following perhaps you would like to have me give a statement in relation to both visions at the time I had the vision of the midnight cry I had given it up in the past & thought

Photographic facsimile of a letter written by Mrs. White, July 13, 1847, to Elder Joseph Bates. Toward the close of the page the date of her first vision is given as December, 1844.

XIV

STRUGGLES WITH POVERTY

At Gorham, Maine, Aug. 26, 1847, our eldest son, Henry Nichols White, was born. In October Brother and Sister Howland, of Topsham, kindly offered us a part of their dwelling, which we gladly accepted, and commenced housekeeping with borrowed furniture. We were poor, and saw close times. We had resolved not to be dependent, but to support ourselves, and have something with which to help others. But we were not prospered. My husband worked very hard hauling stone on the railroad, but could not get what was due him for his labor. Brother and Sister Howland freely divided with us whenever they could; but they also were in close circumstances. They fully believed the first and second messages, and had generously imparted of their substance to forward the work, until they were dependent on their daily labor.

My husband stopped hauling stone, and with his ax went into the woods to chop cordwood. With a continual pain in his side, he worked from early morning till dark to earn about fifty cents a day. We endeavored to keep up good courage, and trust in the Lord. I did not murmur. In the morning I felt grateful to God that He had preserved us through another night, and at night I was thankful that He had kept us through another day.

One day when our provisions were gone, my husband went to his employer to get money or provisions. It was a stormy day, and he walked three miles and back in the rain. He brought home on his back a bag of provisions tied in different compartments, having in this manner passed through the village of Brunswick, where he had often lectured. As he entered the house, very weary, my heart sank within me. My first feelings were that God had forsaken us. I said to my husband: "Have we come to this? Has the Lord left us?" I could not restrain my tears, and wept aloud for hours, until I fainted. Prayer was offered in my behalf. Soon I felt the cheering influence of the Spirit of God, and regretted that I had sunk under discouragement. We desire to follow Christ and to be like Him; but we sometimes faint beneath trials, and remain at a distance from Him. Sufferings and trials bring us near to Jesus. The furnace consumes the dross and brightens the gold.

At this time I was shown that the Lord had been trying us for our good, and to prepare us to labor for others; that He had been stirring up our nest, lest we should settle down at ease. Our work was to labor for souls; if we had been prospered, home would be so pleasant that we would be unwilling to leave it; trials had been permitted to come upon us to prepare us for the still greater conflicts that we would meet in our travels. We soon received letters from brethren in different States, inviting us to visit them; but we had no means to take us out of the State. Our reply was that the way was not open before us. I thought that it would be impossible for me to travel with my child. We did not wish to be dependent, and were careful to live within our means. We were resolved to suffer rather than get in debt.

Little Henry was soon taken very sick, and grew worse so fast that we were much alarmed. He lay in a stupid state; his breathing was quick and heavy. We gave remedies with no success. We then called in a person of experience in sickness, who said that his recovery was doubtful. We had prayed for him, but there was no change. We had made the child an excuse for not traveling and laboring for the good of others, and we feared the Lord was about to remove him. Once more we went before the Lord, praying that He would have compassion upon us, and spare the life of the child, and solemnly pledging ourselves to go forth trusting in God, wherever He might send us.

Our petitions were fervent and agonizing. By faith we claimed the promises of God, and we believed that He listened to our cries. Light from heaven was breaking through the clouds and shining upon us. Our prayers were graciously answered. From that hour the child began to recover.

FIRST VISIT TO CONNECTICUT

While at Topsham we received a letter from Brother E. L. H. Chamberlain, of Middletown, Conn., urging us to attend a conference in that State in April, 1848. We decided to go if we could obtain means. My husband settled with his employer, and found that there was ten dollars due him. With five of this I purchased articles of clothing that we very much needed, and then patched my husband's overcoat, even piecing the patches, making it difficult to tell the original cloth in the sleeves. We had five dollars left to take us to Dorchester, Mass.

Our trunk contained nearly everything we possessed on earth; but we enjoyed peace of mind and a clear conscience, and this we prized above earthly comforts.

In Dorchester we called at the house of Brother Otis Nichols, and as we left, Sister Nichols handed my husband five dollars, which paid our fare to Middletown, Conn. We were strangers in Middletown, having never seen one of the brethren in Connecticut. Of our money there was but fifty cents left. My husband did not dare to use that to hire a carriage, so he threw our trunk upon a high pile of boards in a near-by lumberyard, and we walked on in search of some one of like faith. We soon found Brother Chamberlain, who took us to his home.

CONFERENCE AT ROCKY HILL

The conference at Rocky Hill was held in the large unfinished chamber of Brother Albert Belden's house. In a letter to Brother Stockbridge Howland, my husband wrote of the meeting as follows:

"April 20th Brother Belden sent his two-horse wagon to Middletown for us and the scattered brethren in that city. We arrived at this place about four in the afternoon, and in a few minutes in came Brethren Bates and Gurney. We had a meeting that evening of about fifteen. Friday morning the brethren came in until we numbered about fifty. These were not all fully in the truth. Our meeting that day was very interesting. Brother Bates presented the commandments in a clear light, and their importance was urged home by powerful testimonies. The word had effect to establish those already in the truth, and to awaken those who were not fully decided."

EARNING MEANS TO VISIT WESTERN NEW YORK

Two years before, I had been shown that at some future time we should visit western New York. And now, shortly after the close of the conference at Rocky Hill, we were invited to attend a general meeting at Volney, N. Y., in August. Brother Hiram Edson wrote to us that the brethren were generally poor, and that he could not promise that they would do much toward defraying our expenses, but that he would do what he could. We had no means with which to travel. My husband's health was poor, but the way opened for him to work in the hayfield, and he decided to accept the work.

It seemed then that we must live by faith. When we arose in the morning, we bowed beside our bed, and asked God to give us strength to labor through the day, and we could not be satisfied without the assurance that the Lord heard our prayers. My husband then went forth to swing the scythe in the strength that God gave him. At night when he came home we would again plead with God for strength with which to earn means to spread the truth. In a letter to Brother Howland, written July 2, 1848, he spoke of this experience thus:

"It is rainy to-day, so that I do not mow, or I should not write. I mow five days for unbelievers, and Sunday for believers, and rest on the seventh day, therefore I have but very little time to write. . . . God gives me strength to labor hard all day. . . . Brother Holt, Brother John Belden, and I have taken one hundred acres of grass to mow, at eighty-seven and one half cents per acre, and board ourselves. Praise the Lord! I hope to get a few dollars here to use in the cause of God."

XV

LABORS IN WESTERN NEW YORK IN 1848

As a result of his work in the hayfield, my husband earned forty dollars. With a part of this we purchased some necessary clothing, and had sufficient means left to take us to western New York and return.

My health was poor, and it was impossible for me to travel and have the care of our child. So we left our little Henry, ten months old, at Middletown with Sister Clarissa Bonfoey. It was a severe trial for me to be separated from my child, but we dared not let our affection for him keep us from the path of duty. Jesus laid down His life to save us. How small is any sacrifice we can make compared with His!

On the morning of August 13 we reached New York City, and went to the home of Brother D. Moody. On the following day Brethren Bates and Gurney joined us.

CONFERENCE AT VOLNEY

Our first general meeting in western New York, beginning August 18, was held at Volney, in Brother David Arnold's barn. About thirty-five were present,— all the friends that could be collected in that part of the State. But of this number there were hardly two agreed. Some were holding serious errors, and each strenuously urged his own views, declaring that they were according to the Scriptures.

One brother held that the one thousand years of the twentieth chapter of Revelation were in the past, and that the one hundred and forty-four thousand mentioned in the seventh and fourteenth chapters of Revelation, were those raised at Christ's resurrection.

As we had before us the emblems of our dying Lord, and were about to commemorate His sufferings, this brother arose and said that he had no faith in what we were about to do; that the Lord's supper was a continuation of the Passover, and should be partaken of but once a year.

These strange differences of opinion rolled a heavy weight upon me. I saw that many errors were being presented as truth. It seemed to me that God was dishonored. Great grief pressed upon my spirits, and I fainted under the burden. Some feared that I was dying. Brethren Bates, Chamberlain, Gurney, Edson, and my husband prayed for me. The Lord heard the prayers of His servants, and I revived.

The light of heaven then rested upon me, and I was soon lost to earthly things. My accompanying angel presented before me some of the errors of those present, and also the truth in contrast with their errors. These discordant views, which they claimed were in harmony with the Scriptures, were only according to their opinion of Bible teaching; and I was bidden to tell them that they should yield their errors, and unite upon the truths of the third angel's message.

Our meeting closed triumphantly. Truth gained the victory. Our brethren renounced their errors and united upon the third angel's message, and God greatly blessed them and added many to their numbers.

VISIT TO BROTHER SNOW'S — HANNIBAL

From Volney we journeyed toward Port Gibson, sixty miles distant, to meet another appointment

August 27 and 28. "On our way," wrote my husband in a letter to Brother Hastings dated August 26, "we stopped at Brother Snow's in Hannibal. In that place are eight or ten precious souls. Brother Bates, Brother and Sister Edson, and Brother Simmons stopped all night with them. In the morning Ellen was taken off in vision, and while she was in vision, all the brethren came in. One of the number was not with us on the Sabbath [truth], but was humble and good. Ellen rose up in vision, took the large Bible, held it up before the Lord, talked from it, then carried it to this humble brother, and put it in his arms. He took it while tears were rolling down his bosom. Then Ellen came and sat down by me. She was in vision one and a half hours, in which time she did not breathe at all. It was an affecting time. All wept much for joy. We left Brother Bates with them, and came to this place with Brother Edson."

MEETING AT PORT GIBSON

The meeting at Port Gibson was held in Brother Hiram Edson's barn. There were those present who loved the truth, but were listening to and cherishing error. Before the close of this meeting, however, the Lord wrought for us with power. I was again shown in vision the importance of the brethren laying aside their differences, and uniting upon Bible truth.

VISIT TO BROTHER HARRIS'S — CENTERPORT

We left Brother Edson's intending to spend the following Sabbath in New York City. We were too late for the packet, so we took a line boat, designing to change when the next packet came along. As we saw the packet approaching, we began making preparations to step aboard; but the packet did not stop, and we had to spring on board while the boat was in motion.

Brother Bates was holding the money for our fare in his hand, saying to the captain of the boat, "Here, take your pay." As he saw the boat moving off, he sprang to get aboard, but his foot struck the edge of the boat, and he fell back into the water. He then began swimming to the boat, with his pocketbook in one hand, and a dollar bill in the other. His hat fell off, and in saving it he lost the bill, but held fast to his pocketbook. The packet halted for him to get aboard. His clothes were wet with the dirty water of the canal, and as we were near Centerport, we decided to call at the home of Brother Harris, that Brother Bates might put his clothes in order.

Our visit proved a benefit to this family. For years Sister Harris had suffered from catarrh. She had used snuff for the relief of this affliction, and said that she could not live without it. She suffered much pain in her head. We recommended her to go to the Lord, the great Physician, who would heal her affliction. She decided to do so, and we had a season of prayer for her. She discontinued the use of snuff entirely. Her difficulties were greatly relieved, and from that time her health was better than it had been for years.

While at Brother Harris's I had an interview with a sister who wore gold, and yet professed to be looking for Christ's coming. We spoke of the express declarations of Scripture against the wearing of gold. But she referred to where Solomon was commanded to beautify the temple, and to the statement that the streets of the city of God were pure gold. She said that if we could improve our appearance by wearing gold, so as to have influence in the world, it was right. I replied that we were poor fallen mortals, and instead of decorating these bodies because Solomon's temple was gloriously adorned, we should remember our fallen condition, and that it cost the suffering and death of the Son of God to redeem us. This thought should cause in us self-abasement. Jesus is our pattern. If He would lay aside His humiliation and sufferings, and cry, "If any man will come after Me, let him please himself, and enjoy the world, and he shall be My disciple," the multitude would believe and follow Him. But Jesus will come to us in no other character than that of the meek, crucified One. If we would be with Him in heaven, we must be like Him on earth. The world will claim its own; and whoever will overcome, must leave what belongs to it.

VISIT TO BROTHER ABBEY'S — BROOKFIELD

The next day we resumed our journey by packet, and went as far as Madison Co., N. Y. We then left the packet, hired a carriage, and rode twenty-five miles to Brookfield, where was the home of Brother Ira Abbey. As it was Friday afternoon when we arrived at the house, it was proposed that one should go to the door and make inquiries, so that should we be disappointed in our hope of a welcome, we might return with the driver, and put up at a hotel over the Sabbath.

Sister Abbey came to the door, and my husband introduced himself as one who kept the Sabbath. She said: "I am glad to see you. Come in." He replied: "There are three more in the carriage with me. I thought if we all came in together we might frighten you." "I am never frightened at Christians," was the reply. Sister Abbey expressed much joy at seeing us, and we were heartily welcomed by her and her family. When Brother Bates was introduced, she said: "Can this be Brother Bates, who wrote that hewing book on the Sabbath? And come to see us? I am unworthy to have you come under my roof. But the Lord has sent you to us; for we are starving for the truth."

A child was sent to the field to tell Brother Abbey that four Sabbath keepers had come. He was in no hurry, however, to make our acquaintance; for he had previously been imposed upon by some who had often visited them. These, professing to be God's servants, had scattered error among the little flock who were trying to hold fast the truth. Brother and Sister Abbey had warred against them for so long that they dreaded to come into contact with them. Brother Abbey feared that we were of the same class. When he came into the house, he received us coldly, and then began asking a few plain, direct questions, as to whether we kept the Sabbath and believed the past messages to be of God. When he was satisfied that we had come with truth, he joyfully welcomed us.

Our meetings in this place were cheering to the few who loved the truth. We rejoiced that the Lord in His providence had directed us that way. We enjoyed the presence of God together, and were comforted to find a few who had stood firm all through the scattering time, holding fast the messages of truth through the mist and fog of spiritualizing and fanaticism. This dear family helped us on our way after a godly sort.

XVI

A VIEW OF THE SEALING[1]

At the commencement of the holy Sabbath, Jan. 5, 1849, we engaged in prayer with Brother Belden's family at Rocky Hill, Conn., and the Holy Ghost fell upon us. I was taken off in vision to the most holy place, where I saw Jesus still interceding for Israel. On the bottom of His garment was a bell and a pomegranate, a bell and a pomegranate. Then I saw that Jesus would not leave the most holy place until every case was decided either for salvation or destruction, and that the wrath of God could not come until Jesus had finished His work in the most holy place, laid off His priestly attire, and clothed Himself with the garments of vengeance. Then Jesus

---

[1] Following the return from western New York in September, 1848, Elder and Mrs. White journeyed to Maine, where they held a meeting with the believers, October 20-22. This was the Topsham conference, where the brethren began praying that a way might be opened for publishing the truths connected with the advent message. A month later they were with "a small company of brethren and sisters," writes Elder Joseph Bates in his pamphlet on "The Sealing Message," "assembled in meeting in Dorchester, near Boston, Mass." "Before the meeting commenced," he continues, "some of us were examining some of the points in the sealing message; some difference of opinion existed about the correctness of the view of the word 'ascending' [see Rev. 7: 2], etc."

Elder James White, in an unpublished letter giving his account of this meeting, writes: "We all felt like uniting to ask wisdom from God on the points in dispute; also Brother Bates's duty in writing. We had an exceedingly powerful meeting. Ellen was again taken off in vision. She then began to describe the Sabbath light, which was the sealing truth. Said she: 'It arose from the rising of the sun. It arose back there in weakness, but light after light has shone upon it until the Sabbath truth is clear, weighty, and mighty. Like the sun when it first rises, its rays are cold, but as it comes up, its rays are warming and powerful; so the light and power has increased more and more until its rays are powerful, sanctifying the soul; but, unlike the sun, it will never set. The Sabbath light will be at its brightest when the saints are immortal; it will rise higher and higher until immortality comes.'

"She saw many interesting things about this glorious sealing Sabbath, which I have not time or space to record. She told Brother Bates to write the things he had seen and heard, and the blessing of God would attend it."

It was after this vision that Mrs. White informed her husband of his duty to publish, and that as he should advance by faith, success would attend his efforts. (See page 125.)

will step out from between the Father and men, and God will keep silence no longer, but pour out His wrath on those who have rejected His truth. I saw that the anger of the nations, the wrath of God, and the time to judge the dead, were separate and distinct, one following the other; also that Michael had not stood up, and that the time of trouble, such as never was, had not yet commenced. The nations are now getting angry, but when our High Priest has finished His work in the sanctuary, He will stand up, put on the garments of vengeance, and then the seven last plagues will be poured out.

I saw that the four angels would hold the four winds until Jesus' work was done in the sanctuary, and then will come the seven last plagues. These plagues enraged the wicked against the righteous; they thought that we had brought the judgments of God upon them, and that if they could rid the earth of us, the plagues would then be stayed. A decree went forth to slay the saints, which caused them to cry day and night for deliverance. This was the time of Jacob's trouble. Then all the saints cried out with anguish of spirit, and were delivered by the voice of God. The one hundred and forty-four thousand triumphed. Their faces were lighted up with the glory of God.

Then I was shown a company who were howling in agony. On their garments was written in large characters, "Thou art weighed in the balance, and found wanting." I asked who this company were. The angel said, "These are they who have once kept the Sabbath, and have given it up." I heard them cry with a loud voice, "We have believed in Thy coming, and taught it with energy." And while they were speaking, their eyes would fall upon their garments and see the writing, and then they would wail aloud. I saw that they had drunk of the deep waters, and fouled the residue with their feet,— trodden the Sabbath underfoot,— and that was why they were weighed in the balance and found wanting.

Then my attending angel directed me to the city again, where I saw four angels winging their way to the gate of the city. They were just presenting the golden card to the angel at the gate, when I saw another angel flying swiftly from the direction of the most excellent glory, and crying with a loud voice to the other angels, and waving something up and down in his hand. I asked my attending angel for an explanation of what I saw. He told me that I could see no more then, but he would shortly show me what those things that I then saw meant.

Sabbath afternoon one of our number was sick, and requested prayers that he might be healed. We all united in applying to the Physician who never lost a case, and while healing power came down, and the sick was healed, the Spirit fell upon me, and I was taken off in vision.

I saw four angels who had a work to do on the earth, and were on their way to accomplish it. Jesus was clothed with priestly garments. He gazed in pity on the remnant, then raised His hands, and with a voice of deep pity cried, "*My blood, Father, My blood! My blood! My blood!*" Then I saw an exceeding bright light come from God, who sat upon the great white throne, and was shed all about Jesus. Then I saw an angel with a commission from Jesus, swiftly flying to the four angels who had a work to do in the earth, and waving something up and down in his hand, and crying with a loud voice, "*Hold!*

hold! hold! hold! until the servants of God are sealed in their foreheads.''

I asked my accompanying angel the meaning of what I heard, and what the four angels were about to do. He said to me that it was God that restrained the powers, and that He gave His angels charge over things on the earth; that the four angels had power from God to hold the four winds, and that they were about to let them go; but while their hands were loosening, and the four winds were about to blow, the merciful eye of Jesus gazed on the remnant that were not sealed, and He raised His hands to the Father, and pleaded with Him that He had spilled His blood for them. Then another angel was commissioned to fly swiftly to the four angels, and bid them hold, until the servants of God were sealed with the seal of the living God in their foreheads.

XVII

ENCOURAGING PROVIDENCES

Again I was called to deny self for the good of souls. We must sacrifice the company of our little Henry, and go forth to give ourselves unreservedly to the work. My health was very poor, and should I take my child, he would necessarily occupy a large share of my time. It was a severe trial, yet I dared not let him stand in the way of duty. I believed that the Lord had spared him to us when he was very sick, and that if I should let him hinder me from doing my duty, God would remove him from me. Alone before the Lord, with a sorrowful heart and many tears, I made the sacrifice, and gave up my only child to be cared for by another.

We left Henry in Brother Howland's family, in whom we had the utmost confidence. They were willing to bear burdens, in order that we might be left as free as possible to labor in the cause of God. We knew that they could take better care of Henry than we could should we take him with us on our journeys. We knew that it was for his good to have a steady home and firm discipline, that his sweet temper might not be injured.

It was hard to part with my child. His sad little face, as I left him, was before me day and night; yet in the strength of the Lord I put him out of my mind, and sought to do others good.

For five years Brother Howland's family had the whole charge of Henry. They cared for him without any recompense, providing all his clothing, except a present that I brought him once a year, as Hannah did Samuel.

HEALING OF GILBERT COLLINS

One morning in February, 1849, during family prayers at Brother Howland's, I was shown that it was our duty to go to Dartmouth, Mass. Soon after, my husband went to the post office, and brought a letter from Brother Philip Collins, urging us to come to Dartmouth, for their son was very sick. We went immediately, and found that the boy, who was thirteen years old, had been sick for nine weeks with the whooping cough, and was wasted almost to a skeleton. The parents thought him to be in consumption, and they were greatly distressed to think that their only son must be taken from them.

We united in prayer for the boy, and earnestly besought the Lord to spare his life. We believed that he would get well, though to all appearances there was no possibility of his recovery. My husband raised him in his arms, exclaiming as he walked the room, "You will not die, but live!" We believed that God would be glorified in his recovery.

We left Dartmouth, and were absent about eight days. When we returned, little Gilbert came out to meet us. He had gained four pounds in weight. We found the household rejoicing in God over this manifestation of divine favor.

HEALING OF SISTER TEMPLE

Having received a request to visit Sister Hastings, of New Ipswich, N. H., who was greatly afflicted, we made the matter a subject of prayer, and obtained evidence that the Lord would go with us. On our way we stopped at Dorchester, with Brother Otis Nichols's family, and they told us of the affliction of Sister Temple of Boston. On her arm she had a sore, which caused her much anxiety. It had extended over the bend of the elbow. She had suffered great agony, and had in vain resorted to human means for relief. The last effort had driven the disease to her lungs, and she felt that unless she obtained immediate help, the disease would end in consumption.

Sister Temple had left word for us to come and pray for her. We went with trembling, having sought in vain for the assurance that God would work in her behalf. We went into the sickroom, relying upon the naked promises of God. Sister Temple's arm was in such a condition that we could not touch it, and were obliged to pour the oil upon it. Then we united in prayer, and claimed the promises of God. The pain and soreness left the arm while we were praying, and we left Sister Temple rejoicing in the Lord. On our return, eight days later, we found her in good health, and hard at work at the washtub.

THE FAMILY OF LEONARD HASTINGS

We found Brother Leonard Hastings' family in deep affliction. Sister Hastings met us with tears, exclaiming, "The Lord has sent you to us in a time of great need." She had an infant about eight weeks old, which cried continually when awake. This, added to her wretched state of health. was fast wearing away her strength.

We prayed earnestly to God for the mother, following the directions given in James, and we had the assurance that our prayers were heard. Jesus was in the midst of us to break the power of Satan and release the captive. But we felt sure that the mother could not gain much strength until the cries of the child should cease. We anointed the child and prayed over it, believing that the Lord would give both mother and child peace and rest. It was done. The cries of the child ceased, and we left them both doing well. The gratitude of the mother could not be expressed.

Our interview with that dear family was very precious. Our hearts were knit together; especially was the heart of Sister Hastings knit with mine as were those of David and Jonathan. Our union was not marred while she lived.

MOVING TO CONNECTICUT IN 1849 [1]

In June, 1849, Sister Clarissa M. Bonfoey proposed to live with us. Her parents had recently died, and a division of furniture at the homestead had given her everything necessary for a small family to commence housekeeping. She cheerfully gave us the use of these things, and did our work. We occupied a part of Brother Belden's house at Rocky Hill. Sister Bonfoey was a precious child of God. She possessed a cheerful and happy disposition, never gloomy, yet not light and trifling.

---

[1] NOTE.— After the visit to the Hastings family in New Ipswich, Elder and Mrs. White returned to Maine, going by way of Boston, and arriving at Topsham March 21, 1849. The following Sabbath, while worshiping with the little company in that place, Mrs. White was given a vision in which she saw that the faith of one of the brethren in Paris, Maine, was wavering, and this led her to feel that it was her duty to visit the company there. "We went," she wrote in a letter to Brother and Sister Hastings, "and found they needed strengthening. . . . We spent one week with them. . . . God gave me two visions while there, much to the comfort and strength of the brethren and sisters. Brother Stowell was established in all the present truth he had doubted."

After returning to Topsham, they were in much perplexity as to where they should spend the summer. Invitations had come from brethren in New York and in Connecticut, and in the absence of positive light they decided to respond to the call from New York. They wrote a letter giving directions regarding their arrival at Utica, where some of the brethren might meet them. Soon, however, Mrs. White felt burdened and oppressed. Her husband, seeing her distress, burned the letter they had just written, knelt down, and prayed that the burden might be rolled away. The next day's mail brought to them a letter from Brother Belden, of Rocky Hill, Conn., containing means sufficient to enable them to move to Connecticut, and urging them to accept the invitation. Elder and Mrs. White saw in this hearty invitation the manifest providence of God, and decided to go, believing that the Lord was opening the way before them.

LIVING WATERS — A DREAM

My husband attended meetings in New Hampshire and Maine. During his absence I was much troubled, fearing he might take the cholera, which was then prevailing. But one night I dreamed that while many around us were dying with the cholera, my husband proposed that we should take a walk. In our walk I noticed that his eyes looked bloodshot, his countenance flushed, and his lips pale. I told him that I feared that he would be an easy subject for the cholera. Said he, "Walk on a little further, and I will show you a sure remedy for the cholera."

As we walked on, we came to a bridge over a stream of water, when he abruptly left me and plunged out of sight into the water. I was frightened; but he soon arose, holding in his hand a glass of sparkling water. He drank it, saying, "This water cures all manner of diseases." He plunged in again out of sight, brought up another glass of clear water, and as he held it up repeated the same words.

I felt sad that he did not offer me some of the water. Said he: "There is a secret spring in the bottom of this river which cures all manner of diseases, and all who obtain it must plunge at a venture. No one can obtain it for another. Each must plunge for it himself." As he drank the glass of water, I looked at his countenance. His complexion was fair and natural. He seemed to possess health and vigor. When I awoke, all my fears were dispelled, and I trusted my husband to the care of a merciful God, fully believing that He would return him to me in safety.

XVIII

BEGINNING TO PUBLISH

At a meeting held in Dorchester, Mass., November, 1848, I had been given a view of the proclamation of the sealing message, and of the duty of the brethren to publish the light that was shining upon our pathway.

After coming out of vision, I said to my husband: "I have a message for you. You must begin to print a little paper and send it out to the people. Let it be small at first; but as the people read, they will send you means with which to print, and it will be a success from the first. From this small beginning it was shown to me to be like streams of light that went clear round the world."

While we were in Connecticut in the summer of 1849, my husband was deeply impressed that the time had come for him to write and publish the present truth. He was greatly encouraged and blessed as he decided to do this. But again he would be in doubt and perplexity, as he was penniless. There were those who had means, but they chose to keep it. He at length gave up in discouragement, and decided to look for a field of grass to mow.

As he left the house, a burden was rolled upon me, and I fainted. Prayer was offered for me, and I was blessed, and taken off in vision. I saw that the Lord had blessed and strengthened my husband to labor in the field one year before; that he had made a right disposition of the means he there earned; and that he would have a hundredfold in this life, and, if faithful, a rich reward in the kingdom of God; but that the Lord would not now give him strength to labor in the field, for He had another work for him to do, and that if he ventured into the field, he would be cut down by sickness; but that he must write, write, write, and walk out by faith. He immediately began to write, and when he came to some difficult passage, we would unite in prayer to God for an understanding of the true meaning of His word.

"THE PRESENT TRUTH"

One day in July, my husband brought home from Middletown a thousand copies of the first number of his paper. Several times, while the matter was being set, he had walked to Middletown, eight miles, and back, but this day he had borrowed Brother Belden's horse and buggy with which to bring home the papers.

The precious printed sheets were brought into the house and laid upon the floor, and then a little group of interested ones were gathered in, and we knelt around the papers, and with humble hearts and many tears besought the Lord to let His blessing rest upon these printed messengers of truth.

When we had folded the papers, and my husband had wrapped and addressed copies to all those who he thought would read them, he put them into a carpetbag, and carried them on foot to the Middletown post office.

During July, August, and September, four numbers of the paper were printed at Middletown. Each number contained eight pages.[1] Always before the papers were mailed, they were spread before the Lord, and earnest prayers, mingled with tears, were offered to God that His blessing would attend the silent messengers. Soon after the sending out of the first number,

---

[1] The size of the pages was about six by nine and one half inches.

we received letters bringing means with which to continue publishing the paper, and also the good news of many souls embracing the truth.

With the beginning of this work of publishing, we did not cease our labors in preaching the truth, but traveled from place to place, proclaiming the doctrines which had brought so great light and joy to us, encouraging the believers, correcting errors, and setting things in order in the church. In order to carry forward the publishing enterprise, and at the same time continue our labors in different parts of the field, the paper was from time to time moved to different places.

VISIT TO MAINE

July 28, 1849, my second child, James Edson White, was born. When he was six weeks old we went to Maine. September 14 we attended a meeting at Paris. Brethren Bates, Chamberlain, and Ralph were present, also brethren and sisters from Topsham. The power of God descended something as it did on the day of Pentecost, and five or six who had been deceived and led into error and fanaticism, fell prostrate to the floor. Parents confessed to their children, and children to their parents and to one another. Brother J. N. Andrews with deep feeling exclaimed, "I would exchange a thousand errors for one truth." Such a scene of confession and pleading with God for forgiveness we have seldom witnessed. That meeting, the beginning of better days for the children of God in Paris, was to them a green spot in the desert. The Lord was bringing out Brother Andrews to fit him for future usefulness, and was giving him an experience that would be of great value to him in his future labors.

ADVANCING BY FAITH

At a meeting held at Topsham, some of the brethren present expressed their desire to have us visit New York State again; but feeble health weighed down my spirits. I told them that I dared not venture, unless the Lord should strengthen me for the task. They prayed for me, and the clouds were scattered, yet I did not obtain that strength I so much desired. I resolved to walk out by faith, and go, clinging to the promise, "My grace is sufficient for you."

On the journey to New York, our faith was tried, but we obtained the victory. My strength increased, and I could rejoice in God. Many had embraced the truth since our first visit, but there was much to be done for them, and all our strength was needed in the work as it opened up before us.

RESIDENCE IN OSWEGO

During the months of October and November, while we were traveling, the paper had been suspended; but my husband still felt a burden upon him to write and publish. We rented a house in Oswego, borrowed furniture from our brethren, and began housekeeping. There my husband wrote, published, and preached.[2]

It was necessary for him to keep the armor on every moment, for he often had to contend with professed Adventists who were advocating error. Some set a definite time for the coming of Christ. We took the position that the time they set would pass by. Then they sought to prejudice all against us and what we taught. I was shown that those who were honestly deceived would some day see the deception into which they had fallen, and would be led to search for truth.

---

[2] Nos. 5 and 6 of *Present Truth* were issued from Oswego, N. Y., in December, 1849; Nos. 7 to 10, from the same place, in March to May, 1850. Some tracts also were issued during that time.

XIX

VISITING THE SCATTERED FLOCK

While in Oswego, N. Y., early in 1850, we were invited to visit Camden, a town about forty miles east. Previous to going, I was shown the little company of believers there, and among them I saw a woman who professed much piety, but who was a hypocrite, and was deceiving the people of God.

AT CAMDEN, N. Y.

Sabbath morning quite a number gathered for worship, but the deceitful woman was not present. I inquired of a sister if this was all their company. She said it was. The woman whom I had seen in the vision lived four miles from the place, and the sister did not think of her. But soon she entered, and I immediately recognized her as the woman whose real character the Lord had shown me.

In the course of the meeting, she talked quite lengthily, saying that she had perfect love, and enjoyed holiness of heart, that she did not have trials and temptations, but enjoyed perfect peace and submission to the will of God.

From the meeting I returned to the home of Brother Preston with feelings of great sadness. That night I dreamed that a secret closet filled with rubbish was opened to me, and I was told that it was my work to clear it out. By the light of a lamp I removed the rubbish, and told those with me that the room could be filled with more valuable things.

On Sunday morning we met with the brethren, and my husband arose to preach on the parable of the ten virgins. He had no freedom in speaking, and proposed that we have a season of prayer. We bowed before the Lord, and engaged in earnest prayer. The dark cloud was lifted, and I was taken off in vision, and again shown the case of this woman. She was represented to me as being in perfect darkness. Jesus frowned upon her and her husband. That withering frown caused me to tremble. I saw that she had acted the hypocrite, professing holiness while her heart was full of corruption.

After I came out of vision, I related with trembling, yet with faithfulness, what I had seen. The woman calmly said: "I am glad the Lord knows my heart. He knows that I love Him. If my heart could only be opened that you might see it, you would see that it is pure and clean."

The minds of some were unsettled. They did not know whether to believe what the Lord had shown me, or to let appearance weigh against the testimony I had borne.

Not long after this, terrible fear seized the woman. A horror rested upon her, and she began to confess. She even went from house to house among her unbelieving neighbors, and confessed that the man she had been living with for years was not her husband, that she ran away from England, and left a kind husband and one child. Many other wicked acts she confessed. Her repentance seemed to be genuine, and in some cases she restored what she had taken wrongfully.

As a result of this experience, our brethren and sisters in Camden, and their neighbors, were fully established in the belief that God had revealed to me the things which I had spoken, and that the message was given them in mercy and love, to save them from deception and dangerous error.

IN VERMONT

In the spring of 1850 we decided to visit Vermont and Maine. I left my little Edson, then nine months old, in the care of Sister Bonfoey, while we went on our way to do the will of God. We labored very hard, suffering many privations to accomplish but little. We found the brethren and sisters in a scattered and confused state. Almost every one was affected by some error, and all seemed zealous for their own opinions. We often suffered intense anguish of mind in meeting with so few who were ready to listen to Bible truth, while they eagerly cherished error and fanaticism. We were obliged to make a tedious route of forty miles by stage to get to Sutton, the place of our appointment.

RISING ABOVE DESPONDENCY

The first night after reaching the place of meeting, despondency pressed upon me. I tried to overcome it, but it seemed impossible to control my thoughts. My little ones burdened my mind. We had left one in the State of Maine two years and eight months old, and another babe in New York nine months old. We had just performed a tedious journey in great suffering, and I thought of those who were enjoying the society of their children in their own quiet homes. I reviewed our past life, calling to mind expressions which had been made by a sister only a few days before, who thought it must be very pleasant to be riding through the country without anything to trouble me. It was just such a life as she should delight in. At that very time my heart was yearning for my children, especially my babe in New York, and I had just come from my sleeping-room, where I had been battling with my feelings, and with many tears had besought the Lord for strength to subdue all murmuring, and that I might cheerfully deny myself for Jesus' sake.

In this state of mind I fell asleep, and dreamed that a tall angel stood by my side and asked me why I was sad. I related to him the thoughts that had troubled me, and said, "I can do so little good, why may we not be with our children, and enjoy their society?" Said he: "You have given to the Lord two beautiful flowers, the fragrance of which is as sweet incense before Him, and is more precious in His sight than gold or silver, for it is a heart gift. It draws upon every fiber of the heart as no other sacrifice can. You should not look upon present appearances, but keep the eye single to your duty, single to God's glory, and follow in His opening providence, and the path shall brighten before you. Every self-denial, every sacrifice, is faithfully recorded, and will bring its reward."

IN CANADA EAST

The blessing of the Lord attended our conference at Sutton, and after the meeting closed we went on our way to Canada East. My throat troubled me much, and I could not speak aloud, or even whisper, without suffering. We rode praying as we went, for strength to endure the journey.

Thus we continued until we arrived at Melbourne. We expected to meet opposition there. Many who professed to believe in the near coming of our Saviour fought against the law of God. We felt the need of strength from God. We prayed that the Lord would manifest Himself unto us. My earnest prayer was that the disease might leave my throat, and that my voice might be restored. I had the evidence that the hand of the Lord there touched me. The difficulty was instantly removed, and my voice was clear. The candle of the Lord shone about us during that meeting, and we enjoyed great freedom. The children of God were greatly strengthened and encouraged.

THE MEETING AT JOHNSON, VT.

Soon we returned to Vermont, and held a remarkable meeting at Johnson. On our way we stopped several days at the home of Brother E. P. Butler. We found that he and others of our brethren in northern Vermont had been sorely perplexed and tried by the false teachings and wild fanaticism of a group of people who were claiming entire sanctification, and, under the garb of great holiness, were following a course of life that was a disgrace to the Christian name.

The two men who were leaders in the fanaticism were in life and character much like those we met four years before in Claremont, N. H. They taught the doctrine of extreme sanctification, claiming that they could not sin, and were ready for translation. They practised mesmerism, and claimed to receive divine enlightenment while in a sort of trance.

They did not engage in regular work, but in company with two women, not their wives, they traveled about from place to place, forcing themselves upon the hospitality of the people. Through their subtle, mesmeric influence, they had secured a large degree of sympathy from some of the grown-up children of our brethren.

Brother Butler was a man of stern integrity. He was thoroughly aroused to the evil influence of the fanatical theories, and was active in his opposition to their false teachings and arrogant pretensions.

Moreover, he made it plain to us that he had no faith in visions of any sort.

Rather reluctantly Brother Butler consented to attend the meeting at the home of Brother Lovejoy at Johnson. The two men who were the leaders in the fanaticism, and who had greatly deceived and oppressed God's children, came into the meeting, accompanied by the two women dressed in white linen, with their long black hair hanging loose about their shoulders. The white linen dresses were to represent the righteousness of the saints.

I had a message of reproof for them, and while I was speaking, the foremost of the two men kept his eyes fastened upon me, as mesmerists had done before. But I had no fear of his mesmeric influence. Strength was given me from heaven to rise above their satanic power. The children of God who had been held in bondage began to breathe free and rejoice in the Lord.

As our meeting progressed, these fanatics sought to rise and speak, but they could not find opportunity. It was made plain to them that their presence was not wanted, but they chose to remain. Then Brother Samuel Rhodes seized the back of the chair in which one of the women was sitting, and drew her out of the room and across the porch onto the lawn. Returning to the meeting-room, he drew out the other woman in the same manner. The two men left the meeting-room, but sought to return.

As prayer was being offered at the close of the meeting, the second of the two men came to the door, and began to speak. The door was closed against him. He opened the door and again began to speak. Then the power of God fell upon my husband. The color left his face as he arose from his knees. He lifted his hands before the man, exclaiming: "The Lord does not want your testimony here. The Lord does not want you here to distract and crush His people."

The power of God filled the room. The man looked terrified, and stumbled backward through the hall into another room. He staggered across this room and fell against the wall, then recovered his balance and found the door out of the house. The presence of the Lord, which was so painful to the fanatical sinners, impressed with awful solemnity the company assembled. But after the children of darkness had gone, a sweet peace from the Lord rested upon our company. After this meeting the false and wily professors of perfect holiness were never able to reëstablish their power over our brethren.

The experiences of this meeting won us the confidence and fellowship of Brother Butler.

RETURN TO NEW YORK

After five weeks' absence, we returned to New York. At North Brookfield we found Sister Bonfoey and little Edson. The child was very feeble. A great change had taken place in him. It was difficult to suppress murmuring thoughts. But we knew that our only help was in God, so we prayed for the child, and his symptoms became more favorable, and we journeyed with him to Oswego to attend a conference there.

XX

PUBLISHING AGAIN

From Oswego we went to Centerport, in company with Brother and Sister Edson, and made our home at Brother Harris's, where we published a monthly magazine called the *Advent Review*.[1]

SATAN'S EFFORTS TO HINDER

My child grew worse, and three times a day we had seasons of prayer for him. Sometimes he would be blessed, and the progress of disease would be stayed; then our faith would be severely tried as his symptoms became alarming.

I was greatly depressed in spirit. Such queries as this troubled me: Why was God not willing to hear our prayers and raise the child to health? Satan, ever ready with his temptations, suggested that it was because we were not right. I could think of no particular thing wherein I had grieved the Lord, yet a crushing weight seemed to be on my spirits, driving me to despair. I doubted my acceptance with God, and could not pray. I had not courage so much as to lift my eyes to heaven. I suffered intense anguish of mind until my husband besought the Lord in my behalf. He would not yield until my voice was united with his for deliverance. The blessing came, and I

[1] The *Advent Review*, printed in Auburn, N. Y., during the summer of 1850, should not be confused with the *Advent Review and Sabbath Herald*, the first number of which was issued in Paris, Maine, November, 1850. The *Advent Review* was issued between Nos. 10 and 11 of *Present Truth*. Concerning its purpose, Elder James White wrote in his first page introduction to the 48-page pamphlet edition of the *Advent Review:*

"Our design in this review is to cheer and refresh the true believer, by showing the fulfillment of prophecy in the past wonderful work of God, in calling out, and separating from the world and nominal church, a people who are looking for the second advent of our dear Saviour."

began to hope. My trembling faith grasped the promises of God.

Then Satan came in another form. My husband was taken very sick. His symptoms were alarming. He cramped at intervals, and suffered excruciating pain. His feet and limbs were cold. I rubbed them until I had no strength to do so longer. Brother Harris was away some miles at his work. Sisters Harris and Bonfoey and my sister Sarah were the only ones present; and I was just gathering courage to dare believe in the promises of God. If ever I felt my weakness it was then. We knew that something must be done immediately. Every moment my husband's case was growing more critical. It was clearly a case of cholera. He asked us to pray, and we dared not refuse. In great weakness we bowed before the Lord. With a deep sense of my unworthiness, I laid my hands upon his head, and asked the Lord to reveal His power. A change came immediately. The natural color of his face returned, and the light of heaven beamed upon his countenance. We were all filled with gratitude unspeakable. Never had we witnessed a more remarkable answer to prayer.

That day we were to go to Port Byron to read the proof sheets of the paper that was being printed at Auburn. It appeared to us that Satan was trying to hinder the publication of the truth which we were laboring to place before the people. We felt that we must walk out upon faith. My husband said he would go to Port Byron for the proof sheets. We helped him harness the horse, and I accompanied him. The Lord strengthened him on the way. He received his proof, and a note stating that the paper would be off the press the next day, and we must be at Auburn to receive it.

That night we were awakened by the screams of our little Edson, who slept in the room above us. It was about midnight. Our little boy would cling to Sister Bonfoey, then with both hands fight the air, and then in terror he would cry, "No, no!" and cling closer to us. We knew this was Satan's effort to annoy us, and we knelt in prayer. My husband rebuked the evil spirit in the name of the Lord, and Edson quietly fell asleep in Sister Bonfoey's arms, and rested well through the night.

Then my husband was again attacked. He was in much pain. I knelt at the bedside and prayed the Lord to strengthen our faith. I knew God had wrought for him, and rebuked the disease; and we could not ask Him to do what had already been done. But we prayed that the Lord would carry on His work. We repeated these words: "Thou hast heard prayer. Thou hast wrought. We believe without a doubt. Carry on the work Thou hast begun!" Thus for two hours we pleaded before the Lord; and while we were praying, my husband fell asleep, and rested well till daylight. When he arose he was very weak, but we would not look at appearances.

TRIUMPHING THROUGH FAITH

We trusted the promise of God, and determined to walk out by faith. We were expected at Auburn that day to receive the first number of the paper. We believed that Satan was trying to hinder us, and my husband decided to go, trusting in the Lord. Brother Harris made ready the carriage, and Sister Bonfoey accompanied us. My husband had to be helped into the wagon, yet every mile we rode he gained strength. We kept our minds stayed upon God, and our faith in constant exercise, as we rode on, peaceful and happy.

When we received the paper all finished, and rode back to Centerport, we felt sure that we were in the path of duty. The blessing of God rested upon us. We had been greatly buffeted by Satan, but through Christ strengthening us we had come off victorious. We had a large bundle of papers with us, containing precious truth for the people of God.

Our child was recovering, and Satan was not again permitted to afflict him. We worked early and late, sometimes not allowing ourselves time to sit at the table to eat our meals. With a piece by our side we would eat and work at the same time. By overtaxing my strength in folding large sheets, I brought on a severe pain in my shoulder, which did not leave me for years.

We had been anticipating a journey east, and our child was again well enough to travel. We took the packet for Utica, and there we parted with Sister Bonfoey and my sister Sarah and our child, and went on our way to the East, while Brother Abbey took them home with him. We had to make some sacrifice in order to separate from those who were bound to us by tender ties; especially did our hearts cling to little Edson, whose life had been so much in danger. We then journeyed to Vermont and held a conference at Sutton.

THE "REVIEW AND HERALD"

In November, 1850, the paper was issued at Paris, Maine. Here it was enlarged, and its name changed to that which it now bears, the *Advent Review and Sabbath Herald*. We boarded in Brother A.'s family. We were willing to live cheaply, that the paper might be sustained. The friends of the cause were few in numbers and poor in worldly wealth, and we were still compelled to struggle with poverty and great discouragement. We had much care, and often sat up as late as midnight, and sometimes until two or three in the morning, to read proof sheets.

Excessive labor, care, and anxiety, a lack of proper and nourishing food, and exposure to cold in our long winter journeys, were too much for my husband, and he sank under the burden. He became so weak that he could scarcely walk to the printing office. Our faith was tried to the utmost. We had willingly endured privation, toil, and suffering, yet our motives were misinterpreted, and we were regarded with distrust and jealousy. Few of those for whose good we had suffered, seemed to appreciate our efforts.

We were too much troubled to sleep or rest. The hours in which we should have been refreshed with sleep, were often spent in answering long communications occasioned by envy. Many hours, while others were sleeping, we spent in agonizing tears, and mourning before the Lord. At length my husband said: "Wife, it is of no use to try to struggle on any longer. These things are crushing me, and will soon carry me to the grave. I cannot go any farther. I have written a note for the paper, stating that I shall publish no more." As he stepped out of the door to carry the note to the printing office, I fainted. He came back and prayed for me. His prayer was answered, and I was relieved.

The next morning, while at family prayer, I was taken off in vision and was instructed concerning these matters. I saw that my husband must not give up the paper, for Satan was trying to drive him to take just such a step, and was working through agents to do this. I was shown that we must continue to publish, and the Lord would sustain us.

We soon received urgent invitations to hold conferences in different States, and decided to attend general gatherings at Boston, Mass.; Rocky Hill, Conn.; Camden and West Milton, N. Y. These were all meetings of labor, but very profitable to our scattered brethren.

REMOVAL TO SARATOGA SPRINGS

We tarried at Ballston Spa a number of weeks, until we became settled in regard to publishing at Saratoga Springs. Then we rented a house and sent for Brother and Sister Stephen Belden and Sister Bonfoey, who was then in Maine taking care of little Edson, and with borrowed household stuff began housekeeping. Here my husband published the second volume of the *Advent Review and Sabbath Herald.*

Sister Annie Smith, who now sleeps in Jesus, came to live with us and assist in the work. Her help was needed. My husband expressed his feelings at this time in a letter to Brother Howland, dated Feb. 20, 1852, as follows: "We are unusually well, all but myself. I cannot long endure the labors of traveling and the care of publishing. Wednesday night we worked until two o'clock in the morning, folding and wrapping No. 12 of the *Review and Herald;* then I retired and coughed till daylight. Pray for me. The cause is prospering gloriously. Perhaps the Lord will not have need of me longer, and will let me rest in the grave. I hope to be free from the paper. I have stood by it in extreme adversity; and now when its friends are many, I feel free to leave it, if some one can be found who will take it. I hope my way will be made clear. May the Lord direct."

XXI

IN ROCHESTER, NEW YORK

In April, 1852, we moved to Rochester, N. Y., under most discouraging circumstances. At every step we were obliged to advance by faith. We were still crippled by poverty, and compelled to exercise the most rigid economy and self-denial. I will give a brief extract from a letter to Brother Howland's family, dated April 16, 1852:

"We are just getting settled in Rochester. We have rented an old house for one hundred and seventy-five dollars a year. We have the press in the house. Were it not for this, we should have to pay fifty dollars a year for office room. You would smile could you look in upon us and see our furniture. We have bought two old bedsteads for twenty-five cents each. My husband brought me home six old chairs, no two of them alike, for which he paid one dollar, and soon he presented me with four more old chairs without any seating, for which he paid sixty-two cents. The frames are strong, and I have been seating them with drilling. Butter is so high that we do not purchase it, neither can we afford potatoes. We use sauce in the place of butter, and turnips for potatoes. Our first meals were taken on a fireboard placed upon two empty flour barrels. We are willing to endure privations if the work of God can be advanced. We believe the Lord's hand was in our coming to this place. There is a large field for labor, and but few laborers. Last Sabbath our meeting was excellent. The Lord refreshed us with His presence."

DEATH OF ROBERT HARMON

Soon after our family became settled in Rochester, we received a letter from my mother informing us of the dangerous illness of my brother Robert, who lived with my parents in Gorham, Maine. When the news of his sickness reached us, my sister Sarah decided to go immediately to Gorham.

To all appearance my brother could live but a few days; yet contrary to the expectations of all, he lingered for six months, a great sufferer. My sister faithfully watched over him until the last. We had the privilege of visiting him before his death. It was an affecting meeting. He was much changed, yet his wasted features were lighted up with joy. Bright hope of the future constantly sustained him. We had seasons of prayer in his room, and Jesus seemed very near. We were obliged to separate from our dear brother, expecting never to meet him again this side of the resurrection of the just. Soon afterward my brother fell asleep in Jesus, in full hope of having a part in the first resurrection.

PRESSING ON

We toiled on in Rochester through much perplexity and discouragement. The cholera visited the city, and while it raged, all night long the carriages bearing the dead were heard rumbling through the streets to Mount Hope Cemetery. This disease did not cut down merely the low, but took victims from every class of society. The most skillful physicians were laid low, and borne to Mount Hope. As we passed through the streets in Rochester, at almost every corner we would meet wagons with plain pine coffins in which to put the dead.

Our little Edson was attacked, and we carried him to the great Physician. I took him in my arms, and in the name of Jesus rebuked the disease. He felt relief at once, and as a sister commenced praying for the Lord to heal him, the little fellow of three years looked up in astonishment, and said, "They need not pray any more, for the Lord has healed me." He was very weak, but the disease made no further progress. Yet he gained no strength. Our faith was still to be tried. For three days he ate nothing.

We had appointments out for two months, reaching from Rochester, N. Y., to Bangor, Maine; and this journey we were to perform with our covered carriage and our good horse Charlie, given to us by brethren in Vermont. We hardly dared to leave the child in so critical a state, but decided to go unless there was a change for the worse. In two days we must commence our journey in order to reach our first appointment. We presented the case before the Lord, taking it as an evidence that if the child had appetite to eat we would venture. The first day there was no change for the better. He could not take the least food. The next day about noon he called for broth, and it nourished him.

We began our journey that afternoon. About four o'clock I took my sick child upon a pillow, and we rode twenty miles. He seemed very nervous that night. He could not sleep, and I held him in my arms nearly the whole night.

The next morning we consulted together as to whether to return to Rochester or go on. The family who had entertained us said that if we went on, we would bury the child on the road; and to all appearance it would be so. But I dared not go back to

Rochester. We believed the affliction of the child was the work of Satan, to hinder us from traveling; and we dared not yield to him. I said to my husband: "If we go back, I shall expect the child to die. He can but die if we go forward. Let us proceed on our journey, trusting in the Lord."

We had before us a journey of about one hundred miles, to perform in two days, yet we believed that the Lord would work for us in this time of extremity. I was much exhausted, and feared I should fall asleep and let the child fall from my arms; so I laid him upon my lap, and tied him to my waist, and we both slept that day over much of the distance. The child revived and continued to gain strength the whole journey, and we brought him home quite rugged.

The Lord greatly blessed us on our journey to Vermont. My husband had much care and labor. At the different conferences he did most of the preaching, sold books, and labored to extend the circulation of the paper. When one conference was over, we would hasten to the next. At noon we would feed the horse by the roadside, and eat our lunch. Then my husband, laying his writing paper on the cover of our dinner box or on the top of his hat, would write articles for the *Review* and *Instructor*.

CONVERSION OF THE OFFICE FOREMAN

While we were absent from Rochester on this Eastern tour, the foreman of the Office was attacked with cholera. He was an unconverted young man. The lady of the house where he boarded died with the same disease, also her daughter. He was then brought down, and no one ventured to take care of him, fearing the disease. The Office hands watched over him until the disease seemed checked, then took him to our house. He had a relapse, and a physician attended him, and exerted himself to the utmost to save him, but at length told him that his case was hopeless, that he could not survive through the night. Those interested in the young man could not bear to see him die without hope. They prayed around his bedside while he was suffering great agony. He also prayed that the Lord would have mercy upon him, and forgive his sins. Yet he obtained no relief. He continued to cramp and toss in restless agony. The brethren continued in prayer all night that he might be spared to repent of his sins and keep the commandments of God. He at length seemed to consecrate himself to God, and promised the Lord he would keep the Sabbath and serve Him. He soon felt relief.

The next morning the physician came, and as he entered, said, "I told my wife about one o'clock this morning that in all probability the young man was out of his trouble." He was told that he was alive. The physician was surprised, and immediately ascended the stairs to his room. As he felt the pulse, he said: "Young man, you are better, the crisis is past; but it is not my skill that saved you, but a higher power. With good nursing you may get well." He gained rapidly, and soon took his place in the Office, a converted man.

NATHANIEL AND ANNA WHITE

After we returned from our Eastern journey, I was shown that we were in danger of taking burdens upon us that God did not require us to bear. We had a part to act in the cause of God, and should not add to our cares by increasing our family to gratify the wishes of any. I saw that in order to save souls we should be willing to bear burdens; and that we should open the way for my husband's brother Nathaniel and his sister Anna to come and live with us. They were both invalids, yet we extended to them a cordial invitation to come to our home. This they accepted.

As soon as we saw Nathaniel, we feared that consumption had marked him for the grave. The hectic flush was upon his cheek, yet we hoped and prayed that the Lord would spare him, that his talent might be employed in the cause of God. But the Lord saw fit to order otherwise.

Nathaniel and Anna came into the truth cautiously yet understandingly. They weighed the evidences of our position, and conscientiously decided for the truth.

May 6, 1853, we prepared Nathaniel's supper, but he soon said that he was faint, and did not know but that he was going to die. He sent for me, and as soon as I entered the room, I knew that he was dying, and said to him: "Nathaniel dear, trust in God. He loves you, and you love Him. Trust in Him as a child trusts in its parents. Don't be troubled. The Lord will not leave you." Said he, "Yes, yes." We prayed, and he responded, "Amen, praise the Lord!" He did not seem to suffer pain. He did not groan once, or struggle, or move a muscle of his face, but breathed shorter and shorter until he fell asleep, in the twenty-second year of his age.

XXII

ADVANCING UNDER DIFFICULTIES

After Nathaniel's death in May, 1853, my husband was much afflicted. Trouble and anxiety of mind had prostrated him. He had a high fever, and was confined to his bed. We united in prayer for him; but though relieved, he still remained very weak. He had appointments out for Mill Grove, N. Y., and Michigan, but feared that he could not fill them. We decided, however, to venture as far as Mill Grove, and if he grew no better, to return home. While at Elder R. F. Cottrell's at Mill Grove, he suffered much extreme weakness, and thought he could go no farther.

We were in much perplexity. Must we be driven from the work by bodily infirmities? Would Satan be permitted to exercise his power upon us, and contend for our usefulness and lives, as long as we should remain in the world? We knew that God could limit the power of Satan. He might suffer us to be tried in the furnace, but would bring us forth purified and better fitted for His work.

I went into a log house near by, and there poured out my soul before God in prayer that He would rebuke the disease and strengthen my husband to endure the journey. The case was urgent, and my faith firmly grasped the promises of God. I there obtained the evidence that if we should proceed on our journey to Michigan, the angel of God would go with us. When I related to my husband the exercise of my mind, he said that his own mind had been exercised in a similar manner, and we decided to go, trusting in the Lord. My husband was so weak that he could not buckle the straps to his valise, and called Brother Cottrell to do it for him.

Every mile we traveled he felt strengthened. The Lord sustained him. And while he was preaching the Word, I felt assured that angels of God were standing by his side.

FIRST VISIT TO MICHIGAN

At Jackson, Mich., we found the church in great confusion. While I was among them, the Lord instructed me regarding their condition, and I endeavored to bear a straightforward testimony. Some refused to heed the counsel given, and began to fight against my testimony; and here began what later became known as the Messenger party.

Concerning our labors on this tour among the companies of Sabbath-keeping believers in Michigan, I wrote as follows in a letter dated June 23, 1853:

"While in Michigan we visited Tyrone, Jackson, Sylvan, Bedford, and Vergennes. My husband in the strength of God endured the journey and his labor well. Only once did his strength entirely fail him. He was unable to preach at Bedford. He went to the place of meeting, and stood up in the desk to preach, but became faint and was obliged to sit down. He asked Elder J. N. Loughborough to take the subject where he had left it, and finish the discourse. Then he went out of the house into the open air, and lay upon the green grass until he had somewhat recovered, when Brother Kelsey let him take his horse, and he rode alone one mile and a half to Brother Brooks's.

"Brother Loughborough went through with the subject with much freedom. All were interested in the meeting. The Spirit of the Lord rested upon me, and I had perfect freedom in bearing my testimony.

The power of God was in the house, and nearly every one present was affected to tears. Some took a decided stand for the truth.

"After the meeting closed we rode through the woods to a beautiful lake, where six were buried with Christ in baptism. We then returned to Brother Brooks's, and found my husband more comfortable. While alone that day, his mind had been exercised upon the subject of Spiritualism, and he there decided to write the book entitled 'Signs of the Times.'

"Next day we journeyed to Vergennes, traveling over rough log ways and sloughs. Much of the way I rode in nearly a fainting condition; but our hearts were lifted to God in prayer for strength, and we found Him a present help, and were able to accomplish the journey, and bear our testimony there."

WRITING AND TRAVELING

Soon after our return to Rochester, N. Y., my husband engaged in writing the book "Signs of the Times." He was still feeble, and could sleep but little, but the Lord was his support. When his mind was in a confused, suffering state, we would bow before God, and in our distress cry unto Him. He heard our earnest prayers, and often blessed my husband so that with refreshed spirits he went on with the work. Many times in the day did we thus go before the Lord in earnest prayer. That book was not written in his own strength.

In the fall of 1853 we attended conferences at Buck's Bridge, N. Y.; Stowe, Vt.; Boston, Dartmouth, and Springfield, Mass.; Washington, N. H.; and New Haven, Vt. This was a laborious and rather discouraging journey. Many had embraced the truth who were unsanctified in heart and life; the elements of strife and rebellion were at work, and it was necessary that a movement should take place to purify the church.

DELIVERANCE FROM DISEASE

In the winter and spring I suffered much with heart disease. It was difficult for me to breathe while lying down, and I could not sleep unless raised in nearly a sitting posture. I had upon my left eyelid a swelling which appeared to be a cancer. It had been gradually increasing for more than a year, until it had become quite painful, and affected my sight.

A celebrated physician who gave counsel free visited Rochester, and I decided to have him examine my eye. He thought the swelling would prove to be a cancer; but upon feeling my pulse he said: "You are much diseased, and will die of apoplexy before that swelling shall break out. You are in a dangerous condition with disease of the heart." This did not startle me, for I had been aware that without speedy relief I must go down to the grave. Two other women who had come for counsel were suffering with the same disease. The physician said that I was in a more dangerous condition than either of them, and it could not be more than three weeks before I would be afflicted with paralysis.

In about three weeks I fainted and fell to the floor, and remained nearly unconscious about thirty-six hours. It was feared that I could not live, but in answer to prayer I again revived. One week later I received a shock upon my left side. I had a strange sensation of coldness and numbness in my head, and severe pain in my temples. My tongue seemed heavy and numb; I could not speak plainly. My left arm and side were helpless.

The brethren and sisters came together to make my case a special subject of prayer. I received the blessing of God, and had the assurance that He loved me; but the pain continued, and I grew more feeble every hour. Again the brethren and sisters assembled to present my case to the Lord. I was so weak that I could not pray vocally. My appearance seemed to weaken the faith of those around me. Then the promises of God were arrayed before me as I had never viewed them before. It seemed to me that Satan was striving to tear me from my husband and children and lay me in the grave, and these questions were suggested to my mind: Can you believe the naked promise of God? Can you walk out by faith, let the appearance be what it may? Faith revived. I whispered to my husband, "I believe that I shall recover." He answered, "I wish I could believe it." I retired that night without relief, yet relying with firm confidence upon the promises of God. I could not sleep, but continued my silent prayer. Just before day I fell asleep.

I awoke at sunrise, perfectly free from pain. O, what a change! It seemed to me that an angel of God had touched me while I was sleeping. The pressure upon my heart was gone, and I was very happy. I was filled with gratitude. The praise of God was upon my lips. I awoke my husband, and related to him the wonderful work that the Lord had wrought for me. He could scarcely comprehend it at first; but when I arose and dressed and walked around the house, he could praise God with me. My afflicted eye was free from pain. In a few days the swelling disappeared, and my eyesight was fully restored. The work was complete.

Again I visited the physician, and as soon as he felt my pulse he said, "Madam, an entire change has taken place in your system; but the two women who visited me for counsel when you were last here are dead." After I left, the doctor said to a friend of mine: "Her case is a mystery. I do not understand it."

VISIT TO MICHIGAN AND WISCONSIN — 1854

In the spring of 1854 we visited Michigan again; and though we were obliged to ride over log ways and through mud sloughs, my strength failed not. We felt that the Lord would have us visit Wisconsin, and arranged to board the cars at Jackson late at night.

As we were preparing to take the train, we felt very solemn, and proposed a season of prayer; and as we there committed ourselves to God, we could not refrain from weeping. We went to the depot with feelings of deep solemnity. On boarding the train, we went into a forward car, which had seats with high backs, hoping that we might sleep some that night. The car was full, and we passed back into the next, and there found seats. I did not, as usual when traveling in the night, lay off my bonnet, but held my carpetbag in my hand, as if waiting for something. We both spoke of our singular feelings.

The train had run about three miles from Jackson when its motion became very violent, jerking backward and forward, and finally stopping. I opened the window and saw one car raised nearly upon end. I heard agonizing groans, and there was great confusion. The engine had been thrown from the track, but the car we were in was on the track, and was separated about one hundred feet from those before it. The coupling had not been broken, but our car had been unfastened from the one before it, as if an angel had separated them. The baggage car was not much injured, and our large trunk of books was uninjured. The second-class car was crushed, and the pieces, with the passengers, were thrown on both sides of the track. The car in which we had tried to get a seat was much broken, and one end was raised upon the heap of ruins. Four were killed or mortally wounded, and many were much injured. We could but feel that God had sent an angel to preserve our lives.

We returned to the home of Brother Cyrenius Smith, near Jackson, and the next day took the train for Wisconsin. Our visit to that State was blessed of God. Souls were converted as the result of our efforts. The Lord strengthened me to endure the tedious journey.

RETURN TO ROCHESTER

We returned from Wisconsin much worn, desiring rest, but were distressed to find Sister Anna afflicted. Disease had fastened upon her, and she was brought very low. Trials thickened around us. We had much care. The Office hands boarded with us, and our family numbered from fifteen to twenty. The large conferences and the Sabbath meetings were held at our house. We had no quiet Sabbaths; for some of the sisters usually tarried all day with their children. Our brethren and sisters generally did not consider the inconvenience and additional care and expense brought upon us. As one after another of the Office hands would come home sick, needing extra attention, I was fearful that we should sink beneath the anxiety and care. I often thought that we could endure no more; yet trials increased, and with surprise I found that we were not overwhelmed. We learned the lesson that much more suffering and trial could be borne than we had once thought possible. The watchful eye of the Lord was upon us, to see that we were not destroyed.

August 29, 1854, another responsibility was added to our family in the birth of Willie. He took my mind somewhat from the troubles around me. About this time the first number of the paper falsely called the *Messenger of Truth* was received. Those who slandered us through that paper had been reproved for their faults and errors. They would not bear reproof, and in a secret manner at first, afterward more openly, used their influence against us.

The Lord had shown me the character and final come-out of that party; that His frown was upon those connected with that paper, and His hand was against them, and although they might appear to prosper for a time, and some honest ones be deceived, yet truth would eventually triumph, and every honest soul would break away from the deception which had held them, and come out clear from the influence of these wicked men; as God's hand was against them, they must go down.

DEATH OF ANNA WHITE

Sister Anna continued to fail. Her father and mother and her older sister came from Maine to visit her in her affliction. Anna was calm and cheerful. She had much desired this interview with her parents and sister. She bade them farewell, as they left to return to Maine, to meet them no more until God shall call forth His faithful ones to health and immortality.

In the last days of her sickness, with her own trembling hands she arranged her things, leaving them in perfect order, and disposing of them according to her mind. She expressed a great desire that her parents should embrace the Sabbath, and live near us. "If I thought this would ever be," she said, "I could die perfectly satisfied."

The last office performed by her emaciated, trembling hand, was to trace a few lines to her parents. And did not God regard her last wishes and prayers for her parents? In less than two years, Father and Mother White were keeping the Bible Sabbath, happily situated within less than one hundred feet from our door.

We would have kept Anna with us; but we were obliged to close her eyes in death, and lay her away to rest. Long had she cherished a hope in Jesus, and she looked forward with pleasing anticipation to the morning of the resurrection. We laid her beside dear Nathaniel in Mount Hope Cemetery.

XXIII

REMOVAL TO MICHIGAN

In 1855 the brethren in Michigan opened the way for the publishing work to be removed to Battle Creek. At that time my husband was owing between two and three thousand dollars; and all he had, besides a small lot of books, was accounts for books, and some of these were doubtful. The cause had apparently come to a standstill. Orders for publications were very few and small. My husband's health was very poor. He was troubled with cough and soreness of lungs, and his nervous system was prostrated. We feared that he would die while still in debt.

COMFORTING ASSURANCES

Those were days of sadness. I looked upon my three little boys, soon, as I feared, to be left fatherless, and thoughts like these forced themselves upon me: My husband will die of overwork in the cause of present truth; and who realizes what he has suffered? Who knows the burdens he has for years borne, the extreme care which has crushed his spirits and ruined his health, bringing him to an untimely grave, leaving his family destitute and dependent? I often asked myself the question: Does God have no care for these things? Does He pass them by unnoticed? I was comforted to know that there is One who judgeth righteously, and that every sacrifice, every self-denial, and every pang of anguish endured for His sake, is faithfully chronicled in heaven, and will bring its reward. The day of the Lord will declare and bring to light things that are not yet made manifest.

I was shown that God designed to raise my husband up gradually; that we must exercise strong faith, for in every effort we should be fiercely buffeted by Satan; that we must look away from outward appearances, and believe. Three times a day we went alone before God, and engaged in earnest prayer for the recovery of his health. The Lord graciously heard our earnest cries, and my husband began to recover. I cannot better state my feelings at this time than they are expressed in the following extracts from a letter I wrote to Sister Howland:

"I feel thankful that I can now have my children with me, under my own watchcare.[1] For weeks I have felt a hungering and thirsting for salvation, and we have enjoyed almost uninterrupted communion with God. Why do we stay away from the fountain, when we can come and drink? Why do we die for bread, when there is a storehouse full? It is rich and free. O my soul, feast upon it, and daily drink in heavenly joys! I will not hold my peace. The praise of God is in my heart and upon my lips. We can rejoice in the fullness of our Saviour's love. We can feast upon His excellent glory. My soul testifies to this. My gloom has been dispersed by this precious light, and I can never forget it. Lord, help me to keep it in lively remembrance. Awake, all the energies of my soul! Awake, and adore thy Redeemer for His wondrous love!

"Our enemies may triumph. They may speak bitter words, and their tongue frame slander, deceit, and falsehood; yet will we not be moved. We know in whom we have believed. We have not run in

[1] When returning from an Eastern tour to their Rochester home, in the fall of 1853, Elder and Mrs. White brought with them their eldest child, Henry, who for five years had been tenderly cared for by Brother and Sister Howland.

vain, neither labored in vain. A reckoning day is coming, when all will be judged according to the deeds done in the body. It is true the world is dark. Opposition may wax strong. The trifler and the scorner may grow bold in their iniquity. Yet for all this we will not be moved, but lean upon the arm of the Mighty One for strength."

CAPTIVITY TURNED

From the time we moved to Battle Creek, the Lord began to turn our captivity. We found sympathizing friends in Michigan, who were ready to share our burdens and supply our wants. Old, tried friends in central New York and New England, especially in Vermont, sympathized with us in our afflictions, and were ready to assist us in time of distress. At the conference at Battle Creek in November, 1856, God wrought for us. New life was given to the cause, and success attended the labors of our preachers.

The publications were called for, and proved to be just what the cause demanded. The *Messenger of Truth* soon went down, and the discordant spirits who had spoken through it were scattered. My husband was enabled to pay all his debts. His cough ceased, the pain and soreness left his lungs and throat, and he was gradually restored to health, so that he could preach three times on the Sabbath and on first day with ease. This wonderful work in his restoration was of God, and He should have all the glory.

XXIV

LABORS IN THE MIDDLE WEST—1856-58

In the fall of 1856, while visiting a company of Sabbath-keeping Adventists at Round Grove, Ill., I was shown that the company of brethren at Waukon, Iowa, needed help; that Satan's snare must be broken, and these precious souls rescued. My mind could not be at ease until we had decided to visit them.

A VICTORY AT WAUKON, IOWA

When we reached Waukon, late in December, 1856, we found nearly all the Sabbath keepers sorry we had come. Much prejudice existed against us, for much had been said that tended to injure our influence.

At the evening meeting I was taken off in vision, and the power of God fell upon the company. I related what the Lord had given me for the people. It was this: "Return unto Me, and I will return unto thee, and heal all thy backslidings. Tear down the rubbish from the door of thy heart, and open the door, and I will come in and sup with thee." I saw that if they would clear the way, and confess their wrongs, Jesus would walk through the midst of us in power.

After I had borne my testimony, one sister began to confess in a clear, decided manner; and as she made confession, the floodgates of heaven seemed suddenly opened, and I was prostrated by the power of God. It seemed an awful yet glorious place. The meeting continued till past midnight, and a great work was accomplished.

The next day the meeting began where it had ended the night before. Those who had been blessed at the previous meeting retained the blessing. They had not slept much, for the Spirit of God rested upon them through the night. Some confessed their feeling of disunion with us and their backslidden condition. The meeting continued, without intermission, from ten o'clock in the forenoon till five in the evening.

That evening the burden left us. It was rolled upon the brethren and sisters of Waukon, and they labored for each other with zeal and with the power of God upon them. Countenances that looked sad when we came to the place, now shone with the heavenly anointing. It seemed that heavenly angels were passing from one to another in the room to finish the good work which had begun. Soon we were able to bid farewell to our brethren in Waukon, and to start on our homeward journey.

VIEW AT LOVETT'S GROVE, OHIO

In the spring of 1858, we visited Ohio, and attended conferences at Green Springs, Gilboa, and Lovett's Grove. At Lovett's Grove the Lord's blessing rested upon us in special power. On Sunday afternoon there was a funeral service at the schoolhouse where our meetings were being held. My husband was invited to speak. He was blessed with freedom, and the words spoken seemed to affect the hearers.

When he had closed his remarks, I felt urged by the Spirit of the Lord to bear my testimony. As I was led to speak upon the coming of Christ and the resurrection, and the cheering hope of the Christian, my soul triumphed in God; I drank in rich draughts of salvation. Heaven, sweet heaven, was the magnet to draw my soul upward, and I was wrapped in a vision of God's glory. Many important matters were there revealed to me for the church.

WRITING "SPIRITUAL GIFTS," VOL. 1

In the vision at Lovett's Grove, most of the matter which I had seen ten years before concerning the great controversy of the ages between Christ and Satan, was repeated, and I was instructed to write it out. I was shown that while I should have to contend with the powers of darkness, for Satan would make strong efforts to hinder me, yet I must put my trust in God, and angels would not leave me in the conflict.

Two days afterward, while journeying on the cars to Jackson, Mich., we arranged our plans for writing and publishing, immediately on our return home, the book entitled, "The Great Controversy between Christ and His Angels, and Satan and His Angels," commonly known as "Spiritual Gifts," Vol. 1.[1] I was then as well as usual.

On the arrival of the train at Jackson, we went to Brother Palmer's. We had been in the house but a short time, when, as I was conversing with Sister Palmer, my tongue refused to utter what I wished to say, and seemed large and numb. A strange, cold sensation struck my heart, passed over my head, and down my right side. For a time I was insensible, but was aroused by the voice of earnest prayer. I tried to use my left limbs, but they were perfectly useless. For a short time I did not expect to live. It was my third shock of paralysis; and although

---

[1] NOTE.— This volume, dealing with the fall of man, the plan of redemption, and the history of the church from the time of Christ to the new earth, corresponds with the latter part of "Early Writings," pp. 145-295 (new edition). A portion of the volume, as enlarged in later years, is now published separately under the general title, "The Great Controversy between Christ and Satan."

within fifty miles of home, I did not expect to see my children again. I called to mind the triumphant season I had enjoyed at Lovett's Grove, and thought it was my last testimony, and felt reconciled to die.

Still the earnest prayers of my friends were ascending to heaven for me, and soon a prickling sensation was felt in my limbs, and I praised the Lord that I could use them a little. The Lord heard and answered the faithful prayers of His children, and the power of Satan was broken. That night I suffered much, but the next day I was sufficiently strengthened to return home.

For several weeks I could not feel the pressure of the hand or the coldest water poured upon my head. In rising to walk, I often staggered, and sometimes fell to the floor. In this afflicted condition I began to write on the great controversy. At first I could write but one page a day, and then rest three days; but as I progressed, my strength increased. The numbness in my head did not seem to becloud my mind, and before I closed that work ["Spiritual Gifts," Vol. 1], the effect of the shock had entirely left me.

At the time of the conference at Battle Creek, in June, 1858, I was shown in vision that in the sudden attack at Jackson, Satan intended to take my life, in order to hinder the work I was about to write; but angels of God were sent to my rescue. I also saw, among other things, that I should be blessed with better health than before the attack.

XXV

PERSONAL TRIALS

When my husband became so feeble, before our removal from Rochester, he desired to free himself from the responsibility of the publishing work. He proposed that the church take charge of the work, and that it be managed by a publishing committee whom they should appoint, and that no one connected with the office derive any financial benefit therefrom beyond the wages received for his labor.

EFFORTS TO ESTABLISH THE PUBLISHING WORK

Though the matter was repeatedly urged upon their attention, our brethren took no action in regard to it until 1861. Up to this time my husband had been the legal proprietor of the publishing house, and sole manager of the work. He enjoyed the confidence of the active friends of the cause, who trusted to his care the means which they donated from time to time, as the growing cause demanded, to build up the publishing enterprise. But although the statement was frequently repeated, through the *Review*, that the publishing house was virtually the property of the church, yet as he was the only legal manager, our enemies took advantage of the situation, and under the cry of speculation did all in their power to injure him, and to retard the progress of the cause. Under these circumstances he introduced the matter of organization, which resulted in the incorporation of the Seventh-day Adventist Publishing Association, according to the laws of Michigan, in the spring of 1861.

PARENTAL CARES

Although the cares that came upon us in connection with the publishing work and other branches of the cause involved much perplexity, the greatest sacrifice which I was called to make in connection with the work was to leave my children frequently to the care of others.

Henry had been from us five years, and Edson had received but little of our care. For years at Rochester our family had been very large, and our home like a hotel, and we from that home much of the time. I had felt the deepest anxiety that my children should be brought up free from evil habits, and I was often grieved as I thought of the contrast between my situation and that of others who would not take burdens and cares, who could ever be with their children, to counsel and instruct them, and who spent their time almost exclusively in their own families. And I have inquired: Does God require so much of us, and leave others without burdens? Is this equality? Are we to be thus hurried on from one care to another, one part of the work to another, and have but little time to bring up our children?

LOSS OF CHILDREN

In 1860 death stepped over our threshold, and broke the youngest branch of our family tree. Little Herbert, born Sept. 20, 1860, died December 14 of the same year. When that tender branch was broken, how our hearts did bleed none may know but those who have followed their little ones of promise to the grave.

But oh, when our noble Henry died,[1] at the age of

[1] The death of Henry N. White occurred at Topsham, Maine, Dec. 8, 1863.

sixteen,— when our sweet singer was borne to the grave, and we no more heard his early song,— ours was a lonely home. Both parents and the two remaining sons felt the blow most keenly. But God comforted us in our bereavements, and with faith and courage we pressed forward in the work He had given us, in bright hope of meeting our children who had been torn from us by death, in that world where sickness and death will never come.

We feel the loss of our dear Henry very much
We miss him every where. The youngest
and oldest branches of the family tree has
been broken off. We return from our eastern
journey wounded but not comfortless
It was a great blessing to be permitted
to watch the last painful hours of my
first born My sweet singer is dead
No more will his voice unite with us
around the family altar, no more will
music be called forth by his touch, no
more will his willing feet and hand do
our bidding But we look forward with
with joy to the resurrection morning

Facsimile (slightly reduced) of portion of a page written by Mrs. White shortly after the death of her first-born, Henry N. White, Dec. 8, 1863.

XXVI

BATTLING AGAINST DISEASE

[Historical Note.—"Our people are generally waking up to the subject of health," wrote Elder James White in an editorial in the *Review*, Dec. 13, 1864, "and they should have publications on the subject to meet their present wants, at prices within reach of the poorest." He announced the early issuance of a series of pamphlets, under the general title, "Health: or How to Live."

The strong conviction of Elder and Mrs. White, that the reforms to be outlined in these pamphlets were of great importance, is thus expressed in a note in the *Review*, Jan. 24, 1865, calling attention to the publication of the first of the series:

"We wish to call the attention of the brethren everywhere to these works, prepared with especial care, on the important subject of a reform in our manners of life, which is greatly needed, and as we view it, *will surely be accomplished in whatever people find themselves at last prepared for translation.*"

During the first five months of 1865 this series was completed. These health pamphlets, six in number, contained articles from Mrs. White on "Disease and Its Causes," and on allied subjects; and many extracts from the writings of various physicians and others interested in health reform principles. Hygienic recipes were included, also hints on the use of water as a remedial agency. The harmful effects of alcohol, tobacco, tea and coffee, spices, and other stimulants and narcotics, were further emphasized.

The winter of 1864-65 was a time of stress and trial. While uniting with his wife in the preparation of matter on health and temperance for publication, Elder White found it necessary to labor untiringly in behalf of Sabbath keepers who were being drafted for service in the army. This work was attended with perplexity and anxiety, and drew heavily on his sympathies, besides overtaxing his physical strength. The administrative cares in the session of the General Conference held in May, 1865, added to his weariness.

Worn with the labors of writing and publishing, and of looking after many interests connected with the general work, Elder White and his wife were nevertheless given no rest. Immediately after the Conference session, they were called to Wisconsin and Iowa, where they endured many hardships. Soon after their return to Michigan, he was stricken with partial paralysis. An account of this affliction, and of the impetus it indirectly brought to the health reform movement a few months later, is given by Mrs. White in the *Review*, Feb. 20 and 27, 1866, a portion of which forms the text of this chapter.]

THE SICKNESS OF ELDER JAMES WHITE

One morning, as we were taking our usual walk before breakfast, we stepped into Brother Lunt's garden, and while my husband attempted to open an ear of corn, I heard a strange noise. Looking up, I saw his face flushed, and his right arm hanging helpless at his side. His attempt to raise his right arm was ineffectual — the muscles refused to obey his will.

I helped him into the house, but he could not speak to me until in the house he indistinctly uttered the words, "Pray, pray." We dropped on our knees and cried to God, who had ever been to us a present help in time of trouble. My husband soon uttered words of praise and gratitude to God, because he could use his arm. His hand was partially restored, but not fully.

My husband and myself felt the need of drawing near to God. And as by confession and prayer we drew near to God, we had the blessed assurance that He drew near to us. Precious, exceedingly precious, were these seasons of communion with God.

The first five weeks of our affliction we spent at our own home. For wise purposes our heavenly Father did not see fit to raise my husband to immediate health in answer to our earnest prayers, although He seemed preciously near to comfort and sustain us by His Holy Spirit.

SOJOURN AT DANSVILLE, N. Y.

We had confidence in the use of water as one of God's appointed remedies, but no confidence in drugs. But my own vital energies were too much exhausted for me to attempt to use hydropathic remedies in my husband's case; and we felt that it might be duty to take him to Dansville, N. Y., where he could rest, and where we could have the care of those well skilled as hydropathic physicians. We dared not follow our own judgment, but asked counsel of God, and after prayerful consideration of the matter, decided to go. My husband endured the journey well.

We remained in Dansville about three months. We obtained rooms a short distance from the institution, and were both able to walk out and be in the open air much of the time. Every day, excepting Sabbath and first day, we took treatment.

Some may have thought that when we went to Dansville and placed ourselves under the care of physicians, we had given up our faith that God would raise my husband to health in answer to prayer. But not so. While we did not feel like despising the means that God had placed in our reach for the recovery of health, we felt that God was above all, and that He who had provided remedial agencies would have us use them to assist abused Nature to recover her exhausted energies. We believed that God would bless the efforts we were making in the direction of health.

SEASONS OF PRAYER AND BLESSING

Three times a day we had special seasons of prayer for the Lord to restore my husband to health, and for His special grace to sustain us in our affliction. These seasons of prayer were very precious to us. Our hearts were often filled with unspeakable gratitude that in our affliction we had a heavenly Father in whom we could trust without fear.

Dec. 4, 1865, my husband passed a restless night of suffering. I prayed by his bedside as usual, but the Lord was not pleased to send relief. My husband was troubled in mind. He thought that he might go down into the grave. He stated that death had no terrors for him.

I felt intensely over the matter. I did not believe for a moment that my husband would die. But how was he to be inspired with faith? I prayed God to guide me, and not suffer me to take one wrong step; but to give me wisdom to choose the right course. The more earnestly I prayed, the stronger was my conviction that I must take my husband among his brethren, even if we should again return to Dansville.

In the morning Dr. Lay called, and I told him that unless there should be a decided improvement in the case of my husband in two or three weeks, at most,

I should take him home. He answered: "You cannot take him home. He is not able to endure such a journey." I answered: "I shall go. I shall take my husband by faith, relying upon God, and shall make Rochester my first point, tarry there a few days, and then go on to Detroit, and if necessary, tarry there a few days to rest, and then go on to Battle Creek."

This was the first intimation my husband had of my intentions. He said not a word. That evening we packed our trunks, and the next morning were on our way. My husband rode comfortably.

During the three weeks that we were in Rochester, much of the time was spent in prayer. My husband proposed sending to Maine for Elder J. N. Andrews, to Olcott for Brother and Sister Lindsay, and to Roosevelt, requesting those who had faith in God, and felt it their duty, to come and pray for him. These friends came in answer to his call, and for ten days we had special and earnest seasons of prayer. All who engaged in these seasons of prayer were greatly blessed. We were often so refreshed with heavenly showers of grace that we could say, "My cup runneth over." We could weep and praise God for His rich salvation.

Those who came from Roosevelt were soon obliged to return to their homes. Brother Andrews and Brother and Sister Lindsay remained. We continued our earnest supplications to heaven. It seemed to be a struggle with the powers of darkness. Sometimes the trembling faith of my husband would grasp the promises of God, and sweet and precious was the victory then enjoyed.

Christmas evening, as we were humbling ourselves before God and earnestly pleading for deliverance, the light of heaven seemed to shine upon us, and I was wrapped in a vision of God's glory. It seemed that I was borne quickly from earth to heaven, where all was health, beauty, and glory. Strains of music fell upon my ear, melodious, perfect, and entrancing. I was permitted to enjoy this scene a while before my attention was called to this dark world. Then my attention was called to things taking place upon this earth.[1] I had an encouraging view of the case of my husband.

Circumstances did not seem to favor our starting for Battle Creek, but my mind seemed fixed that we must go.

We were prospered on our journey. On the arrival of the train at Battle Creek, we were met by several of our faithful brethren, who received us gladly. My husband rested well through the night. The next Sabbath, although feeble, he walked to the meetinghouse, and spoke for about three quarters of an hour. We also attended the communion season in the evening. The Lord strengthened him as he walked out by faith.

The long sickness of my husband was a heavy blow, not only to myself and my children, but to the cause of God. The churches were deprived both of my husband's labors and of my own. Satan triumphed as he saw the work of truth thus hindered; but, thank God! he was not permitted to destroy us. After being cut off from all active labor for fifteen months, we ventured out once more together to work among the churches.

---

[1] A portion of the instruction given during this memorable vision, urging the establishment of a health institution by the Seventh-day Adventist denomination, is given in "Testimonies for the Church," Vol. 1, pp. 485-495, 553-564.

XXVII

CONFLICTS AND VICTORY

Having become fully satisfied that my husband would not recover from his protracted sickness while remaining inactive, and that the time had fully come for me to go forth and bear my testimony to the people, I decided to make a tour in northern Michigan, with my husband in his extremely feeble condition, in the severest cold of winter. It required no small degree of moral courage and faith in God to bring my mind to the decision to risk so much; but I knew that I had a work to do, and it seemed to me that Satan was determined to keep me from it. To remain longer from the field seemed to me worse than death, and should we move out, we could but perish. So, on the 19th of December, 1866, we left Battle Creek in a snowstorm for Wright, Mich.

My husband stood the journey of ninety miles much better than I feared, and seemed quite as well when we reached the home of Brother E. H. Root as when we left Battle Creek. We were kindly received by this dear family, and as tenderly cared for as Christian parents can care for invalid children.

LABORS AT WRIGHT, MICH.

Here commenced our first effective labors since my husband's sickness. Here he began to labor as in former years, though in much weakness. He would speak thirty or forty minutes in the forenoon of the Sabbath and on first day, while I would occupy the rest of the time, and then speak in the afternoon of each day, about an hour and a half each time. We were listened to with the greatest attention. I saw that my husband was growing stronger, clearer in mind, and more connected in his discourses. And when on one occasion he spoke one hour with clearness and power, with the burden of the work upon him as before his sickness, my feelings of gratitude were beyond expression.

My labors at Wright were very wearing. I had much care of my husband by day, and sometimes in the night. I gave him baths, and took him out to ride, and twice a day, cold, stormy, or pleasant, walked out with him. I used the pen while he dictated his reports for the *Review,* and also wrote many letters, in addition to personal testimonies, and most of "Testimony for the Church," No. 11.

AT GREENVILLE, MICH.

Jan. 29, 1867, we left Wright, and rode to Greenville, a distance of forty miles. It was a severely cold day, and we were glad to find a shelter from the cold and storm at Brother A. W. Maynard's. This dear family welcomed us to their hearts and to their home. We remained in this vicinity six weeks, laboring with the churches at Greenville and Orleans, and making Brother Maynard's hospitable home our headquarters.

The Lord gave me freedom in speaking to the people. In every effort made I realized His sustaining power. And as I became fully convinced that I had a testimony for the people, which I could bear to them in connection with the labors of my husband, my faith was strengthened that he would yet be raised to health to labor with acceptance in the cause and work of God. As he ventured, trusting in God, regardless of his feebleness, he gained in strength, and improved with every effort.

VISIT TO BATTLE CREEK — MARCH, 1867

It was decided that we should return to Battle Creek, and there remain while the roads were in a muddy, broken-up condition, and that I should there complete Testimony No. 12. My husband was very anxious to see his brethren at Battle Creek, and speak to them, and rejoice with them in the work which God was doing for him.

In a few days we found ourselves again at Battle Creek, after an absence of about three months. On the Sabbath, March 16, my husband spoke with clearness and power, and I also bore my testimony with usual freedom.

I came home to Battle Creek like a weary child, who needed comforting words and encouragement. But on our return we met reports having no foundation in truth. We were humbled into the very dust, and distressed beyond expression.

In this state of things we started to fill an appointment at Monterey. On the journey I tried to explain to myself why it was that our brethren did not understand in regard to our work. I had felt quite sure that when we should meet them, they would know what spirit we were of, and that the Spirit of God in them would answer to the same in us, His humble servants, and there would be union of feeling and sentiment. Instead of this, we were distrusted and suspiciously watched, which was a cause of the greatest perplexity I ever experienced.

LAYING HOLD ON GOD

As I was thus thinking, a portion of the vision given me at Rochester, N. Y., Dec. 25, 1865, came like a flash of lightning to my mind, and I immediately related it to my husband:

I was shown a cluster of trees, standing near together, forming a circle. Running up over these trees was a vine which covered them at the top, and rested upon them, forming an arbor. Soon I saw the trees swaying to and fro, as though moved by a powerful wind. One branch after another of the vine was shaken from its support, until the vine was shaken loose from the trees, except a few tendrils which were left clinging to the lower branches. A person then came up and severed the remaining clinging tendrils of the vine, and it lay prostrated upon the earth.

Many passed and looked pityingly upon it, and I waited anxiously for a friendly hand to raise it; but no help was offered. I inquired why no hand raised the vine. Presently I saw an angel come to the apparently deserted vine. He spread out his arms and placed them beneath the vine, and raised it so that it stood upright, saying: "Stand toward heaven, and let thy tendrils entwine about God. Thou art shaken from human support. Thou canst stand, in the strength of God, and flourish without it. Lean upon God alone, and thou shalt never lean in vain, or be shaken therefrom."

As I saw the neglected vine cared for, I felt inexpressible relief, amounting to joy. I turned to the angel and inquired what these things meant. Said he: "Thou art this vine. All this thou wilt experience, and then, when these things occur, thou shalt fully understand the figure of the vine. God will be to thee a present help in time of trouble."

From this time I was settled as to my duty, and

never more free in bearing my testimony to the people. After we returned from Monterey to Battle Creek, I felt it my duty to move forward in the strength of God, and free myself from the suspicions and reports circulated to our injury. I bore my testimony, and related things which had been shown me in the past history cf some present, warning them of their dangers and reproving their wrong course of action. I stated that I had been placed in most disagreeable positions. When families and individuals were brought before me in vision, it was frequently the case that what was shown me in relation to them was of a private nature, reproving secret sins. I have labored with some for months in regard to wrongs of which others knew nothing. As my brethren see these persons sad, and hear them express doubts in regard to their acceptance with God, also feelings of despondency, they have cast censure upon me, as though I was to blame for their being in trial.

Those who thus censured me were entirely ignorant of what they were talking about. I protested against persons' sitting as inquisitors upon my course of action. It has been the disagreeable work assigned me to reprove private sins. Were I, in order to prevent suspicions and jealousy, to give a full explanation of my course, and make public that which should be kept private, I should sin against God and wrong the individuals. I have to keep private reproofs of private wrongs to myself, locked in my own breast. Let others judge as they may, I will never betray the confidence reposed in me by the erring and repentant, or reveal to others that which should only be brought before the ones that are guilty. I told those assembled that they must take their hands off, and leave me free to act in the fear of God.

XXVIII

AMONG THE CHURCHES IN NEW ENGLAND

Refreshed in spirit over the good result of our labor with the Battle Creek church, which closed in October, 1867, we cheerfully joined Elder J. N. Andrews on a journey to Maine. On the way we held a meeting at Roosevelt, N. Y., October 26 and 27. This meeting was one of hard labor, in which pointed testimonies were given. Confessions were made, followed by a general turning to the Lord on the part of backsliders and sinners.

IN MAINE

Our labors in Maine commenced with the conference at Norridgewock, the first of November. The meeting was large. As usual, my husband and myself bore a plain and pointed testimony in favor of truth and proper church discipline, and against the different forms of error, confusion, fanaticism, and disorder naturally growing out of a want of such discipline. This testimony was especially applicable to the condition of things in Maine. Disorderly spirits who professed to observe the Sabbath, were in rebellion, and labored to diffuse the disaffection through the conference.

In consequence of this spirit of rebellion, our work in Maine required seven weeks of the most trying, laborious, and disagreeable toil. But as we left that State, we were comforted with the fact that all had confessed their rebellion, and that a few had been led to seek the Lord and embrace the truth.

Perhaps I cannot better give an idea of our labors up to the time of the Vermont meeting than by copying a portion of a letter which I wrote to our son at Battle Creek, Dec. 27, 1867:

"My dear Son Edson:

"After our meeting closed at Topsham, Maine, we had an appointment at Westbrook, Maine, to meet the brethren from Portland and vicinity. We made our home with the kind family of Brother Martin. I was not able to sit up during the afternoon; but being urged to attend the meeting in the evening, I went to the schoolhouse, feeling that I had not strength to stand and address the people.

The house was filled with deeply interested listeners. Brother Andrews opened the meeting, and spoke a short time; your father followed with remarks. I then arose, and had spoken but a few words when I felt my strength renewed; all my feebleness seemed to leave me, and I spoke about one hour with perfect freedom. I felt inexpressible gratitude for this help from God at the very time when I so much needed it.

"On Wednesday evening I spoke with freedom nearly two hours. To have my strength so unexpectedly renewed, when I had felt completely exhausted before these two meetings, has been a source of great encouragement to me.

REVIVAL SERVICES AT WASHINGTON, N. H.

"Our journey to Washington, N. H., was tedious. We found shelter at last at the good home of Brother C. K. Farnsworth. They did all they could for our comfort, and everything was arranged so that we could rest as much as possible.

"Sabbath your father spoke in the forenoon, and after an intermission of about twenty minutes I spoke, bearing a testimony of reproof for several. The meeting for the evening was appointed at Brother Farnsworth's. The next morning we attended meetings again in the meetinghouse. We were trying to bring those who professed the truth to see their state of dreadful darkness and backsliding before God, and to make humble confessions.

"Again we held an evening meeting at Brother Farnsworth's. The Lord helped Brother Andrews that night, as he dwelt upon the subject of suffering for Christ's sake. The case of Moses was mentioned, who 'refused to be called the son of Pharaoh's daughter; choosing rather to suffer affliction with the people of God, than to enjoy the pleasures of sin for a season; esteeming the reproach of Christ greater riches than the treasures in Egypt: for he had respect unto the recompense of the reward.' Heb. 11:24-26.

"Meeting commenced Monday at 10 A. M. Again the condition of the church was dwelt upon. With the most earnest entreaties we pleaded with them to be converted to God, and face right about. The Lord aided us in the work. Our morning meeting closed at three or four in the afternoon. All these hours we had been engaged, first one of us, then another, earnestly laboring for the unconverted youth.

"Tuesday evening I spoke an hour with great freedom. Brother Andrews talked in an earnest, touching manner. The Spirit of the Lord was in the meeting. Angels of God seemed drawing very near, driving back the evil angels. Minister and people wept like children. We felt that we had gained ground, and that the powers of darkness had given back. Our meeting closed well.

"We appointed still another meeting for the next day, commencing at 10 A. M. I spoke about an hour upon the humiliation and glorification of Christ. Then we commenced our labors for the youth. Parents had come to the meeting, bringing their children with them to receive the blessing. We pleaded earnestly with the children, until thirteen arose and expressed a desire to be Christians. One young man, about twenty years old, walked forty miles to see us and hear the truth. He had never professed religion, but took his stand on the Lord's side before he left.

"This was one of the very best of meetings. We parted with all with many tears, feeling the blessing of Heaven resting upon us."

IN VERMONT AND NEW YORK

The meeting at West Enosburgh, Vt., was one of deep interest. It seemed good to meet again with, and speak to, our old, tried friends in this State. A great and good work was done in a short time. These friends were generally poor, and toiling for the comforts of life where one dollar is earned with more labor than two in the West, yet they were liberal with us. In no State have the brethren been truer to the cause than in old Vermont.

Our next meeting was at Adams Center, N. Y. It was a large gathering. There were several persons in and around this place whose cases had been shown me, for whom I felt the deepest interest. They were men of moral worth. Some were in positions of life which made the cross of the present truth heavy to bear, or at least they thought so. Others, who had reached the middle age of life, had been brought up from childhood to keep the Sabbath, but had not borne the cross of Christ. These were in a position where it seemed hard to move them. They needed to be shaken from relying on their good works, and to be brought to feel their lost condition without Christ. We could not give up these souls, and labored with our might to help them. They were at last moved, and I have since been made glad to hear from some of them, and good news respecting all of them.

God is converting strong men of wealth, and bringing them into the ranks. If they would prosper in the Christian life, grow in grace, and at last reap a rich reward, they will have to use of their abundance to advance the cause of truth.

RETURN TO MICHIGAN

After leaving Adams Center, we stayed for a few days at Rochester, and from that place came to Battle Creek, where we remained over Sabbath and first day. Thence we returned to our home in Greenville, where we spent the next Sabbath and first day with the brethren who assembled from different places.

Meetinghouse at Washington, N. H.

XXIX

RECLAIMING THE LOST

After we had reached our home, we felt most sensibly the wearing labors of our Eastern tour. Many were urging me by letter to write what I had related to them of what the Lord had shown me concerning them. And there were many others to whom I had not spoken, whose cases were important and urgent. In my weary condition the task of so much writing seemed more than I could endure, and I called in question my duty to write so much, to so many persons, some of them very unworthy. It seemed to me that there was certainly a mistake in this matter somewhere.

AN ENCOURAGING DREAM

One night I dreamed that a person brought to me a web of white cloth, and bade me cut it into garments for persons of all sizes and all descriptions of character and circumstances in life. I was told to cut them out and hang them up all ready to be made when called for. I had the impression that many for whom I was required to cut garments were unworthy. I inquired if that was the last piece of cloth I should have to cut, and was told that it was not; that as soon as I had finished this one, there were others for me to take hold of.

I felt discouraged at the amount of work before me, and stated that I had been engaged in cutting garments for others for more than twenty years, and my labors had not been appreciated, neither did I see that my work had accomplished much good. I spoke to the person who brought the cloth to me, of one woman in particular, for whom he had told me to cut a garment. I stated that she would not prize the garment, and that it would be a loss of time and material to present it to her. She was very poor, of inferior intellect, and untidy in her habits, and would soon soil it.

The person replied: "Cut out the garments; that is your duty. The loss is not yours, but mine. God sees not as man sees. He lays out the work that He would have done, and you do not know which will prosper, this or that. It will be found that many such poor souls will go into the kingdom, while others, who are favored with all the blessings of life, having good intellects and pleasant surroundings, giving them all the advantages of improvement, will be left out. It will be seen that these poor souls have lived up to the feeble light which they had, and have improved by the limited means within their reach, and lived much more acceptably than some others who have enjoyed full light, and ample means for improvement."

I then held up my hands, calloused as they were with long use of the shears, and stated that I could but shrink at the thought of pursuing this kind of labor.

The person again repeated: "Cut out the garments. Your release has not yet come."

With feelings of great weariness I arose to engage in the work. Before me lay new, polished shears, which I commenced using. At once my feelings of weariness and discouragement left me, the shears seemed to cut with hardly an effort on my part, and I cut out garment after garment with comparative ease.

VISITING CHURCHES IN MICHIGAN

With the encouragement which this dream gave me, I at once decided to accompany my husband and

Brother Andrews to Gratiot, Saginaw, and Tuscola counties, and trust in the Lord to give me strength to labor. So, on the 7th of February, we left home, and rode fifty-five miles to our appointment at Alma. Here I labored as usual, with a good degree of freedom and strength. The friends in Gratiot County seemed interested to hear.

At Tittabawassee we found a large house of worship recently built by our people, well filled with Sabbath keepers. The brethren seemed ready for our testimony, and we enjoyed freedom. The next day fifteen were baptized.

At Vassar we held our meetings Sabbath and first day at the union schoolhouse. This was a free place in which to speak, and we saw good fruit of our labors. First day afternoon about thirty backsliders, and children who had made no profession, came forward for prayers.

CARING FOR THE SICK

We returned home from this tour just before a great fall of rain which carried off the snow. This storm prevented the next Sabbath meeting, and I immediately commenced to prepare matter for Testimony No. 14. We also had the privilege of caring for our dear Brother Seneca King, whom we brought to our home with a terrible injury upon the head and face. We took him to our house to die, for we could not think it possible for one with the skull so terribly broken in to recover. But with the blessing of God upon a very gentle use of water, a very spare diet till the danger of fever was past, and well ventilated rooms day and night, in three weeks he was able to return to his home and attend to his farming interests. He did not take one grain of medicine from first to last. Although he was considerably reduced by loss of blood from his wounds and by spare diet, yet when he could take a more liberal amount of food he came up rapidly.

REVIVAL MEETINGS AT GREENVILLE

About this time we commenced labor for our brethren and friends near Greenville. As is the case in many places, our brethren needed help. There were some who kept the Sabbath, yet did not belong to the church, and also some who had given up the Sabbath. We felt disposed to help these poor souls, but the past course and present position of leading members of the church in relation to these persons, made it almost impossible for us to approach them.

In laboring with the erring, some of our brethren had been too rigid, too cutting in remarks. And when some were disposed to reject their counsel, and separate from them, they would say, "Well, if they want to go off, let them go." While such a lack of the compassion and long-suffering and tenderness of Jesus was manifested by His professed followers, these poor, erring, inexperienced souls, buffeted by Satan, were certain to make shipwreck of faith. However great may be the wrongs and sins of the erring, our brethren must learn to manifest not only the tenderness of the Great Shepherd, but also His undying care and love for the poor, straying sheep. Our ministers toil and lecture week after week, and rejoice that a few souls embrace the truth; and yet brethren of a prompt, decided turn of mind may, in five minutes, destroy their work by indulging the feelings which prompt words like these: "Well, if they want to leave us, let them go."

We found that we could do nothing for the scattered sheep near us until we had first corrected the wrongs in many of the members of the church. They had let these poor souls wander. They felt no burden for them. I wrote out pointed testimonies not only for those who had erred greatly and were out of the church, but for those members in the church who had erred greatly in not going in search of the lost sheep.

THE LOST SHEEP

The Lord is giving the erring, the weak and trembling, and even those who have apostatized from the truth, a special call to come fully into the fold. But many have not learned that they have a special duty to go and search for these lost sheep.

The Pharisees murmured because Jesus received publicans and common sinners, and ate with them. In their self-righteousness they despised these poor sinners who gladly heard the words of Jesus. To rebuke this spirit in the scribes and Pharisees, and leave an impressive lesson for all, the Lord gave the parable of the lost sheep. Notice in particular the following points:

The ninety and nine sheep are left, and diligent search is made for the one that is lost. The entire effort is made for the unfortunate sheep. So should the effort of the church be directed in behalf of those members who are straying from the fold of Christ. And have they wandered far away? do not wait till they return before you try to help them, but go in search of them.

When the lost sheep was found, it was borne home with joy, and much rejoicing followed. This illustrates the blessed, joyful work of laboring for the erring. The church that engages successfully in this work, is a happy church. That man or that woman whose soul is drawn out in compassion and love for the erring, and who labors to bring them to the fold of the Great Shepherd, is engaged in a blessed work. And, oh, what a soul-enrapturing thought, that when one sinner is thus reclaimed, there is more joy in heaven than over ninety and nine just persons! Selfish, exclusive, exacting souls who seem to fear to help those in error, as though they would become polluted by so doing, do not taste of the sweets of this missionary work; they do not feel that blessedness which fills all heaven with rejoicing upon the rescue of one who has gone astray.

That church or those persons who shut themselves away from bearing burdens for others, who shut themselves up to themselves, will soon suffer spiritual feebleness. It is labor that keeps the strong man strong. And spiritual labor, toil, and burden bearing, is what will give strength to the church of Christ.

EN ROUTE TO BATTLE CREEK

Sabbath and first day, April 18 and 19, we enjoyed a good season with our people at Greenville. Brethren M. E. Cornell and M. G. Kellogg were with us. My husband baptized eight. The 25th and 26th we were with the church in Wright. This dear people were ever ready to welcome us. Here my husband baptized eight.

May 2 we met a large congregation at the house of worship at Monterey. My husband spoke with clearness and force upon the parable of the lost sheep. The word was greatly blessed to the people. Some who had strayed were out of the church, and there was no spirit of labor to help them. In fact, the stiff, stern, unfeeling position of some in the church was calculated to prevent their return, should they be disposed thus to do. The subject touched the hearts of all, and all manifested a desire to get right. On first day we spoke three times in Allegan to good congregations.

Our appointment was out to meet with the church at Battle Creek the 9th, but we felt that our work in Monterey was but just commenced, and we therefore decided to return to Monterey, and labor with that church another week. The good work moved on, exceeding our expectations. The house was filled, and we never before witnessed such a work in Monterey in so short a time. First day fifty came forward for prayers. Brethren felt deeply for the lost sheep, and confessed their coldness and indifference, and took a good stand. Fourteen were baptized. The work moved on with solemnity, confessions, and much weeping, carrying all before it. Thus closed the arduous labors of the conference year.

THE GENERAL CONFERENCE OF MAY, 1868

The General Conference was a season of deepest interest. The labors of my husband were very great during its numerous sessions. There was manifested to us at the Conference, sympathy, tender care, and benevolence.

XXX

TRAVELING THE NARROW WAY

While at Battle Creek in August, 1868, I dreamed of being with a large body of people. A portion of this assembly started out prepared to journey. We had heavily loaded wagons. As we journeyed, the road seemed to ascend. On one side of this road was a deep precipice; on the other was a high, smooth, white wall, like the hard finish upon plastered rooms.

As we journeyed on, the road grew narrower and steeper. In some places it seemed so very narrow that we concluded that we could no longer travel with the loaded wagons. We then loosed them from the horses, took a portion of the luggage from the wagons and placed it upon the horses, and journeyed on horseback.

As we progressed, the path still continued to grow narrow. We were obliged to press close to the wall, to save ourselves from falling off the narrow road down the steep precipice. As we did this, the luggage on the horses pressed against the wall, and caused us to sway toward the precipice. We feared that we should fall, and be dashed in pieces on the rocks. We then cut the luggage from the horses, and it fell over the precipice. We continued on horseback, greatly fearing, as we came to the narrower places in the road, that we should lose our balance, and fall. At such times, a hand seemed to take the bridle, and guide us over the perilous way.

As the path grew more narrow, we decided that we could no longer go with safety on horseback, and we left the horses and went on foot, in single file, one following in the footsteps of another. At this point small cords were let down from the top of the pure white wall; these we eagerly grasped, to aid us in keeping our balance upon the path. As we traveled, the cord moved along with us. The path finally became so narrow that we concluded that we could travel more safely without our shoes; so we slipped them from our feet, and went on some distance without them. Soon it was decided that we could travel more safely without our stockings; these were removed, and we journeyed on with bare feet.

We then thought of those who had not accustomed themselves to privations and hardships. Where were such now? They were not in the company. At every change, some were left behind, and those only remained who had accustomed themselves to endure hardships. The privations of the way only made these more eager to press on to the end.

Our danger of falling from the pathway increased. We pressed close to the white wall, yet could not place our feet fully upon the path, for it was too narrow. We then suspended nearly our whole weight upon the cords, exclaiming: "We have hold from above! We have hold from above!" The same words were uttered by all the company in the narrow pathway. As we heard the sounds of mirth and revelry that seemed to come from the abyss below, we shuddered. We heard the profane oath, the vulgar jest, and low, vile songs. We heard the war song and the dance song. We heard instrumental music, and loud laughter, mingled with cursing and cries of anguish and bitter wailing, and were more anxious than ever to keep upon the narrow, difficult pathway. Much of the time we were compelled to suspend our whole weight upon the cords. which increased in size as we progressed.

I noticed that the beautiful white wall was stained with blood. It caused a feeling of regret to see the wall thus stained. This feeling, however, lasted but for a moment, as I soon thought that it was all as it should be. Those who are following after will know that others have passed the narrow, difficult way before them, and will conclude that if others were able to pursue their onward course, they can do the same. And as the blood shall be pressed from their aching feet, they will not faint with discouragement; but, seeing the blood upon the wall, they will know that others have endured the same pain.

At length we came to a large chasm, at which our path ended. There was nothing now to guide the feet, nothing upon which to rest them. Our whole reliance must be upon the cords, which had increased in size, until they were as large as our bodies. Here we were for a time thrown into perplexity and distress. We inquired in fearful whispers, "To what is the cord attached?" My husband was just before me. Large drops of sweat were falling from his brow, the veins in his neck and temples were increased to double their usual size, and suppressed, agonizing groans came from his lips. The sweat was dropping from my face, and I felt such anguish as I had never felt before. A fearful struggle was before us. Should we fail here, all the difficulties of our journey had been experienced for naught.

Before us, on the other side of the chasm, was a beautiful field of green grass, about six inches high. I could not see the sun, but bright, soft beams of light, resembling fine gold and silver, were resting upon this field. Nothing I had seen upon earth could compare in beauty and glory with this field. But could we succeed in reaching it? was the anxious inquiry. Should the cord break, we must perish.

Again, in whispered anguish, the words were breathed, "What holds the cord?" For a moment we hesitated to venture. Then we exclaimed: "Our only hope is to trust wholly to the cord. It has been our dependence all the difficult way. It will not fail us now." Still we were hesitating and distressed. The words were then spoken: "God holds the cord. We need not fear." These words were repeated by those behind us, accompanied with: "He will not fail us now. He has brought us thus far in safety."

My husband then swung himself over the fearful abyss into the beautiful field beyond. I immediately followed. And oh, what a sense of relief and gratitude to God we felt! I heard voices raised in triumphant praise to God. I was happy, perfectly happy.

XXXI

BURDEN BEARERS

Oct. 25, 1869, while at Adams Center, N. Y., I was shown that some ministers among us fail to bear all the responsibility that God would have them. This lack throws extra labor upon those who are burden bearers. Some ministers fail to move out and venture something in the cause and work of God. Important decisions are to be made, but as mortal man cannot see the end from the beginning, some shrink from venturing and advancing as the providence of God leads. Some one must advance; some one must venture in the fear of God, trusting the result with Him. Those ministers who shun this part of the labor are losing much. They are failing to obtain that experience which God designed they should have to make them strong, efficient men that can be relied upon in any emergency.

During my husband's affliction, the Lord tested and proved His people, to reveal what was in their hearts; and in so doing He showed to them what was undiscovered in themselves that was not according to the Spirit of God. The Lord proved to His people that the wisdom of man is foolishness, and that unless they possess firm trust and reliance on God, their plans and calculations will prove a failure. We are to learn from all these things. If errors are committed, they should teach and instruct, but not lead to the shunning of burdens and responsibilities. Where much is at stake, and where matters of vital consequence are to be considered, and important questions settled, God's servants should take individual responsibility. They cannot lay off the burden, and yet do the will of God.

Some ministers are deficient in the qualifications necessary to build up the churches, and they are not willing to wear in the cause of God. They should have a disposition to give themselves wholly to the work, with their interest undivided, their zeal unabated, their patience and perseverance untiring. With these qualifications in lively exercise, the churches would be kept in order.

God had cautioned and warned my husband in regard to the preservation of his strength. I was shown that he had been raised up by the Lord, and that he was living as a miracle of mercy — not for the purpose of again gathering upon him the burdens under which he once fell, but that the people of God might be benefited by his experience in advancing the general interests of the cause, and in connection with the work the Lord has given me, and the burden He has laid upon me to bear.

During the years that followed the recovery of my husband, the Lord opened before us a vast field of labor. Though I took the stand as a speaker timidly at first, yet as the providence of God opened the way before me, I had confidence to stand before large audiences. Together we attended our camp meetings and other large gatherings, from Maine to Dakota, from Michigan to Texas and California.

The work begun in feebleness and obscurity has continued to increase and strengthen. Publishing houses and missions in many lands attest its growth. In place of the edition of our first paper carried to the post office in a carpetbag, many hundreds of thousands of copies of our various periodicals are now sent out monthly from the offices of publication. The hand of God has been with His work to prosper and build it up.

The later history of my life would involve the history of many of the enterprises which have arisen among us, and with which my life work has been closely intermingled. For the upbuilding of these institutions, my husband and myself labored with pen and voice. To notice, even briefly, the experiences of these active and busy years, would far exceed the limits of this sketch. Satan's efforts to hinder the work and to destroy the workmen have not ceased; but God has had a care for His servants and for His work.

In reviewing our past history, having traveled over every step of advance to our present standing, I can say, Praise God! As I see what the Lord has wrought, I am filled with astonishment, and with confidence in Christ as leader. We have nothing to fear for the future, except as we shall forget the way the Lord has led us, and His teaching in our past history.

We are debtors to God to use every advantage He has entrusted to us to beautify the truth by holiness of character, and to send the messages of warning, and of comfort, of hope and love, to those who are in the darkness of error and sin.

XXXII

A SOLEMN DREAM

On the night of April 30, 1871, I retired to rest much depressed in spirits. For three months I had been in a state of great discouragement. I had frequently prayed in anguish of spirit for relief. I had implored help and strength from God, that I might rise above the heavy discouragements that were paralyzing my faith and hope, and unfitting me for usefulness.

That night I had a dream which made a very happy impression upon my mind. I dreamed that I was attending an important meeting, at which a large company were assembled. Many were bowed before God in earnest prayer, and they seemed to be burdened. They were importuning the Lord for special light. A few seemed to be in agony of spirit; their feelings were intense; with tears they were crying aloud for help and light. Our most prominent brethren were engaged in this most impressive scene. Brother A. was prostrated upon the floor, apparently in deep distress. His wife was sitting among a company of indifferent scorners. She looked as though she desired all to understand that she scorned those who were thus humiliating themselves.

I dreamed that the Spirit of the Lord came upon me, and I arose amid cries and prayers, and said: "The Spirit of the Lord God is upon me. I feel urged to say to you that you must commence to work individually for yourselves. You are looking to God and desiring Him to do the work for you which He has left for you to do. If you will do the work for yourselves which you know that you ought to do, then God will help you when you need help. You have left undone the very things which God has left for you to do. You have been calling upon God to do your work. Had you followed the light which He has given you, then He would cause more light to shine upon you; but while you neglect the counsels, warnings, and reproofs that have been given, how can you expect God to give you more light and blessings to neglect and despise? God is not as man; He will not be trifled with."

I took the precious Bible, and surrounded it with the several "Testimonies for the Church," given for the people of God. "Here," said I, "the cases of nearly all are met. The sins they are to shun are pointed out. The counsel that they desire can be found here, given for other cases situated similarly to themselves. God has been pleased to give you line upon line and precept upon precept. But there are not many of you that really know what is contained in the Testimonies. You are not familiar with the Scriptures. If you had made God's word your study, with a desire to reach the Bible standard and attain to Christian perfection, you would not have needed the Testimonies. It is because you have neglected to acquaint yourselves with God's inspired book that He has sought to reach you by simple, direct testimonies, calling your attention to the words of inspiration which you had neglected to obey, and urging you to fashion your lives in accordance with its pure and elevated teachings.

"The Lord deigns to warn you, to reprove, to counsel, through the testimonies given, and to impress your minds with the importance of the truth of His word. The written Testimonies are not to give new light, but to impress vividly upon the heart the truths of inspiration already revealed. Man's duty to God and to his fellow man has been distinctly specified in God's word; yet but few of you are obedient to the light given. Additional truth is not brought out; but God has through the Testimonies simplified the great truths already given, and in His own chosen way brought them before the people, to awaken and impress the mind with them, that all may be left without excuse.

"Pride, self-love, selfishness, hatred, envy, and jealousy have beclouded the perceptive powers, and the truth, which would make you wise unto salvation, has lost its power to charm and control the mind. The very essential principles of godliness are not understood, because there is not a hungering and thirsting for Bible knowledge, purity of heart, and holiness of life. The Testimonies are not to belittle the word of God, but to exalt it and attract minds to it, that the beautiful simplicity of truth may impress all."

I said further: "As the word of God is walled in with these books and pamphlets, so has God walled you in with reproofs, counsel, warnings, and encouragements. Here you are crying before God, in the anguish of your souls, for more light. I am authorized from God to tell you that not another ray of light through the Testimonies will shine upon your pathway, until you make a practical use of the light already given. The Lord has walled you about with light; but you have not appreciated the light; you have trampled upon it. While some have despised the light, others have neglected it, or followed it but indifferently. A few have set their hearts to obey the light which God has been pleased to give them.

"Some that have received special warnings through testimony, have forgotten in a few weeks the reproof given. The testimonies to some have been several times repeated; but they have not thought them of sufficient importance to be carefully heeded. They have been to them like idle tales. Had they regarded the light given, they would have avoided losses and trials which they think are hard and severe. They have only themselves to censure. They have placed upon their own necks a yoke which they find grievous to be borne. It is not the yoke which Christ has bound upon them. God's care and love were exercised in their behalf; but their selfish, evil, unbelieving souls could not discern His goodness and mercy. They rush on in their own wisdom, until, overwhelmed with trials and confused with perplexity, they are ensnared by Satan. When you gather up the rays of light which God has given in the past, then will He give an increase of light."

I referred them to ancient Israel. God gave them His law; but they would not obey it. He then gave them ceremonies and ordinances, that in the performance of these God might be kept in remembrance. They were so prone to forget Him and His claims upon them, that it was necessary to keep their minds stirred up to realize their obligations to obey and honor their Creator. Had they been obedient, and loved to keep God's commandments, the multitude of ceremonies and ordinances would not have been required.

If the people who now profess to be God's peculiar treasure would obey His requirements, as specified in His word, special testimonies would not be given to awaken them to their duty, and impress upon them their sinfulness and their fearful danger in neglecting to obey the word of God. Consciences have been blunted, because light has been set aside, neglected, and despised. And God will remove these Testimonies from the people, and will deprive them of strength, and humble them.

I dreamed that, as I was speaking, the power of God fell upon me in a most remarkable manner, and I was deprived of all strength, yet I had no vision. I thought that my husband stood up before the people, and exclaimed: "This is the wonderful power of God. He has made the Testimonies a powerful means of reaching souls, and He will work yet more mightily through them than He has hitherto done. Who will be on the Lord's side?"

I dreamed that quite a number instantly sprang to their feet, and responded to the call. Others sat sullen, some manifested scorn and derision, and a few seemed wholly unmoved. One stood by my side, and said:

"God has raised you up, and has given you words to speak to the people and to reach hearts, as He has given to no other one. He has shaped your testimonies to meet cases that are in need of help. You must be unmoved by scorn, derision, reproach, and censure. In order to be God's special instrument, you should lean to no one, but hang upon Him alone, and, like the clinging vine, let your tendrils entwine about Him. He will make you a means through which to communicate His light to the people. You must daily gather strength from God, in order to be fortified, that your surroundings may not dim or eclipse the light that He has permitted to shine upon His people through you. It is Satan's special object to prevent this light from coming to the people of God, who so greatly need it amid the perils of these last days.

"Your success is in your simplicity. As soon as you depart from this, and fashion your testimony to meet the minds of any, your power is gone. Almost everything in this age is glossed and unreal. The world abounds in testimonies given to please and charm for the moment, and to exalt self. Your testimony is of a different character. It is to come down to the minutiæ of life, keeping the feeble faith from dying, and pressing home upon believers the necessity of shining as lights in the world.

"God has given you your testimony to set before the backslider and the sinner his true condition, and the immense loss he is sustaining by continuing a life of sin. God has impressed this upon you by opening it before your vision as He has to no other one now living; and according to the light He has given you, will He hold you responsible. 'Not by might, nor by power, but by My Spirit, saith the Lord of hosts.' 'Lift up thy voice like a trumpet, and show My people their transgression, and the house of Jacob their sins.' " Zech. 4:6; Isa. 58:1.

This dream had a powerful influence upon me. When I awoke, my depression was gone, my spirits were cheerful, and I realized great peace. Infirmities that had unfitted me for labor were removed, and I realized a strength and vigor to which I had for months been a stranger. It seemed to me that angels of God had been commissioned to bring me relief. Unspeakable gratitude filled my heart for this great change from despondency to light and happiness. I knew that help had come from God. This manifestation appeared to me like a miracle of God's mercy, and I will not be ungrateful for His loving-kindness.

XXXIII

MISSIONARY WORK[1]

Dec. 10, 1871, I was shown that God would accomplish a great work through the truth, if devoted, self-sacrificing men would give themselves unreservedly to the work of presenting it to those in darkness. Those who have a knowledge of the precious truth, and who are consecrated to God, should avail themselves of every opportunity where there is an opening to press in the truth. Angels of God are moving on the hearts and consciences of the people of other nations, and honest souls are troubled as they witness the signs of the times in the unsettled state of the nations. The inquiry arises in their hearts, What will be the end of all these things? While God and angels are at work to impress hearts, the servants of Christ seem to be asleep. But few are working in unison with the heavenly messengers.

If ministers and people were sufficiently aroused, they would not rest thus indifferently, while God has honored them by making them the depositaries of His law, by printing it in their minds and writing it upon their hearts. These truths of vital importance

---

[1] NOTE.— At times during the early days of the message, Seventh-day Adventists caught glimpses of a broadening work that would eventually embrace many nationalities. Not until the early 70's, however, did the leaders in the advent movement begin to comprehend that theirs was a mission to the whole world. Even as late as in 1872, the scripture, "This gospel of the kingdom shall be preached in all the world for a witness unto all nations; and then shall the end come," was regarded simply as a "prominent sign of the last day," meeting fulfillment in the extension of Protestant missions. Its complete fulfillment was in no way associated with the spread of the advent movement throughout the world. (See *Review and Herald*, April 16 and July 16, 1872.) But in 1873 a marked change of sentiment began to appear in the utterances of leaders among Seventh-day Adventists regarding their duty to warn the world. (See editorial *Review and Herald*, August 26, 1873; and many other articles of similar import in the issues that followed.) By the close of the year 1874, this transformation of sentiment seems to have been effected almost completely.

are to test the world; and yet in our own country there are cities, villages, and towns that have never heard the warning message. Young men who feel stirred by the appeals that have been made for help in this great work of advancing the cause of God, make some advance moves, but do not get the burden of the work upon them sufficiently to accomplish what they might.

If young men who commence to labor in this cause would have the missionary spirit, they would give evidence that God has indeed called them to the work. But when they do not go out into new places, but are content to go from church to church, they give evidence that the burden of the work is not upon them. The ideas of our young preachers are not broad enough. Their zeal is too feeble. Were the young men awake and devoted to the Lord, they would be diligent every moment of their time, and would seek to qualify themselves to become laborers in the missionary field.

Young men should be qualifying themselves by becoming familiar with other languages, that God may use them as mediums to communicate His saving truth to those of other nations. These young men may obtain a knowledge of other languages even while engaged in laboring for sinners. If they are economical of their time, they can be improving their minds, and qualifying themselves for more extended usefulness. If young women who have borne but little responsibility would devote themselves to God, they could qualify themselves for usefulness by studying and becoming familiar with other languages. They could devote themselves to the work of translating.

Our publications should be printed in other languages, that foreign nations may be reached.[2] Much can be done through the medium of the press, but still more can be accomplished if the influence of the labors of the living preachers goes with our publications. Missionaries are needed to go to other nations to preach the truth in a guarded, careful manner. The cause of present truth can be greatly extended by personal effort.

When the churches see young men possessing zeal to qualify themselves to extend their labors to cities, villages, and towns that have never been aroused to the truth, and missionaries volunteering to go to other nations to carry the truth to them, the churches will be encouraged and strengthened far more than to themselves receive the labors of inexperienced young men. As they see their ministers' hearts all aglow with love and zeal for the truth and with a desire to save souls, the churches will arouse themselves. These generally have the gifts and power within themselves to bless and strengthen themselves, and to gather the sheep and lambs into the fold. They need to be thrown upon their own resources, that all the gifts that are lying dormant may thus be called into active service.

The Lord has moved upon men of other tongues, and has brought them under the influence of the truth, that they might be qualified to labor in His cause. He has brought them within reach of the Office of publication, that its managers might avail themselves of their services, if they were awake to the wants of the cause. Publications are needed in other languages, to raise an interest and the spirit of inquiry among other nations.

As the preaching of Noah warned, tested, and

---

[2] When these words were penned, in 1871, only a beginning had been made in the preparation and publication of denominational literature in the various languages of Europe and of other lands.

proved the inhabitants of the world before the flood of waters destroyed them from off the face of the earth, so the truth of God for these last days is doing a similar work of warning, testing, and proving the world. The publications which go forth from the Office bear the signet of the Eternal. They are being scattered all through the land, and are deciding the destiny of souls. Men are now greatly needed who can translate and prepare our publications in other languages, so that the message of warning may go to all nations and test them by the light of the truth, that men and women, as they see the light, may turn from transgression to obedience of the law of God.

Every opportunity should be improved to extend the truth to other nations. This will be attended with considerable expense, but expense should in no case hinder the performance of this work. Means are of value only as they are used to advance the interest of the kingdom of God. The Lord has lent men means for this very purpose, to use in sending the truth to their fellow men.

Now is the time to use means for God. Now is the time to be rich in good works, laying up in store for ourselves a good foundation against the time to come, that we may lay hold on eternal life. One soul saved in the kingdom of God is of more value than all earthly riches. We are answerable to God for the souls of those with whom we are brought in contact, and the closer our connections with our fellow men, the greater our responsibility. We are one great brotherhood, and the welfare of our fellow men should be our great interest. We have not one moment to lose. If we have been careless in this matter, it is high time we were now in earnest to redeem the time, lest the blood of souls be found on our garments. As children of God, none of us are excused from taking a part in the great work of Christ in the salvation of our fellow men.

It will be a difficult work to overcome prejudice, and to convince the unbelieving that our efforts to help them are disinterested. But this should not hinder our labor. There is no precept in the word of God that tells us to do good to those only who appreciate and respond to our efforts, and to benefit those only who will thank us for it. God has sent us to work in His vineyard. It is our business to do all we can. "In the morning sow thy seed, and in the evening withhold not thine hand: for thou knowest not whether shall prosper, either this or that." Eccl. 11:6.

We have too little faith. We limit the Holy One of Israel. We should be grateful that God condescends to use any of us as His instruments. For every earnest prayer put up in faith for anything, answers will be returned. They may not come just as we have expected; but they will come—not perhaps as we have devised, but at the very time when we most need them. But, oh, how sinful is our unbelief! "If ye abide in Me, and My words abide in you, ye shall ask what ye will, and it shall be done unto you." John 15:7.

XXXIV

BROADER PLANS

While in California in the year 1874, I was given an impressive dream, in which was represented the instrumentality of the press in the work of giving the third angel's message to the world

I dreamed that several of the brethren in California were in council, considering the best plan for labor during the coming season. Some thought it wise to shun the large cities, and work in smaller places. My husband was earnestly urging that broader plans be laid, and more extended efforts made, which would better compare with the character of our message.

Then a young man whom I had frequently seen in my dreams, came into the council. He listened with deep interest to the words that were spoken, and then, speaking with deliberation and authoritative confidence, said:

"The cities and villages constitute a part of the Lord's vineyard. They must hear the messages of warning. The enemy of truth is making desperate efforts to turn the people from the truth of God to falsehood. . . . You are to sow beside all waters.

"It may be that you will not at once see the result of your labor, but this should not discourage you. Take Christ as your example. He had many hearers, but few followers. Noah preached for one hundred and twenty years to the people before the flood; yet out of the multitudes on the earth at that time only eight were saved."

The messenger continued: "You are entertaining too limited ideas of the work for this time. You are trying to plan the work so that you can embrace it in your arms. You must take broader views. Your light must not be put under a bushel or under a bed, but on a candlestick, that it may give light to all that are in the house. Your house is the world. . . .

"The verity and truth of the binding claims of the fourth commandment must be presented in clear lines before the people. 'Ye are My witnesses.' The message will go in power to all parts of the world, to Oregon, to Europe, to Australia, to the islands of the sea, to all nations, tongues, and peoples. Preserve the dignity of the truth. It will grow to large proportions. Many countries are waiting for the advanced light the Lord has for them; and your faith is limited, it is very small. Your conception of the work needs to be greatly enlarged. Oakland, San Francisco, Sacramento, Woodland, and the large cities in the United States must hear the message of truth. Go forward. God will work with great power if you will walk in all humility of mind before Him. It is not faith to talk of impossibilities. Nothing is impossible with God. The light of the binding claims of the law of God is to test and prove the world." . . .

In my last vision I was shown that we should have a part to act in California in extending and confirming the work already commenced. I was shown that missionary labor must be put forth in California, Australia, Oregon, and other territories far more extensively than our people have imagined, or ever contemplated and planned. I was shown that we do not at the present time move as fast as the opening providence of God leads the way. I was shown that the present truth might be a power in California if the believers in the message would give no place to the enemy in unbelief and selfishness, but would concentrate their efforts to one object,— the upbuilding of the cause of present truth.

I saw that there would be a paper published upon the Pacific coast. There would be a health institute established there, and a publishing house created.

Time is short; and all who believe this message, should feel a solemn obligation resting upon them to be disinterested workers, exerting their influence on the right side, and never by word or action be found arrayed against those who are seeking to advance the interests of God's cause. The ideas of our brethren are altogether too narrow. They expect but little. Their faith is too small.

A paper published on the Pacific coast would give strength and influence to the message. The light God has given us isn't worth much to the world unless it can be seen by being presented before them. I declare to you our vision must be extended. We see things nigh, but not afar off.

XXXV

INTO ALL THE WORLD

I deeply feel the necessity of our making more thorough and earnest efforts to bring the truth before the world. In the last vision given me, I was shown that we were not doing one twentieth part of the work we should for the salvation of souls. We labor for them indifferently, as though it was not a question of very great importance whether they received or rejected the truth. General efforts are made, but we fail to work to the point by personal effort. We do not approach men and women in a manner that impresses them that we have a personal interest for them, and that we feel deeply in earnest for their salvation, and do not mean to give them up.

We hold too much at a distance those who do not believe the truth. We call them and wait for them to come to us to inquire for the truth. Many will not be inclined to do this, for they are in darkness and error, and cannot discern the truth and its vital importance. Satan holds them with his firm power, and if we would help them, we must show a personal interest and love for their souls, and take hold of them in earnest. We must work in prayer and love, with faith and unwearied patience, hoping all things and believing all things, having the wisdom of the serpent and the meekness of the dove, in order to win souls to Christ.

SPECIAL PREPARATION

We are not, as a people, sufficiently aroused to the short time in which we have to work, and we do not understand the magnitude of the work for the time.

The night soon cometh, in which no man can work. God calls for men and women to qualify themselves, by consecration to His will and earnest study of the Scriptures, to do His special work for these last days. He calls for men now who can work. As they engage in the work in sincerity and humility to do all they can, they will be obtaining a more thorough experience. They will have a better knowledge of the truth and better know how to reach souls and help them just where they need to be helped. Workmen are needed now, just now, to labor for God. The fields are already white for the harvest, and yet laborers are few.

OPENING PROVIDENCES

I have been shown that, as a people, we have been asleep as to our duty in regard to getting the light before those of other nations. Is it because God has excused us, as a people, from having any burden or special work to do for those of other tongues, that we have no missionaries to-day in foreign countries? Why is this negligence and delay? There are those of superior minds in many other nations whom God is impressing with the lack of spirituality and genuine godliness in the Christian denominations of the land. They cannot harmonize the life and character of professed Christians generally with the Bible standard. Many are praying for light and knowledge. They are not satisfied. God will answer their prayers through us, as a people, if we are not at such a distance from Him that we cannot hear His voice, and so selfish that we do not wish to be disturbed in our ease and agreeable associations.

We are not keeping pace with the opening providence of God. Jesus and angels are at work. This cause is onward, while we are standing still and being left in the rear. If we would follow the opening providence of God, we should be quick to discern every opening, and make the most of every advantage within our reach, to let the light extend and spread to other nations. God, in His providence, has sent men to our very doors, and thrust them, as it were, into our arms, that they might learn the truth more perfectly, and be qualified to do a work we could not do in getting the light before men of other tongues. We have too often failed to discern God's hand, and we have not received the very ones God had provided for us to work in union with, and act a part in sending the light to other nations.

SOWING BESIDE ALL WATERS

There has been a slothful neglect and a criminal unbelief among us as a people, which has kept us back from doing the work God has left us to do in letting our light shine forth to those of other nations. There is a fearfulness to venture out and to run risks in this great work, fearing that the expenditure of means would not bring returns. What if means are used and yet we cannot see that souls have been saved by it? What if there is a dead loss of a portion of our means? Better work and keep at work than to do nothing. You know not which shall prosper, this or that.

God will have men who will venture anything and everything to save souls. Those who will not move until they can see every step of the way clearly before them, will not be of advantage at this time to forward the truth of God. There must be workers now who will push ahead in the dark as well as in the light, and who will hold up bravely under discouragements and disappointed hopes, and yet work on with faith, with tears and patient hope, sowing beside all waters, trusting the Lord to bring the increase. God calls for men of nerve, of hope, faith, and endurance, to work to the point.

PUBLICATIONS IN MANY LANGUAGES

I have been shown that our publications should be printed in different languages and sent to every civilized country, at any cost. What is the value of money at this time, in comparison with the value of souls? Every dollar of our means should be considered as the Lord's, not ours; and as a precious trust from God to us; not to be wasted for needless indulgences, but carefully used in the cause of God, in the work of saving men and women from ruin.

I have been shown that the press is powerful for good or evil. This agency can reach and influence the public mind as no other means can. The press, controlled by men who are sanctified to God, can be a power indeed for good in bringing men to the knowledge of the truth. The pen is a power in the hands of men who feel the truth burning upon the altar of their hearts, and who have an intelligent zeal for God, balanced with sound judgment. The pen, dipped in the fountain of pure truth, can send the beams of light to dark corners of the earth, which will reflect its rays back, adding new power, and giving increased light to be scattered everywhere.

A HARVEST OF PRECIOUS SOULS

I have been shown that the publications already have been doing a work upon some minds in other countries, in breaking down the walls of prejudice and superstition. I was shown men and women studying with intense interest papers and a few pages of tracts upon present truth. They would read the evidences so wonderful and new to them, and would open their Bibles with a deep and new interest, as subjects of truth that had been dark to them were made plain, especially the light in regard to the Sabbath of the fourth commandment. As they searched the Scriptures to see if these things were so, a new light shone upon their understanding, for angels were hovering over them, and impressing their minds with the truths contained in the publications they had been reading.

I saw them holding papers and tracts in one hand, and the Bible in the other, while their cheeks were wet with tears; and bowing before God in earnest, humble prayer, to be guided into all truth,—the very thing He was doing for them before they called upon Him. And when the truth was received in their hearts, and they saw the harmonious chain of truth, the Bible was to them a new book; they hugged it to their hearts with grateful joy, while their countenances were all aglow with happiness and holy joy.

These were not satisfied with merely enjoying the light themselves, and they began to work for others. Some made great sacrifices for the truth's sake and to help those of the brethren who were in darkness. The way is thus preparing to do a great work in the distribution of tracts and papers in other languages.

XXXVI

CIRCULATING THE PRINTED PAGE[1]

Several speakers had addressed large and attentive congregations at the camp meeting at Rome, N. Y., on first day, Sept. 12, 1875. The following night I dreamed that a young man of noble appearance came into the room where I was, immediately after I had been speaking. He said:

"You have called the attention of the people to important subjects, which, to a large number, are strange and new. To some they are intensely interesting. The laborers in word and doctrine have done what they could in presenting the truth. But unless there is a more thorough effort made to fasten these impressions upon minds, your efforts will prove nearly fruitless. Satan has many attractions ready to divert the mind; and the cares of this life and the deceitfulness of riches all combine to choke the seed of truth sown in the heart.

"In every effort such as you are now making, much more good would result from your labors if you had appropriate reading matter ready for circulation. Tracts upon the important points of truth for the present time should be handed out freely to all who will accept them. You are to sow beside all waters.

"The press is a powerful means to move the minds and hearts of the people. The men of this world seize the press, and make the most of every opportunity to get poisonous literature before the people. If men, under the influence of the spirit of the world and of Satan, are earnest to circulate books, tracts,

[1] These words of counsel regarding the circulation of literature were among the first calling for trained colporteur-evangelists.

and papers of a corrupting nature, you should be more earnest to get reading matter of an elevating and saving character before the people.

"God has placed at the command of His people advantages in the press, which, combined with other agencies, will be successful in extending the knowledge of the truth. Tracts, papers, and books, as the case demands, should be circulated in all the cities and villages in the land. Here is missionary work for all.

"There should be men trained for this branch of the work who will be missionaries, and will circulate publications. They should be men of good address, who will not repulse others or be repulsed. This is a work which would warrant men to give their whole time and energies as the occasion demands. God has committed to His people great light. This is not for them to selfishly enjoy alone, but to let its rays shine forth to others who are in the darkness of error.

"You are not as a people doing one twentieth part of what might be done in spreading the knowledge of the truth. Very much more can be accomplished by the living preacher with the circulation of papers and tracts than by the preaching of the word alone without the publications. The press is a powerful instrumentality which God has ordained to be combined with the energies of the living preacher to bring the truth before all nations, kindreds, tongues, and peoples. Many minds can be reached in no other way.

"Here is true missionary work in which labor and means can be invested with the best results. There has been too great fear of running risks, and moving out by faith, and sowing beside all waters. Opportunities have been presented which have not been grasped and made the most of. There has been too great fear of venturing. True faith is not presumption, but it ventures much. Precious light and powerful truth need to be brought out in publications without delay."

Said he: "Your husband must not be discouraged in his efforts to encourage men to become workers, and responsible for important work. Every man whom God will accept, Satan will attack. If they disconnect from heaven, and imperil the cause, their failures will not be set to his account or to yours, but to the perversity of the nature of the murmuring ones, which they would not understand and overcome. These men whom God has tried to use to do His work, and who have failed, and brought great burdens upon those who were unselfish and true, have hindered and discouraged more than all the good they have done. And yet this should not hinder the purpose of God in having this growing work, with its burden of cares, divided into different branches, and laid upon men who should do their part, and lift the burdens when they ought to be lifted. These men must be willing to be instructed, and then God can fit them and sanctify them, and impart to them sanctified judgment, that what they undertake they may carry forward in His name."

XXXVII

PUBLIC LABORS IN 1877

May 11, 1877, we left Oakland, Cal., for Battle Creek, Mich. A telegram had been sent to my husband, requesting his presence at Battle Creek, to give attention to important business relative to the cause. In answer to this summons, he went, and engaged earnestly in preaching, writing, and holding board meetings at the Review Office, the College, and the Sanitarium, often working into the night. This wore him fearfully. His constant mental anxiety was preparing the way for a breakdown. We both felt our danger, and decided to go to Colorado to enjoy retirement and rest.

While planning for the journey, a voice seemed to say to me: "Put the armor on. I have work for you to do in Battle Creek." The voice seemed so plain that I involuntarily turned to see who was speaking. I saw no one; and at the sense of the presence of God my heart was broken in tenderness before Him. When my husband entered the room, I told him the exercises of my mind. We wept and prayed together. Our arrangements had been made to leave in three days; but now all our plans were changed.

SPECIAL SERVICES FOR COLLEGE STUDENTS

The close of the school year of the Battle Creek College was at hand. I had felt very anxious for the students, many of whom were either unconverted or backslidden from God. I spent a week laboring for them, holding meetings every evening and on the Sabbath and first day. My heart was touched to see the house of worship nearly filled with the students of our school. I tried to impress upon them that a life of purity and prayer would not be a hindrance to them in obtaining a thorough knowledge of the sciences, but that it would remove many hindrances to their progress in knowledge. By becoming connected with the Saviour, they are brought into the school of Christ; and if they are diligent students in this school, vice and immorality will be expelled from the midst of them. These being crowded out, increased knowledge will be the result.

Our school is to take a higher position in an educational point of view than any other institution of learning, by opening before the young nobler views, aims, and objects in life, and educating them to have a correct knowledge of human duty and eternal interests. The great object in the establishment of our College was to give correct views, showing the harmony of science and Bible religion.

The Lord strengthened me and blessed the efforts made in behalf of the youth. A large number came forward for prayers. Some of these, through lack of watchfulness and prayer, had lost their faith and the evidence of their connection with God. Many testified that in taking this step they received the blessing of God. As a result of the meetings, quite a number presented themselves for baptism.

TEMPERANCE MEETINGS

But my work was not yet done in Battle Creek. We were earnestly solicited to take part in a temperance mass meeting, a very praiseworthy effort in progress among the better portion of the citizens of Battle Creek. This movement embraced the Battle Creek Reform Club, six hundred strong, and the Woman's Christian Temperance Union, two hundred and sixty strong. God, Christ, the Holy Spirit, and the Bible were familiar words with these earnest workers. Much good had already been accomplished, and the activity of the workers, the system by which they labored, and the spirit of their meetings, promised greater good in time to come.

It was on the occasion of the visit of Barnum's great menagerie to this city, on the 28th of June, that the ladies of the Woman's Christian Temperance Union struck a telling blow for temperance and reform by organizing an immense temperance restaurant to accommodate the crowds of people who gathered in from the country to visit the menagerie, thus preventing them from visiting the saloons and groggeries, where they would be exposed to temptation. The mammoth tent, capable of holding five thousand people, used by the Michigan Conference for camp meeting purposes, was tendered for the occasion. Beneath this immense canvas temple were erected fifteen or twenty tables for the accommodation of guests.

By invitation I spoke in the tent Sunday evening, July 1, upon the subject of Christian temperance, to fully five thousand persons.

ON THE INDIANA CAMP GROUND

August 9-14, I attended the camp meeting near Kokomo, Ind., accompanied by my daughter-in-law, Mary K. White. My husband found it impossible for him to leave Battle Creek. At this meeting the Lord strengthened me to labor most earnestly. He gave me clearness and power to appeal to the people. As I looked upon the men and women assembled here, noble in appearance and commanding in influence, and compared them with the little company assembled six years before, who were mostly poor and uneducated, I could but exclaim, "What hath the Lord wrought!"

The refining influence that the truth has upon the life and character of those who receive it, was exemplified very strongly here. While speaking, we asked those to arise who had been addicted to the use of tobacco, but had entirely discontinued its use because of the light they had received through the truth. In response, between thirty-five and forty arose to their feet, ten or twelve of whom were women. We then invited those to rise who had been told by physicians that it would be fatal for them to stop the use of tobacco, because they had become so accustomed to its false stimulus that they would not be able to live without it. In reply, eight persons, whose countenances indicated health of mind and body, arose to their feet. How wonderful is the sanctifying influence which this truth has upon the human life, making staunch temperance men of those who have indulged in tobacco, wine, and other fashionable dissipation.

On Sunday Elder J. H. Waggoner spoke with great freedom in the forenoon to a good congregation, on the subject of the Sabbath. Three excursion trains poured their living freight upon the grounds. The people here were very enthusiastic on the temperance question. At 2:30 P. M. I spoke to about eight thousand people on the subject of temperance viewed from a moral and Christian standpoint. I was blessed with remarkable clearness and liberty, and was heard with the best of attention from the large audience present.

We left the beaten track of the popular lecturer, and traced the origin of the prevailing intemperance

The work of God seems so important
to me in every department. I must be
connected with Jesus in order to do good
to others. I believe there is great blessing
for God's people if they will only come up
to their privilege. What is lacking is
living faith. Every moment is precious
now. I cannot endure the thought of
time passing and we not doing as
a people the very things God would
have us to do. Our time to work
will soon be over. May God help us
all to work in wisdom. My prayer to God
is continually for wisdom and grace
to move according to his opening
providence. I dare not choose my own
course or follow my own pleasure.
God is my counseller. I must look to
him for guidance. I ~~must~~ must cling
to my Saviour with firm grasp.
The Lord is precious to me. The truths in
the life of Christ is truly rich and

Photographic facsimile of a page from a letter written by Mrs. White from Oakland, Cal., May 12, 1876, to her husband while he was in attendance at Eastern camp meetings.

to the home, the family board, and the indulgence of appetite in the child. Stimulating food creates a desire for still stronger stimulants. The boy whose taste is thus vitiated, and who is not taught self-control, is the drunkard or tobacco slave of later years. The duty of parents was pointed out to train their children to right views of life and its responsibilities, and to lay the foundation for their upright Christian characters. The great work of temperance reform, to be thoroughly successful, must begin in the home.

In the evening Elder Waggoner spoke upon the signs of the times, to a large and attentive audience. Many remarked that this discourse, and his sermon upon the Sabbath, had awakened new thoughts in their minds, and that they were determined to investigate these subjects.

Monday I appealed to the people to give their hearts to God. About fifty came forward for prayers. The deepest interest was manifested. Fifteen were buried with Christ in baptism as the result of the meeting.

WALKING OUT BY FAITH

We had planned to attend the Ohio and Western camp meetings; but our friends thought that, considering my state of health, it would be presumptuous; so we decided to remain at Battle Creek. Being much of the time a great sufferer, I placed myself under treatment at the Sanitarium.

My husband labored incessantly to advance the interests of the cause of God in the various departments of the work centering in Battle Creek. Before we were aware of it, he was very much worn. Early one morning, he was attacked with giddiness, and was threatened with paralysis. We greatly feared this dreadful disease; but the Lord was merciful, and spared us the affliction. However, his attack was followed by great physical and mental prostration; and now, indeed, it seemed impossible for us to attend the Eastern camp meetings, or for me to attend them, and leave my husband depressed in spirits and in feeble health.

I could not, however, find rest and freedom in the thought of remaining away from the field of labor. We took the matter to the Lord in prayer. We knew that the mighty Healer could restore both my husband and myself to health, if it was for His glory so to do. We both decided to walk out by faith, and to venture all on the promises of God.

THE EASTERN CAMP MEETINGS

When we arrived at the camp ground at Groveland, Mass., we found an excellent meeting in progress. There were forty-seven tents on the ground, besides three large tents, the one for the congregation being 80x125 feet in dimensions. The meetings on the Sabbath were of the deepest interest. The church was revived and strengthened, while sinners and backsliders were aroused to a sense of their danger.

Sunday morning boats and trains poured their living freight upon the ground in thousands. Elder Smith spoke in the morning upon the Eastern question. The subject was of special interest, and the people listened with the most earnest attention.

In the afternoon it was difficult to make my way to the desk through the standing crowd. Upon reaching it, a sea of heads was before me. The mammoth tent was full, and thousands stood outside, making a living wall several feet deep. My lungs and throat pained me very much; yet I believed that God would help me upon this important occasion. The Lord gave me great freedom in addressing that immense crowd upon the subject of Christian temperance. While speaking, my weariness and pain were forgotten, as I realized that I was speaking to a people that did not regard my words as idle tales. The discourse occupied over an hour, and the very best attention was given throughout.

Monday morning we had a season of prayer in our tent in behalf of my husband. We presented his case to the Great Physician. It was a precious season; the peace of heaven rested upon us. These words came forcibly to my mind: "This is the victory that overcometh the world, even our faith." 1 John 5:4. We all felt the blessing of God resting upon us.

We then assembled in the large tent; my husband met with us, and spoke for a short time, uttering precious words from a heart softened and aglow with a deep sense of the mercy and goodness of God.

We then took up the work where we had left it on the Sabbath, and the morning was spent in special labor for sinners and backsliders, of whom two hundred came forward for prayers, ranging in years from the child of ten to gray-headed men and women. More than a score of these were setting their feet in the way of life for the first time. In the afternoon thirty-eight persons were baptized; and quite a number delayed baptism until they should return to their homes.

Monday evening I stood in the stand at a tent meeting in progress at Danvers, Mass. A large congregation was before me. I was too weary to arrange my thoughts in connected words; I felt that I must have help, and asked for it with my whole heart. I knew if any degree of success attended my labors, it would be through the strength of the Mighty One.

The Spirit of the Lord rested upon me as I attempted to speak. Like a shock of electricity I felt it upon my heart, and all pain was instantly removed. I had suffered great pain in the nerves centering in the brain; this also was entirely removed. My irritated throat and sore lungs were relieved. My left arm and hand had become nearly useless in consequence of pain in my heart; but natural feeling was now restored. My mind was clear; my soul was full of the light and love of God. Angels of God seemed to be on every side, like a wall of fire.

Before me were a people whom I might not meet again until the judgment; and the desire for their salvation led me to speak earnestly and in the fear of God, that I might be free from their blood. Great freedom attended my effort, which occupied one hour and ten minutes. Jesus was my helper, and His name shall have all the glory. The audience was very attentive.

We returned to Groveland on Tuesday to find the camp breaking up, tents being struck, our brethren saying farewell, and ready to step on board the cars to return to their homes. This was one of the best camp meetings I ever attended.

In the afternoon Elder Haskell took us in his carriage, and we started for South Lancaster, to rest at his home for a time.

We decided to travel by private conveyance a part of the way to the Vermont camp meeting, as we thought this would be beneficial to my husband. At noon we would stop by the roadside, kindle a fire, prepare our lunch, and have a season of prayer. These precious hours spent in company with Brother and

Sister Haskell, Sister Ings, and Sister Huntley, will never be forgotten. Our prayers went up to God all the way from South Lancaster to Vermont. After traveling three days, we took the cars, and thus completed our journey.

This meeting was of especial benefit to the cause in Vermont. The Lord gave me strength to speak to the people as often as once each day.

We went directly from Vermont to the New York camp meeting. The Lord gave me great freedom in speaking to the people. But some were not prepared to be benefited by the meeting. They failed to realize their condition, and did not seek the Lord earnestly, confessing their backslidings and putting away their sins. One of the great objects of holding camp meetings is that our brethren may feel their danger of being overcharged with the cares of this life. A great loss is sustained when these privileges are not improved.

RETURN TO MICHIGAN AND CALIFORNIA

We returned to Michigan, and after a few days went to Lansing to attend the camp meeting there, which continued two weeks. Here I labored very earnestly, and was sustained by the Spirit of the Lord. I was greatly blessed in speaking to the students, and in laboring for their salvation. This was a remarkable meeting. The Spirit of God was present from the beginning to the close. As the result of the meeting, one hundred and thirty were baptized. A large part of these were students from our College. We were rejoiced to see the salvation of God in this meeting. After spending a few weeks in Battle Creek, we decided to cross the plains to California.

XXXVIII

VISIT TO OREGON

By the close of the winter of 1877-78, which was spent in California, my husband had improved in health; and as the weather in Michigan had become mild, he returned to Battle Creek, that he might have the benefit of treatment at the Sanitarium.

I dared not accompany my husband across the plains; for constant care and anxiety, and inability to sleep, had brought upon me heart difficulties which were alarming. We felt keenly as the hour of separation drew on. We knew not that we should meet again in this world. My husband was returning to Michigan, and we had decided that it was advisable for me to visit Oregon, and bear my testimony there to those who had never heard me.

THE VOYAGE

In company with a lady friend and Elder J. N. Loughborough, I left San Francisco on the afternoon of June 10, 1878, upon the steamer *Oregon*. Captain Conner, who had charge of this splendid steamer, was very attentive to his passengers. As we passed through the Golden Gate into the broad ocean, it was very rough. The wind was against us, and the steamer pitched fearfully, while the ocean was lashed into fury by the wind. I watched the clouded sky, the rushing waves leaping mountain high, and the spray reflecting the colors of the rainbow. The sight was fearfully grand, and I was filled with awe while contemplating the mysteries of the deep. It is terrible in its wrath. There is a fearful beauty in the lifting up of its proud waves with roaring, and then falling back in mournful sobs. I could see the exhibition of God's power in the movements of the restless waters, groaning beneath the action of the merciless winds, which tossed the waves up on high as if in convulsions of agony.

As I looked upon the white-capped, roaring billows, I was reminded of that scene in the life of Christ, when the disciples, in obedience to the command of their Master, went in their boats to the farther side of the sea.

When nearly all had left for their staterooms, I continued on deck. The captain had provided me a deck chair, and blankets to serve as a protection from the chilly air. I knew that if I went into the cabin, I should be sick. Night came on, darkness covered the sea, and the plunging waves were pitching our ship fearfully. This great vessel was as a mere chip upon the merciless waters; but she was guarded and protected on her course by the heavenly angels, commissioned of God to do His bidding. Had it not been for this, we might have been swallowed up in a moment, leaving not a trace of that splendid ship. But that God who feeds the ravens, who numbers the hairs of our heads, will not forget us.

The last night we were on the boat I felt most grateful to my heavenly Father. I there learned a lesson I shall never forget. God had spoken to my heart in the storm, and in the waves, and in the calm following. And shall we not worship Him? Shall man set up his will against the will of God? Shall we be disobedient to the commands of so mighty a Ruler? Shall we contend with the Most High, who is the source of all power, and from whose heart flows infinite love and blessing to the creatures of His care?

MEETINGS OF SPECIAL INTEREST

My visit to Oregon was one of special interest. I here met, after a separation of four years, my dear friends Brother and Sister Van Horn, whom we claim as our children. I was somewhat surprised, and very much pleased, to find the cause of God in so prosperous a condition in Oregon.

Tuesday evening, June 18, I met a goodly number of the Sabbath keepers in this State. I gave my testimony for Jesus, and expressed my gratitude for the sweet privilege that is ours of trusting in His love, and of claiming His power to unite with our efforts to save sinners from perdition. If we would see the work of God prosper, we must have Christ dwelling in us; in short, we must work the works of Christ. Wherever we look, the whitening harvest appears; but the laborers are so few. I felt my heart filled with the peace of God, and drawn out in love for His dear people with whom I was worshiping for the first time.

On Sunday, June 23, I spoke in the Methodist church of Salem, on the subject of temperance. On the next Tuesday evening, I again spoke in this church. Many invitations were tendered me to speak on temperance in various cities and towns of Oregon, but the state of my health forbade my complying with these requests.

We entered upon the camp meeting with feelings of deepest interest. The Lord gave me strength and grace as I stood before the people. As I looked upon the intelligent audience, my heart was broken before God. This was the first camp meeting held by our people in the State. I tried to present before the people the gratitude we should feel for the tender compassion and great love of God. His goodness and glory impressed my mind in a remarkable manner.

I had felt very anxious about my husband, on account of his poor health. While speaking, there came vividly before my mind's eye a meeting in the church at Battle Creek, my husband being in the midst, with the mellow light of the Lord resting upon and surrounding him. His face bore the marks of health, and he was apparently very happy.

I was overwhelmed with a sense of God's unparalleled mercies, and of the work He was doing, not only in Oregon, and in California and Michigan, where our important institutions are located, but also in foreign countries. I can never represent to others the picture that vividly impressed my mind on that occasion. For a moment the extent of the work came before me, and I lost sight of my surroundings. The occasion and the people I was addressing passed from my mind. The light, the precious light from heaven, was shining in great brilliancy upon those institutions which are engaged in the solemn and elevated work of reflecting the rays of light that heaven has let shine upon them.

All through this camp meeting the Lord seemed very near me. When it closed, I was exceedingly weary, but free in the Lord. It was a season of profitable labor, and strengthened the church to go on in their warfare for the truth.

On the Sunday following the camp meeting, I spoke in the afternoon in the public square, upon the simplicity of gospel religion.

A PRISON SERVICE

During my stay in Oregon, I visited the prison in Salem, in company with Brother and Sister Carter and Sister Jordan. When the time arrived for service, we were conducted to the chapel, which was made cheerful by an abundance of light and pure, fresh air. At a signal from the bell, two men opened the great iron gates, and the prisoners came flocking in. The doors were securely closed behind them, and for the first time in my life I was immured in prison walls.

I had expected to see a set of repulsive looking men, but was happily disappointed; many of them seemed to be intelligent, and some to be men of ability. They were dressed in the coarse but neat prison uniform, their hair smooth, and their boots brushed. As I looked upon the varied physiognomies before me, I thought, "To each of these men have been committed peculiar gifts, or talents, to be used for the glory of God and the benefit of the world; but they have despised these gifts of Heaven, abused and misapplied them." As I looked upon young men from eighteen to twenty and thirty years of age, I thought of their unhappy mothers, and of the grief and remorse which was their bitter portion. Many of these mothers' hearts had been broken by the ungodly course pursued by their children.

When all the company were assembled, Brother Carter read a hymn. All had books, and joined heartily in singing. One, who was an accomplished musician, played the organ. I then opened the meeting by prayer, and again all joined in singing. I spoke from the words of John: "Behold, what manner of love the Father hath bestowed upon us, that we should be called the sons of God: therefore the world knoweth us not, because it knew Him not. Beloved, now are we the sons of God, and it doth not yet appear what we shall be: but we know that, when He shall appear, we shall be like Him; for we shall see Him as He is." 1 John 3: 1, 2.

I exalted before them the infinite sacrifice made by the Father in giving His beloved Son for fallen men, that they might through obedience be transformed, and become the acknowledged sons of God.

THE RETURN JOURNEY

While in Salem, I formed the acquaintance of Brother and Sister Donaldson, who desired that their daughter should return to Battle Creek with us, and attend the College. Her health was poor, and it was quite a struggle for them to part with her, their only daughter; but the spiritual advantages she would there receive induced them to make the sacrifice. Not long afterward, at a camp meeting in Battle Creek, she was buried with Christ in baptism. This was another proof of the importance of Seventh-day Adventists' sending their children to our school, where they can be brought directly under a saving influence.

On our voyage from Oregon, we made many pleasant acquaintances, and distributed our publications to different ones, which led to profitable conversation.

When we arrived at Oakland, we found that the tent was pitched there, and that quite a number had embraced the truth under the labors of Elder Wm. Healey. We spoke several times under the tent. Sabbath and first day the churches of San Francisco and Oakland met together, and we had interesting and profitable meetings.

XXXIX

FROM STATE TO STATE

I was very anxious to attend the camp meeting in California; but there were urgent calls for me to attend the Eastern camp meetings. As the condition of things in the East had been presented before me, I knew that I had a testimony to bear, especially to our brethren in the New England Conference; and I could not feel at liberty to remain longer in California.

July 28, 1878, accompanied by my daughter-in-law, Mrs. Emma L. White, and Edith Donaldson, I left Oakland, Cal., for the East. On the way I spoke at Sacramento Sunday, to an attentive congregation, and the Lord gave me freedom in speaking to them from His word. Monday we again took the cars, stopping at Reno, Nevada, where I spoke Tuesday evening.

IN COLORADO

On the way from Denver to Walling's Mills, the mountain retreat where my husband was spending the summer months, we stopped in Boulder City, and beheld with joy our canvas meetinghouse, where Elder Cornell was holding a series of meetings. We found a quiet retreat in the comfortable home of Sister Dartt. The tent had been loaned to hold temperance meetings in; and by special invitation, I spoke to a tent full of attentive hearers.

Monday, August 8, I met my husband, and found him much improved in health, cheerful and active, for which I felt thankful to God.

Our family were all present in the mountains but our son Edson. My husband and children thought that as I was much worn, having labored almost constantly since the Oregon camp meeting, it was my privilege to rest; but my mind was impressed to attend the Eastern camp meetings, especially the one in Massachusetts.

We received a letter from Brother Haskell, urging us both to attend the camp meeting; but if my husband could not come, he wished me to come if possible. I read the letter to my husband, and after a few moments' silence, he said, "Ellen, you will have to attend the New England camp meeting."

The next day Edith Donaldson and I packed our trunks. At two o'clock in the morning, favored with the light of the moon, we started for the cars, and at half past six we stepped on board the train at Black Hawk. The journey was anything but pleasant, for the heat was intense.

Upon arriving at Battle Creek, we learned that an appointment had been made for me to speak Sunday evening in the mammoth tent pitched on the College grounds. The tent was filled to overflowing, and my heart was drawn out in earnest appeals to the people

I tarried in Battle Creek but a very short time, and then, accompanied by Sister Mary Smith Abbey and Elder E. W. Farnsworth, I was again on the wing, bound for the East.

THE NEW ENGLAND CONFERENCE

When we arrived at Boston, Brethren Wood and Haskell met us, and accompanied us to Ballard Vale, the place of meeting. There we were welcomed by our old friends with a heartiness that was restful. Much labor was required at this meeting. New churches had been raised up since our last camp meeting. Precious souls had accepted the truth, and these needed to be carried forward to a deeper and more thorough knowledge of practical godliness.

On one occasion I spoke in reference to genuine sanctification, which is nothing less than a daily dying to self and daily conformity to the will of God. While in Oregon I had been shown that some of the young churches of the New England Conference were in danger through the blighting influence of what is called sanctification. Some would become deceived by this doctrine, while others, knowing its deceptive influence, would realize their danger and turn from it. Paul's sanctification was a constant conflict with self. Said he, "I die daily." 1 Cor. 15:31. His will and his desires every day conflicted with duty and the will of God. Instead of following inclination, he did the will of God, however unpleasant and crucifying to his nature.

We called on those who desired to be baptized, and those who were keeping the Sabbath for the first time, to come forward. Twenty-five responded. These bore excellent testimonies; and before the close of the camp meeting twenty-two received baptism.

We were pleased to meet here our old friends of the cause whose acquaintance we made thirty years before. Our much esteemed Brother Hastings was as deeply interested in the truth as ever. We were pleased to meet Sister Temple, and Sister Collins of Dartmouth, Mass., and Brother and Sister Wilkinson, at whose house we were entertained during our first labors in connection with the third angel's message.

MEETING IN MAINE

We left Ballard Vale Tuesday morning, September 3, to attend the Maine camp meeting. We enjoyed a quiet rest at the home of Brother Morton, near Portland. He and his good wife made our tarry with them very pleasant. We were upon the Maine camp ground before the Sabbath, and were happy to meet here some of the tried friends of the cause. There are some who are ever at their post of duty, come sunshine or come storm. There is also a class of sunshine Christians. When everything goes well and is agreeable to their feelings, they are fervent and zealous; but when there are clouds and disagreeable things to meet, these will have nothing to say or do. The blessing of God rested upon the active workers, while those who did nothing were not benefited by the meeting as they might have been. The Lord was with His ministers, who labored faithfully in presenting both doctrinal and practical subjects.

AT BATTLE CREEK

The General Conference was held at Battle Creek, Oct. 2-14, 1878. More than forty ministers were present. We were all happy to meet here Elders Andrews and Bourdeau from Europe, and Elder Loughborough from California. At this meeting was represented the cause in Europe, California, Texas, Alabama, Virginia, Dakota, Colorado, and in all of the Northern States from Maine to Nebraska.

Here I was happy to join my husband in labor. As the meeting progressed, my strength increased.

On Wednesday of the second week of the meeting, a few of us united in prayer for a sister who was afflicted with despondency. While praying, I was greatly blessed. The Lord seemed very near. I was taken off in a vision of God's glory, and shown many things.

These were meetings of solemn power and of the deepest interest. Several connected with our Office of publication were convicted, and converted to the truth, and bore clear, intelligent testimonies. Infidels were convicted, and took their stand under the banner of Prince Immanuel. This meeting was a decided victory. One hundred and twelve were baptized before its close.

KANSAS CAMP MEETINGS

Accompanied by my daughter-in-law, Emma White, I left Battle Creek, October 23, for the Kansas camp meeting. At Topeka we left the cars and rode by private conveyance twelve miles to Richland, the place of meeting. We found the settlement of tents in a grove. It was late in the season, and faithful preparation had been made for cold weather. Every tent had a stove.

Sabbath morning it commenced snowing; but not one meeting was suspended. About an inch of snow fell, and the air was piercing cold. Women with little children clustered about the stoves. It was touching to see one hundred and fifty people assembled for a convocation meeting under these circumstances. Some had come two hundred miles by private conveyance. All seemed hungry for the bread of life, and thirsty for the water of salvation.

Elder Haskell spoke Friday afternoon and evening. Sabbath morning I spoke encouraging words to those who had made so great an effort to attend the meeting. I told them that the more inclement the weather, the greater the necessity of our obtaining the sunshine of God's presence. This life at best is but the Christian's winter; and the bleak winds of winter — disappointments, losses, pain, and anguish — are our lot here; but our hopes are reaching forward to the Christian's summer, when we shall change climate, leave all the wintry blasts and fierce tempests behind, and be taken to those mansions Jesus has gone to prepare for those that love Him.

Tuesday morning the meeting closed, and we went to Sherman, Kansas, where another camp meeting had been appointed. This was an interesting and profitable meeting, although there were only about one hundred brethren and sisters present. It was designed for a general gathering of the scattered ones. Some were present from southern Kansas, Arkansas, Kentucky, Missouri, Nebraska, and Tennessee. At this meeting my husband joined me, and from here, with Elder Haskell and our daughter, we went to Dallas, Texas.

VISIT TO TEXAS

Thursday we went to Brother McDearman's at Grand Prairie. Here our daughter met her parents and her brother and sister, who had all been brought near to the door of death by the fever which had prevailed in the State during the past summer. We took great pleasure in ministering to the wants of this afflicted family, who had in years past liberally assisted us in our affliction. They were somewhat improved in health when we left them to attend the Plano camp meeting, held November 12-19. Here we were happy to meet our old friends Elder R. M. Kilgore and his wife. And we were highly pleased to find a large and intelligent body of brethren on the ground. My testimony was never received more readily and heartily than by this people. I became deeply interested in the work in the great State of Texas.

XL

A VIEW OF THE JUDGMENT

On the morning of Oct. 23, 1879, about two o'clock, the Spirit of the Lord rested upon me, and I beheld scenes in the coming judgment. Language fails me in which to give an adequate description of the things which passed before me, and of the effect they had upon my mind.

The great day of the execution of God's judgment seemed to have come. Ten thousand times ten thousand were assembled before a large throne, upon which was seated a Person of majestic appearance. Several books were before Him, and upon the covers of each was written in letters of gold, which seemed like a burning flame of fire, "Ledger of Heaven."

One of these books, containing the names of those who claim to believe the truth, was then opened. Immediately I lost sight of the countless millions about the throne, and only those who were professedly children of the light and of the truth engaged my attention. As these persons were named, one by one, and their good deeds mentioned, their countenances would light up with a holy joy that was reflected in every direction. But this did not seem to rest upon my mind with the greatest force.

Another book was opened, wherein were recorded the sins of those who profess the truth. Under the general heading of "Selfishness" came every other sin. There were also headings over every column, and underneath these, opposite each name, were recorded, in their respective columns, the lesser sins. Under "Covetousness" came falsehood, theft, robbery, fraud, and avarice; under "Ambition" came pride and extravagance; "Jealousy" stood at the head of malice, envy, and hatred; and "Intemperance" headed a long list of fearful crimes, such as lasciviousness, adultery, indulgence of animal passions, etc. As I beheld, I was filled with inexpressible anguish, and exclaimed: "Who can be saved? Who will stand justified before God? Whose robes are spotless? Who are faultless in the sight of a pure and holy God?"

As the Holy One upon the throne slowly turned the leaves of the ledger, and His eyes rested for a moment upon individuals, His glance seemed to burn into their very souls, and at the same moment every word and action of their lives passed before their minds as clearly as though traced before their vision in letters of fire. Trembling seized them and their faces turned pale. . . .

One class were registered as cumberers of the ground. As the piercing eye of the Judge rested upon these, their sins of neglect were distinctly revealed. With pale, quivering lips they acknowledged that they had been traitors to their holy trust. They had had warnings and privileges, but they had not heeded nor improved upon them. They could now see that they had presumed too much upon the mercy of God. . . .

The names of all who profess the truth were mentioned. . . . Upon one page of the ledger, under the head of "Fidelity," was the name of my husband. His life, character, and all the incidents in our experience, seemed to be brought vividly before my mind. A very few items which impressed me, I will mention. I was shown that God had qualified my husband for a specific work, and in His providence had united us to carry forward this work. Through the Testimonies of His Spirit, He had imparted to him great light. He had cautioned, warned, reproved, and encouraged;

and it was due to the power of His grace that we had been enabled to bear a part in the work from its very commencement. God had miraculously preserved his mental faculties, notwithstanding his physical powers had given out again and again.

God should have the glory for the unbending integrity and noble courage to vindicate the right and condemn the wrong which my husband has had. Just such firmness and decision were necessary at the commencement of the work, and they have been needed all along, as it progressed step by step. He has stood in defense of the truth without yielding a single principle to please the best friend. He has had an ardent temperament, bold and fearless in acting and speaking. This has often led him into difficulties which he might frequently have avoided. He has been obliged to stand more firmly, to be more decided, to speak more earnestly and boldly, because of the very different temperament of the men connected with him in his labor.

God has given him the power to form and execute plans with the needed firmness, because he did not refuse to exercise these qualities of the mind, and to venture in order to advance the work of God. Self has at times been mingled with the work; but when the Holy Spirit has controlled his mind, he has been a most successful instrument in the hands of God for the upbuilding of His cause. He has had elevated views of the Lord's claims upon all who profess His name,— of their duty to stand in defense of the widow and the fatherless, to be kind to the poor, to help the needy. He would jealously guard the interests of his brethren, that no unjust advantage should be taken of them.

The earnest efforts of my husband to build up the institutions in our midst I also saw registered in the Ledger of Heaven. The truth sent out from the press was like rays of light emanating from the sun in all directions. This work was commenced and carried forward at a great sacrifice of strength and means.

TIMES OF TEST AND TRIAL

When affliction came upon my husband, other men were selected to take his place. They commenced with a good purpose, but they had never learned the lesson of self-denial. Had they felt the necessity of earnestly agonizing before God daily, and thrown their souls unselfishly into the work, not depending upon self, but upon the wisdom of God, they would have shown that their works were wrought in God. Had they heeded the reproofs and counsels given, when they did not meet the mind of the Spirit of God, they would have been saved from sin.

A man who is honest before God will deal justly with his fellow men, whether or not it is for his own personal interest to do so. The outward acts are a fair transcript of the principles within. Many whom God called to His work have been tested and proved; and there are others whom He is now testing and proving.

After God had tested and proved us in the furnace of affliction, he raised up my husband and gave him greater clearness of mind and power of intellect to plan and execute than he had before his affliction. When my husband felt his own weakness and moved in the fear of God, then the Lord was his strength. Prompt in speech and action, he has pushed forward reforms where they would otherwise have languished. He has made very liberal donations, fearing that his means would prove a snare to him.

A CALL FOR BURDEN BEARERS

While God has given us our work to do in bearing our testimony to the people by pen and voice, others must come to bear burdens in connection with the cause. They should not become discouraged, but should endeavor to learn by every apparent failure how to make a success of the next effort. And if they connect with the Source of wisdom, they will surely succeed.

God is putting burdens upon more inexperienced shoulders. He is fitting them to be care-taking, to venture, to run risks.

All who have responsible positions must realize that they must first have power with God, in order that they may have power with the people. Those who devise and execute plans for our institutions must connect with heaven, if they would have wisdom, foresight, discernment, and keen perception. The Lord is left out of the question altogether too much, when everything depends upon His blessing. God listens to the appeals of His self-denying workers who labor to advance His cause. He has even condescended to talk with feeble mortals, face to face.

The close intercourse which Moses had with God, and the glorious manifestation vouchsafed to him, caused his face to shine so brightly with heavenly luster that the people of Israel could not look upon him. He appeared like a bright angel from heaven. This personal experience of the knowledge of God was of more value to him as a man bearing responsibilities as a leader than all his former education in the learning of the Egyptians. The most brilliant intellect, the most earnest study, the highest eloquence, can never be substituted for the wisdom and power of

God in those who are bearing the responsibilities connected with His cause. Nothing can be substituted for the grace of Christ and the knowledge of God's will.

God has made every provision for man to have help which He alone can give him. If he allows his work to hurry, drive, and confuse, so that he has no time for devotional thought or for prayer, he will make mistakes. If a standard is not lifted up by Jesus Christ against Satan, the enemy will overcome those who are engaged in the important work for this time.

It is the privilege of every one connected with our denominational institutions to be connected in close relationship with God; and if they fail to do this, they show themselves unfitted for their work of trust. The provision made for us all through Christ was a full and perfect sacrifice,— a sinless offering. His blood can cleanse the foulest stain. Had He been but a man, we would be excusable for our lack of faith and obedience. He came to save that which was lost. We are not qualified for the great work for this time, except when we labor in God, when our prayers, earnest and fervent, are continually ascending to the throne of grace.

God is fitting up men to bear burdens, to plan and execute, and my husband must not stand in the way. He cannot encircle the cause of God in his arms; it is too broad. Many heads and many hands are needed to plan and labor, not saving themselves. For want of experience, mistakes will be made; but if the workers connect with God, He will give them an increase of wisdom. Never since the creation of the world were such important interests at stake as now depend upon the action of men who believe and are giving the last message of warning to the world.

XLI

THE DEATH OF ELDER JAMES WHITE

Notwithstanding the labors, cares, and responsibilities with which my husband's life had been crowded, his sixtieth year found him active and vigorous in mind and body. Three times had he fallen under a stroke of paralysis; yet by the blessing of God, a naturally strong constitution, and strict attention to the laws of health, he had been enabled to rally. Again he traveled, preached, and wrote with his wonted zeal and energy. Side by side we had labored in the cause of Christ for thirty-five years; and we hoped that we might stand together to witness the triumphant close. But such was not the will of God. The chosen protector of my youth, the companion of my life, the sharer of my labors and afflictions, was taken from my side, and I was left to finish my work and to fight the battle alone.

The spring and early summer of 1881 we spent together at our home in Battle Creek. My husband hoped to arrange his business so that we could go to the Pacific coast and devote ourselves to writing. He felt that we had made a mistake in allowing the apparent wants of the cause and the entreaties of our brethren to urge us into active labor in preaching when we should have been writing. My husband desired to present more fully the glorious subject of redemption, and I had long contemplated the preparation of important books. We both felt that while our mental powers were unimpaired we should complete these works,— that it was a duty which we owed to ourselves and to the cause of God to rest from the heat of battle, and give to our people the precious light of truth which God had opened to our minds.

Some weeks before the death of my husband, I urged upon him the importance of seeking a field of labor where we would be released from the burdens necessarily coming upon us at Battle Creek. In reply he spoke of various matters which required attention before we could leave,— duties which some one must do. Then with deep feeling he inquired: "Where are the men to do this work? Where are those who will have an unselfish interest in our institutions, and who will stand for the right, unaffected by any influence with which they may come in contact?"

With tears he expressed his anxiety for our institutions at Battle Creek. Said he: "My life has been given to the upbuilding of these institutions. It seems like death to leave them. They are as my children, and I cannot separate my interest from them. These institutions are the Lord's instrumentalities to do a specific work. Satan seeks to hinder and defeat every means by which the Lord is working for the salvation of men. If the great adversary can mould these institutions according to the world's standard, his object is gained. It is my greatest anxiety to have the right man in the right place. If those who stand in responsible positions are weak in moral power and vacillating in principle, inclined to lead toward the world, there are enough who will be led. Evil influences must not prevail. I would rather die than live to see these institutions mismanaged, or turned aside from the purpose for which they were brought into existence.

"In my relations to this cause I have been longest and most closely connected with the publishing work. Three times have I fallen, stricken with paralysis, through my devotion to this branch of the cause. Now that God has given me renewed physical and mental strength, I feel that I can serve His cause as I have never been able to serve it before. I must see the publishing work prosper. It is interwoven with my very existence. If I forget the interests of this work, let my right hand forget her cunning."

We had an appointment to attend a tent meeting at Charlotte, Sabbath and Sunday, July 23 and 24. We decided to travel by private conveyance. On the way, my husband seemed cheerful, yet a feeling of solemnity rested upon him. He repeatedly praised the Lord for mercies and blessings received, and freely expressed his own feelings concerning the past and future: "The Lord is good, and greatly to be praised. He is a present help in time of need. The future seems cloudy and uncertain, but the Lord would not have us distressed over these things. When trouble comes, He will give us grace to endure it. What the Lord has been to us, and what He has done for us, should make us so grateful that we would never murmur or complain.

"It has seemed hard to me that my motives should be misjudged, and that my best efforts to help, encourage, and strengthen my brethren should again and again be turned against me. But I should have remembered Jesus and His disappointments. His soul was grieved that He was not appreciated by those He came to bless. I should have dwelt upon the mercy and loving-kindness of God, praising Him more, and complaining less of the ingratitude of my brethren. Had I ever left all my perplexities with the Lord, thinking less of what others said and did against me, I should have had more peace and joy. I will now seek first to guard myself, that I offend not in word or deed, and then to help my brethren make straight paths for their feet. I will not stop to mourn over any wrong done to me. I have expected more of men than I ought. I love God and His work, and I love my brethren also."

Little did I think, as we traveled on, that this was the last journey we should ever make together. The weather changed suddenly from oppressive heat to chilling cold. My husband took cold, but thought his health so good that he would receive no permanent injury. He labored in the meetings at Charlotte, presenting the truth with great clearness and power. He spoke of the pleasure he felt in addressing a people who manifested so deep an interest in the subjects most dear to him. "The Lord has indeed refreshed my soul," he said, "while I have been breaking to others the bread of life. All over Michigan the people are calling eagerly for help. How I long to comfort, encourage, and strengthen them with the precious truths applicable to this time!"

On our return home, my husband complained of slight indisposition, yet he engaged in his work as usual. Every morning we visited the grove near our home, and united in prayer. We were anxious to know our duty. Letters were continually coming in from different places, urging us to attend the camp meetings. Notwithstanding our determination to devote ourselves to writing, it was hard to refuse to meet with our brethren in these important gatherings. We earnestly pleaded for wisdom to know the right course.

Sabbath morning, as usual, we went to the grove together, and my husband prayed most fervently three times. He seemed reluctant to cease pleading with God for special guidance and blessing. His prayers were heard, and peace and light came to our hearts. He praised the Lord, and said: "Now I give it all up to Jesus. I feel a sweet, heavenly peace, an assurance that the Lord will show us our duty; for we desire to do His will." He accompanied me to the Tabernacle, and opened the services with singing and prayer. It was the last time he was ever to stand by my side in the pulpit.

On the following Monday he had a severe chill, and the next day I too was attacked. Together we were taken to the Sanitarium for treatment. On Friday my symptoms became more favorable. The doctor then informed me that my husband was inclined to sleep, and that danger was apprehended. I was immediately taken to his room, and as soon as I looked upon his countenance I knew that he was dying. I tried to arouse him. He understood all that was said to him, and responded to all questions that could be answered by yes or no, but seemed unable to say more. When I told him I thought he was dying, he manifested no surprise. I asked if Jesus was precious to him. He said, "Yes, oh, yes." "Have you no desire to live?" I inquired. He answered, "No." We then knelt by his bedside, and I prayed for him. A peaceful expression rested upon his countenance. I said to him: "Jesus loves you. The everlasting arms are beneath you." He responded, "Yes, yes."

Brother Smith and other brethren then prayed around his bedside, and retired to spend much of the night in prayer. My husband said he felt no pain; but he was evidently failing fast. Dr. Kellogg and his helpers did all that was in their power to hold him back from death. He slowly revived, but continued very weak.

The next morning he seemed slightly to revive, but about noon he had a chill, which left him unconscious. At 5 P. M., Sabbath, August 6, 1881, he quietly breathed his life away, without a struggle or a groan.

The shock of my husband's death — so sudden, so unexpected — fell upon me with crushing weight. In my feeble condition I had summoned strength to remain at his bedside to the last; but when I saw his eyes closed in death, exhausted nature gave way, and I was completely prostrated. For some time I seemed balancing between life and death. The vital flame burned so low that a breath might extinguish it. At night my pulse would grow feeble, and my breathing fainter and fainter till it seemed about to cease. Only by the blessing of God and the unremitting care and watchfulness of physician and attendants was my life preserved.

Though I had not risen from my sick-bed after my husband's death, I was borne to the Tabernacle on the following Sabbath to attend his funeral. At the close of the sermon I felt it a duty to testify to the value of the Christian's hope in the hour of sorrow and bereavement. As I arose, strength was given me, and I spoke about ten minutes, exalting the mercy and love of God in the presence of that crowded assembly. At the close of the services I followed my husband to Oak Hill Cemetery, where he was laid to rest until the morning of the resurrection.

My physical strength had been prostrated by the blow, yet the power of divine grace sustained me in my great bereavement. When I saw my husband breathe his last, I felt that Jesus was more precious to me than He ever had been in any previous hour of my life. When I stood by my first-born, and closed his eyes in death, I could say, "The Lord gave, and the

Lord hath taken away; blessed be the name of the Lord." And I felt then that I had a comforter in Jesus. And when my latest born was torn from my arms, and I could no longer see its little head upon the pillow by my side, then I could say, "The Lord gave, and the Lord hath taken away; blessed be the name of the Lord." And when he upon whose large affections I had leaned, with whom I had labored for thirty-five years, was taken away, I could lay my hands upon his eyes, and say, "I commit my treasure to Thee until the morning of the resurrection."

When I saw him passing away, and saw the many friends sympathizing with me, I thought: What a contrast to the death of Jesus as He hung upon the cross! What a contrast! In the hour of His agony, the revilers were mocking and deriding Him. But He died, and He passed through the tomb to brighten it, and to lighten it, that we might have joy and hope even in the event of death; that we might say, as we lay our friends away to rest in Jesus, "We shall meet them again."

At times I felt that I could not have my husband die. But these words seemed to be impressed on my mind: "Be still, and know that I am God." Ps. 46:10. I keenly feel my loss, but dare not give myself up to useless grief. This would not bring back the dead. And I am not so selfish as to wish, if I could, to bring him from his peaceful slumber to engage again in the battles of life. Like a tired warrior, he has lain down to sleep. I will look with pleasure upon his resting place. The best way in which I and my children can honor the memory of him who has fallen, is to take the work where he left it, and in the strength of Jesus carry it forward to completion. We will be thankful for the years of usefulness that were granted to him; and for his sake, and for Christ's sake, we will learn from his death a lesson which we shall never forget. We will let this bereavement make us more kind and gentle, more forbearing, patient, and thoughtful toward the living.

I take up my life work alone, in full confidence that my Redeemer will be with me. We have only a little while to wage the warfare; then Christ will come, and this scene of conflict will close. Then our last efforts will have been made to work with Christ, and advance His kingdom. Some who have stood in the forefront of the battle, zealously resisting incoming evil, fall at the post of duty; the living gaze sorrowfully at the fallen heroes, but there is no time to cease work. They must close up the ranks, seize the banner from the hand palsied by death, and with renewed energy vindicate the truth and the honor of Christ.

As never before, resistance must be made against sin — against the powers of darkness. The time demands energetic and determined activity on the part of those who believe present truth. If the time seems long to wait for our Deliverer to come; if, bowed by affliction and worn with toil, we feel impatient to receive an honorable release from the warfare, let us remember — and let the remembrance check every murmur — that we are left on earth to encounter storms and conflicts, to perfect Christian character, to become better acquainted with God our Father, and Christ our elder Brother, and to do work for the Master in winning many souls to Christ. "They that be wise shall shine as the brightness of the firmament; and they that turn many to righteousness as the stars forever and ever." Dan. 12:3.

XLII

FORTITUDE UNDER AFFLICTION

Sabbath afternoon, Aug. 20, 1881, two weeks after the death of her husband, Mrs. White met with the Battle Creek church, and spoke to the people for nearly an hour. Reporting this service, Elder Uriah Smith wrote:

"Her theme was the lesson we are to learn from the recent experience through which we have passed. The uncertainty of life is the thought first impressed upon us. . . . We should also consider what manner of persons we ought to be while we live. . . .

"The speaker's mind then turned to those blessed exhortations of the apostles in reference to the relation which the members of the body of Christ should sustain one to another, and their bearing, words, and actions toward one another. We were pointed to such passages as these: 'Be at peace among yourselves;' 'be kindly affectioned one to another;' 'be kind;' 'be courteous;' 'speak the same thing;' 'be perfectly joined together in the same mind and in the same judgment;' 'speak not evil one of another;' 'live in peace; and the God of love and peace shall be with you.' "[1]

PERSONAL REFLECTIONS

Regarding her journey westward, en route to California, and her reflections while tarrying a few weeks at her summer retreat in the Rocky Mountains, Mrs. White wrote:

"August 22, in company with my daughters, Emma and Mary White, I left Battle Creek for the West, hoping to receive benefit from a change of climate.

[1] *Review and Herald*, Aug. 23, 1881.

Though still suffering from the effects of a severe attack of malarial fever, as well as from the shock of my husband's death, I endured the journey better than I had expected. We reached Boulder, Colo., on Thursday, August 25, and on the following Sunday left that place by private carriage for our home in the mountains.

"From our cottage I could look out upon a forest of young pines, so fresh and fragrant that the air was perfumed with their spicy odor. In former years, my husband and myself made this grove our sanctuary. Among these mountains we often bowed together in worship and supplication. All around me were the places which had been thus hallowed; and as I gazed upon them, I could recall many instances in which we there received direct and remarkable answers to prayer. . . .

"How near we seemed to God, as in the clear moonlight we bowed upon some lonely mountain side to ask for needed blessings at His hand! What faith and confidence were ours! God's purposes of love and mercy seemed more fully revealed, and we felt the assurance that our sins and errors were pardoned. Upon such occasions I have seen my husband's countenance lighted up with a radiance that seemed reflected from the throne of God, as in changed voice he praised the Lord for the rich blessings of His grace. Amid earth's gloom and darkness, we could still discern on every hand gleams of brightness from the Fount of light. Through the works of creation we communed with Him who inhabiteth eternity. As we looked upon the towering rocks, the lofty mountains, we exclaimed, 'Who is so great a God as our God?'

"Surrounded, as we often were, with difficulties, burdened with responsibilities, finite, weak, erring mortals at best, we were at times almost ready to yield to despair. But when we considered God's love and care for His creatures, as revealed both in the book of nature and on the pages of inspiration, our hearts were comforted and strengthened. Surrounded by the evidences of God's power and overshadowed by His presence, we could not cherish distrust or unbelief. Oh, how often have peace, and hope, and even joy, come to us in our experience amid these rocky solitudes!

"Again I have been among the mountains, but alone. None to share my thoughts and feelings as I looked once more upon those grand and awful scenes! Alone, alone! God's dealings seem mysterious, His purposes unfathomable; yet I know that they must be just, and wise, and merciful. It is my privilege and my duty to wait patiently for Him, the language of my heart at all times being, 'He doeth all things well.' . . .

"My husband's death was a heavy blow to me, more keenly felt because so sudden. As I saw the seal of death upon his countenance, my feelings were almost insupportable. I longed to cry out in my anguish. But I knew that this could not save the life of my loved one, and I felt that it would be unchristian to give myself up to sorrow. I sought help and comfort from above, and the promises of God were verified to me. The Lord's hand sustained me. . . .

"Let us learn a lesson of courage and fortitude from the last interview of Christ with His apostles. They were about to be separated. Our Saviour was entering the bloodstained path which would lead Him to Calvary. Never was scene more trying than that through which He was soon to pass. The apostles had heard the words of Christ foretelling His sufferings and death, and their hearts were heavy with sorrow, their minds distracted with doubt and fear. Yet there were no loud outcries; there was no abandonment of grief. Those last solemn, momentous hours were spent by our Saviour in speaking words of comfort and assurance to His disciples, and then all united in a hymn of praise. . . . What a prelude to the agony in Gethsemane, the abuse and mockery of the judgment hall, and the awful scenes of Calvary, were those last hours spent in chanting the praises of the Most High!

"When Martin Luther received discouraging news, he would often say, 'Come, let us sing the forty-sixth psalm.' This psalm commences with the words: 'God is our refuge and strength, a very present help in trouble. Therefore will not we fear, though the earth be removed, and though the mountains be carried into the midst of the sea.' Instead of mourning, weeping, and despairing, when troubles gather about us like a flood and threaten to overwhelm us, if we would not only pray for help from God, but would praise Him for so many blessings left,—praise Him that He is able to help us,—our course would be more pleasing to Him, and we would see more of His salvation."[2]

FINDING REST IN LABOR FOR SOULS

Scarcely a week passed following her arrival at the home of her son, Elder W. C. White, in Oakland, Cal., before Mrs. White attended a camp meeting held in Sacramento, October 13-25. On nearly every day of the meeting she spoke to the people, and during the

---

[2] *Review and Herald,* Nov. 1, 1881.

last Sunday afternoon gave a temperance address to an audience numbering upwards of five thousand.

Often during the winter months of 1881-82, Mrs. White met with local churches and small companies of believers in Sonoma and Napa valleys and vicinity. "I was in feeble health," she wrote in her first published report of these labors among the churches; "but the precious evidence of the favor of God more than repaid me for the effort made.

"Would that our smaller churches could be more often visited. The faithful ones, who stand firmly in defense of the truth, would be cheered and strengthened by the testimony of their brethren.

"I would encourage those who assemble in little companies to worship God. Brethren and sisters, be not disheartened because you are so few in number. The tree that stands alone upon the plain, strikes its roots deeper into the earth, spreads out its branches farther on every side, and grows stronger and more symmetrical while wrestling singly with the tempest or rejoicing in the sunshine. So the Christian, cut off from earthly dependence, may learn to rely wholly upon God, and may gain strength and courage from every conflict.

"May the Lord bless the scattered and lonely ones, and make them efficient workers for Him. . . . Brethren, do not forget the wants of these small and isolated companies. Christ will be found a guest at their little gatherings."[3]

In a report concerning her labors in the church at Healdsburg, where a few weeks later a beginning was made in the establishment of Healdsburg College, Mrs. White wrote particularly of her effort to reach the

[3] *Signs of the Times,* Jan. 12, 1882.

hearts of the children and youth — a marked feature of her labors in the California churches at this period of her experience:

SPECIAL EFFORTS FOR THE YOUTH

"On the Sabbath I attended meeting, trusting in God for support. In speaking to the church, I was comforted and refreshed. The Lord gave me peace and rest in Him. I felt burdened for the youth, and my words were addressed especially to them. They listened attentively, with serious faces and tearful eyes. At the close of my remarks I requested all who wished to become Christians to come forward. Thirteen responded. These were all children and youth, from eight to fifteen years of age, who thus manifested their determination to begin a new life. Such a sight was enough to soften the hardest heart. The brethren and sisters, especially the parents of the children, seemed to feel deeply. Christ has told us that there is joy in heaven over one sinner that repenteth. Angels were looking with gladness upon this scene. Nearly all who came forward spoke in a few words their hope and determination. Such testimonies ascend like incense to the throne of God. All hearts felt that this was a precious season. The presence of God was with us."[4]

---

[4] *Signs of the Times,* Jan. 19, 1882.

XLIII

RESTORATION OF HEALTH

In April, 1882, the California Conference opened a school in Healdsburg, which was soon incorporated as the Healdsburg College. Desiring to be near this institution, Mrs. White purchased a home on the outskirts of the town, and made this her residence for several years.

One year after her husband's death, she was at this new home, and friends remarked about how well she appeared, and spoke of her active labors.

August 22 she went to Oakland to welcome from the East Elder Uriah Smith, Elder and Mrs. Wm. Ings, and Prof. C. C. Ramsey and family. Three days later, at the home of her son, W. C. White, she had a severe chill, followed with fever, and notwithstanding thorough treatments by Mrs. Dr. C. F. Young, and faithful nursing by Mrs. Ings and Mary Chinnock, the malarial chills continued till September 10. Although very weak, she desired to be taken to the St. Helena Sanitarium, believing that the superior climate of the mountains would be favorable to her recovery.

September 15 the journey was made in a wheel chair, which was lifted into the baggage car at the station. After a few days of treatment at the Sanitarium, without any apparent benefit, she pleaded to be taken to her home in Healdsburg. A bed was arranged in a spring wagon, and, accompanied by her son and Mrs. Ings, she accomplished the wearisome journey of thirty-five miles.

The annual camp meeting of the California Conference was to be held at Healdsburg October 6-16.

At this meeting important decisions were to be made regarding the work of the Healdsburg College. Would our people rally to its support, and make liberal gifts for the building of the students' home? or would the work of the school be crippled for lack of proper facilities?

Mrs. White greatly desired health and vigor, that she might attend the meeting and bear her testimony; but the outlook was discouraging. She had a bad cough, and her left lung was very sore. She was weak, and without energy or courage. Nevertheless she said, "Prepare me a place at the meeting, for I shall attend if possible." She expressed the hope that when she got on the camp ground there would be some reviving influence.

Sabbath forenoon she was very feeble, hardly able to leave her bed. But at noon she said: "Prepare me a place in the large tent where I can hear the speaker. Possibly the sound of the speaker's voice will prove a blessing to me. I am hoping for something to bring new life."

A sofa was arranged for her near the speaker's stand, with its back toward the congregation. Elder Waggoner spoke on the rise and early work of the message, and its progress up to 1882. There was a large congregation, and several of the business men of Healdsburg were present. When Elder Waggoner had finished speaking, Mrs. White said, "Help me onto my feet." Sister Ings and her son lifted her up, and she was led to the desk. Laying hold of the pulpit with both hands, she began, in a feeble way, to tell the people that this might be the last time they would hear her voice at camp meeting. After she had spoken a few sentences, there was a change in her voice and attitude. She felt a thrill of healing power.

Her voice strengthened, and her sentences came clear and full. As she proceeded with her address, her strength was manifest. She stood firmly, and did not need to hold onto the desk for support.

The large congregation witnessed the healing. All noticed the change in her voice, and many observed the change in her countenance. They saw the sudden transition from a deathlike paleness to the flush of health, as the natural color was seen, first in her neck, then in the lower part of the face, and then in the forehead. One of the business men of Healdsburg exclaimed, "A miracle is being wrought in sight of this whole congregation!" After the meeting she testified to inquiring friends that the Lord had healed her. With the healing came strength and courage to labor, and during the remainder of the meeting she spoke five times.

In the *Signs of the Times* of Oct. 26, 1882, the editor, Elder J. H. Waggoner, relating this experience, said:

"At the close of the discourse [Sabbath afternoon], . . . she arose and began to address the people. Her voice and appearance changed, and she spoke for some time with clearness and energy. She then invited those who wished to make a start in the service of God, and those who were far backslidden, to come forward, and a goodly number answered the call. . . .

"After the first attempt of Sister White to speak, as noticed above, her restoration was complete."

Regarding the miracle wrought in her behalf, Mrs. White herself testified in the *Signs* of Nov. 2, 1882:

"For two months my pen has been resting; but I am deeply grateful that I am now able to resume my writing. The Lord has given me an additional evidence of His mercy and loving-kindness by again restoring me to health. By my recent illness I was brought very near to the grave; but the prayers of the Lord's people availed in my behalf.

"About two weeks before our camp meeting the disease from which I had been suffering was checked, yet I gained little strength. As the time for the meeting drew near, it seemed impossible that I could take any part in it. . . . I prayed much over the matter, but still remained very feeble. . . . In my suffering condition I could only fall helpless into the arms of my Redeemer, and there rest.

"When the first Sabbath of the meeting came, I felt that I must be upon the camp ground, for I might there meet the divine Healer. In the afternoon I lay upon a lounge under the large tent, while Elder Waggoner addressed the people, presenting the signs that show the day of God very near. At the close of his discourse, I decided to rise to my feet, hoping that if I thus ventured out by faith, doing all in my power, God would help me to say a few words to the people. As I began to speak, the power of God came upon me, and my strength was instantly restored.

"I had hoped that my feebleness might gradually pass away, but had looked for no immediate change. The instantaneous work wrought for me was unexpected. It cannot be attributed to imagination. The people saw me in my feebleness, and many remarked that to all appearance I was a candidate for the grave. Nearly all present marked the change which took place in me while I was addressing them. They stated that my countenance changed, and the deathlike paleness gave place to a healthy color.

"I testify to all who read these words, that the Lord has healed me. Divine power has wrought a great work for me, whereof I am glad. I was able to labor every day during the meeting, and several times spoke more than one hour and a half. My whole system was imbued with new strength and vigor. A new tide of emotions, a new and elevated faith, took possession of my soul.

"During my sickness I learned some precious lessons,—learned to trust where I cannot see; while unable to do anything, to rest quietly, calmly, in the arms of Jesus. We do not exercise faith as we should. We are afraid to venture upon the word of God. In the hour of trial, we should strengthen our souls with the assurance that God's promises can never fail. Whatever He has spoken, will be done. . . .

"Before my sickness, I thought that I had faith in the promises of God; yet I find myself surprised at the great change wrought in me, so far exceeding my expectations. I am unworthy of this manifestation of the love of God. I have reason to praise God more earnestly, to walk in greater humility before Him, and to love Him more fervently than ever before. I am placed under renewed obligation to give to the Lord all that there is of me. I must shed upon others the blessed radiance which He has permitted to shine upon me.

"I do not now expect to be lifted above all infirmities and tribulations, and to have an unruffled sea on the journey heavenward. I expect trials, losses, disappointments, and bereavements; but I have the Saviour's promise, 'My grace is sufficient for thee.' We must not count it a strange thing if we are assaulted by the enemy of all righteousness. Christ has promised to be a present help in every time of need; but He has not told us that we shall be exempt from trials. On the contrary, He has plainly informed us that we shall have tribulation. To be tried and tested is a part of our moral discipline. Here we may learn the most valuable lessons, and obtain the most precious graces, if we will draw near to God, and endure all in His strength.

"My sickness has taught me my own weakness, and my Saviour's patience and love, and His power to save. When passing sleepless nights, I have found hope and comfort in considering the forbearance and tenderness of Jesus toward His weak, erring disciples, and remembering that He is still the same,— unchangeable in mercy, compassion, and love. He sees our weakness, He knows how we lack faith and courage; yet He does not cast us off. He is pitiful and of tender compassion toward us.

"I may fall at my post before the Lord shall come; but when all that are in their graves shall come forth, I shall, if faithful, see Jesus, and be made like Him. Oh, what joy unspeakable, to see Him whom we love,— to see Him in His glory who so loved us that He gave Himself for us,— to behold those hands once pierced for our redemption, stretched out to us in blessing and welcome! What will it matter though we toil and suffer here, if we may only attain to the resurrection of life! We will patiently wait till our time of trial ends, and then we shall raise the glad shout of victory."

XLIV

WRITING AND SPEAKING

"From Washington Territory and from the East," wrote Mrs. White from her Healdsburg, Cal., home March 26, 1883, "come urgent requests that I attend the camp meetings. . . . I am now engaged in important writing that I have for six years been trying to accomplish. Year after year I have broken away from this work to attend camp meetings. . . .

"The last two summers I was brought very near to the gates of death, and as I felt that it might please the Lord to let me rest in the grave, I had most painful regrets that my writings were not completed. In the providence of God my life is spared, and my health once more restored. I thank the Lord for His mercy and loving-kindness to me. I have felt ready to go east or west, if my duty were made plain; but in answer to my prayer, 'Lord, what wilt Thou have me to do?' the answer comes to me, 'Rest in peace until the Lord bids you go.'

"I have not been idle. Since the Lord raised me up at the camp meeting in Healdsburg, I have visited Santa Rosa, Oakland, San Francisco, Petaluma, Forestville, and Ukiah, and have labored in Healdsburg, frequently speaking on the Sabbath and on Sunday evening. In four weeks I gave ten discourses, traveled two hundred miles, and wrote two hundred pages. . . .

"My brethren who urge me to attend camp meeting and to visit them are anxiously inquiring, 'When shall we have Volume 4, "Spirit of Prophecy?"' I can now answer them. In a few weeks my work on this book will be completed. But there are other important works that require attention as soon as this shall be finished. . . . While I have physical and mental ability, I will do the work which is most needed by our people. . . . I have, when traveling, labored at great disadvantage. I have written in the depot, on the cars, under my tent at camp meeting, often speaking until exhausted, and then rising at three o'clock in the morning and writing from six to fifteen pages before breakfast. . . .

"It would give me great pleasure to meet my dear brethren and sisters in camp meeting. I feel the love of Jesus burning in my soul. I love to talk this out and to write it out. My prayers shall be, that God may bless you at your camp meetings, and that your souls may be refreshed by His grace. If God bids me leave my writing to attend these meetings or to speak to the people in different places, I hope to hear and obey His voice."[1]

During the spring and summer of 1883, Mrs. White spent much time in an effort to complete Volume 4 of "Spirit of Prophecy," known in later years as "Great Controversy." Not until early August did she break away from her writing to attend some of the fall camp meetings in the East, and the General Conference session following. Of these public labors in 1883, she wrote:

VISIT TO BATTLE CREEK

"Sunday, August 12, in company with Sister Sara McEnterfer, I left the Pacific coast on my way to the East. Although we suffered considerably from heat and dust, we had a pleasant journey across the plains. We found conductor and porters ready to do all in their power for our comfort and convenience.

"From the time that we stepped on board the train,

[1] *Signs of the Times,* April 5, 1883.

I felt perfectly satisfied that I was in the way of duty. I have had sweet communion with my Saviour, and have felt that He is my refuge and my fortress, and that no harm can come to me while engaged in the work which He has given me to do. I have an abiding trust in the promises of God, and enjoy that peace which comes only from Jesus. . . .

"We reached Battle Creek on Friday, August 17. The following night I found it impossible to sleep. I had not visited this place since I left it in great feebleness after my husband's funeral. Now the great loss which the cause had sustained in his death, the great loss which I had sustained in being deprived of his society and assistance in my work, came up vividly before me, and I could not compose myself to sleep. I recalled the covenant which I had made with God at my husband's deathbed,—that I would not become discouraged under the burden, but would labor more earnestly and devotedly than ever before to present the truth both by pen and voice; that I would set before the people the excellence of the statutes and precepts of Jehovah, and would point them to the cleansing fountain where we may wash away every stain of sin.

"All night I wrestled with God in prayer that He would give me strength for my work, and imbue me with His Spirit, that I might keep my solemn covenant. I desired nothing so much as to spend my time and strength in urging those who profess the truth to come into closer relationship with God, that they may enjoy more perfect communion with Him than did ancient Israel in their most prosperous days.

"Sabbath morning I spoke to the large congregation assembled in the Tabernacle. The Lord gave me strength and freedom as I presented the words found in Rev. 7:9-17. . .

THE PATH OF OBEDIENCE

"On Sunday morning I spoke to about seventy-five of the workers connected with the Office of the *Review and Herald*. One week before, August 12, I had stood before a similar company at the Pacific Press, and urged upon them the importance of acting from principle. Now I presented the same subject, admonishing all to allow nothing to sway them from the right. I warned them that they would have opposing influences to meet, and would be pressed by temptations, and every one who was not rooted and grounded in the truth would be moved from the sure foundation. . . .

"Sunday evening, August 19, I spoke by invitation at the Sanitarium. . . . I addressed the crowded congregation from the words: 'He that will love life, and see good days, let him refrain his tongue from evil, and his lips that they speak no guile: let him eschew evil, and do good; let him seek peace, and ensue it. For the eyes of the Lord are over the righteous, and His ears are open unto their prayers: but the face of the Lord is against them that do evil.' 1 Peter 3:10-12. . . .

"The path of obedience to God is the path of virtue, of health and happiness. The plan of salvation, as revealed in the Holy Scriptures, opens up a way whereby man may secure happiness and prolong his days upon the earth, as well as enjoy the favor of heaven, and secure that future life which measures with the life of God. . . .

"The assurance of God's approval will promote physical health. It fortifies the soul against doubt, perplexity, and excessive grief, that so often sap the vital forces and induce nervous diseases of a most debilitating and distressing character. The Lord has pledged His unfailing word that His eye shall be over the righteous, and His ear open to their prayer. . . .

"Monday evening, August 20, I spoke again to those employed at the Review Office. . . .

"There are some, even connected with our institutions, who are in great danger of making shipwreck of faith. Satan will work in disguise, in his most deceptive manner, in these branches of God's work. He makes these important instrumentalities his special points of attack, and he will leave no means untried to cripple their usefulness. . . . In these days of peril we should be exceedingly careful not to reject the rays of light which heaven in mercy sends us; for it is by these that we are to discern the devices of the enemy. We need light from heaven every hour, that we may distinguish between the sacred and the common, the eternal and the temporal.

"All who remain pure and uncorrupted from the spirit and influence prevailing at this time, will have stern conflicts. They will come through great tribulation; they will wash their robes of character, and make them white in the blood of the Lamb. These will sing the song of triumph in the kingdom of glory. Those who suffer with Christ will be partakers of His glory."[2]

RIPENING FOR THE HARVEST

"The camp meeting at Worcester, Mass., August 22-28, . . . was an occasion of special interest to me. I there met a large number of believers, some of whom have been connected with the work from the

[2] *Review and Herald,* Oct. 16, 1883.

very rise of the third angel's message. Since our last camp meeting, Brother Hastings, one of the faithful standard bearers, had fallen at his post. I felt sad as I saw others weighed down by the infirmities of age, yet I was glad to see them eagerly listening to the words of life. The love of God and His truth seemed to glow in their hearts and to light up their countenances. Their eyes were often filled with tears, not of sorrow but of joy, as they heard the message from God by the mouth of His servants. These aged pilgrims were present at nearly all the meetings; as if they feared that, like Thomas, they might be absent when Jesus should come in, and say, 'Peace be unto you.'

"Like ripening grain these precious tried and faithful ones are fitting for the harvest. Their work is nearly done. They may be permitted to remain till Christ shall be revealed in the clouds of heaven with power and great glory. They may drop out of the ranks at any time, and sleep in Jesus. But while darkness covers the earth and gross darkness the people, these children of the light can lift up their heads and rejoice, knowing that their redemption draweth nigh. . . .

LAY MEMBERS AS MISSIONARIES FOR GOD

"As I looked over the congregation of believers, and marked the serious, earnest expression upon their countenances, . . . my eyes rested upon not a few who had a knowledge of the truth, and who, if this knowledge were but sanctified, might accomplish a work for God. I thought: If all these realized their accountability to God and their duty to their fellow men, and would work as the Lord has given them ability, what a light would shine forth from them in

Portland Oregon June 17/84.

Dear Bro and Sister Smith I have received an urgent letter from Bro. Haskell to come to the important meetings east, I would be glad to go but as I look over the work that must be done I cannot see any consistency in my going east this ~~fall~~ summer. I have been very much exhausted but this would not deter me from going, if I could see it to be duty I have not been able to discover duty in going east up to this time, Marian and Eliza ~~to~~ are the best help I could have and appreciated highly by me there are many works I wish to complete, if I went east I would have to return in the winter to do the very work that I should leave undone in the spring Willie and I will go east in May to remain one year and perhaps two years.

The meeting closed up well in Walla Walla it was a success and a great change has taken place in the feelings of the upper Columbia conference, Sunday, I spoke upon the subject of temperance If ever the Lord helped me he did at this time I was free and free indeed the Lord let the power of his spirit rest upon me

Ellen G White

Photographic facsimile of a letter written by Mrs. White, June 17, 1884, to Elder and Mrs. Uriah Smith, in which she expresses her hesitancy over attending the Eastern camp meetings, because of the press of book work.

Massachusetts, and even extend to other States! If every one who has professed faith in the third angel's message would make the word of God his rule of action, and with strict fidelity perform his work as a servant of Christ, this people would be a power in the world.

"It is not alone those who labor in word and doctrine who are responsible for souls. Every man and every woman who has a knowledge of the truth should be a coworker with Christ. . . . He requires the lay members to act as missionaries. Brethren, go out with your Bibles, visit the people at their firesides, read the word of God to the family, and as many more as will come in. Go with a contrite heart and an abiding trust in God's grace and mercy, and do what you can. . . .

"There are men who never gave a discourse in their lives, who ought to be laboring to save souls. Neither great talents nor high position is required. But there is urgent need of men and women who are acquainted with Jesus, and familiar with the story of His life and death. . . .

"We do not need eminent men so much as good, true, and humble men. God calls for those of all classes and all trades to work in His cause. Those are wanted who will begin at the lower rounds of the ladder, who will, if need be, eat their own bread and quietly perform their duty; men who will not shrink from diligent labor to acquire means, or from rigid economy in its expenditure, and who will devote both time and means to work for the Master in their own families and their own neighborhoods. If the work of reformation be begun and carried forward in each family, there will be a living and prosperous church. Things must first be set in order at home.

The cause needs those who can work at home, who will study the Bible and practise its teachings, and who will train up their children in the fear of God. Then let diligent, persevering effort be put forth for others, with earnest prayer for the aid of divine grace and power, and great results will follow missionary labor.

"No matter who you are, it is the mind, the heart, the sincere purpose, and the daily life that mark the value of the man. Restless, talkative, dictatorial men are not needed in this work. There are too many of them springing up everywhere. Many youth who have but little experience, push themselves forward, manifest no reverence for age or office, and take offense if counseled or reproved. We have already more of these self-important ones than we want. God calls for modest, quiet, sober-minded youth, and men of mature age, who are well balanced with principle, who can pray as well as talk, who will rise up before the aged, and treat gray hairs with respect.

"The cause of God is suffering for want of laborers of understanding and mental power. My brethren and sisters, the Lord has blessed you with intellectual faculties capable of vast improvement. Cultivate your talents with persevering earnestness. Train and discipline the mind by study, by observation, by reflection. You cannot meet the mind of God unless you put to use every power. The mental faculties will strengthen and develop if you will go to work in the fear of God, in humility, and with earnest prayer. A resolute purpose will accomplish wonders. Be open, firm, decided Christians. Exalt Jesus, talk of His love, tell of His power, and thus let your light shine forth to the world."[3]

[3] *Review and Herald*, Nov. 13, 1883.

AN EXAMPLE OF SELF-SACRIFICE

"I was glad of the privilege of attending the Vermont camp meeting, which was held in Montpelier, August 30 to September 4. . . . My mind was carried back thirty years, to the time when, in company with my sister, I visited Fairhaven, Mass., to bear my message to the little company in that place. Elder Bates was then living there, and expressed his conviction that it was his duty to visit Vermont, and preach the truth in that State. But he added: 'I have no means, and cannot tell where the money is coming from to take me there. I think I will walk out by faith, start on foot, and go as far as God will give me strength.' My sister said to me: 'I think the Lord will help me to open the way for Elder Bates to go to Vermont. Sister F. is looking for a girl to do her housework, and . . . I will earn the money necessary.' She carried out her purpose, and, requesting her pay in advance, placed the money in Elder Bates's hand. He started the next morning, and my sister remained to work for a dollar and a quarter a week. Quite a number were brought into the truth in Vermont, and Elder Bates returned with great joy because the Lord had indeed blessed his labors. . . .

FILLING UP THE RANKS OF WORKERS

"As I looked in the faces of the tried ones who are precious in the sight of the Lord, and saw that some of them seemed almost ready to lay off their armor, . . . the question arose in my mind: Who are coming up to take the places of these aged, worn soldiers of the cross? Who will consecrate themselves to the work of God? . . . Where are those who have the knowledge of the truth, and who love Jesus and the souls for whom He died well enough to deny self, to choose the suffering part of religion, and to go without the camp, bearing the reproach of Christ? . . .

"Who will put to use the talents lent them of God, be they great or small, and work in humility, learning daily in the school of Christ, and then imparting that precious knowledge to others? Who will see what ought to be done, and do it? And how many will make excuses, become tied up with worldly interests? Cut the cords that bind you, and go into the vineyard to work for the Master.

"In every department of the cause of God, consecrated, God-fearing, willing helpers are needed; men of brains, men of intellect, who will go forth as ministers, canvassers, and colporteurs. Brethren and sisters, let the earnest prayer of faith ascend to God that He will raise up laborers, and send them into the harvest field; for the harvest is great, and the laborers are few."[4]

ESTABLISHING FAITH IN BIBLE TRUTH

"I attended the camp meeting held at Waterville, Maine, September 6-11. Here in my native State I met dear brethren and sisters whose interest has for years been identified with the cause and work of present truth. . . . We had some very precious seasons at this camp meeting. Many cheering testimonies were borne; but there was not that thorough work which we greatly desired to have accomplished. . . . There is a kind of faith that takes it for granted that we have the truth; but the faith that takes God

---

[4] *Review and Herald,* Nov. 20, 1883.

at His word, which works by love and purifies the heart, is very rare."

"In His word, God has revealed saving truths. As a people we should be earnest students of prophecy; we should not rest until we become intelligent in regard to the subject of the sanctuary, which is brought out in the visions of Daniel and John. This subject sheds great light on our present position and work, and gives us unmistakable proof that God has led us in our past experience. It explains our disappointment in 1844, showing us that the sanctuary to be cleansed was not the earth, as we had supposed, but that Christ then entered into the most holy apartment of the heavenly sanctuary, and is there performing the closing work of His priestly office, in fulfillment of the words of the angel to the prophet Daniel, 'Unto two thousand and three hundred days; then shall the sanctuary be cleansed.' Dan. 8:14.

"Our faith in reference to the messages of the first, second, and third angels was correct. The great way marks we have passed are immovable. Although the hosts of hell may try to tear them from their foundation, and triumph in the thought that they have succeeded, yet they do not succeed. These pillars of truth stand firm as the eternal hills, unmoved by all the efforts of men combined with those of Satan and his host. We can learn much, and should be constantly searching the Scriptures to see if these things are so. God's people are now to have their eyes fixed on the heavenly sanctuary, where the final ministration of our great High Priest in the work of the judgment is going forward,— where He is interceding for His people."[5]

---

[5] *Review and Herald*, Nov. 27, 1883.

THE GENERAL CONFERENCE OF 1883

The fall camp meetings were followed by the twenty-second annual session of the General Conference, during which Mrs. White gave many "morning talks" to the ministers, published first in the *Review,* and later in the 1893 edition of "Gospel Workers." Concerning the Conference, Mrs. White reported:

"The meetings at Battle Creek were fraught with deeper interest than similar meetings ever held among our people. Many prayers had ascended to heaven in behalf of this session of the General Conference; and we can testify that Jesus came up to the feast, and was an honored guest at this important gathering. The Bible readings afforded valuable instruction to ministers, licentiates, and people. The morning meetings, designed especially for the benefit of ministers and other workers in the cause of God, were intensely interesting. Faith and love were awakened in many hearts. Spiritual and eternal things became a reality, and not a mere sentiment; a glorious substance, and not a fitful shadow. This precious meeting is in the past, but its results are to be seen in the future. We shall never know the good accomplished during the twenty days of its continuance until we meet around the great white throne."[6]

CLOSING LABORS IN THE EAST

Appointments were out for a ten days' Bible and Missionary Institute at South Lancaster, Mass., and a general meeting for the believers in the Pennsylvania Conference at Wellsville, N. Y. These Mrs. White was persuaded to attend, and upon her return

[6]*Review and Herald,* Jan. 15, 1884.

to Battle Creek she spoke on Friday night to the helpers at the Sanitarium, and on Sabbath day to a large congregation in the Tabernacle.

"These were my closing labors in the East on this journey," wrote Mrs. White of the Bible Institutes attended; "and I have to say to the praise of God, that He has sustained me at every step. I have prayed in the night season; and in the day, when traveling, I have been pleading with God for strength, for grace, for light from His presence; and I know in whom I have believed. I return to California with more strength and better courage than I had when I left Oakland the 12th of August.[7]

"I desire the love of Jesus as I never desired it before. I see reason to praise God for His goodness, His preserving care, and for the sweet peace, joy, and courage He gave me on this journey. I started out by faith, and not by sight; and I have seen the hand of God in every day's labor, and daily His praise has been in my heart and on my lips. His Spirit has helped my infirmities in so marked a manner that I cannot fear to commit myself to His keeping. I have the perfect assurance of His love. He has heard and answered my prayers, and I will praise Him."[8]

---

[7] Mrs. White reached her Healdsburg home Dec. 30, 1883, having been absent nearly five months.

[8] *Review and Herald,* Feb. 5, 1884.

XLV

LABORS IN CENTRAL EUROPE

The second session of the European Missionary Council was held in Basel, Switzerland, May 28 to June 1, 1884, Elder George I. Butler, from America, presiding. At this meeting, resolutions were adopted, requesting the General Conference to ask Mrs. E. G. White and her son, W. C. White, to visit the European missions. At the General Conference held in Battle Creek, Mich., the following November, the request was acted upon, and they were recommended to go.

In harmony with this action, Mrs. White and her secretary, Miss Sara McEnterfer, and W. C. White and his family, left America August 8, 1885, sailing from Boston on the steamer *Cephalonia,* and arriving in Liverpool August 19. Two weeks were spent in England, visiting companies of Sabbath keepers at Grimsby, Ulceby, Riseley, and Southampton. Several addresses were given in public halls.

Leaving London September 2, the party arrived in Basel, Switzerland, the following morning. Here the annual meeting of the Swiss Conference and the third session of the European Missionary Council were soon to be held.

THE "IMPRIMERIE POLYGLOTTE"

The Basel publishing house, afterward named the "Imprimerie Polyglotte" (the printing house of many languages), was just completed. The land had been secured and the building planned during the visit of Elder Butler early in 1884. The structure had been erected under the watchful supervision of Elder

B. L. Whitney, the superintendent of the European Mission; and its equipment had been purchased and installed by Brother H. W. Kellogg, for many years the manager of the Review and Herald Publishing Association at Battle Creek, Mich.

The new publishing house was a large, substantial building, 46x76 feet, with four stories above the basement. The upper stories were so constructed that, until required by the growth of the business, they could be used as residence suites for families. It was in one of these suites that Mrs. White made her home during a greater part of the two years she spent in Europe.

PUBLISHING HOUSES IN MANY LANDS

When Mrs. White and her party reached the publishing house, Elder Whitney said, "Look at our meeting-hall before going upstairs." It was a fine room on the first floor, well lighted and well furnished. Mrs. White looked searchingly at all features of the place, and then said: "It is a good meeting-hall. I feel that I have seen this place before."

Not long after this, those parts of the building occupied by the printing business were visited. When the pressroom was reached, the press was running, and Mrs. White said: "I have seen this press before. This room looks very familiar to me." Soon the two young men who were working in the pressroom came forward, and were introduced to the visitors. Mrs. White shook hands with them, and then inquired, "Where is the other one?"

"What other one?" Elder Whitney asked.

"There is an older man here," Mrs. White replied, "and I have a message for him."

Elder Whitney explained that the foreman of the pressroom was in the city on business.

It had been a little more than ten years since Mrs. White, in relating before a large audience in the Battle Creek church what had been shown her in vision regarding the work to be done in many foreign lands, had said that she had seen printing presses running in many foreign countries, printing periodicals and tracts and books on present truth for the people of these countries. At this point in her narrative, Elder James White had interrupted her, asking if she could name some of these countries. She said she could not, because they had not been named to her, "except one; I remember the angel said Australia." But she stated that although she could not name the countries, she would recognize the places should she ever see them, because the picture was very distinct in her mind.

In the pressroom of the new publishing house at Basel she recognized one of these places. A few months after this, during her visit to Norway, she recognized in the pressroom of the Christiania publishing house another of these places; and six years later, during her visit to Australia, she saw, in the Bible Echo Office in Melbourne, still another pressroom where she recognized the place and the presses as among those she had seen in the vision at Battle Creek, Jan. 3, 1875.

THE SALE OF LITERATURE

The Swiss Conference was held Sept. 10-14, 1885. There were about two hundred in attendance. This meeting was immediately followed by the European Missionary Council, which continued for two weeks.

At these meetings very interesting reports were received from Scandinavia, Great Britain, Germany, France, Italy, and Switzerland, where the cause of present truth was beginning to gain a foothold. The reports elicited some animated discussions of such subjects as these: The most effective plans for the circulation of our literature; the illustrating of our periodicals and books; the use of tents; and the bearing of arms.

The Scandinavian brethren reported that the sales of literature in their conferences during the preceding fiscal year had amounted to $1,033. The delegates from Great Britain reported sales amounting to $550. The Basel office had received on its German and French periodicals $1,010.

Much time was occupied by the colporteurs who had been laboring in Catholic Europe, in relating their experiences and in telling the Council why our literature could not be sold in Europe on the plans that were very successfully followed in America; and it was urged by them that the colporteur must be given a salary, as was done by the leading evangelical societies that were operating in Catholic countries.

During the nineteen days covered by the Conference and the Council, Mrs. White was an attentive listener to the reports, which were given mostly in English. She spoke words of encouragement and cheer in the business meetings, and in the early morning meetings gave a series of instructive addresses, dealing with such subjects as love and forbearance among brethren; manner of presenting the truth; unity among laborers; courage and perseverance in the ministry; how to work in new fields. Addressing the missionary workers, she said:

"Remember, brethren, in every perplexity, that God has angels still. You may meet opposition; yea, even persecution. But if steadfast to principle, you will find, as did Daniel, a present helper and deliverer in the God whom you serve. Now is the time to cultivate integrity of character. The Bible is full of rich gems of promise to those who love and fear God.

"To all who are engaged in the missionary work I would say, Hide in Jesus. Let not self but Christ appear in all your labors. When the work goes hard, and you become discouraged and are tempted to abandon it, take your Bible, bow upon your knees before God, and say, 'Here, Lord, Thy word is pledged.' Throw your weight upon His promises, and every one of them will be fulfilled."[1]

When the discouraging reports of the colporteurs had reached a climax, she would urge that notwithstanding all these difficulties, the workers must have faith that success would attend their labors. Repeatedly she assured the disheartened colporteurs that it had been shown her that books could be sold in Europe in such a way as to give support to the workers, and bring to the publishing house sufficient returns to enable it to produce more books.

THE TRAINING OF COLPORTEURS

Encouraged by her assurance that special help would be given those who would persevere in faith, a number of young men were persuaded to make another effort to do self-supporting work in the sale of literature, but they pointed out that they must be furnished with a better supply of salable books.

Elder J. G. Matteson testified that he had made every effort to encourage and train colporteurs, and

[1] "Historical Sketches," page 153.

that they had succeeded in selling the periodicals and smaller books; but the returns were not sufficient to support them properly, and he was in great perplexity to know what could be done to bring better results. He said that, with the encouragement received from Mrs. White, he was resolved to try once more.

Accordingly, during the winter of 1885-86 special efforts were made in Scandinavia to educate and train colporteurs. Training schools were held in Sweden, Norway, and Denmark. The school in Stockholm continued four months. Twenty persons were in attendance. Six hours in the middle of the day they spent in canvassing; the mornings and evenings were spent in study. The sales of books and tracts in Scandinavia in 1886 amounted to $5,386, and subscriptions to periodicals to $3,146.

Years afterward, Elder Matteson declared that in his efforts in behalf of the colporteur work soon after his return from the Basel conference, he was so fully convinced that his workers must live on a very meager income, that he persuaded each one to keep a strict cash account, and to let him examine this account once a week, and advise economies. Soon the scale was turned, for the colporteurs were spending less and earning more, and a number earned enough to support themselves without drawing anything from the conference treasury.[2]

---

[2] NOTE.— The earnest endeavors put forth to establish the canvassing work on a substantial basis in Scandinavia, bore early fruit. At the 1889 General Conference, Elder O. A. Olsen was able to report fifty canvassers in Scandinavia, who were having good success. (See 1889 *Bulletin*, p. 4.) The book sales for 1889 amounted to about $10,000, and in later years these figures were swelled to upwards of $20,000. During the 1891 General Conference, the general agent for Scandinavia declared: "The canvassers are supporting themselves, and besides this, are helping to support the cause by their gifts. Several hundred kroner have come into the treasury of the Swedish Conference through the donations of our canvassers, and I presume this is also true of Norway and Denmark. . . . The more our canvassers sell, the more they can sell. . . . Many have already accepted the truth by reading our publications." (*Bulletin*, 1891, p. 84.)

In central Europe the canvassing work waited for books and for a teacher and leader. The "Life of Christ," which was proving to be a popular book in the Scandinavian countries, was translated into German and French, and was ready for the people early in 1887.

Elder L. R. Conradi had come from America early in 1886, and having visited the churches and companies of Sabbath keepers in Germany, Russia, and Switzerland, he reported that one of the most urgent needs of the European fields was books on present truth, carried to the homes of the people by consecrated and well trained colporteurs. He saw clearly that our literature must be used to carry the advent message to the multitudes of Europe, and that because the mission funds would not make it possible to pay even a small salary to colporteurs, an effort must be made to inaugurate in central Europe what had been begun in Scandinavia,— the education of colporteurs to sell the literature and live upon their commission, without salary. He also saw that our young men needed employment of a character that would educate and train them to become efficient workers in the cause of Christ.

Beginning at Basel, Elder Conradi gathered a group of six or eight young people, and began to train them for success. He declared that the people needed the saving truths in our books; that Mrs. White said that with well trained effort these books could be sold; that Elder Matteson had proved this true; and that he and his young associates must find the way. They studied their book until they were enthusiastic about its great truths, and then as they went out under his encouragement and instruction, they met with success.[3]

[3] NOTE.— At the General Conference of 1887 it was stated: "The publishing work at Basel has steadily increased. From the very first, it was evident that our publications must act a leading part in the central Euro-

DEVELOPMENT THROUGH FAITHFUL SERVICE

The action of the General Conference Committee in making liberal appropriations for the translation and printing of several large books in German and French at Basel, had given much work to the Imprimerie Polyglotte. This opened the way for the employment of a score of young men and women who were very glad to connect with so educational a work.

Seeing that the young people were eager to study the Bible and the languages, the management arranged classes in Bible, history, Bible doctrines, and English grammar, for those who wished to attend. These classes were usually held from 6:30 to 7:30 in the morning. With marvelous rapidity the French boys mastered both the German and the English language, and the German boys both the French and the English. At the same time they grew in stature and in wisdom.

Several times the morning classes gave place for a week or ten days to a series of religious meetings. In these Mrs. White took a leading part, and she seemed never to weary in her efforts to encourage the young people to fit themselves for efficient service in the cause of Christ. She urged them to improve their opportunities, to be diligent in work and in study; and she told them that it had been shown her that if they were faithful, God would use them to carry the

pean field. The denominational books, tracts, and periodicals issued in various languages are having a powerful influence for good wherever they are circulated." (S. D. A. Year Book, 1888, p. 120.)

So prospered were the workers for the larger books and for the periodicals published at the Imprimerie Polyglotte, that in 1889 Elder O. A. Olsen was able to report a substantial gain in its operation. "The publishing house at Basel . . . has done a good business the past year," he declared to the delegates assembled at the 1889 General Conference. "The annual report shows a gain of $1,559.55 for the year. When we consider the fact that this office has never before been self-sustaining, this report is very encouraging. The aggressive work of the Central European Conference this year has been largely in the direction of Germany." (*General Conference Daily Bulletin,* 1889, p. 3.)

truth to many people near and afar off; that if they kept near the Lord, they would become mighty in His work; and that some of them would be called to positions of large responsibility.

There are many who can bear witness to the remarkable fulfillment of this prediction. In later years, one of these young men held for several terms the presidency of the Latin Union Conference; another, the presidency of the Swiss Conference; another has been superintendent of the Levant Union Mission. Others have been preachers, translators, editors, teachers, and managers of large publishing interests.[4]

VISITS TO ITALY

Nov. 26, 1885, Mrs. White left Basel for Torre Pellice, Italy. She was accompanied by her daughter-in-law, Mary K. White, and Elder B. L. Whitney. Regarding this trip she wrote:

"It was my fifty-eighth birthday, and surely it was to be celebrated in a way and place that I had little dreamed of. It seemed hard for me to realize that I was in Europe; that I had borne my testimony in England, Switzerland, Denmark, Norway, and Sweden, and was on my way to labor in Italy.

"Our course over the Alps lay through the great St. Gothard pass. We reached Torre Pellice Friday, about 9 A. M., and were welcomed to the hospitable home of Elder A. C. Bourdeau. The next day, Sab-

[4] NOTE.— As reported in 1915, the following positions of trust were held by some of those in that company at Basel, Switzerland:

a. Manager of publishing work in the Latin Union Conference.
b. Manager of the Gland Sanitarium.
c. President of the Latin Union Conference.
d. Superintendent of the Levant Union Mission.
e. Director of the northern France field.
f. Teacher in Latin Union school.
g. Matron of the Gland Sanitarium.
h. Editor and evangelist in Quebec.

bath, I spoke to the brethren and sisters in the hired hall in which they held their regular Sabbath meetings.''

Mrs. White remained in Torre Pellice three weeks. She spoke to the people ten times, and visited some of the noted places where the Waldenses, fleeing from their persecutors, had been followed and captured, tortured, and slain. Referring to these experiences, she wrote:

''If their voices could be heard, what a history the everlasting mountains surrounding these valleys could give of the sufferings of God's people because of their faith! What a history of the visits of angels unrecognized by these Christian fugitives! Again and again have angels talked with men, as man speaketh with a friend, and led them to places of security. Again and again have the encouraging words of angels renewed the drooping spirits of the faithful, and, carrying their minds above the tops of the highest mountains, caused them to behold by faith the white robes, the crowns, the palm branches of victory, which the overcomers will receive when they surround the great white throne.''

Twice after this, Mrs. White visited the Waldensian valleys,— once in April, 1886, when, in company with her son and his wife, she devoted two weeks to speaking to little congregations in many places; and again, in company with Elder and Mrs. Wm. Ings, in November, as they were returning to Basel after laboring two weeks at Nimes, France.

XLVI

LABORS IN GREAT BRITAIN AND SCANDINAVIA

The fourth European Missionary Council was held in Great Grimsby, England, Sept. 27 to Oct. 4, 1886. The reports of the laborers showed that great difficulties were attending every branch of the work. One morning, before the meeting, a group of workers gathered about the stove in the meeting-hall, and related some of their experiences and disappointments. Good halls for public services were very expensive. To the inexpensive halls the class of people they desired to reach would not come. Tents soon wore out in the damp climate. In their efforts to do house-to-house work, the doors of the best homes did not open to the Bible worker; and in the houses where the doors opened readily, minds were slow to comprehend the importance of obedience to unpopular truths. "What can be done?" was the inquiry.

CONSECRATION, COURAGE, CONFIDENCE

During a series of meetings held in Great Grimsby just before the Council, Mrs. White had given several discourses teaching consecration, courage, and confidence. In closing a sermon on the experience of the disciples in connection with the resurrection of Jesus, she said:

"We should improve every opportunity given us day by day to overcome the temptations of the enemy. This life is a conflict, and we have a foe who never sleeps, who is watching constantly to destroy our minds and lure us away from our precious Saviour, who has given His life for us. Shall we lift the cross given us? or shall we go on in selfish gratification, and lose the eternity of bliss? We cannot afford to sin; we cannot afford to disgrace the law of God.

"The question should not be with us, How shall I make the most money in this world? The question should not be, Shall I serve God? Shall we serve God, or Baal? 'Choose you this day whom ye will serve;' 'as for me and my house, we will serve the Lord.' Joshua 24:15.

"I do not look to the end for all the happiness; I get happiness as I go along. Notwithstanding I have trials and afflictions, I look away to Jesus. It is in the strait, hard places that He is right by our side, and we can commune with Him, and lay all our burdens upon the Burden Bearer, and say, 'Here, Lord, I cannot carry these burdens longer.' Then He says to us, 'My yoke is easy, and My burden is light.' Matthew 11:30. Do you believe it? I have tested it. I love Him; I love Him. I see in Him matchless charms. And I want to praise Him in the kingdom of God.

"Will we break the stony heart? Will we travel the thorny path that Jesus trod all the way from the manger to the cross? We see the tracks of blood. Shall the pride of the world come in? Shall we seek to make the world our standard? or shall we come out from among them? The invitation is, 'Come out from among them, and be ye separate, . . . and touch not the unclean; and I will receive you, and will be a Father unto you, and ye shall be My sons and daughters.' 2 Cor. 6:17, 18.

"O, what an exaltation is this,— to be members of the royal family, children of the heavenly King; to have the Saviour of the universe, the King over all kings, to know us by name, and we to be heirs of God to the immortal inheritance, the eternal substance! This is our privilege. Will we have the prize? Will we fight the battles of the Lord? Will we press the battle to the gate? Will we be victorious?

"I have decided that I must have heaven, and I want you to have it. I never would have come from California to Europe, had I not wanted to tell you how precious the Saviour is, and what a precious truth we have.

"You should search the Bible; for it tells you of Jesus. As you read the Bible, you will see the matchless charms of Jesus. You will fall in love with the Man of Calvary, and at every step you can say to the world, 'His ways are ways of pleasantness, and all His paths are peace.' You are to represent Christ to the world. You may show to the world that you have a hope big with immortality. You may drink of the waters of salvation. Teach your children to love and fear God. You want the heavenly angels to be in your dwelling. You want the Sun of Righteousness shining in the darkened chambers of your mind, then your lips will speak thanksgiving to God.

"Jesus has gone to prepare mansions for us. He said: 'Let not your heart be troubled: ye believe in God, believe also in Me. In My Father's house are many mansions: if it were not so, I would have told you. I go to prepare a place for you. And if I go and prepare a place for you, I will come again, and receive you unto Myself; that where I am, there ye may be also.' John 14: 1-3. It is these mansions that I am looking to; it is not the earthly mansions here, for erelong they are to be shaken down by the mighty earthquake; but those heavenly mansions that Christ has gone to prepare for the faithful.

"We have no home here; we are only pilgrims and

strangers, passing to a better country, even a heavenly. Place your mind upon these things, and while you are doing this, Christ will be right by your side. May God help us to win the precious boon of eternal life.''

Some of the workers responded with testimonies showing faith and determination. Some felt that she did not understand the difficulties of the field. Others were searching for some ground on which to base their hopes of future success.

DISPELLING THE DARKNESS

During the early days of the Council, one of the speakers, after referring to some of the barriers to the progress of the message, appealed to Mrs. White to state her views as to what more could be done, and if there might be expected changes in the conditions under which the laborers were struggling.

In answer to this question, Mrs. White said that there would come changes that would open doors that were closed and barred, changes in many things that would alter conditions and arouse the minds of the people to understand and appreciate present truth. Political upheavals would come, and changes in the industrial world, and great religious awakenings, that would prepare minds to listen to the third angel's message. ''Yes, there will be changes,'' she assured them, ''but *nothing for you to wait for.* Your work is to go forward, presenting the truth in its simplicity, holding up the light of truth before the people.''

Then she told them how the matter had been presented to her in vision. Sometimes the multitudes in our world, to whom is sent the warning message from the word of God that Christ is soon coming, were presented to her as enveloped in mists and clouds and dense darkness, even as described by Isaiah, who wrote, "Behold, the darkness shall cover the earth, and gross darkness the people." Isa. 60:2.

As in the vision she looked upon this scene with intense sorrow, her accompanying angel said, "Look ye," and as she looked again, there were to be seen little jets of light, like stars shining dimly through the darkness. As she watched them, their light grew brighter, and the number of lights increased, because each light kindled other lights. These lights would sometimes come together as if for the encouragement of one another; and again they would scatter out, each time going farther and lighting more lights. Thus the work went on until the whole world was illuminated with their brightness.

In conclusion, she said: "This is a picture of the work you are to do. 'Ye are the light of the world.' Matt. 5:14. Your work is to hold up the light to those around you. Hold it firmly. Hold it a little higher. Light other lights. Do not be discouraged if yours is not a great light. If it is only a penny taper, hold it up. Let it shine. Do your very best, and God will bless your efforts."[1]

---

[1] NOTE.— In the official reports of the progress of the third angel's message in Great Britain, frequent acknowledgment has been made from time to time of the influence that the sale of penny periodicals has had on the development of a strong constituency in that field of labor. "Publications have been sent to all parts of the kingdom," the workers reported in 1888, "and faithful souls are being aroused to embrace the truth, and scores are candidly investigating it." (S. D. A. Year Book, 1888, p. 130.) At the 1895 General Conference, it was stated that "the average weekly sales of *Present Truth* [the missionary journal published by Seventh-day Adventists in Great Britain since 1884] have run from nine thousand to ten thousand." "Nothing that has been done in Great Britain has had such marked effect on the people as the circulation of this paper." (*Bulletin*, 1895, pp. 314, 315.) And in 1897 the brethren from Europe were rejoicing in a still larger circulation of their missionary journal. "The *Present Truth* has an average circulation of thirteen thousand copies weekly," they declared, "and many are coming to a knowledge of the truth in reading this medium."

During the 1909 General Conference, Brother W. C. Sisley, in charge of the British publishing house, reviewed the results of the past four years thus:

FIRST VISIT TO SCANDINAVIA

During the two years spent by Mrs. White in Europe, she visited Denmark, Sweden, and Norway three times. At the close of the Missionary Council held in Basel during September, 1885, the delegates from Scandinavia pleaded that she should visit their field as soon as possible; and although her friends in Switzerland pointed out that summer was a better time to travel in northern Europe, she decided to venture out by faith, trusting in God for strength to endure the hardships of the journey.

October and the first half of November were spent in Copenhagen, Stockholm, Grythyttehed, Orebro, and Christiania. Mrs. White was accompanied by her secretary, Miss Sara McEnterfer, by her son, W. C. White, and by Elder J. G. Matteson, who was guide, interpreter, and fellow laborer. In the various places where believers assembled to hear, her message was received with reverential interest. The congregations were not large, excepting in Christiania, where the church membership numbered one hundred and twenty. On Sabbath day, October 31, when the brethren from other churches gathered in, there were about two hundred in attendance. On Sunday she spoke in the workingmen's hall to an audience of eight hundred. The next Sunday, by request of the president of a strong temperance society, she spoke

---

"We have sold, during the last four years, exclusive of our considerable foreign trade, 168,947 books, 6,871,649 periodicals, 23,382 pamphlets, and 964,163 tracts, at a total retail value of $310,221.57; or a yearly average of 42,237 books, 1,717,912 periodicals, 5,840 pamphlets, 241,041 tracts, at an average annual retail value of $77,555.

"We have 207 regular book and periodical canvassers, an average of one out of every eight of our members. . . .

"The net profits of our publishing work during the past four years have been $19,878. The tract society has donated that sum, and $12,832 more of its former profits, or a total of $32,710, to the British Union property fund." (*Bulletin*, 1909, p. 96.)

to about one thousand three hundred assembled in the soldiers' military gymnasium, on the importance of home training in the principles of temperance. This subject was presented from a Biblical standpoint, and illustrated by the experiences of Bible characters.

SECOND VISIT TO SCANDINAVIA

Mrs. White's second visit to Scandinavia was made in the summer of 1886, in company with her son and Miss McEnterfer. During the first part of the journey, Miss Christine Dahl acted as guide and interpreter.

The most important of the meetings attended on this trip was at Orebro, Sweden. Here the Swedish Conference held its annual session, June 23 to 28, during which a tract society and a Sabbath school association were organized, each including the work in Denmark, Sweden, and Norway.

A week before the opening of this Conference, Elder Matteson had begun a school for colporteurs and Bible workers. In the carrying on of this school he was joined by Elder A. B. Oyen, of Christiania, and Elder O. A. Olsen, just from America. Education was the watchword among the leaders in those days, and the people were eager to learn. The workers' institute was opened each morning at 6:30 with a prayer and social meeting. At 9 o'clock there was a class in bookkeeping; at 11:30 instruction was given in home missionary work. Instruction on the holding of Bible readings was given at 4 o'clock in the afternoon; and at 8 P. M. there was a preaching service. Every hour of the day was counted as precious by both teachers and students.

At the conference session following, about sixty-five Sabbath keepers were in regular attendance. Of the ten churches in Sweden, nine were represented by twenty-three delegates. Mrs. White spoke six times in the early morning meetings, and five times on other occasions. Addressing the small but resolute band of believers, she said:

"In the beginning, the work goes hard and slow. Now is the time when all should bend their shoulders to raise the load and carry it forward. Advance we must, though the Red Sea be before us, and impassable mountains on either hand. God has been with us and has blessed our efforts. We must work by faith. 'The kingdom of heaven suffereth violence, and the violent take it by force.' Matt. 11:12. We are to pray, believe that our prayers are heard, and then work.

"The work may now seem small; but there must be a beginning before there can be any progress. 'First the blade, then the ear, after that the full corn in the ear.' The work may start in weakness, and its progress may for a time be slow; yet if it is commenced in a healthy manner, there will be a steady and substantial gain.[2] A high standard should be placed before those who are newly come to the faith. They should be educated to be careful in speech and circumspect in conduct, giving evidence that the truth has accomplished something for them, and thus by their example shedding light upon those who are in darkness. . . .

"Those who have received the truth may be poor, but they should not remain ignorant or defective in character, to give the same mould, by their influence, to others. When the church fully receives the light, darkness will be dispelled; and if in holi-

[2] In confirmation of this, witness the development of the work in the Scandinavian Union Conference, at the close of 1914, to a membership of 3,807, divided into six local conferences and three missions.

ness of character they keep pace with the truth revealed, their light will grow brighter and brighter. The truth will do its refining work, restoring the moral image of God in man, and the darkness and confusion and strife of tongues which is the curse of so many churches, will cease. The power that God will give to His church, if they will only walk in the light as fast as it shines upon them, is scarcely conceived of.

"The Lord is soon to come, and the message of warning is to go forth to all nations, tongues, and peoples. While God's cause is calling for means and laborers, what are those doing who live under the full light of the present truth?"[3]

The Conference in Sweden having closed, two weeks were spent in Christiania, in earnest labor for the church and for the workers in the publishing house. At that time the new publishing house had been completed, and the various departments of the printing work had been moved in and were in operation.

When Mrs. White was shown through the several departments of the new printing plant, she expressed great joy over the thought that with the facilities thus provided, periodicals and books suitable for the field could now be printed in acceptable form and sent forth on their mission. It was on the occasion of this visit, when reaching the pressroom, that she declared that this very room, with its presses running as they were seen that day, had been shown her in vision years before.

The meetings in Christiania were followed by ten days of labor in Copenhagen, after which the party returned to Basel.

---

[3] *Review and Herald*, Oct. 5, 1886.

FIFTH EUROPEAN MISSIONARY COUNCIL

Again, in 1887, Mrs. White spent the month of June in Scandinavia. In company with Mrs. Ings she had attended very interesting meetings with the little companies of Sabbath keepers in Voh-winkel and Gladbach, Germany. In these meetings Elder L. R. Conradi had acted as guide, interpreter, and fellow laborer.

At Copenhagen there was seen an encouraging growth in the church since the last visit. A busy week was spent there.

The fifth annual session of the European Council of Seventh-day Adventist Missions was to be held June 14-21 in Norway. The place selected for this meeting was Moss, a beautiful town of eight thousand inhabitants, about two hours' ride from Christiania. The delegates were as follows:

Central Europe: B. L. Whitney, Mrs. E. G. White. W. C. White, and L. R. Conradi.

England: S. H. Lane, Wm. Ings, J. H. Durland.

Norway: O. A. Olsen, K. Brorsen, and N. Clausen.

Denmark: E. G. Olsen.

Sweden: J. G. Matteson.

Russia: J. Laubhan.

United States: S. N. Haskell, J. H. Waggoner, D. A. Robinson, and C. L. Boyd.

In conjunction with the Missionary Council was held the first camp meeting of the Norway Conference. Ten tents had been pitched in a beautiful grove, and in these about one hundred were accommodated, while fifty more found lodgings in near-by houses. The delegates from America and Central Europe were cared for in a large, comfortable house overlooking the Christiania Fiord.

In the camp the prevailing language was the Norwegian, and there the usual program of a local camp meeting was followed. In the big house the prevailing language was English, and there very many precious seasons of prayer were enjoyed, also profitable councils were held regarding the means to be used for broadening and strengthening the work in all the countries of Europe.

Tuesday, June 14, cheering reports were made regarding the marvelous development during the year in the colporteur work. Elder Matteson related wonderful experiences during the preceding winter in his school for colporteurs and Bible workers; Elder Conradi reported the success of workers in Germany and Switzerland; Elder Olsen gave cheering reports from Norway, and Elder Hendrickson from Denmark. Elder Lane reported good progress on the part of the colporteurs in England.

The Missionary Council went busily on with its work for several days after the people from the churches in Norway had returned to their homes. Plans were laid and resolutions adopted looking to the education of men for the ministry, and the establishment of a ship mission in Hamburg. The subject commanding the most enthusiastic attention was the development of schools in each conference for the training of colporteurs. That which called for the most anxious study was the question of preparing and publishing the most suitable literature.

Much interest was added to the meetings of the Council by the presence of Elders C. L. Boyd and D. A. Robinson, who were on their way from America to the great South African field. They joined heartily in the study of the difficult questions regarding the work in Europe; and they also brought in many of their South African problems for informal consideration.

EFFICIENCY IN MISSIONARY SERVICE

In writing to these brethren concerning the great work before them, Mrs. White emphasized the importance of their starting in right at the beginning of their work. She spoke of fields where much more might have been done if the work had not been bound about by unwise economies; and she declared that if the work had been begun right, less means would actually have been drawn from the treasury. She said:

"We have a great and sacred trust in the elevated truths committed to us. We are glad that there are men who will enter into our mission fields who are willing to work with small remuneration. Money does not weigh with them in the scale against the claims of conscience and duty, to open the truth to those who are in the darkness of error in far-off countries for the love of Christ and their fellow men.

"The men who will give themselves to the great work of teaching the truth are not the men who will be bribed with wealth or frightened by poverty. But God would have His delegated servants constantly improving. In order for the work to be carried forward with efficiency, the Lord sent forth His disciples two and two. . . . No one man's ideas, one man's plans, are to have a controlling power in carrying forward the work. . . . One is not to stand apart from the other, and argue his own ways and plans; for he may have an education in a certain direction, and possess certain traits of character, which will be detrimental to the interests of the work if allowed to become the controlling power.

"The workers are not to stand apart from one another, but work together in everything that interests the cause of God. And one of the most important things to be considered is self-culture. There is too little attention given to this matter. There should be a cultivation of all the powers to do high and honorable work for God. Wisdom may be gained in a much larger measure than many suppose who have been laboring for years in the cause of God. . . .

"Keep up the elevated character of the missionary work. Let the inquiry of both men and women associated in the missionary work be, What am I? and what ought I to be and do? Let each worker consider that he cannot give to others that which he does not possess himself. Therefore he should not settle down into his own set ways and habits, and make no change for the better. Paul says, I have not attained, but I press forward. It is constant advancement and improvement and reformation that is to be made with individuals, to perfect a symmetrical, well balanced character. . . .

"There is little that any of you can do alone. Two or more are better than one if you will each esteem the other better than yourself. If any of you consider your plans and modes of labor perfect, you greatly deceive yourselves. Counsel together with much prayer and humbleness of mind, willing to be entreated and advised. This will bring you where God will be your counselor. . . .

"We are not to make the world's manner of dealing ours. We are to give to the world a nobler example, showing that our faith is of a high and elevated character. Do unto others as you would that others should do unto you. Let every action reveal the nobility of truth. Be true to your faith, and you will be true to God. Come to the Word, that you may learn what its claims really are. When God speaks, it is our duty to listen and obey. . . .

"From the very first establishment of your work, begin in a dignified, Godlike manner, that you may give character to the influence of the truth which you know to be of heavenly birth. But remember that great care is to be exercised in regard to the presentation of truth. Carry the minds along guardedly. Dwell upon practical godliness, weaving the same into doctrinal discourses. The teachings and love of Christ will soften and subdue the soil of the heart for the good seed of truth, and you will obtain the confidence of the people by working to obtain acquaintance with them. But keep up the elevated character of the work. Let the publications, the papers, the pamphlets, be working among the people, and preparing the minds of the reading class for the preaching of the truth. Let no stinted efforts be made in this line, and the work, if begun wisely and prosecuted wisely, will result in success. But do be humble and teachable, if you would teach others and lead them in the way of truth and righteousness."

"GO FORWARD!"

In reviewing the progress attained up to the close of the year 1887, Mrs. White wrote freely concerning the opening providences of God in Europe, and the opportunities of the future. She said:

"A great work is committed to those who present the truth in Europe. . . . There are France and Germany, with their great cities and teeming population. There are Italy, Spain, and Portugal, after so many centuries of darkness, . . . opened to the word of God — opened to receive the last message of warning to the world. There are Holland, Austria, Roumania, Turkey, Greece, and Russia, the home of millions upon millions, whose souls are as precious in the sight of God as our own, who know nothing of the special truths for this time. . . .

"A good work has already been done in these countries. There are those who have received the truth, scattered as light bearers in almost every land. . . . But how little has been done in comparison with the great work before us! Angels of God are moving upon the minds of the people, and preparing them to receive the warning. Missionaries are needed in fields that have yet been scarcely entered. New fields are constantly opening. The truth must be translated into different languages, that all nations may enjoy its pure, life-giving influences. . . .

"Colporteurs are meeting with encouraging success in the sale of our books. The light is thus brought to the people, while the colporteur — who in many cases has been thrown out of employment by accepting the truth — is enabled to support himself, and the sales are a financial help to the office. In the days of the Reformation, monks who had left their convents, and who had no other means of support, traversed the country, selling Luther's works, which were thus rapidly circulated throughout Europe. Colportage work was one of the most efficient means of spreading the light then, and so it will prove now. . . .

"There will be obstacles to retard. . . . These we have had to meet wherever missions have been established. Lack of experience, imperfections, mistakes, unconsecrated influences, have had to be overcome. How often have these hindered the advancement of the cause in

America! We do not expect to meet fewer difficulties in Europe. Some connected with the work in these foreign fields, as in America, become disheartened, and, following the course of the unworthy spies, bring a discouraging report. Like the discontented weaver, they are looking at the wrong side of the web. They cannot trace the plan of the Designer; to them all is confusion, and instead of waiting till they can discern the purpose of God, they hastily communicate to others their spirit of doubt and darkness.

"But we have no such report to bring. After a two years' stay in Europe we see no more reason for discouragement in the state of the cause there than at its rise in the different fields in America. There we saw the Lord testing the material to be used. Some would not bear the proving of God. They would not be hewed and squared. Every stroke of the chisel, every blow of the hammer, aroused their anger and resistance. They were laid aside, and other material was brought in, to be tested in like manner. All this occasioned delay. Every fragment broken away was regretted and mourned over. Some thought that these losses would ruin the building; but, on the contrary, it was rendered stronger by the removal of these elements of weakness. The work went steadily forward. Every day made it plainer that the Lord's hand was guiding all, and that a grand purpose ran through the work from first to last. So we see the cause being established in Europe.

"One of the great difficulties there is the poverty that meets us at every turn. This retards the progress of the truth, which, as in earlier ages, usually finds its first converts among the humbler classes. Yet we had a similar experience in our own country, both east and west of the Rocky Mountains. Those who first accepted this message were poor, but as they set to work in faith to accomplish what they could with their talents of ability and means, the Lord came in to help. In His providence He brought men and women into the truth who were willing-hearted; they had means, and they wanted to send the light to others. So it will be now. But the Lord would have us labor earnestly in faith till that time comes.

"The word has gone forth to Europe, 'Go forward!' The humblest toiler for the salvation of souls is a laborer together with God, a coworker with Christ. Angels minister unto him. As we advance in the opening path of His providence, God will continue to open the way before us. The greater the difficulties to be overcome, the greater will be the victory gained."[4]

A REMARKABLE DEVELOPMENT

Mrs. White lived to see the day when a strong constituency of Seventh-day Adventist believers had been raised up in Europe through the untiring effort put forth by many laborers. She rejoiced over the prosperity attending many lines of work in the various countries, and over the reports of rapidly increasing numbers of believers, totaling in 1914 upwards of thirty-three thousand,— more than the entire number of Sabbath-keeping Adventists throughout the world at the time of her sojourn in Europe.

And great was Mrs. White's rejoicing whenever there were brought to her attention sample copies of books and other publications in the various languages of the European field, the product of many publish-

[4] *Review,* Dec. 6, 1887.

ing centers, where was issued denominational literature with a total annual sale in 1913 of $482,000.

MESSAGES OF HOPE AND COURAGE

The messages that Mrs. White has sent from time to time to the workers in Europe, have encouraged the following of broad policies that would bring strength and prosperity to all branches of the work. In 1902 she wrote:

"My brethren, bind up with the Lord God of hosts. Let Him be your fear, and let Him be your dread. The time has come for His work to be enlarged. Troublous times are before us; but if we stand together in Christian fellowship, none striving for supremacy, God will work mightily for us.

"Let us be hopeful and courageous. Despondency in God's service is sinful and unreasonable. He knows our every necessity. He has all power. He can bestow upon His servants the measure of efficiency that their need demands. His infinite love and compassion never weary. With the majesty of omnipotence He unites the gentleness and care of a tender shepherd. We need have no fear that He will not fulfill His promises. He is eternal truth. Never will He change the covenant that He has made with those that love Him. His promises to His church stand fast forever. He will make her an eternal excellence, a joy of many generations."[5]

---

[5] "Testimonies for the Church," Vol. 3, pp. 38, 39.

XLVII

IN CONFIRMATION OF CONFIDENCE

During the summer of 1890, Mrs. White devoted much of her time to writing. In October she was urged to attend general meetings in Massachusetts, New York, Virginia, and Maryland. After a few days spent in Adams Center, N. Y., she attended a general meeting at South Lancaster, Mass. On the journey from South Lancaster to Salamanca, N. Y., she caught a severe cold, and found herself at the beginning of the Salamanca meeting much wearied as the result of ten days of arduous labor at South Lancaster, and heavily burdened with hoarseness and a sore throat.

About two hundred had assembled from all parts of Pennsylvania and southwestern New York. The meetings were held mostly in the opera house, but Sabbath afternoon and evening they were held in the Congregational church. Mrs. White spoke Sabbath afternoon on the necessity of a greater effort on the part of our churches to cherish faith and love. Sunday morning she spoke in the opera house. There was a large audience, filling all the seats and aisles, and crowding about the platform close to the speaker. Her subject was temperance, and she dwelt largely upon the duty of parents so to train their children to habits of fidelity and self-denial, that they need not be overcome when tempted to drink intoxicating liquors.

After this meeting, Mrs. White was so thoroughly exhausted that her secretary, Miss Sara McEnterfer, urged her to return to her home in Battle Creek, and take treatment at the Sanitarium. Elder A. T.

Robinson, and others interested in the remaining meetings which she had promised to attend, pleaded that she should not abandon hope for health and strength to continue her labors.

With great difficulty she filled an appointment Monday afternoon, and then felt that she must decide what course she should take about attending the Virginia meeting, which immediately followed.

At the home of Brother Hicks, where she was entertained, she was visited by an old lady who was violently opposed in her Christian life by her husband. This interview lasted an hour. After this, weary, weak, and perplexed, she thought to retire to her room and pray. Climbing the stairs, she knelt by the bed, and before the first word of petition had been offered she felt that the room was filled with the fragrance of roses. Looking up to see whence the fragrance came, she saw the room flooded with a soft, silvery light. Instantly her pain and weariness disappeared. The perplexity and discouragement of mind vanished, and hope and comfort and peace filled her heart.

Then, losing all consciousness regarding her surroundings, she was shown in vision many things relating to the progress of the cause in different parts of the world, and the conditions which were helping or hindering the work.

Among the many views presented to her, were several showing the conditions existing in Battle Creek. In a very full and striking manner, these were laid out before her.

Tuesday forenoon, November 4, was the time set for the departure from Salamanca. In the morning Elders A. T. Robinson and W. C. White called to see what Mrs. White had decided to do. Then she told them of her experience of the evening before, and of her peace and joy through the night. She said that during the night she had had no inclination to sleep; for her heart was so filled with joy and gladness. Many times she had repeated the words of Jacob: "Surely the Lord is in this place; and I knew it not." "This is none other but the house of God, and this is the gate of heaven." Gen. 28:16, 17.

She was fully decided to attend the meetings according to appointment. Then she proposed to tell the brethren what had been shown her regarding the work in Battle Creek; but her mind immediately turned to other matters, and she did not relate the vision. Not until the General Conference held in Battle Creek the following March, did she relate it.

The remainder of November and the month of December were spent in the Eastern States, at meetings in Washington and Baltimore, and in Norwich, Lynn, and Danvers, Mass. January and February were spent in labors at Battle Creek, and in preparation for the General Conference.

PROPOSALS REGARDING CENTRALIZATION

During the year 1890, much thought had been given by leading men connected with the management of the Review and Herald Publishing Association, to a proposal for the consolidation of the work of the publishing houses under one board of control. The proposed union of the publishing interests was advocated as a means of securing unity, economy, and efficiency. At the same time the hope was expressed that at no distant day all the sanitariums might be brought under one ownership and control. By the same ones who advocated consolidation of the publishing houses and the medical institutions, the theory was advanced that the surest way to establish confidence in the work that Seventh-day Adventists were doing was to strengthen the institutions at headquarters, by providing them with large and substantial buildings and with ample facilities.

But those who were personally acquainted with the conditions existing in the home and foreign mission fields, felt that there was greater need for broadening the field work and establishing many centers of influence. They felt that already a disproportionate amount of means had been expended at headquarters. Moreover, the men bearing responsibility at the publishing house in California did not approve of any plan of consolidation which might result in the crippling of the work on the Pacific coast.

SUGGESTED CHANGES IN POLICY

Among those working in the cause of religious liberty there had arisen serious differences of opinion regarding the best way to conduct that rapidly developing work. For several years the *American Sentinel*, and the ministers of the denomination, had treated the question of religious liberty as a vital part of the third angel's message. But during the year 1890 the leading speakers of the National Religious Liberty Association had found an open door to present the principles that they were advocating, and their protest against religious legislation, before large audiences of secular and non-Christian people, and it appeared to them that it would be a wise plan to improve these opportunities, and also that it would be consistent to let these principles stand out very clearly, unassociated with the teachings of the Scriptures regarding the sacredness of the Sabbath and the nearness of the second advent of Christ. They urged that the policy of the *Sentinel* be changed, and declared that if this could not be effected, they would propose that another paper be published in Battle Creek, the editorial policy of which should be more in harmony with their manner of presenting truth.

FORMAL CONSIDERATION OF PROPOSED CHANGES

The General Conference for 1891 was held in Battle Creek March 5-25. Sunday forenoon, March 15, the committee of twenty-one appointed at the preceding General Conference to consider the consolidation of the publishing interests, presented its report. The committee spoke favorably of the objects to be gained by consolidation, but advised that the Conference move cautiously. They then proposed that the General Conference Association be reorganized, with a view to its eventually securing control of all the publishing work of the denomination.

In harmony with the advice of this committee, the General Conference Association, intended at first as an agency for the holding of church property, was reorganized with a board of twenty-one members, and was given control of many lines of work, of which publishing interests stood first.

A SPECIAL COMMITTEE COUNCIL

Early in the meeting an effort had been made by the officers of the National Religious Liberty Association and the representatives of the *American Sentinel*, to come to an agreement regarding policies and plans. To this end a joint council was arranged to be held Saturday night, March 7, after the regular meeting in the Tabernacle.

At this council meeting men with strong convictions and fixed determination expressed their views and feelings very freely, and at last the representatives of the National Religious Liberty Association voted that unless the policy of the *American Sentinel* was changed, the Association would establish another periodical to be its organ. This joint meeting continued until after one o'clock Sunday morning.

THE SABBATH SERVICE

Sabbath, March 7, was a day of deep solemnity. In the forenoon Elder Haskell spoke on the world-wide proclamation of the gospel. As in the apostolic age the gospel was proclaimed in its purity, with a power which carried it into all the world, so in the last days God is to bring out every ray of light in the everlasting gospel, and send it with the power of His Spirit into all the earth.

In the afternoon Mrs. White spoke on the importance of preaching the Word, and the danger of covering up, and keeping in the background, the distinctive features of our faith, under the impression that prejudice will thereby be avoided. If there is committed to us a special message, as we believe, that message must go, without reference to the customs or prejudices of the world, not governed by a policy of fear or favor. Some will receive it and be sanctified through it, though multitudes will oppose and reject it. But it must go everywhere till the very earth is lightened with its glory. She dwelt especially upon the danger of leaving our first love, and upon the importance of all, especially those connected with our leading institutions, having a vital connection with Christ, the true vine. Patterning after the world and adopting a worldly policy, must be guarded against. Men in responsible positions should go to

God as often as did Daniel in earnest supplication for divine help.

Two or three times during the discourse she began to tell the story of her experience at Salamanca, and each time she hesitated, and leaving the story untold proceeded with other lines of thought. This discourse made a profound impression on the large congregation.

Late in the afternoon a ministers' meeting was held in the east vestry of the Tabernacle. Mrs. White was present, and pleaded for a deeper consecration. At the close of this special meeting she was asked by Elder O. A. Olsen if she would attend the ministers' meeting Sunday morning. She replied that she had done her part, and would leave the burden with him. Then it was planned that Elders Olsen and Prescott should lead the meeting.

Sunday morning, about 5 : 20, Brethren A. T. Robinson, W. C. White, and Ellery Robinson were passing Mrs. White's residence on their way to the early meeting. They saw a light in her room, and her son ran up to inquire about her health.

He found her busily engaged in writing. She then told him that an angel of God had wakened her about three o'clock, and had bidden her go to the ministers' meeting and relate some things shown her at Salamanca. She said that she arose quickly, and had been writing for about two hours.

At the ministers' meeting an earnest season of prayer had just closed when Mrs. White entered with a package of manuscripts in her hand. With evident surprise Elder Olsen said: "We are glad to see you, Sister White. Have you a message for us this morning?"

"Indeed I have," was her reply. She then said that it had not been her plan to attend the morning meeting, but she had been awakened very early, and instructed to prepare to relate to the brethren some things shown her at Salamanca.

She told briefly the story of her experience at the Salamanca meeting, and said that in the vision given her there the Lord had opened before her the condition and perils of the work in many places. Warnings were given her which she was commanded to present to men in responsible positions. Especially in Battle Creek great perils surrounded the work, but men knew it not, because impenitence blinded their eyes.

With regard to one occasion, her guide said, "Follow me," and she was ushered into a council meeting where men were advocating their views and plans with great zeal and earnestness, but not according to knowledge. One brother stood before the council with a paper in his hand and criticized the character of its contents. The paper was the *American Sentinel.* Pointing to certain articles, he said: "This must come out, and that must be changed. If the *Sentinel* did not contain such articles as these, we could use it." The articles pointed out as objectionable were upon the Sabbath and the second coming of Christ.

With clearness Mrs. White spoke of the views and the attitude of the chief speakers in this council meeting. She referred to the harsh spirit manifested by some, and to the wrong positions taken by others. She closed her remarks with a most earnest appeal that all should hold forth the truth in its perfection, and that the watchmen should give the trumpet a certain sound. A solemn conviction rested upon the assembly, and all felt that they had been listening to a message from Heaven.

Elder Olsen was bewildered, and knew not what to say. He had not heard of the special committee council which had been continued into the early hours of that very morning, and which had closed less than two hours before the angel bade Mrs. White tell the vision given her four months before, in which this very meeting was minutely described. But he had not long to wait for an explanation. Soon the men who had been in the council of the night before arose and testified regarding their committee meeting.

One said: "I was in the meeting last night, and I am sorry to say that I was on the wrong side. And I take this early opportunity to place myself on the right side."

The president of the National Religious Liberty Association bore a clear testimony. He said that the night before, a number of brethren had met in his room at the Review Office, and there discussed the very matters just referred to by Mrs. White. Their deliberations had continued till after one o'clock in the morning. He said he would not undertake to describe the meeting. That was unnecessary, because the description as given by Mrs. White was correct, and more exact than he could give it. He freely acknowledged that the position he had held was not right, and that he could now see his error.

Another brother stated that he had been in the meeting, and that the description given by Mrs. White was true and correct in every particular. He was profoundly thankful that light had been given, because the differences of opinion had created a very serious situation. He believed that all were honest in their convictions, and sincerely desired to do what was right, yet their views were at variance, and they could not agree. Others who had been present at the late committee counsel over the *Sentinel,* bore testimony that the meeting had been correctly described by Mrs. White.

Other testimonies were borne, expressing thankfulness that light had been given on this question which was attended with so much perplexity. They also expressed their gratitude that the message had been given in such a way that all could see not only the wisdom of God in the message, but also the goodness of God in sending it at such a time that none could doubt its being a message from Heaven.

This experience confirmed the faith of those who believed, and deeply impressed those who had felt that their own experienced judgment about business matters was safer to follow than the plans for the distribution of responsibility and the establishment of many centers of influence that had been called for by their brethren in the field and by the Testimonies.

XLVIII

DANGER IN ADOPTING WORLDLY POLICY IN THE WORK OF GOD

Regarding some of the counsels given during the Salamanca vision, and the experiences and admonitions that came to workers in the cause of God during the next few weeks, Mrs. White wrote:

"Nov. 3, 1890, while laboring at Salamanca, N. Y., as I was in communion with God in the night season, I was taken out of and away from myself to assemblies in different States, where I bore decided testimony of reproof and warning. In Battle Creek a council of ministers and responsible men from the publishing house and other institutions was convened, and I heard those assembled, in no gentle spirit, advance sentiments and urge measures for adoption that filled me with apprehension and distress.

"Years before, I had been called to pass through a similar experience, and the Lord then revealed to me many things of vital importance, and gave me warnings that must be delivered to those in peril. On the night of November 3, these warnings were brought to my mind, and I was commanded to present them before those in responsible offices of trust, and to fail not nor be discouraged. There were laid out before me some things which I could not comprehend; but the assurance was given me that the Lord would not allow His people to be enshrouded in the fogs of worldly skepticism and infidelity, bound up in bundles with the world; but if they would only hear and follow His voice, rendering obedience to His commandments, He would lead them above the mists of skepticism and unbelief, and place their feet upon the Rock, where they might breathe the atmosphere of security and triumph.

"While engaged in earnest prayer, I was lost to everything around me; the room was filled with light, and I was bearing a message to an assembly that seemed to be the General Conference. I was moved by the Spirit of God to make a most earnest appeal; for I was impressed that great danger was before us at the heart of the work. I had been, and still was, bowed down with distress of mind and body, burdened with the thought that I must bear a message to our people at Battle Creek, to warn them against a line of action that would separate God from the publishing house.

"The eyes of the Lord were bent upon the people in sorrow mingled with displeasure, and the words were spoken: 'I have somewhat against thee, because thou hast left thy first love. Remember therefore from whence thou art fallen, and repent, and do the first works; or else I will come unto thee quickly, and will remove thy candlestick out of his place, except thou repent.' Rev. 2:4, 5.

"He who wept over impenitent Israel, noting their ignorance of God, and of Christ their Redeemer, looked upon the heart of the work at Battle Creek. Great peril was about the people, but some knew it not. Unbelief and impenitence blinded their eyes, and they trusted to human wisdom in the guidance of the most important interests of the cause of God relating to the publishing work. In the weakness of human judgment, men were gathering into their finite hands the lines of control, while God's will, God's way and counsel, were not sought as indispensable. Men of stubborn, iron-like will, both in and out of the Office, were confederating together, determined to drive certain measures through in accordance with their own judgment.

"I said to them: 'You cannot do this. The control of these large interests cannot be vested wholly in those who make it manifest that they have little experience in the things of God, and have not spiritual discernment. The people of God throughout our ranks must not, because of mismanagement on the part of erring men, have their confidence shaken in the important interests at the great heart of the work, which have a decided influence upon our churches in the United States and in foreign lands. If you lay your hand upon the publishing work, this great instrumentality of God, to place your mould and superscription upon it, you will find that it will be dangerous to your own souls, and disastrous to the work of God. It will be as great a sin in the sight of God as was the sin of Uzzah when he put forth his hand to steady the ark. There are those who have entered into other men's labors, and all that God requires of them is to deal justly, to love mercy, and walk humbly with God, to labor conscientiously as men employed by the people to do work entrusted to their hands. Some have failed to do this, as their works testify. Whatever may be their position, whatever their responsibility, if they have as much authority even as had Ahab, they will find that God is above them, that His sovereignty is supreme.' . . .

"No confederacy should be formed with unbelievers, neither should you call together a certain chosen number who think as you do, and who will say Amen to all that you propose, while others are excluded, who you think will not be in harmony. I was shown that there was great danger of doing this.

"'For the Lord spake thus to me with a strong hand, and instructed me that I should not walk in the way of this people, saying, Say ye not, A confederacy, to all them to whom this people shall say, A confederacy; neither fear ye their fear, nor be afraid. Sanctify the Lord of hosts Himself; and let Him be your fear, and let Him be your dread.' 'To the law and to the testimony: if they speak not according to this word, it is because there is no light in them.' Isa. 8:11-13, 20. The world is not to be our criterion. Let the Lord work, let the Lord's voice be heard.

"Those employed in any department of the work whereby the world may be transformed, must not enter into alliance with those who know not the truth. The world know not the Father or the son, and they have no spiritual discernment as to the character of our work, as to what we shall do or shall not do. We must obey the orders that come from above. We are not to hear the counsel or follow the plans suggested by unbelievers. Suggestions made by those who know not the work that God is doing for this time, will be such as to weaken the power of the instrumentalities of God. By accepting such suggestions, the counsel of Christ is set at naught. . . .

"The eye of the Lord is upon all the work, all the plans, all the imaginings of every mind; He sees beneath the surface of things, discerning the thoughts and intents of the heart. There is not a deed of darkness, not a plan, not an imagination of the heart, not a thought of the mind, but that He reads it as an open book. Every act, every word, every motive, is faithfully chronicled in the records of the great Heart-searcher, who said, 'I know thy works.'

"I was shown that the follies of Israel in the days of Samuel will be repeated among the people of God to-day, unless there is greater humility, less confidence in self, and more trust in the Lord God of Israel, the Ruler of the people. It is only as divine power is combined with human effort that the work will abide the test. When men lean no longer on men or on their own judgment, but make God their trust, it will be made manifest in every instance by meekness of spirit, by less talking and much more praying, by the exercise of caution in their plans and movements. Such men will reveal the fact that their dependence is in God, that they have the mind of Christ.

"Again and again I have been shown that the people of God in these last days could not be safe in trusting in men, and making flesh their arm. The mighty cleaver of truth has taken them out of the world as rough stones that are to be hewed and squared and polished for the heavenly building. They must be hewed by the prophets with reproof, warning, admonition, and advice, that they may be fashioned after the divine Pattern; this is the specified work of the Comforter, to transform heart and character, that men may keep the way of the Lord. . . .

"Since 1845 the dangers of the people of God have from time to time been laid open before me, and I have been shown the perils that would thicken about the remnant in the last days. These perils have been revealed to me down to the present time. Great scenes are soon to open before us. The Lord is coming with power and great glory. And Satan knows that his usurped authority will soon be forever at an end. His last opportunity to gain control of the world is now before him, and he will make most decided efforts to accomplish the destruction of the inhabitants of the earth. Those who believe the truth must be as faithful sentinels on the watchtower, or Satan will suggest specious reasonings to them, and they will give utterance to opinions that will betray sacred, holy trusts. The enmity of Satan against good, will be manifested more and more, as he brings his forces into activity in his last work of rebellion; and every soul that is not fully surrendered to God, and kept by divine power, will form an alliance with Satan against heaven, and join in battle against the Ruler of the universe.

"In a vision in 1880 I asked, 'Where is the security for the people of God in these days of peril?' The answer was, 'Jesus maketh intercession for His people, though Satan standeth at His right hand to resist Him.' 'And the Lord said unto Satan, The Lord rebuke thee, O Satan; even the Lord that hath chosen Jerusalem rebuke thee: is not this a brand plucked out of the fire?' As man's Intercessor and Advocate, Jesus will lead all who are willing to be led, saying, 'Follow Me upward, step by step, where the clear light of the Sun of Righteousness shines.'

"But not all are following the light. Some are moving away from the safe path, which at every step is a path of humility. God has committed to His servants a message for this time; but this message does not in every particular coincide with the ideas of all the leading men, and some criticize the message and the messengers. They dare even to reject the words of reproof sent to them from God through His Holy Spirit.

"What reserve power has the Lord with which to reach those who have cast aside His warnings and reproofs, and have accredited the Testimonies of the Spirit of God to no higher source than human wisdom? In the judgment, what can you who have done this, offer to God as an excuse for turning from the evidences He has given you that God was in the work? 'By their fruits ye shall know them.' I would not now rehearse before you the evidences given in the past two years of the dealings of God by His chosen servants; but the present evidence of His working is revealed to you, and you are now under obligation to believe. You cannot neglect God's messages of warning, you cannot reject them or treat them lightly, but at the peril of infinite loss.

"Caviling, ridicule, and misrepresentation can be indulged in only at the expense of the debasement of your own souls. The use of such weapons does not gain precious victories for you, but rather cheapens the mind, and separates the soul from God. Sacred things are brought down to the level of the common, and a condition of things is created that pleases the prince of darkness, and grieves away the Spirit of God. Caviling and criticism leave the soul as devoid of the dew of grace as the hills of Gilboa were destitute of rain. Confidence cannot be placed in the judgment of those who indulge in ridicule and misrepresentation. No weight can be attached to their advice or resolutions. You must bear the divine credentials before you make decided movements to shape the working of God's cause.

"To accuse and criticize those whom God is using, is to accuse and criticize the Lord, who has sent them. All need to cultivate their religious faculties, that they may have a right discernment of religious things. Some have failed to distinguish between pure gold and mere glitter, between the substance and the shadow.

"The prejudices and opinions that prevailed at Minneapolis are not dead by any means; the seeds sown there in some hearts are ready to spring into life and bear a like harvest. The tops have been cut down, but the roots have never been eradicated, and they still bear their unholy fruit to poison the judgment, pervert the perceptions, and blind the understanding of those with whom you connect, in regard to the message and the messengers. When, by thorough confession, you destroy the root of bitterness, you will see light in God's light. Without this thorough work you will never clear your souls. You need to study the word of God with a purpose, not to confirm your own ideas, but to bring them to be trimmed, to be condemned or approved, as they are or are not in harmony with the word of God. The Bible should be your constant companion. You should study the Testimonies, not to pick out certain sentences to use as you see fit, to strengthen your assertions, while you disregard the plainest statements given to correct your course of action.

"There has been a departure from God among us, and the zealous work of repentance and return to our first love essential to restoration to God and regeneration of heart, has not yet been done. Infidelity has been making its inroads into our ranks; for it is the fashion to depart from Christ, and give place to skepticism. With many the cry of the heart has been, 'We will not have this man to reign over us.' Baal, Baal, is the choice. The religion of many among us will be the religion of apostate Israel, because they love their own way, and forsake the way of the Lord. The true religion, the only religion of the Bible, that teaches forgiveness only through the merits of a crucified and risen Saviour, that advocates righteousness by the faith of the Son of God, has been slighted, spoken against, ridiculed, and rejected. It has been denounced as leading to enthusiasm and fanaticism. But it is the life of Jesus Christ in the soul, it is the active principle of love imparted by the Holy Spirit, that alone will make the soul fruitful unto good works. The love of Christ is the force and power of every message for God that ever fell from human lips. What kind of a future is before us, if we shall fail to come into the unity of the faith?

"When we are united in the unity for which Christ prayed, this long controversy that has been kept up through satanic agency will end, and we shall not see men framing plans after the order of the world because they have not spiritual eyesight to discern spiritual things. They now see men as trees walking, and they need the divine touch, that they may see as God sees, and work as Christ worked. Then will Zion's watchmen unitedly sound the trumpet in clearer, louder notes; for they will see the sword coming, and realize the danger in which the people of God are placed.

"You will need to make straight paths for your feet, lest the lame be turned out of the way. We are surrounded by the lame and halting in the faith, and you are to help them, not by halting yourselves, but by standing, like men who have been tried and proven, in principle firm as a rock. I know that a work must be done for the people, or many will not be prepared to receive the light of the angel sent down from heaven to lighten the whole earth with His glory. Do not think that you will be found as vessels unto honor in the time of the latter rain, to receive the glory of God, if you are lifting up your souls unto vanity, speaking perverse things, in secret cherishing roots of bitterness. The frown of God will certainly be upon every soul who cherishes these roots of dissension, and possesses a spirit so unlike the Spirit of Christ.

"As the Spirit of the Lord rested upon me, I seemed to be present in one of your councils. One of your number rose; his manner was very decided and earnest as he held up a paper before you. I could read plainly the heading of the paper; it was the *American Sentinel*. Criticisms were then passed upon the paper and the character of the articles therein published. Those in council pointed to certain passages, declaring that this must be cut out, and that must be changed. Strong words were uttered in criticism of the methods of the paper, and a strong unchristlike spirit prevailed. Voices were decided and defiant.

"My guide gave me words of warning and reproof to speak to those who took part in this proceeding, who were not slow to utter their accusations and condemnation. In substance this was the reproof given: The Lord has not presided at this council, and there is a spirit of strife among the counselors. The minds and hearts of these men are not under the controlling influence of the Spirit of God. Let the adversaries of our faith be the ones to suggest and develop such plans as you are now discussing. From the world's point of view some of these plans are not objectionable; but they are not to be adopted by those who have had the light of heaven. The light which God has given should be respected, not only for our own safety, but also for the safety of the church of God. The steps now being taken by the few cannot be followed by the remnant people of God. Your course cannot be sustained by the Lord. It is made evident by your course of action that you have laid your plans without the aid of Him who is mighty in counsel;

but the Lord will work. Those who have criticized the work of God need to have their eyes anointed, for they have felt mighty in their own strength; but there is One who can bind the arm of the mighty, and bring to naught the counsels of the prudent.

"The message we have to bear is not a message that men need to cringe to declare. They are not to seek to cover it, to conceal its origin and purpose. Its advocates must be men who will not hold their peace day nor night. As those who have made solemn vows to God, and who have been commissioned as the messengers of Christ, as stewards of the mysteries of the grace of God, we are under obligation to declare faithfully the whole counsel of God. We are not to make less prominent the special truths that have separated us from the world and made us what we are; for they are fraught with eternal interests. God has given us light in regard to the things that are now taking place in the last remnant of time, and with pen and voice we are to proclaim the truth to the world, not in a tame, spiritless way, but in demonstration of the Spirit and power of God. The mightiest conflicts are involved in the furtherance of the message, and the results of its promulgation are of moment to both heaven and earth.

"The controversy between the two great powers of good and evil is soon to be ended; but to the time of its close, there will be continual and sharp contests. We should now purpose, as did Daniel and his fellows in Babylon, that we will be true to principle, come what may. The flaming fiery furnace heated seven times hotter than it was wont to be heated, did not cause these faithful servants of God to turn aside from allegiance to the truth. They stood firm in the time of trial, and were cast into the furnace; and they were not forsaken of God. The form of the Fourth was seen walking with them in the flames, and they came forth not having even the smell of fire upon their garments."

"To-day the world is full of flatterers and dissemblers; but God forbid that those who claim to be guardians of sacred trusts, shall betray the interests of God's cause through the insinuating suggestions and devices of the enemy of all righteousness.

"There is no time now to range ourselves on the side of the transgressors of God's law, to see with their eyes, to hear with their ears, and to understand with their perverted senses. We must press together. We must labor to become a unit, to be holy in life and pure in character. Let those who profess to be servants of the living God no longer bow down to the idol of men's opinions, no longer be slaves to any shameful lust, no longer bring a polluted offering to the Lord, a sin-stained soul."

XLIX

ACROSS THE PACIFIC

In his reports and addresses to the General Conference of 1891, Elder S. N. Haskell made very earnest appeals for laborers to be sent to distant lands that he had recently visited; and he was especially urgent that provision be made for the establishment in Australia of a training school for Christian workers. He was profoundly impressed with the importance of having the young people in each great division of the world, trained in their own land for service as colporteurs, teachers, and preachers. He pleaded that teachers be chosen to open a school in Australasia; and also that Mrs. Ellen G. White and her son, W. C. White, spend some time in that field.

Action was taken by the Mission Board, immediately after the Conference, inviting them to go in the autumn. This would bring them to the new field of labor in Australia's summer. The steamer sailing in October was found to be overcrowded, and the departure from San Francisco was delayed till the sailing of the *Alameda,* November 12.

Elder and Mrs. Geo. B. Starr, who had been selected to act a part in the proposed Australian school, had gone in advance to the Hawaiian Islands, where they spent seven busy weeks before the arrival of the *Alameda.* The other members of the party were W. C. White, Mary A. Davis, May Walling, Fannie Bolton, and Emily Campbell.

THE VOYAGE

The weather during most of the twenty-five days of the voyage was good.

At Honolulu the ship remained nineteen hours—and what enjoyable hours they were! Here the party were met by several of the brethren and sisters, were shown the beauties of the place, and were given a feast at the home of Sister Kerr. Meanwhile, notices were circulated, and in the evening Mrs. White spoke to a large audience in the hall of the Young Men's Christian Association.

On her sixty-fourth birthday, one day before the ship reached Samoa, Mrs. White wrote:

"As I contemplate the past year, I am filled with gratitude to God for His preserving care and loving-kindness. We are living in a perilous time, when all our powers must be consecrated to God. We are to follow Christ in His humiliation, His self-denial, His suffering. We owe everything to Jesus, and renewedly I consecrate myself to His service, to lift Him up before the people, to proclaim His matchless love."

About noon, December 3, the *Alameda* tied up to the Auckland wharf. Very soon a number of representative members of the Auckland church were on board, welcoming the party to New Zealand. All were invited to the home of Brother Edward Hare. During dinner many incidents of Elder Haskell's first visit were related. In the afternoon an inspection was made of the city and its beautiful suburbs. In the evening, in the first Seventh-day Adventist meetinghouse built south of the equator, Mrs. White spoke to an eager congregation, on the love of Jesus.

Early the next morning the *Alameda* proceeded on her way, and entered Sydney harbor at 7 A. M., December 8. Elder and Mrs. A. G. Daniells were waiting at the wharf. During the week spent at their home Mrs. White spoke twice to the Sydney church.

December 16, the party reached Melbourne, and were given a most hearty welcome by Elder Geo. C. Tenney and his associates in the publishing house. In anticipation of Mrs. White's arrival, Elder Tenney had vacated his new house, and insisted that she and her helpers walk in and make themselves at home.

THE AUSTRALIAN CONFERENCE MEETING

It was only a week till the time of the opening of the Australian Conference, which was to be held in Federal Hall, North Fitzroy, Melbourne, beginning December 24. There were in regular attendance about one hundred representatives from the companies of Sabbath keepers in Victoria, Tasmania, South Australia, and New South Wales.

At that time there were about four hundred and fifty Sabbath keepers in all Australia and Tasmania. At the capital of each of the colonies entered, a church had been established; and it was in these leading cities that the bulk of the membership was located.

During the Conference, much thought was given to the question as to how the message should be carried to all parts of the great Australian continent by the handful of believers upon whom rested the responsibility of holding up the light of the message. Thousands of truth-filled books had been placed in the homes of the people by faithful colporteurs, and plans were now laid for the employment of Bible workers to follow up the interests awakened by the reading of these books.

CONSIDERATION OF SCHOOL INTERESTS

The majority of those who had embraced the truth in Australia, were tradesmen living in the cities. As their children reached the age when they must leave the public schools and prepare to assist in the support of the family, it was found, because of their observance of the Sabbath, exceedingly difficult for them to secure employment or to learn trades.

Some desired that their children should be trained to become laborers in the cause. But how could this be accomplished? The colonies were passing through a severe financial depression; and many of the Sabbath keepers, with thousands of others, were greatly perplexed and overtaxed with the work of supplying their families with the necessities of life. Then how could they, at such a time, enter upon the expensive enterprise of establishing and supporting a denominational training school?

The canvassers pleaded that the school be organized without delay. Many of them had been thrown upon their own resources in early life, with but little school education; and their work among the people had led them to feel that they must have opportunity to fit themselves for more efficient service. These urged that if a school was not established soon in Australia, they would be obliged to bear the great expense of going to America to get the education necessary for the best success in their work. They also said that while a few of them might be able to do this, there were scores who might attend a school in Australia, but who could not go to the schools across the sea.

The Conference appointed a committee to outline plans, and another committee to study the question of location; and it authorized the holding of a workers' training school while waiting for the selection of a site and the erection of buildings.

SICKNESS, AND CHANGE OF PLANS

It had been planned that Mrs. White, with her son and Elders Daniells and Starr, should attend the New Zealand Conference, to be held in April, 1892; but shortly after the close of the Melbourne meeting, she suffered a severe attack of neuritis. When it became evident that she could not attend the New Zealand meeting, she rented a roomy cottage in Preston, a northern suburb of Melbourne, and said that she would do what she could to complete her long promised work on the life of Christ.

From time to time, when the weather was favorable, Mrs. White spoke at the Sabbath meetings of the Melbourne church. Sometimes, when unable to ascend the stairs leading up to Federal Hall, she was carried to the platform; and on two or three occasions, when unable to stand, she spoke while sitting in an easy-chair.

THE OPENING OF THE AUSTRALASIAN BIBLE SCHOOL

During the winter of 1892, Mrs. White watched with eager interest the efforts that were made for the opening of the proposed school. In April, she pleaded with the brethren in responsibility in America to recognize the possibilities of the future, and provide facilities for the training of a large force of workers who could advance into unentered territory. "O, what a vast number of people have never been warned!" she wrote. "Is it right that such a superabundance of opportunities and privileges should be provided for the work in America, while there is such a destitution of the right kind of workers here in this field? Where are God's missionaries?"

"Our field is the world," she urged. "The Saviour directed the disciples to begin their work in Jerusalem, and then pass on through Judea and Samaria, and unto the uttermost part of the earth. Only a small proportion of the people accepted the doctrines; but the messengers bore the message rapidly from place to place, passing from country to country, lifting the standard of the gospel in all the near and far-off places of the earth."

In June, the committee having the matter in charge announced that on St. Kilda Road, Melbourne, two large houses in George's Terrace had been rented for the school.

Early in August, Elder and Mrs. L. J. Rousseau arrived from America, and on August 24 a term of sixteen weeks was begun. The teachers were Elder Rousseau, principal; Elder Starr, Bible; W. L. H. Baker and Mrs. Rousseau, assistants in common branches; Mrs. Starr, matron. Soon twenty-four students were in attendance. Nearly all were adults. Twelve had been canvassers or were preparing for that work. Half of the remaining twelve had been laborers in some other line of Christian service.

On the opening day, short addresses were made by Elders Daniells, Tenney, Starr, White, and Rousseau; also by Mrs. White, who in the course of her remarks outlined with clearness the broad scope of a denominational training school, and the vital relation that it sustains to the task of finishing the work of God in the earth without delay. But her special burden seemed to be to impress upon the minds of teachers and students the fact that God by His providence is opening country after country to the heralds of the cross, and that in these lands of gospel opportunity the honest in heart are groping eagerly after the light of saving truth.

"The plans and work of men," she said, "are not keeping pace with the providence of God; for while some in these countries who claim to believe the truth declare by their attitude, 'We want not Thy way, O Lord, but our own way,' there are many who are pleading with God that they may understand what is truth. In secret places they are weeping and praying that they may see light in the Scriptures, and the Lord of heaven has commissioned His angels to co-operate with human agencies in carrying forward His vast design, that all who desire life may behold the glory of God."

"We are to follow where God's providence opens the way," the speaker continued; "and as we advance, we shall find that Heaven has moved before us, enlarging the field for labor far beyond the proportion of our means and ability to supply. The great want of the field open before us, should appeal to all to whom God has entrusted means or ability, that they may devote themselves and their all to God."

Nor were those who should receive a training, to be limited in their missionary endeavors by racial or national barriers. Wherever they labored, their efforts were to be crowned with speedy triumph. "The purpose and ends to be attained by consecrated missionaries," Mrs. White declared, "are very comprehensive. The field for missionary operation is not limited by caste or nationality. The field is the world, and the light of truth is to go to all the dark places of the earth in a much shorter time than many think possible."[1]

[1] *Bible Echo,* Supplement, Sept. 1. 1892.

It was on this same occasion of the opening of the Australasian Bible School, which afterward developed into the Australasian Missionary College, that Mrs. White said:

"The missionary work in Australia and New Zealand is yet in its infancy, but the same work must be accomplished in Australia, New Zealand, in Africa, India, China, and the islands of the sea, as has been accomplished in the home field."[2]

ENCOMPASSED BY INFIRMITIES

The suffering from neuritis which began in January, continued till the following November. Very faithful and vigorous treatment for checking the disease was given her by her nurse and secretaries; but during the winter months the ailment made steady advance. Still she continued her writing. Propped up in bed, she wrote letters to friends, testimonies to leading workers in the cause, and many chapters for "The Desire of Ages."

As spring approached, there was some improvement; and in October she decided to try the drier climate of Adelaide, South Australia. There she spent six weeks, with beneficial results.

A REVIEW OF EXPERIENCE

In a letter written from Melbourne Dec. 23, 1892, to the brethren assembled in General Conference, Mrs. White reviewed her experience during this long sickness, as follows:

"I am rejoiced to report to you the goodness, the mercy, and the blessing of the Lord bestowed upon me. I am still compassed with infirmities, but I am improving. The great Restorer is working in my

---

[2] *Bible Echo*, Supplement, Sept. 1, 1892.

behalf, and I praise His holy name. My limbs are gaining in strength, and although I suffer pain, it is not nearly as severe as it has been during the past ten months. I am now so far restored that by taking hold of the balusters I can walk up and down stairs without assistance. All through my long affliction I have been most signally blessed of God. In the most severe conflicts with intense pain, I realized the assurance, 'My grace is sufficient for you.' At times when it seemed that I could not endure the pain, when unable to sleep, I looked to Jesus by faith, and His presence was with me, every shade of darkness rolled away, a hallowed light enshrouded me, the very room was filled with the light of His divine presence.

"I have felt that I could welcome suffering if this precious grace was to accompany it. I knew the Lord is good and gracious and full of mercy and compassion and tender, pitying love. In my helplessness and suffering, His praise has filled my soul and has been upon my lips. My meditation has been so comforting and so strengthening as I have thought how much worse condition I should be in without the sustaining grace of God. My eyesight is continued to me, my memory has been preserved, and my mind has never been more clear and active in seeing the beauty and preciousness of truth.

"What rich blessings are there! With the psalmist I could say: 'How precious also are Thy thoughts unto me, O God! how great is the sum of them! If I should count them, they are more in number than the sand: when I awake, I am still with Thee.' Ps. 139:17, 18. These last words express my feelings and experience. When I awake, the first thought and expression of my heart is: 'Praise the Lord! I love Thee, O Lord, Thou knowest that I love Thee! Precious Saviour, Thou hast bought me with the price of Thine own blood. Thou hast considered me of value, or Thou wouldst not have paid an infinite price for my salvation. Thou, my Redeemer, hast given Thy life for me, and Thou shalt not have died for me in vain.' . . .

"Since the first few weeks of my affliction, I have had no doubts in regard to my duty in coming to this distant field; and more than this, my confidence in my heavenly Father's plan in my affliction has been greatly increased. I cannot now see all the purpose of God, but I am confident it was a part of His plan that I should be thus afflicted, and I am content and perfectly at ease in the matter. With the writings that shall go in this mail, I have since leaving America written twenty hundred pages of letter paper. I could not have done all this writing if the Lord had not strengthened and blessed me in large measure. Never once has that right hand failed me. My arm and shoulder have been full of suffering, hard to bear, but the hand has been able to hold the pen and trace words that have come to me from the Spirit of the Lord.

"I have had a most precious experience, and I testify to my fellow laborers in the cause of God, 'The Lord is good, and greatly to be praised.' "[3]

THE AUSTRALIAN CONFERENCE OF JANUARY, 1893

The fifth session of the Australian Conference was held in North Fitzroy, Melbourne, Jan. 6-15, 1893. During this meeting Mrs. White spoke seven times, on themes relating to practical godliness.

---

[3] *Daily Bulletin of the General Conference,* 1893, pp. 407, 408.

One day she reviewed the rise and progress of the denominational publishing work. She urged that the brethren in Australia put forth their best efforts to develop into strong laborers in this and every other line of Christian endeavor.

LABORS IN NEW ZEALAND

At the close of the Australian Conference, Mrs. White decided to undertake the long deferred visit to New Zealand. She was accompanied by Emily Campbell, who assisted her both as secretary and as nurse. Her son, W. C. White, and Elder and Mrs. Starr were also with her during much of the time.

Arriving in Auckland February 8, they were met by Elder M. C. Israel, and conducted to a furnished cottage which the Auckland church had placed at their disposal.

During the twelve days spent in earnest labor for the Auckland church, Mrs. White spoke eight times. After this she spent three weeks with the brethren and sisters in Kaeo, the oldest Seventh-day Adventist church in New Zealand. Here she found a number of promising young people, for whom she labored earnestly.

Both in Auckland and in Kaeo Mrs. White urged the brethren and sisters to go with their families to the annual conference which was to be held the last of March, in Napier. This conference was to be a camp meeting, the first undertaken by Seventh-day Adventists south of the equator. Regarding this experience she wrote:

"We felt that this first camp meeting must be, as far as possible, a sample of what every other camp meeting held in the future ought to be. Over and over again I said to the people: 'See, saith He, that thou make all things according to the pattern showed to thee in the mount.' Heb. 8:5. . . . Jesus said to His disciples, 'Be ye therefore perfect, even as your Father which is in heaven is perfect.' Matt. 5:48."

But regarding this proposed camp meeting it seemed impossible to arouse much enthusiasm. Logging camps, and groups of tents for road builders, were well-known institutions, not much to be desired; but a comfortable camp for a company of people gathered to worship God, was an entirely new thing for New Zealand.

On account of the financial depression, it was unusually difficult for many to attend. Up to the beginning of the meeting, there was little promise that more than thirty would be encamped on the grounds. For that number tents were provided. But just as the meeting was opening, the people from the different churches came in, unannounced, until there were twice as many as had been expected. During the last week of the meeting there were eighteen tents in the encampment, occupied by fifty-three persons. Many others occupied rooms near by. These, with the membership of the Napier church, made a good sized congregation during the day. Every evening the large tent was well filled.

As the meeting progressed, the camp meeting plan was heartily approved, and it was voted that the next annual conference be held in camp. Resolutions were adopted endorsing the Australasian Bible School, and funds were contributed,— five hundred dollars for the furniture, and four hundred dollars as a students' aid fund. Two hundred and seventy dollars was subscribed as a camp meeting fund.

"After the close of the camp meeting in Napier," wrote Mrs. White, "we decided to visit Wellington, and also to spend a few days at Palmerston North to labor for a little company of Sabbath keepers there who were pleading for help. Although infirmities were still my companions by night and day, the Lord gave grace to bear them. Sometimes when I felt unable to fill my appointments, I would say, 'In faith I will place myself before the people;' and when I did this, strength was given me to rise above my infirmities, and to bear the message the Lord had given me."

At Wellington, Mrs. White was welcomed to the home of Mrs. M. H. Tuxford, where she spent several months, and from which headquarters she went out from time to time to speak to little companies of believers in Petone, Ormondville, Dannevirke, Palmerston North, and Gisborne.

Before returning to Australia, Mrs. White attended the second New Zealand camp meeting, held Nov. 30 to Dec. 12, 1893, in a sheltered suburb of Wellington. There were in attendance double the number that had been present at the Napier meeting. Elder O. A. Olsen, president of the General Conference, arrived during the early days of the meeting, and his labors and timely instruction were of untold value. He brought cheering reports from the great mission fields that he had recently visited; and he appealed to the young people to fit themselves for service in the closing work of the gospel.

From Wellington, Mrs. White, in company with Elder Olsen and other laborers, hastened to Melbourne to attend the first camp meeting in Australia.

L

THE FIRST AUSTRALIAN CAMP MEETING

"We are glad to announce to our people," wrote Elder A. G. Daniells late in September, 1893, to the brethren and sisters throughout Australia, "that the time has come when the executive committee of the Conference see their way clear to carry out the wishes of so many to hold a camp meeting." Some had been waiting eagerly for such an announcement, and it came as welcome news to the rank and file of the believers scattered far and wide through the Australian colonies.

Among the general laborers advertised to attend were Elder O. A. Olsen, president of the General Conference; Mrs. Ellen G. White; and some brethren whom the Mission Board were sending over from America to supplement the small force of workers in the Australian field. The promise of ample help led Elder Daniells to add to his appeal the words, "This will be a rare occasion,— one which we may not have again for years,— and we truly hope that but few of our people will be denied the privilege of being present."[1]

Much faith was required to plan for a general camp meeting to which the brethren and sisters from all the colonies should be invited to come. The traveling expenses alone seemed almost prohibitive because of the great distances to be traversed. But the need of getting together was imperative, and therefore the believers were urged strongly to attend. "This meeting," Mrs. White declared, "will mark a new era in the history of the work of God in this field. It is im-

[1] *Bible Echo,* Oct. 1, 1893, p. 320.

portant that every member of our churches should be present, and I urge you all to come."

"I am afraid that some will say," she continued, " 'It is expensive to travel, and it would be better for me to save the money, and give it for the advancement of the work, where it is so much needed.' Do not reason in this way; for God calls upon you to take your place among the rank and file of His people. You are to be there in person, and to strengthen the meeting all you possibly can. . . . We know that the believers in the truth are scattered widely; but make no excuse that will keep you from gaining every spiritual advantage possible. Come to the meeting, and bring your families. . . .

"We should use every power at our command to make this meeting a success, and suit it to the needs of those who shall attend. The work of the Lord is above every temporal interest, and we must not misrepresent His cause. Watching, waiting, working, must be our motto. . . .

"God has committed to our hands a most sacred work, and we need to meet together to receive instruction as to what is personal religion and family piety; we need to understand what part we shall individually be called upon to act in the grand and important work of building up the cause and work of God in the earth, in vindicating God's holy law, and in lifting up the Saviour as 'the Lamb of God, which taketh away the sin of the world.' John 1:29. We need to receive the divine touch, that we may understand our work in the home. Parents need to understand how they may send forth from the sanctuary of the home, Christian children, trained and educated so that they shall be fitted to shine in the world. We need the Holy Spirit, in order that we may not misrepresent our faith. . . . It is now fully time that an advance move was made in Australia. . . . Let us move forward with well concentrated effort, and overcome every difficulty.''[2]

Thirty-five family tents were manufactured by some of the brethren, in advance, for the Conference. It was thought that these would meet all requirements. But as the orders came rolling in, more tents were purchased, and others were hired for the meeting. When completed, the camp had over one hundred tents, and five hundred and eleven people. The grounds were well laid out and faithfully cared for. Many of the tents were furnished with bedsteads, tables, chairs, and bureaus; and the whole camp was a model of cleanliness and good order.

''We felt that the eye of God was upon all our arrangements,'' Mrs. White wrote when referring afterward to these painstaking efforts to make the grounds appear attractive and inviting; ''and in the order of our camp we sought to show forth the praises of Him who hath called us out of darkness into His marvelous light.'' 1 Peter 2:9. The results attained were much greater than the toilers had dared expect. ''The encampment made the impression upon those who visited it,'' Mrs. White wrote further, ''that the truth we advocated was of great importance, that the missionary spirit is the true spirit of the gospel.

''This was the first camp meeting that Melbourne had seen, and it was a marvel of wonders to the people. Far and near the sound went out concerning this city of tents, and a most wonderful interest was awakened. Every afternoon and evening the tent was filled to its utmost capacity, not with a cheap order of society, but

[2] *Bible Echo,* Dec. 8, 1893.

with people of intelligence, physicians of note, ministers, and business men. We saw that with the blessing of God this camp meeting would do more to bring our work before the people than years of labor could possibly do.

"Thousands visited the encampment, and expressed their delight and astonishment at the order of the grounds, and the nicety of arrangements in the clean, white tents. No stubborn opposition seemed to be awakened as men and women listened to the truth for the first time. The power of God was among us. Brighton was stirred from one end to the other. An interest was awakened in Melbourne also, and the surrounding suburbs, greater than anything we had witnessed since the movement of 1844. The truth was new and strange; yet it took hold upon the people; for we preached the word of God, and the Lord sent it home to the hearts of the hearers.

"Many visitors came from long distances, and, as it was in the 1843 and 1844 movement, they would bring their lunch and remain through the day. A number of the citizens of the place declared that if they were not living close by, they would hire tents and camp with us on the ground. They valued the privilege of hearing the word of God so clearly explained. They said the Bible seemed to be full of new and precious things, and was like a new book to them. We heard from many such expressions as these: 'This is more than we hoped for.' 'Our faith is confirmed; our hope brightened; our belief in the testimony of the Scriptures made strong.'"

"I have attended many camp meetings," testified Elder O. A. Olsen concerning the Brighton meeting, "but I have never before witnessed such an outside interest. This is more like what in my imagination

I have thought would be the loud voice of the third angel's message, than anything I have seen heretofore. A most profound impression is made on the city of Melbourne. Wherever one goes, the leading topic of conversation is the camp meeting and what is seen and heard there. From all around come most earnest appeals for meetings. . . .

"To our brethren this meeting has been of the greatest value possible. It has given them much broader ideas of the work for this time, and a much deeper Christian experience. After they had been here one week, they voted almost unanimously to continue yet another week."[3]

"As an outgrowth of the Brighton camp meeting," Mrs. White afterward testified, "several churches were raised up. I visited the church in Williamstown, and rejoiced to see that many had moral courage to manifest their loyalty to the commandments of God in spite of the continual opposition and contempt that have been heaped upon them and upon God's holy law.

"A church was raised up in Hawthorne, and another in Brighton. About sixty belonged to these two churches. A large number of new members have been added to the Prahan church, and to the church in North Fitzroy. Persons are continually coming in who heard the truth at the Brighton camp meeting.

"Some will say that these camp meetings are very expensive, and that the Conference cannot afford to support another such meeting; but when we look at the three churches that have been organized, and are prospering in the faith, can we hesitate in answering the question, 'Will it pay?' Shall we not raise our voices in decided affirmation, 'It will pay'?"

[3] *Review and Herald,* March 6, 1894.

LI

THE AVONDALE SCHOOL

During the closing days of the Australian camp meeting, much time was devoted to a study of educational problems. The committee having charge of the Australasian Bible School, and the committee on location, made their reports. It was generally felt that the three short terms held in rented quarters had been of great value, and should be counted as a marked success. At the same time, it was seen that if the school was continued in rented buildings, the expense to the students would be too great to permit of that large attendance which was desirable. It was also evident that with a small attendance, the expense to the promoters of the enterprise would be very heavy. How could the school be put on such a basis as would open the way for a large number of students to attend at moderate expense?

Mrs. White spoke often regarding educational work, and presented the views which had been given her from time to time concerning the character of the work to be undertaken and of the places that should be selected for the training of Christian workers. She also spoke of the advantages to be gained by combining study with work in the acquirement of a well balanced education.

Shortly after camp meeting, she prepared for publication a comprehensive statement regarding the advisability of placing the school away from the large cities, and outlining the kind of education that should be sought for and given in the proposed school. The main features of these counsels are embodied in the following extracts:

WORK AND EDUCATION

"Our minds have been much exercised day and night in regard to our schools. How shall they be conducted? And what shall be the education and training of the youth? Where shall our Australasian Bible School be located? I was awakened this morning at one o'clock with a heavy burden upon my soul. The subject of education has been presented before me in different lines, in varied aspects, by many illustrations, and with direct specification, now upon one point, and again upon another. I feel, indeed, that we have much to learn. We are ignorant in regard to many things.

"In writing and speaking upon the life of John the Baptist and the life of Christ, I have tried to present that which has been presented to me in regard to the education of our youth. We are under obligation to God to study this subject candidly; for it is worthy of close, critical examination upon every side. . . .

"Those who claim to know the truth and understand the great work to be done for this time, are to consecrate themselves to God, soul, body, and spirit. In heart, in dress, in language, in every respect, they are to be separate from the fashions and practices of the world. They are to be a peculiar and holy people. It is not their dress that makes them peculiar; but because they are a peculiar and holy people, they cannot carry the marks of likeness to the world.

"Many who suppose they are going to heaven, are blindfolded by the world. Their ideas of what constitutes a religious education and religious discipline are vague, resting only on probabilities. There are many who have no intelligent hope, and are running great risk in practising the very things which Jesus has taught that they should not do, in eating, drinking, and dressing, binding themselves up with the world in a variety of ways. They have yet to learn the serious lessons so essential to growth in spirituality, to come out from the world and be separate. The heart is divided; the carnal mind craves conformity, similarity to the world in so many ways that the mark of distinction from the world is scarcely distinguishable. Money, God's money, is expended in order to make an appearance after the world's customs; the religious experience is contaminated with worldliness; and the evidence of discipleship — Christ's likeness in self-denial and cross-bearing — is not discernible by the world or by the universe of heaven. . . .

"Never can the proper education be given to the youth in this country, or any other country, unless they are separated a wide distance from the cities. The customs and practices in the cities unfit the minds of the youth for the entrance of truth. The liquor-drinking, the smoking and gambling, the horse-racing, the theater-going, the great importance placed upon holidays,— all are a species of idolatry, a sacrifice upon idol altars. . . .

"It is not the correct plan to locate school buildings where the students will have constantly before their eyes the erroneous practices that have moulded their education during their lifetime, be it longer or shorter. . . . Should schools be located in the cities or within a few miles from them, it would be most difficult to counteract the influence of the former education which students have received in regard to these holidays and the practices connected with them, such as horse-racing, betting, and the offering of prizes. The very atmosphere of these cities is full of poisonous malaria. . . .

"We shall find it necessary to establish our schools out of, and away from, the cities, and yet not so far away that they cannot be in touch with them, to do them good, to let light shine amid the moral darkness. Students need to be placed under the most favorable circumstances to counteract very much of the education they have received. . . .

"We need schools in this country to educate children and youth that they may be *masters* of labor, and not *slaves* of labor. Ignorance and idleness will not elevate one member of the human family. Ignorance will not lighten the lot of the hard toiler. Let the worker see what advantage he may gain in the humblest occupation, by using the ability God has given him as an endowment. Thus he can become an educator, teaching others the art of doing work intelligently. He may understand what it means to love God with the heart, the soul, the mind, and the strength. The physical powers are to be brought into service for love to God. The Lord wants the physical strength, and you can reveal your love for Him by the right use of your physical powers, doing the very work which needs to be done. There is no respect of persons with God. . . .

"There is in the world a great deal of hard, taxing work to be done; and he who labors without exercising the God-given powers of mind and heart and soul, he who employs the physical strength alone, makes the work a wearisome tax and burden. There are men with mind, heart, and soul who regard work as a drudgery, and settle down to it with self-complacent ignorance, delving without thought, without taxing the mental capabilities in order to do the work better.

"There is science in the humblest kind of work; and if all would thus regard it, they would see nobility in labor. Heart and soul are to be put into work of any kind; then there is cheerfulness and efficiency. In agricultural or mechanical occupations, men may give evidence to God that they appreciate His gift in the physical powers, and the mental faculties as well. Let the educated ability be employed in devising improved methods of work. This is just what the Lord wants. There is honor in any class of work that is essential to be done. Let the law of God be made the standard of action, and it ennobles and sanctifies all labor. Faithfulness in the discharge of every duty makes the work noble, and reveals a character that God can approve. . . .

"Schools should be established where there is as much as possible to be found in nature to delight the senses and give variety to the scenery. While we shun the false and artificial, discarding horse-racing, card-playing, lotteries, prize fights, liquor-drinking, and tobacco-using, we must supply sources of pleasure that are pure and noble and elevating. We should choose a location for our school apart from the cities, where the eye will not rest continually upon the dwellings of men, but upon the works of God; where there shall be places of interest for them to visit, other than what the city affords. Let our students be placed where nature can speak to the senses, and in her voice they may hear the voice of God. Let them be where they can look upon His wondrous works, and through nature behold her Creator. . . .

"Manual occupation for the youth is essential. The mind is not to be constantly taxed to the neglect of the physical powers. The ignorance of physiology, and a neglect to observe the laws of health, have brought many to the grave who might have lived to labor and study intelligently. The proper exercise of mind and body will develop and strengthen all the powers. Both mind and body will be preserved, and will be capable of doing a variety of work. Ministers and teachers need to learn in regard to these things, and they need to practise as well. The proper use of their physical strength, as well as of the mental powers, will equalize the circulation of the blood, and keep every organ of the living machinery in running order. Minds are often abused; they are goaded on to madness by pursuing one line of thought; the excessive employment of the brain power and the neglect of the physical organs create a diseased condition of things in the system. Every faculty of the mind may be exercised with comparative safety if the physical powers are equally taxed, and the subject of thought varied. We need a change of employment, and nature is a living, healthful teacher. . . .

"Habits of industry will be found an important aid to the youth in resisting temptation. Here is opened a field to give vent to their pent-up energies, that, if not expended in useful employment, will be a continual source of trial to themselves and to their teachers. Many kinds of labor adapted to different persons may be devised. But the working of the land will be a special blessing to the worker. There is a great want of intelligent men to till the soil, who will be thorough. This knowledge will not be a hindrance to the education essential for business or for usefulness in any line. To develop the capacity of the soil requires thought and intelligence. Not only will it develop muscle, but capability for study, because the action of brain and muscle is equalized.

We should so train the youth that they will love to work upon the land, and delight in improving it. The hope of advancing the cause of God in this country is in creating a new moral taste in love of work, which will transform mind and character. . . .

"The school to be established in Australia should bring the question of industry to the front, and reveal the fact that physical labor has its place in God's plan for every man, and that His blessing will attend it. The schools established by those who teach and practise the truth for this time, should be so conducted as to bring fresh and new incentives into all kinds of practical labor. There will be much to try the educators, but a great and noble object has been gained when students shall feel that love for God is to be revealed, not only in the devotion of heart and mind and soul, but in the apt, wise appropriation of their strength. Their temptations will be far less; from them by precept and example a light will radiate amid the erroneous theories and fashionable customs of the world. . . .

"The question may be asked, How can he get wisdom that holdeth the plow, and driveth the oxen?—By seeking her as silver, and searching for her as for hid treasures. 'For his God doth instruct him to discretion, and doth teach him.' 'This also cometh forth from the Lord of hosts, which is wonderful in counsel, and excellent in working.'

"He who taught Adam and Eve in Eden how to tend the garden, would instruct men to-day. There is wisdom for him who holds the plow, and plants and sows the seed. The earth has its concealed treasures, and the Lord would have thousands and tens of thousands working upon the soil who are crowded into the cities to watch for a chance to earn a trifle. In many cases that trifle is not turned into bread, but is put into the till of the publican [saloon-keeper], to obtain that which destroys the reason of man formed in the image of God. Those who will take their families into the country, place them where they have fewer temptations. The children who are with parents that love and fear God, are in every way much better situated to learn of the Great Teacher, who is the source and fountain of wisdom. They have a much more favorable opportunity to gain a fitness for the kingdom of heaven."[1]

LOOKING FOR A SUITABLE PROPERTY

Elder Olsen remained in Australia about six weeks after the close of the 1894 camp meeting. During that time he joined heartily in the search for a suitable place for the school. The officers of the Conference and the locating committee were hoping that some good property might be found before his departure for America, but in this they were disappointed. Mrs. White visited many of the places under consideration. As the search advanced, it became evident that great difficulty would be experienced in securing, at moderate cost, a property suitable for the broad lines of work it was thought should be carried on by the school.

In May, five members of the committee visited Dora Creek and Cooranbong, and examined the tract of land which was afterward purchased for $4,500. This tract contained 1,450 acres of wild land, about 500 acres of which was thought to be suitable for the cultivation of grains, fruits, and vegetables, and for pasture. After its purchase, the estate was

[1] "Special Testimonies on Education," pp. 84-104.

named "Avondale," because of the numerous creeks and the abundance of flowing water. The place chosen for school buildings is about three miles west from the Dora Creek railway station, and one and a quarter miles southeast of the Cooranbong post office.

In January and February of 1895, the friends of the school were favored with a visit from Mrs. A. E. Wessels, of Cape Town, South Africa, accompanied by three of her children. They were well pleased with many features of the Avondale estate; and being deeply in sympathy with the objects and aims of the work, her daughter Anna gave $5,000 to help make a beginning.

AN INDUSTRIAL EXPERIMENT

From the time the property came into full possession of the Australasian Union Conference, to the time of the opening of the school, there was much to be done. Land must be cleared, a swamp drained, an orchard planted, and buildings erected. For the accomplishment of this, a number of students were gathered,— sturdy young men who were glad to work six hours a day, and receive their board, and instruction in two studies. The school opened March 6, 1895, and continued thirty weeks.

For the accommodation of the twenty young men who entered into this work, an old hotel was rented in Cooranbong, and several tents were pitched beside this building. In April, Brother Metcalfe Hare, who had been chosen as treasurer and business manager of the school enterprise, moved his family to Cooranbong, and, desiring to be close to the work, pitched his tents near the sawmill and the site set apart for school buildings. For nearly two years the tent, covered with a galvanized iron roof, served as his habitation.

Many parents wishing to send their children to the school, thought it ought to be located near one of the large cities where many Seventh-day Adventists were living. They believed that thirty or forty acres of land not far from Sydney or Melbourne would be much better than a large tract of wild land near Newcastle. Others were opposed to the place because they thought the land was so poor that little would be gained in its cultivation. Mrs. White had a more encouraging view of the value of the land; and when the liberal gift of $5,000 by the friends from Africa made it possible to pay for the tract, she wrote: "I felt my heart bound with gratitude, when I knew that in the providence of God the land was in our possession; and I longed to shout the high praises of God for so favorable a situation."

In July, 1895, Mrs. White determined to manifest her interest in the school enterprise and her confidence in the Avondale estate, by purchasing a piece of the land, and making Cooranbong her home. She selected sixty-six acres, and in a few weeks had a portion of her family living in tents on the tract, which she named "Sunnyside." The erection of an eight-roomed cottage was begun; and as soon as a clearing could be made, land was plowed, and fruit trees were planted. Of this experience she wrote:

"When the foundation of the house was laid, preparations were made for the raising of fruit and vegetables. The Lord had shown me that the poverty which existed about Cooranbong need not be; for with industry the soil could be cultivated, and made to yield its treasure for the service of man."

Mrs. White's unbounded enthusiasm regarding the improvement of the Avondale estate, did much to cheer and encourage others. She was particularly insistent that no time be lost by the school men in the planting of an orchard; and she greatly rejoiced when in October one thousand choice fruit trees were

A view of "Sunnyside," the Australian home of Mrs. White at Cooranbong, New South Wales, 1895-1900.

planted on a favorable piece of land occupied a year before by a thick forest of eucalyptus trees.

After the close of the industrial school in November, several months passed without material progress being made. The people felt very keenly the financial depression under which the colonies were still staggering. Criticism regarding the effort to build up a school in such a wild, out-of-the-way place, grew more and more general. Then came the unfavorable termination of a lawsuit into which the school had been dragged by the hasty action of its solicitor, which cost two thousand dollars, besides causing serious delay in the work.

What could be done? The work seemed to be at a standstill, with little prospect of more favorable conditions. The loss of two thousand dollars would have been very discouraging at any time, but at such a time as this it was most disheartening.

A BEAUTIFUL DREAM

In this crisis, when the faith of many was being sorely tried, Mrs. White had a dream which brought to her and to others the sweet assurance that God had not forsaken them. In relating this experience, she wrote:

"On the night of July 9, 1896, I had a beautiful dream. My husband, James White, was by my side. We were upon our little farm in the woods in Cooranbong, consulting in regard to the prospect of the future returns of the labor put forth.

"My husband said to me, 'What are you doing in reference to a school building?'

"'We can do nothing,' I said, 'unless we have means, and I know not where means are coming from. We have no school building. Everything seems to be at a standstill. But I am not going to encourage unbelief. I will work in faith. I have been tempted to tell you a discouraging chapter in our experience; but I will talk faith. If we look at things which are seen, we shall be discouraged. We have to break the soil at a venture, plow in hope, in faith. We would see a measure of prosperity ahead, if all would work intelligently, and with earnest endeavor put in the seed. The present appearance is not flattering, but all the light that I can obtain is that now is the sowing time. The working of the grounds is our lesson book; for in exactly the way we treat the fields with the hope of future returns, so we must sow this missionary soil with the seeds of truth.'

"We went the whole length of the grounds we were cultivating. We then returned, conversing as we walked along; and I saw that the vines we had passed were bearing fruit. Said my husband, 'The fruit is ready to be gathered.'

"As I came to another path, I exclaimed: 'Look, look at the beautiful berries. We need not wait until to-morrow for them.' As I gathered the fruit, I said: 'I thought these plants were inferior, and hardly worth the trouble of putting into the ground. I never looked for such an abundant yield.'

"My husband said: 'Ellen, do you remember when we first entered the field in Michigan, and traveled in a wagon to the different localities to meet with the humble companies who were observing the Sabbath,— how forbidding the prospect was? In the heat of summer our sleeping-room was often the kitchen, where the cooking had been done through the day, and we could not sleep. Do you remember how, in one instance, we lost our way, and when we could find no water, you fainted? With a borrowed ax we cut our way through the forest until we came to a log shanty, where we were given some bread and milk and a lodging for the night. We prayed and sang with the family, and in the morning left them one of our pamphlets.

" 'We were greatly troubled over this circumstance. Our guide knew the way, and that we should get lost was something we could not understand. Years afterward, at a camp meeting, we were introduced to several persons who told us their story. That visit made, as we thought, by mistake, that book we left, was seed sown. Twenty in all were converted by what we supposed was a mistake. This was the work of the Lord, that light might be given to those who desired to know the truth.'

"My husband continued: 'Ellen, you are on missionary ground. You are to sow in hope and faith, and you will not be disappointed. One soul is worth more than all that was paid for this land, and already you have sheaves to bring to the Master. The work commenced in other new fields,— in Rochester, N. Y., in Michigan, in Oakland, in San Francisco, and in the European fields,— was quite as unpromising as the work in this field. But the work you do in faith and hope will bring you into fellowship with Christ and His faithful servants. It must be carried on in simplicity and faith and hope, and eternal results will be the reward of your labors.' "

HELP FROM FRIENDS IN AFRICA

In April, 1896, Mrs. White had written to the Wessels brothers, of Cape Town, asking them to lend her $5,000 at a low rate of interest, that she might lend it to the school board to help and encourage in the beginning of the necessary buildings. In one of her letters to these friends in South Africa, she wrote:

"We must build a school here, where students may be educated to form characters for eternal life, and where they may receive such an education in the Scriptures that they will go out from the school to educate others. This is the Lord's work; and when we know that we are doing the very work He has specified, we must have faith to believe that He will open the way. . . . The King's business requires haste. The youth in this country are expecting a school, and we do not want them to wait longer.

"Would you know how you can best please your Saviour? It is by putting your money to the exchangers, to be used in the Lord's service and to advance His work. By doing this, you make the very best outlay of the means God has entrusted to you. I have consecrated all I possess to the Lord, and have expended means in various lines, helping to sustain camp meetings, and building meetinghouses in those places where people have accepted the truth. I find many openings where I can help to save perishing souls. . . .

"It pays us to labor for those for whom Christ has died. Our strength and resources can be expended in no better way. If, by the help of the Spirit of God, we can build a structure which will last through the eternal ages, what a work we have done! Coöperating with God in this work, we can think of Christ's words, so full of assurance, 'I say unto you, that likewise joy shall be in heaven over one sinner that repenteth, more than over ninety and nine just persons, which need no repentance.' God cares for the human souls to whom He gave His only-begotten Son, and we must see all men through the eyes of divine compassion."

Not long after the dream about the ripening fruit, letters came from Africa, stating that Mrs. A. E. Wessels would lend to Sister White the money she had asked for. Joyfully this news was communicated to the school board, and immediately the cutting and sawing of timber for the buildings was hastened along.

Oct. 5, 1896, at 5:30 P. M., a group of about thirty-five gathered on the school campus, and Mrs. White laid the first brick of the foundation of Bethel Hall, which was to be the young ladies' dormitory. She then briefly related her experience, as follows:

"Often during this time of financial straits, I awakened in the night sorely distressed over the situation. To what source could we look for help? I earnestly prayed that the Lord would open the way for us to build, and that although there seemed no prospect of securing means, He would send the needed help. One night I fell asleep, and dreamed that I was weeping and praying before the Lord. A hand touched me on the shoulder, and a voice said: 'I have means in many families in Africa that is being bound up in worldly enterprises. Send to the Wessels brothers. Tell them the Lord has need of money. It will do them good to help to advance My work here with their entrusted means. Tell them to lay up treasure for themselves in heaven, where moth will not corrupt, and where thieves do not break through nor steal; for where their treasure is, there will their heart be also.' "

PUTTING UP THE FIRST BUILDINGS

For four months the sawmill and the carpenters made very good progress. The ladies' dormitory was nearly completed, and the foundation pillars for the Dining Hall were being laid. According to the architect's plans, this was to be a one-story structure, eighty by twenty-six feet in size, for the accommodation of dining- and serving-rooms, pantry, kitchen, and storerooms. But the school board, fearing that a third building could not be erected soon, planned to add a second story, one end of which, left unfinished, could be used for a time as a chapel, while the remaining portion could be made to accommodate a dozen boys with sleeping quarters.

When the work on this building was about two thirds done, the treasurer reported that the funds were exhausted, and that the work must move slowly. But the time was nearing when the school was to be opened, and the friends of the enterprise felt that unpreparedness to care properly for those who should come would be disastrous. "The school must open on the date advertised," Mrs. White insisted, when told of the difficulties surrounding the school board. To this the builders replied, "It is impossible; it cannot be done."

There remained one resource,— the united and unselfish coöperation of all in a supreme effort to bring about that which seemed so utterly impossible. Mrs. White determined to appeal direct to the people. "We appointed a meeting for Sunday morning at six o'clock, and called the church together," she afterward wrote of the experiences of the weeks that followed. "We laid the situation before the brethren and sisters, and called for donated labor. Thirty men and women offered themselves for work; and although it was hard for them to spare the time, a strong company continued at work day after day, till the buildings were completed, cleaned, and furnished, ready to be used at the day set for the opening of the school."

At the time appointed, April 28, 1897, the school was opened, with Elder and Mrs. S. N. Haskell and Prof. and Mrs. H. C. Lacey as teachers. On the first day, there were only ten students. When the word went abroad that the school had actually opened and begun work, others came; and a month later, when Prof. and Mrs. C. B. Hughes came to join the teaching force, there were nearly thirty students in attendance. As the term advanced, and the character of the instruction given was told in the churches, others made great efforts to join them, and before the close of the term there were sixty students in all. About forty of these were accommodated in the school home.

ANOTHER TEST OF FAITH

As the school term advanced, and families gathered in so that their children might have its advantages, the Sabbath congregations became much too large for the temporary chapel above the dining-hall, in which seats had been provided for one hundred. In former years the Sabbath meetings had been held, first, in the dining-room of the Healey Hotel; and later on, in the dark, uncomfortable loft of the sawmill. The little chapel was a much better meeting-hall than the mill loft; but now it was too small. There was much discussion as to what could be done; and finally the brethren determined to erect a neat and commodious church, sufficiently large for the needs of all.

Referring to this experience while speaking in the church during the week of prayer held in June, 1898, Mrs. White said:

"When the time came for this meetinghouse to be built, there was another test of faith and loyalty. We had a council to consider what should be done. The way seemed hedged about with difficulties. Some said, 'Inclose a small building, and when money shall come in, enlarge; for we cannot possibly complete at this time such a house as we desire.' Others said, 'Wait till we have money with which to build a commodious house.' This we thought to do. But the word of the Lord came to me in the night season, 'Arise, and build without delay.'

"We then decided that we would take hold of the work, and walk out by faith to make a beginning. The very next night there came from South Africa a draft for two hundred pounds, . . . to help us in building the meetinghouse. Our faith had been tested, we had decided to begin the work, and now the Lord put into our hands this large gift with which to begin. With this encouragement the work began in earnest. The school board gave the land and one hundred pounds, two hundred pounds was received from the Union Conference, and the members of the church gave what they could. Friends outside of the church helped; and the builders gave a part of their time, which was as good as money. Thus the work was completed, and we have this beautiful house, capable of seating four hundred people."[2]

Meanwhile the school prospered, and a goodly number of young men and young women were prepared to enter the service of the Master. At the Queensland camp meeting, held in Brisbane Oct. 14-24, 1898, Mrs. White reviewed this most encouraging feature of the development of the school, as follows:

"During the first year, . . . with an attendance of sixty students, there were about thirty who were over sixteen years of age; and from this number, ten were employed during the vacation in various branches of our religious work. During the second year, there were one hundred in attendance; and from among fifty who were over sixteen years of age, definite work was found for thirty-two during the vacation. Twenty-five of these were employed by the conferences and societies in religious work."[3]

---

[2] *Review and Herald,* Nov. 1, 1898.
[3] *Idem,* March 28, 1899.

AIMS AND OBJECTS

It was primarily for the purpose of giving the students a practical fitting up for service in many lines of Christian endeavor, that the managers of the Avondale School had been planning all through the years. Clearly and forcefully Mrs. White emphasized, over and over again, the work before the school, and the great advantages accruing to students and teachers through daily contact with the practical affairs of everyday life. In September, 1898, she wrote:

"We need more teachers and more talent to educate the students in various lines, that many persons may go from this place willing and able to carry to others the knowledge which they have received. Orphan boys and girls are to find a home here. Buildings should be erected for a hospital, and boats should be provided to accommodate the school. A competent farm manager should be employed, also wise, energetic men to act as superintendents of the several industrial enterprises, men who will use their undivided talents in teaching the students how to work.

"Many young people will come to school who desire a training in industrial lines. The industrial instruction should include the keeping of accounts, carpentry, and everything that is comprehended in farming. Preparation should also be made for teaching blacksmithing, painting, shoemaking, cooking, baking, laundering, mending, typewriting, and printing.[4]

---

[4] NOTE.— Some of the industries undertaken at the Avondale school have developed to large proportions. Concerning the printing plant and the health food factory, it was reported at the 1909 General Conference: "The work in our printing plant and in our food factory has grown until at the present time we have an income of from two to three thousand dollars a month [gross] from these departments. This amount in cash each month helps us out considerably. But if we had not acted upon the instruction God gave us on this matter, we would not have had this income, and would not have been able to help so many students." (*Bulletin*, 1909, p. 83.)

At the 1913 General Conference, the principal of the Avondale School

Every power at our command is to be brought into this training work, that students may go out equipped for the duties of practical life. . . .

MISSIONARY LABOR THE HIGHEST TRAINING

"The Lord will surely bless all who seek to bless others. The school is to be so conducted that teachers and students will be continually gaining in power through the faithful use of the talents given them. By putting to a practical use that which they have learned, they will constantly increase in wisdom and knowledge. We are to learn from the Book of books the principles upon which we are to live and labor. By consecrating all our God-given abilities to Him who has the first right to them, we may make precious advances in everything that is worthy of our attention. . . .

"Our schools must be conducted under the supervision of God. There is a work to be done for young men and women that is not yet accomplished. There are much larger numbers of young people who need to have the advantages of our training schools. They need the manual training course, that will teach them how to lead an active, energetic life. All kinds of labor must be connected with our schools. Under wise, judicious, God-fearing directors, the students are to be taught. Every branch of the work is to be conducted in the most thorough and systematic ways that long experience and wisdom can enable us to plan and execute.

reported: "As a missionary and educational factor, the printing department is proving to be of great importance. It is self-supporting, and employs about twenty-five students. Several others are members of the industrial class. Literature has been produced by the press up to the present time in Fijian, Tongan, Tahitian, Rarotongan, Maori, Singapore-Malay, Java-Malay, Niue, Samoan, and English. Six monthly publications and one weekly journal are issued." (*Bulletin*, 1913, pp. 149, 150.)

"Let the teachers wake up to the importance of this subject, and teach agriculture and other industries that it is essential for the students to understand. Seek in every department of labor to reach the very best results. Let the science of the word of God be brought into the work, that the students may understand correct principles, and may reach the highest possible standard. Exert your God-given abilities, and bring all your energies into the development of the Lord's farm. Study and labor, that the best results and the greatest returns may come from the seed-sowing, that there may be an abundant supply of food, both temporal and spiritual, for the increased number of students that shall be gathered in to be trained as Christian workers."[5]

FIELDS WHITE UNTO THE HARVEST

As the workers in the Australasian colonies and in the islands of the Pacific kept advancing into new territory, there came to them a deepening conviction that every effort possible must be put forth to train many laborers for the harvest.

"All about us," declared Mrs. White on one occasion in 1898, while attending a wonderfully inspiring camp meeting in the newly formed Queensland Conference, "are fields white unto the harvest; and we all feel an intense desire that these fields shall be entered, and that the standard of truth shall be raised in every city and village.

"As we study the vastness of the work, and the urgency of entering these fields without delay, we see that hundreds of workers are needed where there are now but two or three, and that we must lose no

[5] "Testimonies for the Church," Vol. 6, pp. 182, 189, 191, 192.

time in building up those institutions where workers are to be educated and trained."[6]

And as the Australasian Union Conference Committee studied anew, in the light of the opening providences of God, their duty to occupy new territory, they "recognized the school, the sanitarium, and the food factory as three agencies working in harmony for the education and training of home and foreign missionaries, who should go forth prepared to minister to the physical, mental, and moral needs of their fellow men." In her report to the readers of the *Review* of this advance step on the part of her brethren in Australia, Mrs. White wrote: "We all feel that the work is urgent. There is no part that can wait. All must advance without delay."

At times through the years of toil spent in raising up a strong constituency in Australasia, and in establishing centers where the youth might be trained as workers for God, Mrs. White and her associates caught glimpses of what the future had in store for that portion of the broad harvest field. The pioneers in that field,— Elders Haskell, Corliss, Israel, Daniells, and others,— had early recognized the possibility of raising up workers there who should be able to enter the surrounding islands of Polynesia, Melanesia, and Micronesia. But late in the nineties, when the various branches of the cause of present truth,— publishing, educational, and medical,— were becoming well established, and many youth were being raised up as workers, the brethren in charge of the Australasian Union Conference saw more and still more clearly the opportunities for service with which they were surrounded.

---

[6] *Review and Herald*, March 28, 1899.

These possibilities of the future were outlined at length by Mrs. White in communications addressed to the leaders of the cause of God who were assembling in General Conference early in 1899. "Our brethren have not discerned that in helping us," she wrote to them concerning the value of maintaining strong training centers for workers in Australasia, "they would be helping themselves. That which is given to start the work here, will result in strengthening the work in other places. As your gifts free us from continual embarrassment, our labors can be extended; there will be an ingathering of souls, churches will be established, and there will be increasing financial strength. We shall have a sufficiency not only to carry on the work here, but to impart to other fields. Nothing is gained by withholding the very means that would enable us to work to advantage, extending the knowledge of God and the triumphs of truth in regions beyond."[7]

A TRAINING GROUND FOR MISSION FIELDS

In behalf of the brethren and sisters in Australasia who were eager to share the burdens of missionary endeavor in the regions beyond, Elder A. G. Daniells, at that time the president of the Australasian Union Conference, reported to the 1899 General Conference the rapid developments taking place, and the strong faith of all in their ability to unite with their fellow workers in America and Europe in carrying the third angel's message into missionary territory.

"We in Australasia," he wrote, "have been slow to grasp the meaning of God's providence in keeping His servant, Sister White, in this country. When

[7] The *Daily Bulletin of the General Conference,* 1899, p. 131.

she came, we all thought she was making us only a brief visit. She thought so. But the Lord knew better. He placed her in this land, and does not cause the cloud to lift and move elsewhere.

"Ever since she came, God has been instructing her regarding the work here. He has pointed out the mistakes in our methods of labor. He has caused another mould to be placed upon the work throughout the entire field. He has constantly admonished to 'go forward,' to break forth on every side. All the time He is directing us to enlarge our work. He has given His servant a great burden regarding the educational work. The struggle it has taken to carry out what God has plainly revealed should be done, has been terrible. Satan has contested every inch of the ground; but God has given us many victories. He has planted the Avondale School, and we have the plainest evidences that He will be glorified by it. He has given minute instructions regarding its location, object, and management. *Now He is telling us that if we will walk in the light He has given, Avondale will become the training ground for many missionary fields.* The hand of God is in all these things. We are endeavoring to arouse our people to understand the situation, and do all in their power to sustain the work. They are responding nobly; but our visible resources are small for the great work we are urged to do. . . .

"We have an army of intelligent young men and women, anxious to fit themselves for the work of God. We believe that in a short time we shall be able to furnish a large number of valuable workers for various mission fields under the British flag. The

Lord is revealing this to us through the Spirit of prophecy, *and He will bring it to pass.*"[8]

In a talk on the Avondale School and its work, given Sabbath afternoon, July 22, 1899, before the Australasian Union Conference session of that year, Mrs. White emphasized at considerable length the missionary character of the work to be done there. She said:

"God designs that this place shall be a center, an object lesson. Our school is not to pattern after any school that has been established in America, or after any school that has been established in this country. We are looking to the Sun of Righteousness, trying to catch every beam of light that we can. . . .

"From this center we are to send forth missionaries. Here they are to be educated and trained, and sent to the islands of the sea and other countries. The Lord wants us to be preparing for missionary work. . . .

"There is a great and grand work to be done. Some who are here may feel that they must go to China or other places to proclaim the message. These should first place themselves in the position of learners, and thus be tested and tried."[9]

And this ideal—the training of many Christian workers for the needy mission fields lying beyond—was continually held before the supporters of the Avondale School, and is the ideal that has characterized the work there in the years that have followed, as indicated by the very name the school now bears, "The Australasian Missionary College."

"We have moved out by faith and have made large advancement," Mrs. White wrote at the close of 1899,

---

[8] The *Daily Bulletin of the General Conference*, 1899, pp. 141, 142.
[9] *Australasian Union Conference Record*, July 28, 1899, pp. 8, 9.

"because we saw what needed to be done, and we dared not hesitate. But we have not done the half of that which should be done. We are not yet on vantage ground. There is a great work before us. All about us are souls longing for light and truth; and how are they to be reached? . . .

"My brethren and sisters in Australasia, there is in every city and every suburb a work to be done in presenting the last message of mercy to a fallen world. And while we are trying to work these destitute fields, the cry comes from far-off lands, 'Come over and help us.' These are not so easily reached, and perhaps not so ready for the harvest, as the fields within our sight, but they must not be neglected. We want to push the triumphs of the cross. Our watchword is to be, 'Onward, ever onward!' Our burden for the 'regions beyond' can never be laid down until the whole earth shall be lightened with the glory of the Lord.

"But what can we do? We sit down and consider, we pray, and plan how to begin the work in the places all around us. Where are the faithful missionaries who will carry it forward? and how shall they be sustained?

"Above all, how shall missionaries be trained? How shall workers be prepared to enter the opening fields? Here is now our greatest burden. Therefore our special anxiety is for our school in Avondale. We must here provide suitable facilities for educating workers in different lines. We see young men possessing qualifications that, if they can be rightly educated, will enable them to become laborers together with God. We must give them the opportunity. Some are placing students in our school, and are assisting them in defraying their expenses, that they may become workers in some part of the Lord's vineyard. Much more should be done in this line, and special efforts should be made in behalf of those whom our workers shall send from the islands to be trained as missionaries.

"In the future, more than in the past, our school must be an active missionary agency, as the Lord has specified. . . . Workers we must have, and in twenty-fold greater numbers, to supply the need in both the home and the foreign field. Therefore, the Avondale School must not be restricted in its facilities."[10]

AFTER MANY YEARS

From 1901 to 1909 Prof. C. W. Irwin acted as principal of the Avondale School; and in his report to the General Conference of 1909 he bore witness of the fulfillment of that which had been said would come to pass on the Avondale estate, as follows:

"As time has gone on, and we have had an opportunity to watch the work develop, we can say most assuredly, from our experience, that God led in the selection of this place. Everything that has been said about the location of the school in this place, has been fulfilled,— everything."

Professor Irwin declared further: "The brethren, in counsel with Sister White, had made such broad and liberal plans for the school, that through my eight years' connection with it I have never yet needed to change a single plan they had laid down. God guided in the establishment of the work there; and all we have endeavored to do during these eight years, has simply been to develop more fully the plans

---

[10] *Australian Union Conference Record,* Jan. 1, 1900, p. 2.

already made. I believe the working out of this has proved that God's instruction was true.

"It would necessarily follow that in starting a school of that kind, in a field where the constituency was small, and where the people had been passing through serious difficulty financially, there would be a large indebtedness of about $23,000 on the school. It was about this time that the plan of selling the book 'Christ's Object Lessons' was launched, and our brethren in that country took hold of this work with an earnest purpose to carry out the instruction regarding it. As a result of their efforts, up to the present time, something over $20,000 has been received from the sale of 'Christ's Object Lessons' for the school. The indebtedness being $23,000 when we started, practically all the original indebtedness has been liquidated by the sale of 'Christ's Object Lessons.' . . .

"At the beginning of the 'Object Lessons' campaign, the present worth of the Avondale School was about $23,000. The present worth of the school today [1909] is about $67,000. Adding $20,000, the amount that has been received, to the $23,000 present worth, makes $43,000. Subtract this from $67,000, the present worth, and you will notice that the school has made, during the past eight years, about $24,000. This proves that industrial schools can be made to pay.

"When we began our work at this school, eight years ago, the students were earning about $2,000 a year in the industrial work; that is, they were working sufficient to receive a credit of $2,000 a year. That work has steadily grown from that day to this, until, when our last statement was drawn, Sept. 30,

1908, it was shown that the students, during the preceding year, had earned $20,000 on their education."[11] . . . Since the inauguration of the 'Christ's Object Lessons' work, we have never called for a penny of donations from the field. We believe that when the Lord says that an industrial school can be conducted successfully, financially as well as otherwise, the only thing for us to do is to take hold and prove that what He has said is true.

"I am aware, however, that financial figures are not necessarily the best sign of success in a school. It was said at that time, also, that this school was to prepare missionaries to go out into various fields; and, as you know, we in Australia have a large missionary field, representing many millions of people, . . . between sixty-five and seventy millions. Most of these are natives, who must be reached by this present truth. Five years ago we did not have more than two or three from the Avondale School in these mission fields, but to-day nearly thirty from our school are engaged in active labor in these fields."[12]

During the 1913 General Conference, Elder J. E. Fulton reported concerning the Avondale School: "Each year, this institution supplies new recruits for our field. Many who in former years were students in this school are now doing successful work both in home and foreign fields."[13]

---

[11] NOTE.— At the 1913 General Conference, Professor Machlan reported continued prosperity in the industrial departments at Avondale. "The industrial feature of the college," he declared, "is a most interesting as well as a most valuable one. Last year fifty-five per cent of the students paid their entire expenses in labor, thirty-five per cent paid one half their school fees, while only ten per cent were full-paying students." (*Bulletin*, 1913, p. 154.)

[12] *General Conference Bulletin*, 1909, pp. 82, 83. During the year 1915, the number of workers in mission fields outside of Australasia, who received a training at Avondale, reached nearly one hundred.

[13] *Idem*, 1913, pp. 149, 150.

LII

THROUGH THE SOUTH TO THE CONFERENCE OF 1901

"Our efforts in missionary lines must become far more extensive," wrote Mrs. White shortly before her return to America in 1900. "A more decided work than has been done must be done prior to the second appearing of our Lord Jesus Christ. God's people are not to cease their labors until they shall encircle the world."

"Let the gospel message ring through our churches, summoning them to universal action. Let the members of the church have increased faith, gaining zeal from their unseen, heavenly allies, from a knowledge of their exhaustless resources, from the greatness of the enterprise in which they are engaged, and from the power of their Leader. Those who place themselves under God's control, to be led and guided by Him, will catch the steady tread of the events ordained by Him to take place. Inspired with the Spirit of Him who gave His life for the life of the world, they will no longer stand still in impotency, pointing to what they cannot do. Putting on the armor of heaven, they will go forth to the warfare, willing to do and dare for God, knowing that His omnipotence will supply their need."[1]

CENTERS OF INFLUENCE AND OF TRAINING

With the rapid development of missionary operations in many lands during the nineties, there had arisen perplexing administrative problems regarding the distribution of workers and of means. Some advocated one policy, some another. There were those

[1] "Testimonies for the Church," Vol. 6, p. 14.

who urged the immediate occupation of the strongholds of heathenism by large forces of workers, while others held to the policy of carrying on a vigorous campaign in unoccupied regions of the home land, as, for example, the Southern States of America, and in those countries where the efforts of the workers were rewarded with encouraging and substantial results. These advocated that difficult heathen lands be entered only as the providence of God might plainly open the way.

For several years Mrs. White had been writing concerning the advantages to be gained by establishing centers of influence and of training in England and in some of the Continental countries of Europe, and in such fields as Australasia, where the prospects were good for raising up and educating many workers to enter the less favored regions beyond. She had also been counseling the brethren to carry forward an aggressive campaign in the Southern States, and had often pleaded that this portion of the field be dealt with liberally.

"It is the very essence of all right faith," she wrote, "to do the right thing at the right time. God is the great Master Worker, and by His providence He prepares the way for His work to be accomplished. He provides opportunities, opens up lines of influence and channels of working. If His people are watching the indications of His providence, and stand ready to coöperate with Him, they will see a great work accomplished. Their efforts, rightly directed, will produce a hundredfold greater results than can be accomplished with the same means and facilities in another channel where God is not so manifestly working. . . .

"Certain countries have advantages that mark them as centers of education and influence. In the English-speaking nations and the Protestant nations of Europe it is comparatively easy to find access to the people, and there are many advantages for establishing institutions and carrying forward our work. In some other lands, such as India and China, the workers must go through a long course of education before the people can understand them, or they the people. And at every step there are great difficulties to be encountered in the work. In America, Australia, England, and some other European countries, many of these impediments do not exist."[2]

SPECIAL OPPORTUNITIES IN THE SOUTH

During her journey to the General Conference of 1901, Mrs. White took occasion to pass through the Southern States, and to speak words of courage and counsel to those who were laboring there. At Vicksburg, Miss., she came in direct contact with the work carried forward from that center in behalf of the colored people. At Nashville she met with a larger group of workers, diligently studying the necessities of the cause in the Southern States, and inaugurating many lines of work.

The *Gospel Herald,* formerly printed in Battle Creek, had been moved to Nashville, and the advantages in publishing tracts and books for the Southland, at Nashville, were being considered. Regarding these things, Mrs. White testified:

"Many lines of business will open up as the work is carried forward. There is much work to be done in the South, and in order to do this work the laborers must have suitable literature, books telling the

[2] "Testimonies for the Church," Vol. 6, pp. 24, 25 (published in 1901).

truth in simple language, and abundantly illustrated. This kind of literature will be the most effective means of keeping the truth before the people. A sermon may be preached and soon forgotten, but a book remains."[3]

In communications written a few months later on the necessity of planning wisely for the conduct of the publishing work in the South, it was plainly pointed out that the brethren in responsibility in that field would find rich blessing in preparing and publishing a line of literature specially adapted to the peculiar needs of the various classes living within their borders.

In May, 1901, the Southern Publishing Association was organized, and plans were laid for the strengthening of the colporteur work throughout the Southern Union Conference. But the issuance and circulation of specially prepared literature would not alone meet the demands of the field. "We need schools in the South," declared Mrs. White. "They must be established away from the city, in the country. There must be industrial and educational schools, where the colored people can teach colored people, and schools where the white people can teach the white people. Missions must be established."[4] The medical missionary work also was to be undertaken, and many small centers for the carrying forward of this line of endeavor were to be established at strategic points.

INSTITUTIONAL TRAINING IN MANY LANDS

Not only in the South were institutions called for, for the education of workers; centers of training were to be established in many lands,—in "England, Aus-

---

[3] *Review and Herald*, May 28, 1901, p. 11.
[4] *General Conference Bulletin*, 1901, p. 483.

tralia, Germany, and Scandinavia, and other Continental countries as the work advances."

"In these countries," Mrs. White pointed out, "the Lord has able workmen, laborers of experience. These can lead out in the establishment of institutions, the training of workers, and the carrying forward of the work in its different lines. God designs that they shall be furnished with means and facilities. The institutions established would give character to the work in these countries, and would give opportunity for the training of workers for the darker heathen nations. In this way the efficiency of our experienced workers would be multiplied a hundredfold."[5]

While broad foundations were to be laid in lands whence many workers might quickly be prepared to go forth to the ends of the earth, the less favored regions were not to be neglected. In this connection Mrs. White wrote: "The cry comes from far-off countries, 'Come over and help us.' These are not so easily reached, and not so ready for the harvest, as are the fields more nearly within our sight; but they must not be neglected."[6]

It was her great desire to see the message of present truth proclaimed in every land, that led Mrs. White during the 1901 General Conference to outline very clearly God's purpose in building up the work along broad lines in the favored regions of the earth. It was her desire to see the message proclaimed in heathen lands, that led her to urge the establishment of institutional training centers in Great Britain, and on the Continent of Europe, as well as in Australia and in the Southern States of America. She pointed out the folly of restricting the work in such places.

---

[5] "Testimonies for the Church," Vol. 6, p. 25.
[6] *Idem*, p. 27.

"Let us not forget the English-speaking countries," she pleaded, "where, if the truth were presented, many would receive and practise it. London has been presented to me again and again as a place in which a great work is to be done. . . . Why have not workers been sent there, men and women who could have planned for the advancement of the work?

SELF-SUPPORTING MISSIONARIES

"I have wondered why our people, those who are not ordained ministers, but who have a connection with God, who understand the Scriptures, do not open the Word to others. If they would engage in this work, great blessing would come to their own souls. . . .

"Let no one suppose that the work in London can be carried forward by one or two. This is not the right plan. While there must be those who can oversee the work, there is to be an army of workers striving to reach the different classes of people. . . .

"God calls upon His people to awake. There is much work to do, and no one is to say: 'We do not want this one. He will stand in our way. He will hinder us.' Cannot God take care of that? Are there not those in this congregation who will settle in London to work for the Master? Are there not those who will go to that great city as self-supporting missionaries? But while missionaries are to do all they can to be self-supporting, let those who remain here, who Sabbath after Sabbath come to the Tabernacle to hear the word of God, who have every convenience and advantage, let them beware how they say to those they send to foreign fields, destitute of every facility and advantage, 'You must be self-supporting.' . . .

"The European field must receive the attention it should have. And we are not to forget the needy fields close at hand. Look at New York! What representation for the truth is there in that city? How much help has been sent there? Our educational and health work must be established there, and this work must be given financial aid. . . .

"God wants the work to go forward in New York. There ought to be thousands of Sabbath keepers in that place, and there would be if the work were carried on as it should be. But prejudices spring up. Men want the work to go in their lines, and they refuse to accept broader plans from others. Thus opportunities are lost. In New York there should be several small companies established, and workers should be sent out. It does not follow that because a man is not ordained as a preacher, he cannot work for God. Let such ones as these be taught how to work, then let them go out to labor. On returning, let them tell what they have done. Let them praise the Lord for His blessing, and then go out again. Encourage them. A few words of encouragement will be an inspiration to them."[7]

REORGANIZATION

In order that the cause of God might prosper, it was imperative that the administration of affairs be such as to permit the widest possible development in all lines of service. "God desires His work to be a rising, broadening, enlarging power," Mrs. White declared during a council meeting held the day preceding the formal opening of the Conference session. "But the management of the work is becoming confused in itself. . . . God calls for a change."[8]

---

[7] *General Conference Bulletin,* 1901, pp. 396-399.
[8] Unpublished MS.

On the opening day of the Conference, Mrs. White spoke further regarding these matters:

"Greater strength must be brought into the managing force of the Conference. . . . God has not put any kingly power in our ranks to control this or that branch of the work. The work has been greatly restricted by the efforts to control it in every line. Here is a vineyard presenting its barren places that have received no labor. And if one should start out to till these places in the name of the Lord, unless he should get the permission of the men in a little circle of authority he would receive no help. But God means that His workers shall have help. If a hundred should start out on a mission to these destitute fields, crying unto God, He would open the way before them. . . . If the work had not been so restricted, . . . it would have gone forward in its majesty. It would have gone in weakness at first, but the God of heaven lives; the great Overseer lives. . . .

"There must be a renovation, a reorganization; a power and strength must be brought into the committees that are necessary."[9]

A few days later, when it was proposed to organize the Southern field into a strong union conference, Mrs. White, in another talk before the delegates, said:

"The arrangements which are being made for that field are in accordance with the light which has been given me. God desires the Southern field to have a conference of its own. The work there must be done on different lines from the work in any other field. The laborers there will have to work on peculiar lines, nevertheless the work will be done. . . .

"The Lord God of Israel will link us all together. The organizing of new conferences is not to separate

[9] *General Conference Bulletin*, 1901, pp. 25, 26.

us. It is to bind us together. The conferences that are formed are to cling mightily to the Lord, so that through them He can reveal His power, making them excellent representations of fruit bearing.''[10]

In later years, as these plans were carried out more or less fully by brethren in responsibility, Mrs. White on many occasions rejoiced in the success that was crowning the efforts of an army of workers whose preparation for service had been gained in strong training centers in North America, Europe, and Australasia.

And great was Mrs. White's rejoicing when the reports from our missionaries in China indicated that the Lord was going before our workers in that land in a special manner, and preparing the hearts of the heathen for the reception of present truth. As God opened the way in fields that in former years had been difficult to enter, she urged the brethren in responsibility to do all in their power to coöperate with the heavenly agencies manifestly at work in the dark places of earth. At the same time she continued to encourage those having to do with institutional work, to hold before the youth in training the high ideals for which our denominational institutions have ever stood, and to redouble their efforts to train many workers to enter the fields whitening unto the harvest. Thus the home land, whether in America, in Europe, in Australasia, or in other favored lands, was to be linked closely with the regions beyond; and all the agencies established for the advancement of the cause of God were to coöperate for the accomplishment of one purpose,—the preparing of a people for the coming of their Lord.

[10] *General Conference Bulletin,* 1901, pp. 69, 70.

LIII

AT THE NATION'S CAPITAL

The destruction in one year, by fire, of the main buildings of two of the leading Seventh-day Adventist institutions at Battle Creek, Mich., led to a study of the advantages that might accrue to the cause of God through a removal of the denominational headquarters and of the Review and Herald printing office to some other place.

This problem was spread before the delegates assembled at the 1903 General Conference. The brethren were urged to express freely their convictions as to the proper course to pursue. While they had the matter under advisement, Mrs. White, who was in attendance as one of the delegates, bore a decided testimony in favor of adopting a policy that would result in a widespread dissemination of the truths of the third angel's message. She called attention to oft repeated counsels to establish centers of influence at strategic points, and to arrange for a wise distribution of the working forces, rather than to follow plans tending toward centralization. The stakes were to be strengthened, but only that the cords might be lengthened. From established centers the influence of present truth was to be extended into all the world. Mrs. White said, in part:

"Will those who have collected in Battle Creek hear the Voice speaking to them, and understand that they are to scatter out into different places, where they can spread abroad a knowledge of the truth, and where they can gain an experience different from the experience that they have been gaining?

"In reply to the question that has been asked in regard to settling somewhere else, I answer, Yes. Let the General Conference offices and the publishing work be moved from Battle Creek. I know not where the place will be, whether on the Atlantic coast or elsewhere; but this I will say: Never lay a stone or a brick in Battle Creek to rebuild the Review Office there. God has a better place for it."[1]

FROM BATTLE CREEK TO THE EAST

Before the close of the 1903 General Conference, the delegates voted:

"That the General Conference offices be removed from Battle Creek, Mich., to some place favorable for its work in the Atlantic States."[2]

Soon after the close of the Conference session, the General Conference Committee took the following action:

"*Voted,* That we favor locating the headquarters of the General Conference in the vicinity of New York City."[3]

And in the forty-third annual meeting of the Review and Herald Publishing Association, held April 21, 1903, recommendations were adopted looking toward the transfer of the work of the Association to some point in the Eastern States.

In the discussion of these recommendations, the object set forth during the General Conference session — placing the institution where it could best share the burden of giving the third angel's message world-wide publicity — was reiterated. As one of the members of the Committee on Resolutions declared, in support of the recommendations offered:

---

[1] *General Conference Bulletin,* 1903, p. 85.
[2] *Idem,* pp. 67, 103.
[3] *Review and Herald,* May 12, 1903, p. 16.

"Why do we talk about moving this institution? Is it not to place ourselves where we can do the work entrusted to us to better advantage? Is it not to place ourselves where . . . we can hasten on to the whole wide world with our message, and bring the glorious consummation of our work?"[4]

IN SEARCH OF A SITE

As a preliminary step toward the carrying out of the recommendations of the General Conference and of the stockholders of the Review and Herald, representative men were chosen to serve as a locating committee. Before proceeding with their work, they wrote to Mrs. White, requesting her to communicate to them any definite light she might have regarding the exact place where they should transfer the publishing interests. In her first response to their request, Mrs. White wrote:

"I have no special light, except what you have already received, in reference to New York and the other large cities that have not been worked. Decided efforts should be made in Washington, D. C. It is a sad thing that the record stands as it does, showing so little accomplished there. It will be best to consider what can be done for this city, and see what ways of working will be the best.

"In the past, decided testimony has been borne in regard to the need of making decided efforts to bring the truth before the people of Washington. . . .

"May the Lord help us to move understandingly and prayerfully. I am sure that He is willing that we should know, and that right early, where we should locate our publishing house. I am satisfied that our

[4] Supplement to *Review and Herald*, April 28, 1903, p. 7.

only safe course is to be ready to move just when the cloud moves. Let us pray that He will direct us. He has signified, by His providence, that He would have us leave Battle Creek. . . .

"New York needs to be worked, but whether our publishing house should be established there, I cannot say. I should not regard the light I have received as definite enough to favor the movement.

"Let us all lift our hearts to God in prayer, having faith that He will guide us. What more can we do? Let Him indicate the place where the publishing house should be established. We are to have no will of our own, but are to seek the Lord, and follow where He leads the way."[5]

The locating committee met in New York City, May 18, 1903, formed their plans, and began at once an investigation of properties in suburban places, and along the Sound and up the Hudson. Day after day they continued their search, until finally they began to despair of finding anything suitable for their needs. Two or three of their number had already returned to Battle Creek, when a second letter was received from Mrs. White, in which she gave further counsel, as follows:

"During the past night many things have been presented to me regarding our present dangers, and some things about our publishing work have been brought most distinctly to my mind.

"As our brethren search for a location for the Review and Herald publishing house, they are earnestly to seek the Lord. They are to move with great caution, watchfulness, and prayer, and with a constant sense of their own weakness. We must not depend upon

---

[5] *Review and Herald,* Aug. 11, 1903, p. 6.

human judgment. We must seek for the wisdom that God gives. . . .

"In regard to establishing the institution in New York, I must say, Be guarded. I am not in favor of its being near New York. I cannot give all my reasons, but I am sure that any place within thirty miles of that city would be too near. Study the surroundings of other places. I am sure that the advantages of Washington, D. C., should be closely investigated.

"The workers connected with the publishing house must be closely guarded. Our young men and young women must not be placed where they will be in danger of being ensnared by Satan.

"We should not establish this institution in a city, nor in the suburbs of a city. It should be established in a rural district, where it can be surrounded by land. In the arrangements made for its establishment, the climate must be considered. The institution should be placed where the atmosphere is most conducive to health. This point should be given an important place in our considerations, for wherever the office of publication is established, preparation must also be made to fit up a small sanitarium and to establish a small agricultural school. We must, therefore, find a place that has sufficient land for these purposes. We must not settle in a congested center.

"My brethren, open up the work intelligently. Let every point be carefully and prayerfully considered. After much prayer and frequent consultation together, act in accordance with the best judgment of all. Let each worker sustain the other. Do not fail or become discouraged. Keep your perceptive faculties keen and clear by learning constantly of Christ, the Teacher who cannot err."[6]

---

[6] *Review and Herald*, Aug. 11, 1903.

As the locating committee had found nothing in the vicinity of New York City that seemed to meet their requirements, and as they had been counseled in both letters to study the advantages of Washington, some members of the committee decided to go to that city, although with but little hope of finding the advantages desired. But they were happily surprised.

"We had not looked about the place long," wrote one of the committeemen, "before there began to steal over us a conviction that, after all, Washington might be the place for our headquarters. The longer we continued to search, the deeper this conviction grew. We found conditions here far more in harmony with the counsel . . . received, than we had found anywhere else."[7]

It was not long after the brethren had come to this conviction, when they received a third letter from Mrs. White, in which she stated:

"We have been praying for light regarding the location of our work in the East, and light has come to us in a very decided way. Positive light has been given me that there will be offered to us for sale places upon which much money has been expended by men who had money to use freely. The owners of these places die, or their attention is called to some other object, and their property is offered for sale at a very low price.

"In regard to Washington, I will say that twenty years ago memorials for God should have been established in that city, or rather, in its suburbs. . . .

"We are many years behind in giving the message of warning in the city that is the capital of our nation. Time and time again the Lord has presented Washing-

[7] *Review and Herald*, Aug. 20, 1903.

ton to me as a place that has been strangely neglected. . . . If there is one place above another where a sanitarium should be established, and where gospel work should be done, it is Washington. . . .

"I present this to you as a matter that is stirring me mightily. One thing is certain: we shall not be clear unless we at once do something in Washington to represent our work. I shall not be able to rest until I see the truth going forth as a lamp that burneth. . . .

"From the light given me, I know that, for the present, the headquarters of the Review and Herald should be near Washington. If there is on our books and papers the imprint of Washington, D. C., it will be seen that we are not afraid to let our light shine. Let the publishing house be established near Washington. Thus we shall show that we are trying to do what God has bidden us do to proclaim the last message of mercy to a perishing world."[8]

FAVORABLE CONDITIONS AT TAKOMA PARK, D. C.

During the latter part of July, 1903, representative brethren from many parts of the field met in Washington, D. C., and proceeded at once to inspect the outlying portions of the District of Columbia for suitable properties. Morning by morning, before going out, they met to pray earnestly for divine guidance. And their prayers were signally answered. In Takoma Park, one of the most attractive and healthful of the towns near Washington, was found a tract of fifty acres, which seemed to meet all requirements. With an altitude of about three hundred feet, the tract was only seven miles from the capitol building, and within

[8] *Review and Herald*, Aug. 20, 1903.

the limits of Takoma Park, thus having the advantages of postal services, gas, water, sewerage, and streets; and at the same time it was sufficiently isolated by dense forests to have the added advantages of a retired country estate. The property was covered with hundreds of native trees; and across one side of it, yet inside the boundary line, ran a picturesque stream fed by living springs.

In former years this property had been selected by a Boston physician for a sanitarium site, and upon it he had expended, including purchase price, about sixty thousand dollars. At heavy cost he had had cleared away the underbrush, logs, and rubbish; but he had been unable to finance his proposed enterprise, and after his death the property had fallen into the hands of a gentleman who held a $15,000 mortgage against it, and who was now offering it for $6,000.

The brethren felt clear in securing, without delay, this beautiful property, thereby making practicable the establishment of a sanitarium and a school near the proposed denominational headquarters. Though the fifty-acre tract in Takoma Park was situated a mile or so beyond the District line, yet the locating committee were able to purchase in the same village sufficient land lying within the District line to serve as a site for the factory building of the Review and Herald Publishing Association. Adjacent lots were secured for the General Conference administration building and for the local church edifice and church school.

Thus the way was opening, step by step, for the early removal of the Review and Herald printing plant and the General Conference offices from Battle Creek, Mich., to the nation's capital. Only a few weeks elapsed before actual transfers were made, and the brethren established themselves in temporary rented quarters in the heart of the city, pending the erection of buildings at Takoma Park.

AN ADVANCE STEP

"The removal to Washington of work hitherto carried on in Battle Creek," wrote Mrs. White to those who had ventured to make the transfer, "is a step in the right direction. We are to continue to press into the regions beyond, where the people are in spiritual darkness."[9]

Those who had advanced by faith were richly rewarded; and as they labored on, they could see more and still more clearly the wisdom of the step they had taken. "As the months go by," wrote the editor of the *Review*, in a last-page note, bearing date of Feb. 25, 1904, "we are able to see more clearly the meaning of the removal of the headquarters of our work to Washington, and to appreciate the opportunity offered here to establish such memorials for the truth as will exert a wide influence in behalf of this message. From the instruction given through the Spirit of prophecy, it is plain that each line of institutional work — publishing, educational, and medical — is to be established here in a representative way, and that a continuous evangelical effort is to be carried forward, so that at the capital of the nation and at the headquarters of our denominational work there may be a proper representation of this message as a missionary movement."

WORDS OF ENCOURAGEMENT

Early in 1904 Mrs. White decided to go to Washington herself, to spend some months there while foundations were being laid. In the course of her first sermon, on Sabbath day, April 30, 1904, she said:

---

[9] *Review and Herald*, Oct. 1, 1903.

"In the city of Washington there is much to be done. I am thankful to God for the privilege of seeing the land that has been purchased for our institutional work in this place. The securing of this land was in the Lord's providence, and I praise God that our brethren had the faith to take this forward step. As I look over this city, I realize the magnitude of the work to be accomplished. . . .

"God now calls upon every believer in this center to act his individual part in helping to build up the work that must be done."[10]

A few days later, Mrs. White wrote:

"The location that has been secured for our school and sanitarium is all that could be desired. The land resembles representations that have been shown me by the Lord. It is well adapted for the purpose for which it is to be used. There is on it ample room for a school and a sanitarium, without crowding either institution. . . .

"A good location for the printing office has been chosen within easy distance of the post office; and a site for a meetinghouse, also, has been found. It seems as if Takoma Park has been specially prepared for us, and that it has been waiting to be occupied by our institutions and their workers.

"My hopes for this place are high. The country for miles and miles around Washington is to be worked from here. I am so thankful that our work is to be established in this place. Were Christ here upon the ground, He would say, 'Lift up your eyes, and look on the fields; for they are white already to harvest.' John 4:35."[11]

---

[10] *Review and Herald*, May 26, 1904.
[11] Unpublished MS., May 10, 1904.

"ARISE, AND BUILD"

In order to bring into existence a strong training center at the denominational headquarters, the brethren found it necessary to plan for the raising of a fund of $100,000. "God's word to His workers in Washington is, 'Arise, and build,' " wrote Mrs. White in one of her published appeals in behalf of this fund; "and His word to His people in all the conferences is, 'Strengthen the hands of the builders.' The work in Washington is to advance in straight lines, without delay or hindrance. Let it not be kept back for lack of means." [12]

Nobly did the brethren and sisters throughout the world respond to the appeals sent forth for funds to establish a strong training center for workers at the nation's capital,— so nobly, in fact, that when the delegates to the 1905 General Conference met in the beautiful grove that had been purchased at Takoma Park, and presented the gifts of the conferences for the closing up of the fund, they found that the amount called for had been exceeded, and that a large overflow was available for appropriation to missions.

"We feel very grateful to our heavenly Father," declared Mrs. White during the 1905 Conference session where the fund was made up, "because He has moved by His Holy Spirit upon the minds of His people to give so liberally for the establishment of His work here in Washington. . . . He will place His approval on the efforts made to carry forward His work on the lines that He has marked out." [13]

---

[12] *Review and Herald,* July 14, 1904.
[13] *Idem,* June 1, 1905, p. 13.

LIV

IN SOUTHERN CALIFORNIA

"All our medical institutions are established as Seventh-day Adventist institutions, to represent the various features of gospel medical missionary work, and thus to prepare the way for the coming of the Lord,"[1] wrote Mrs. White in 1903, when the development of medical missionary work in southern California was under consideration.

"If we are to go to the expense of building sanitariums in order that we may work for the salvation of the sick and afflicted, we must plan our work in such a way that those we desire to help will receive the help they need. We are to do all in our power for the healing of the body; but we are to make the healing of the soul of far greater importance. Those who come to our sanitariums as patients are to be shown the way of salvation, that they may repent, and hear the words, Thy sins are forgiven thee; go in peace and sin no more."[2]

It was because of extraordinary opportunities presenting themselves for the winning of souls, that Mrs. White bore a decided testimony in favor of establishing a group of medical institutions in southern California. "From the light given me when I was in Australia, and renewed since I came to America," she wrote in 1902, "I know that our work in southern California must advance more rapidly. The people flocking to that place in search of health must hear the last message of mercy. . . .

"From many places in southern California the light

---

[1] "Testimonies for the Church," Vol. 7, p. 107.

[2] *Idem*, p. 96.

is to shine forth to the multitudes. Present truth is to be as a city set on a hill, which cannot be hid.

"In southern California there are many properties for sale on which buildings suitable for sanitarium work are already erected. Some of these properties should be purchased, and medical missionary work carried forward on sensible, rational lines. Several small sanitariums are to be established in southern California for the benefit of the multitudes drawn there in the hope of finding health. Instruction has been given me that now is our opportunity to reach the invalids flocking to the health resorts of southern California, and that a work may be done also in behalf of their attendants. . . .

"Instead of investing in one medical institution all the means obtainable, we ought to establish smaller sanitariums in many places. Soon the reputation of the health resorts in southern California will stand even higher than it stands at present. Now is our time to enter that field for the purpose of carrying forward medical missionary work."[3]

During the years when such counsels as these were being given, Mrs. White visited southern California on several occasions, in the hope of encouraging the brethren to persevere in their search for properties suitable for use as medical institutions. At times, in visions of the night there were given her flash-light pictures of sanitariums in running order. These representations she endeavored to write out and pass on to the brethren in responsibility. At other times there was brought vividly before her mind instruction given in past years as to the aim and object of medical missionary work, and as to the pattern that should be

[3] MS. as published in the *Medical Evangelist*, Vol. 1, No. 2.

followed in establishing and maintaining sanitarium enterprises in different parts of the world.

While the eyes of some of the brethren were turned toward the cities, Mrs. White called attention to the advantages of country locations, and the benefits that would come to patients far removed from the distracting influences of modern city life. Considerable portions of this instruction were published in "Testimonies for the Church," Volume 7.[4] Among the presentations set forth were the following:

"In the night season I was given a view of a sanitarium in the country. The institution was not large, but it was complete. It was surrounded by beautiful trees and shrubbery, beyond which were orchards and groves. Connected with the place were gardens, in which the lady patients, when they chose, could cultivate flowers of every description, each patient selecting a special plot for which to care. Outdoor exercise in these gardens was prescribed as a part of the regular treatment.

"Scene after scene passed before me. In one scene a number of suffering patients had just come to one of our country sanitariums. In another I saw the same company, but, oh, how transformed their appearance! Disease had gone, the skin was clear, the countenance joyful; body and mind seemed animated with new life. . . .

"Many of the sick and suffering will turn from the cities to the country, refusing to conform to the habits, customs, and fashions of city life; they will seek to regain health in some one of our country sanitariums. Thus, though we are removed from the cities twenty or thirty miles, we shall be able to reach

---

[4] See section entitled "Our Sanitarium Work," pp. 57-109, in "Testimonies for the Church," Vol. 7.

the people, and those who desire health will have opportunity to regain it under conditions most favorable.

"God will work wonders for us if we will in faith coöperate with Him. Let us, then, pursue a sensible course, that our efforts may be blessed of heaven, and crowned with success."[5]

The counsels regarding the extension of medical missionary work were not limited to any one favored section. "God has qualified His people to enlighten the world," Mrs. White wrote while her mind was especially exercised concerning the opportunities before Seventh-day Adventists in southern California. "He has entrusted them with faculties by which they are to extend His work until it shall encircle the globe. In all parts of the earth, they are to establish sanitariums, schools, publishing houses, and kindred facilities for the accomplishment of His work. . . . In many lands medical missions are to be established, to act as God's helping hand in ministering to the afflicted.

"Christ coöperates with those who engage in medical missionary work. Men and women who unselfishly do what they can to establish sanitariums and treatment rooms in many lands will be richly rewarded. Those who visit these institutions will be benefited physically, mentally, and spiritually — the weary will be refreshed, the sick restored to health, the sin-burdened relieved. In far-off countries, from those whose hearts are by these agencies turned from the service of sin unto righteousness, will be heard thanksgiving and the voice of melody. By their songs of grateful praise a testimony will be borne that will win others to allegiance to and fellowship with Christ."[6]

---

[5] "Testimonies for the Church," Vol. 7, pp. 78, 79.
[6] *Idem*, pp. 51, 52.

At the time of the dedication of the Loma Linda Sanitarium, April 15, 1906, Mrs. White reviewed some of the remarkable providences that had attended the efforts of the brethren to secure sanitarium properties in southern California. She also outlined briefly the divine purpose that is to be wrought out through such agencies. In the course of her remarks, she declared:

"Solemn is the responsibility resting upon medical missionaries. They are to be missionaries in the true sense of the term. The sick and the suffering who entrust themselves to the care of the helpers in our medical institutions, must not be disappointed. They are to be taught how to live in harmony with heaven. As they learn to obey God's law, they will be richly blessed in body and in spirit.

"The advantage of outdoor life must never be lost sight of. How thankful we should be that God has given us beautiful sanitarium properties at Paradise Valley and Glendale and Loma Linda! 'Out of the cities! out of the cities!'—this has been my message for years. We cannot expect the sick to recover rapidly when they are shut in within four walls, in some city, with no outside view but houses, houses, houses,—nothing to animate, nothing to enliven. And yet how slow some are to realize that the crowded cities are not favorable places for sanitarium work!

"Even in southern California, not many years ago, there were some who favored the erection of a large sanitarium building in the heart of Los Angeles. In the light of the instruction God had given, we could not consent to the carrying out of any such plan. In the visions of the night the Lord had shown me unoccupied properties in the country, suitable for sanitarium purposes, and for sale at a price far below the original cost.

"It was some time before we found these places. First we secured the Paradise Valley Sanitarium, near San Diego. A few months later, in the good providence of God, the Glendale property came to the notice of our people, and was purchased and fitted up for service. But light came that our work of establishing sanitariums in southern California was not complete; and on several different occasions testimonies were given that medical missionary work must be done somewhere in the vicinity of Redlands.

"In an article published in the *Review* of April 6, 1905, I wrote:

" 'On our way back to Redlands, as our train passed through miles of orange groves, I thought of the efforts that should be made in this beautiful valley to proclaim the truth for this time. I recognized this section of southern California as one of the places that had been presented to me with the word that it should have a fully equipped sanitarium.

" 'Why have such fields as Redlands and Riverside been left almost unworked? . . . The Lord would have brave, earnest men and women take up His work in these places. The cause of God is to make more rapid advancement in southern California than it has in the past. Every year thousands of people visit southern California in search of health, and by various methods we should seek to reach them with the truth. They must hear the warning to prepare for the great day of the Lord, which is right upon us. . . . Workers who can speak to the multitudes are to be located where they can meet the people, and give them the warning message. . . . Let them be quick to seize opportunities to place present truth before those who know it not. Let them give the message with clearness and power, that those who have ears to hear may hear.'

"These words were written before I had learned anything about the property at Loma Linda. Still the burden of establishing another sanitarium rested upon me. In the fall of 1903 I had a vision of a sanitarium in the midst of beautiful grounds, somewhere in southern California, and no property I had visited answered to the presentation given in this vision. At the time, I wrote about this vision to our brethren and sisters assembled at the Los Angeles camp meeting early in September, 1903.

"While attending the General Conference of 1905, at Washington, D. C., I received a letter from Elder J. A. Burden, describing a property he had found four miles west of Redlands, five and one half miles southeast of San Bernardino, and eight miles northeast of Riverside. As I read his letter, I was impressed that this was one of the places I had seen in vision. . . .

"Later, when I visited this property, I recognized it as one of the places I had seen nearly two years before in vision. How thankful I am to the Lord our God for this place, which is all prepared for us to use to the honor and glory of His name!"[7]

To the delegates assembled at the 1909 General Conference, Mrs. White outlined some of the experiences connected with the establishment of medical missionary work on a solid basis in southern California, and referred particularly to the prospering hand of God in providing facilities for the training of many medical missionary evangelists for world-wide service. In this connection she said:

"One of the chief advantages of Loma Linda is the pleasing variety of charming scenery on every side.

[7] *Review and Herald,* June 21, 1906.

The extensive view of valley and mountain is magnificent. But more important than magnificent scenery and beautiful buildings and spacious grounds is the close proximity of this institution to a densely populated district, and the opportunity thus afforded of communicating to many, many people a knowledge of the third angel's message. We are to have clear spiritual discernment, else we shall fail of discerning the opening providences of God that are preparing the way for us to enlighten the world.

"With the possession of this place comes the weighty responsibility of making the work of the institution educational in character. Loma Linda is to be not only a sanitarium, but an educational center. A school is to be established here for the training of gospel medical missionary evangelists. . . .

"In Loma Linda we have an advantageous center for the carrying on of various missionary enterprises. We can see that it was in the providence of God that this sanitarium was placed in the possession of our people. We should appreciate Loma Linda as a place which the Lord foresaw we should need and which He gave us. There is a very precious work to be done in connection with the interests of the sanitarium and the school at Loma Linda, and this will be done, when we all work to that end, moving unitedly in God's order."[8]

---

[8] *Review and Herald*, June 21, 1906, pp. 173, 174, 176, 177.

LV

THE SAN FRANCISCO EARTHQUAKE

Thursday afternoon, April 12, 1906, Mrs. White left her home to attend the annual meeting of the Southern California Conference, at Los Angeles, and the dedicatory exercises of two sanitariums — Paradise Valley, near San Diego, and Loma Linda, in the San Bernardino Valley. The first few days were spent in Loma Linda, and during this time she had a remarkable experience, which she has briefly described thus:

RETRIBUTIVE JUDGMENTS

"While at Loma Linda, Cal., April 16, 1906, there passed before me a most wonderful representation. During a vision of the night, I stood on an eminence, from which I could see houses shaken like a reed in the wind. Buildings, great and small, were falling to the ground. Pleasure resorts, theaters, hotels, and the homes of the wealthy were shaken and shattered. Many lives were blotted out of existence, and the air was filled with the shrieks of the injured and the terrified.

"The destroying angels of God were at work. One touch, and buildings so thoroughly constructed that men regarded them as secure against every danger, quickly became heaps of rubbish. There was no assurance of safety in any place. I did not feel in any special peril, but the awfulness of the scenes that passed before me I cannot find words to describe. It seemed that the forbearance of God was exhausted, and that the judgment day had come.

"The angel that stood by my side then instructed me that but few have any conception of the wickedness existing in our world to-day, and especially the wickedness in the large cities. He declared that the Lord has appointed a time when He will visit transgressors in wrath for persistent disregard of His law.

"Terrible as was the representation that passed before me, that which impressed itself most vividly upon my mind was the instruction given me in connection with it. The angel that stood by my side declared that God's supreme rulership, and the sacredness of His law, must be revealed to those who persistently refuse to render obedience to the King of kings. Those who choose to remain disloyal, must be visited in mercy with judgments, in order that, if possible, they may be aroused to a realization of the sinfulness of their course.

"Throughout the following day I pondered the scenes that had passed before me, and the instruction that had been given. During the afternoon we journeyed to Glendale, near Los Angeles; and the following night . . . I seemed to be in an assembly, setting before the people the requirements of God's law. I read the scriptures regarding the institution of the Sabbath in Eden at the close of the creation week, and regarding the giving of the law at Sinai; and then declared that the Sabbath is to be observed 'for a perpetual covenant,' as a sign between God and His people forever, that they may know that they are sanctified by the Lord, their Creator.

"Then I further dwelt upon the supreme rulership of God above all earthly rulers. His law is to be the standard of action. Men are forbidden to pervert their senses by intemperance, or by yielding their minds to satanic influences; for this makes impossible the keeping of God's law. While the divine Ruler bears long with perversity, He is not deceived, and will not always keep silence. His supremacy, His authority as Ruler of the universe, must finally be acknowledged, and the just claims of His law vindicated.

"Much more instruction regarding the long-sufferance of God and the necessity of arousing transgressors to a realization of their perilous position in His sight, was repeated to the people, as received from my instructor."[1]

"It has taken me many days to write out a portion of that which was revealed those two nights at Loma Linda and Glendale."[2]

"On April 18, two days after the scene of falling buildings had passed before me, I went to fill an appointment in the Carr Street church, Los Angeles. As we neared the church, we heard the newsboys crying, 'San Francisco destroyed by an earthquake!' With a heavy heart I read the first hastily printed news of the terrible disaster."[3]

WORKING THE CITIES FROM OUTPOST CENTERS

In the course of her talk before the conference, Mrs. White exalted the sacredness of God's law, and spoke decidedly regarding the necessity of prompt action and of acquainting the people with the meaning of the things coming upon the earth. She referred particularly to the advantages to be gained by working the cities from outpost centers.

"Out of the cities, out of the cities!" she declared; "this is the message the Lord has been giving me. The earthquakes will come; the floods will come; and we are not to establish ourselves in the wicked cities,

---

[1] "Testimonies for the Church," Vol. 9, pp. 92-94.
[2] *Review and Herald*, July 5, 1906.
[3] "Testimonies for the Church," Vol. 9, p. 94.

where the enemy is served in every way, and where God is so often forgotten. The Lord desires that we shall have clear spiritual eyesight. We must be quick to discern the peril that would attend the establishment of institutions in these wicked cities. We must make wise plans to warn the cities, and at the same time live where we can shield our children and ourselves from the contaminating and demoralizing influences so prevalent in these places."[4]

SCENES OF DESTRUCTION

Two weeks later Mrs. White returned to her St. Helena home by way of San Jose, Mountain View, and San Francisco. "As we traveled northward," she wrote in an account of this journey, "we saw some of the effects of the earthquake; and when we entered San Jose, we could see that large buildings had collapsed, and that others had been seriously damaged.

"At Mountain View, the new post office and some of the largest stores in town had been leveled to the ground. Other buildings had partially collapsed, and were badly wrecked."[5]

"On our way home from Mountain View, we passed through San Francisco, and, hiring a carriage, spent an hour and a half in viewing the destruction wrought in that great city. Buildings that were thought to be proof against disaster, were lying in ruins. In some instances, buildings were partially sunken in the ground. The city presented a most dreadful picture of the inefficiency of human ingenuity to frame fireproof and earthquake-proof structures."[6]

---

[4] *Review and Herald,* July 5, 1906.
[5] *Idem,* May 24, 1906.
[6] "Testimonies for the Church," Vol. 9, pp. 94, 95.

WARNINGS AND EXHORTATIONS

As regards her teachings and warnings concerning the necessity of earnest endeavor in proclaiming the third angel's message in the cities, in view of the calamities that were to befall populous centers as the end of the world draws nigh, Mrs. White has written thus:

"Since the San Francisco earthquake, many rumors have been current regarding statements I have made. Some have reported that while in Los Angeles, I claimed that I had predicted the San Francisco earthquake and fire, and that Los Angeles would be the next city to suffer. This is not true. The morning after the earthquake, I said no more than that 'the earthquakes will come; the floods will come;' and that the Lord's message to us is that we shall 'not *establish* ourselves in the wicked cities.'

"Not many years ago, a brother laboring in New York City published some very startling notices regarding the destruction of that city. I wrote immediately to the ones in charge of the work there, saying that it was not wise to publish such notices; that thus an excitement might be aroused which would result in a fanatical movement, hurting the cause of God. It is enough to present the truth of the word of God to the people. Startling notices are detrimental to the progress of the work."[7]

Under date of Aug. 3, 1903, Mrs. White further wrote regarding this sensational report:

"Now comes the word that I have declared that New York is to be swept away by a tidal wave. This I have never said. I have said, as I looked at the great buildings going up there, story after story:

[7] *Review and Herald,* July 5, 1906.

'What terrible scenes will take place when the Lord shall arise to shake terribly the earth! Then the words of Rev. 18:1-3 will be fulfilled.' The whole of the eighteenth chapter of Revelation is a warning of what is coming on the earth. But I have no light in particular in regard to what is coming on New York, only I know that one day the great buildings there will be thrown down by the turning and overturning of God's power. From the light given me, I know that destruction is in the world. One word from the Lord, one touch of His mighty power, and these massive structures will fall. Scenes will take place the fearfulness of which we cannot imagine."

On Sept. 1, 1902, Mrs. White wrote:

"Well equipped tent meetings should be held in the large cities, such as San Francisco; for not long hence these cities will suffer under the judgments of God. San Francisco and Oakland are becoming as Sodom and Gomorrah, and the Lord will visit them in wrath."

June 20, 1903: "The judgments of God are in our land. The Lord is soon to come. In fire and flood and earthquake, He is warning the inhabitants of this earth of His soon approach. O that the people may know the time of their visitation! We have no time to lose. We must make more determined efforts to lead the people of the world to see that the day of judgment is at hand."

June 3, 1903: "There are many with whom the Spirit of God is striving. The time of God's destructive judgments is the time of mercy for those who have no opportunity to learn what is truth. Tenderly will the Lord look upon them. His heart of mercy is touched; His hand is still stretched out to save."

Nov. 12, 1902: "The time is nearing when the great crisis in the history of the world will have come, when every movement in the government of God will be watched with intense interest and inexpressible apprehension. In quick succession the judgments of God will follow one another,— fire and flood and earthquakes, with war and bloodshed. Something great and decisive will soon of necessity take place."[8]

Feb. 15, 1904: "When I was last in New York, I was in the night season called upon to behold buildings rising story after story toward heaven. These buildings were warranted to be fireproof, and they were erected to glorify the owners. Higher and still higher these buildings rose, and in them the most costly material was used. . . .

"As these lofty buildings went up, the owners rejoiced with ambitious pride that they had money to use in glorifying self. . . . Much of the money that they thus invested had been obtained through exaction, through grinding the faces of the poor. In the books of heaven, an account of every business transaction is kept. There every unjust deal, every fraudulent act, is recorded. The time is coming when in their fraud and insolence men will reach a point that the Lord will not permit them to pass, and they will learn that there is a limit to the forbearance of Jehovah.

"The scene that next passed before me was an alarm of fire. Men looked at lofty and supposedly fireproof buildings, and said, 'They are perfectly safe.' But these buildings were consumed as if made of pitch. The fire engines could do nothing to stay the destruction. The firemen were unable to operate the engines.

[8] These and several other extracts of like nature were published in an article by Mrs. White in the *Review* bearing date of July 5, 1906.

"I am instructed that when the Lord's time comes, should no change have taken place in the hearts of proud, ambitious human beings, men will find that the hand that has been strong to save will be strong to destroy. No earthly power can stay the hand of God. No material can be used in the erection of buildings that will preserve them from destruction when God's appointed time comes to send retribution on men for their insolence and their disregard of His law."[9]

CALLS TO REPENTANCE

The mercy of God in sparing so many lives during the dreadful calamity befalling San Francisco and near-by communities, was pointed out by Mrs. White as constituting a strong appeal to all classes to recognize the supreme rulership of Jehovah and the binding claims of His law. She urged that evangelistic efforts be carried on in the cities about the bay, in order that the people might have every opportunity to learn the meaning of the judgments coming upon the inhabitants of the earth.

Accordingly, for many months following the earthquake, special and continued efforts were made to proclaim the third angel's message in San Francisco and Oakland and other bay cities. Mrs. White did what she could to encourage the workers stationed in these places, and made several visits herself to the companies of laborers busily engaged in teaching the people. When meeting with those who were familiar with the truths of God's word, she appealed to them to lend willing assistance to the efforts of the workers. At the same time she wrote also of the far-reaching work that is to be done in every land.

---

[9] Quoted in *Review and Herald*, April 26, 1906.

"The world is filled with transgression," she declared. "A spirit of lawlessness pervades every land, and is especially manifest in the great cities of the earth. The sin and crime to be seen in our cities is appalling. God cannot forbear much longer. Already His judgments are beginning to fall on some places, and soon His signal displeasure will be felt in other places.

"There will be a series of events revealing that God is master of the situation. The truth will be proclaimed in clear, unmistakable language. As a people we must prepare the way of the Lord under the overruling guidance of the Holy Spirit. The gospel is to be given in its purity. The stream of living water is to deepen and widen in its course. In all fields, nigh and afar off, men will be called from the plow and from the more common commercial business vocations that largely occupy the mind, and will be educated in connection with men of experience. As they learn to labor effectively, they will proclaim the truth with power. Through most wonderful workings of divine Providence, mountains of difficulty will be removed, and cast into the sea. The message that means so much to the dwellers upon the earth, will be heard and understood. Men will know what is truth. Onward and still onward the work will advance, until the whole earth shall have been warned; and then shall the end come."[10]

---

[10] *Review and Herald,* July 5, 1906. The closing paragraph, with many similar counsels given during those busy months spent in soul-winning service in the great cities of the land following the San Francisco earthquake, may be found in the section on "The Work in the Cities," in "Testimonies for the Church," Vol. 9.

LVI

AT THE 1909 GENERAL CONFERENCE

Thursday evening, Sept. 9, 1909, Mrs. White returned to her home near St. Helena, California, after an absence of five months and four days, during which time she had traveled more than eight thousand miles, and spoken to audiences, large and small, seventy-two times, in twenty-seven places, from California to Maine, and from Alabama to Wisconsin.

The chief purpose of this journey was to attend the quadrennial session of the General Conference, which convened at Washington, D. C., in the spring of 1909. Her visits to other places were in response to urgent invitations, and were made possible by the merciful bestowal of strength and courage, as she proceeded from place to place.

A few days before starting on her journey, she remarked that as she was eighty-one years of age and in feeble health, it would doubtless be best for her to take the most direct route to Washington; but that she could not disregard the calls to visit Los Angeles, Loma Linda, and Paradise Valley, in southern California, nor the invitation to stop in College View, Neb., and speak to the five hundred students in Union College. She said: "I must also visit my son Edson, in Nashville, Tenn., and if the Lord gives me strength, I should be pleased to visit Brethren Sutherland and Magan at the Madison school." She also expressed a desire to stop off a day at Asheville, N. C., where Prof. S. Brownsberger lived, and where Sister Rumbaugh had built and given to the conference a commodious meetinghouse and parsonage.

During the four weeks occupied with the journey to Washington, Mrs. White was able to speak four times at College View; twice each at Loma Linda, Nashville, and Asheville; and once each at Paradise Valley, Madison, Hillcrest, Huntsville, and the Alden mission school near Hilltop. Upon her arrival at Washington, she went at once to Takoma Park, where she was entertained at the home of Elder G. A. Irwin.

A REPRESENTATIVE GATHERING

The General Conference of 1909 was attended by representatives from many lands. The delegations from abroad were unusually large, nearly if not quite a full quota being present from the conferences and missions across the seas. The attendance from the home field also was large.

From the opening day of the session, Mrs. White bore a heavy burden in behalf of the spiritual interests of the various classes of believers encamped on the grounds. In several of her public talks she urged the brethren and sisters to lay hold on God, and to seek Him most earnestly for guidance and blessing. Those in attendance were to gather courage and inspiration for the carrying forward of a mighty work throughout the world. In all their planning, they were to keep constantly before their minds the needs of the perishing, and the importance of occupying places where God is marvelously opening the way for the entrance of present truth.

THE WORK IN THE CITIES

Particularly was this pointed out to be the case with the great cities of the nations. "Behold our cities," she urged, "and their need of the gospel. The need for earnest labor among the multitudes in the cities has been kept before me for more than twenty years. Who is carrying a burden for our large cities? Some will say, We need all the money we can get to carry on the work in other places. Do you not know that unless you carry the truth to the cities, there will be a drying up of means? When you carry this message to those in cities who are hungry for truth, and they accept the light, they will go earnestly to work to bring that light to others. Souls who have means will bring others into the truth, and will give of their means to advance the cause of God."[1]

The necessity of planning in an extraordinary way for the preaching of the third angel's message in the crowded centers of population, constituted one of the chief burdens of Mrs. White's discourses throughout the Conference.

"A little is being done in our world," she declared; "but, O that the good work might spread abroad and reach every needy soul! O that the present truth might be proclaimed in every city! This great need is kept before me night and day. . . .

"Men and women are going forth more and more to carry the gospel message. We thank God for this, but we need a greater awakening. . . . It is our privilege to see the work of God advancing in the cities. Christ is waiting, waiting for places to be entered. Who are preparing for this work? We will not say that we are destitute of laborers. We are glad that there are some; but there is a greater, a far greater work to be done in our cities."[2]

SPECIAL EFFORTS IN NEW ENGLAND

"The work we have to do is a wonderfully great work," she said in another of her discourses during the Conference. "There is a world to be saved."

[1] *General Conference Bulletin*, 1909, p. 136. [2] *Idem*, p. 98.

In this connection she referred especially to the blessing that would come to the cause of God through a strong and united effort to proclaim the message in the cities of New England, where the first and second angels' messages had been given with mighty power. "We must bring to these same cities the glory of the third angel's message," she said. "Who among us is trying to scatter the rays of light where the truth was so favorably received in the early days of the message?"[3]

In one of her appeals regarding the work to be done in the cities of New England and the Atlantic States, she said:

"What is being done in the Eastern cities where the advent message was first proclaimed? The cities of the West have had advantages, but who in the East have been burdened to take up the work of going over the ground that in the early days of the message was baptized with the truth of the Lord's soon coming? The light has been given that the truth should go again to the Eastern States, where we first began our work, and where we had our first experiences. We must make every effort to spread a knowledge of the truth to all who will hear, and there are many who will listen. All through our large cities God has honest souls who are interested in what is truth. There is earnest work to be done in the Eastern States. 'Repeat the message, repeat the message,' were the words spoken to me over and over again. 'Tell My people to repeat the message in the places where it was first preached, and where church after church took their position for the truth, the power of God witnessing to the message in a remarkable manner.' "[4]

---

[3] *General Conference Bulletin,* 1909, pp. 225, 226. [4] *Idem,* p. 136.

DELEGATIONS FROM ABROAD

The presence at the 1909 General Conference of over a hundred delegates from abroad, gave Mrs. White opportunity to meet old friends with whom in former years she had been associated in labor. Often during the Conference she was visited by groups of brethren present from some foreign conference or mission field, who conveyed to her personally their greetings, and reported the progress of the third angel's message in the fields they represented. Thus opportunity was afforded nearly all from abroad, both old friends and those who had never before made her acquaintance, to assure her of their courage in God and of their determination to do their part in the finishing of the work.

"I felt very deeply," Mrs. White said publicly, after enjoying one of these occasions, "when our brethren who had come from foreign fields told me a little of their experiences and of what the Lord is doing in bringing souls to the truth."[5] And at another time, addressing them especially while speaking before the Conference, she said:

"Here are workers who have come from foreign countries. They have come to see and to understand. They are determined to improve every privilege, that they may go back to their fields of labor with a renewal of grace and the power of the Spirit of God. As teachers and leaders in the work, they are to gather precious truths which they will, if faithful, present to their fellow laborers who are working in many places and in various ways to bring souls to a knowledge of the truth. My brethren, in your fields of labor, you may be surrounded by unfavorable

[5] *General Conference Bulletin*, 1909, p. 105.

circumstances; but the Lord knows all about this, and He will supply your lack by His own Holy Spirit. We need to have much more faith in God.''[6]

STRIFE AMONG THE NATIONS

Mrs. White solemnly charged the brethren who had come to the meeting as representatives of the cause of present truth from every part of Europe, from Asia, Africa, South America, Australasia, and the islands of the sea, to prepare their hearts for terrible scenes of strife and oppression beyond anything they had conceived of, soon to be witnessed among the nations of earth. ''Very soon,'' she declared, ''the strife and oppression of foreign nations will break forth with an intensity that you do not now anticipate. You need to realize the importance of becoming acquainted with God in prayer. When you have the assurance that He hears you, you will be cheerful in tribulation; you will rise above despondency, because you experience the quickening influence of the power of God in your hearts. What we need is the *truth*. Nothing can take the place of this,— the sacred, solemn truth that is to enable us to stand the test of trial, even as Christ endured.''[6]

And in the farewell service marking the close of the Conference, she once more appealed to the delegates assembled from all parts of the world, to endure as beholding the Invisible. She exhorted every worker to go forth in the strength of the Mighty One of Israel. She declared that while she might never have the privilege of meeting her brethren in another Conference like this one, yet she would pray for them, and prepare to meet them all in the kingdom of glory.

[6] *General Conference Bulletin,* 1909, p. 57.

IMPORTANT COUNSELS

It was during the 1909 General Conference that Mrs. White read a manuscript calling for loyalty to the principles of health reform;[7] and she also spoke to the delegates on the same subject.[8] Another manuscript read was "A plea for Medical Missionary Evangelists;" and still another "The Loma Linda College of Evangelists"[9]

Following the Conference session, Mrs. White met twice with the members of the General Conference Committee, before going on to Philadelphia and other cities of the East, and thence to camp meetings and institutions in the Central States and the Middle West, en route to her California home.

In her interviews with the General Conference Committee, Mrs. White read manuscripts dealing with some of the problems that were perplexing the brethren. The call to do a much larger work in the cities at home and abroad, than had hitherto been attempted, could be responded to only as men and means could be found to use in the carrying forward of such work. In order that a broad and far-reaching campaign might be inaugurated quickly and effectively, Mrs. White suggested the advisability of releasing for evangelistic service some of the workers bearing heavy burdens in institutional centers. She said:

"For the conduct of affairs at the various centers of our work, we must endeavor, as far as possible, to find consecrated men who have been trained in business lines. We must guard against tying up at these centers of influence men who could do a more im-

[7] This manuscript was afterward published in "Testimonies for the Church," Vol. 9, pp. 153-166.
[8] See *General Conference Bulletin*, 1909, pp. 213-215.
[9] For these, see "Testimonies for the Church," Vol. 9, pp. 167-178.

portant work on the public platform, in presenting before unbelievers the truths of God's word. . . .

"To us, as God's servants, has been entrusted the third angel's message, the binding-off message, that is to prepare a people for the coming of our King. Time is short. The Lord desires that everything connected with His cause shall be brought into order. He desires that the solemn message of warning and of invitation shall be proclaimed as widely as His messengers can carry it. The means that shall come into the treasury, is to be used wisely in supporting the workers. Nothing that would hinder the advance of the message, is to be allowed to come into our planning. . . .

"For years the pioneers of our work struggled against poverty and manifold hardships, in order to place the cause of present truth on vantage ground. With meager facilities, they labored untiringly; and the Lord blessed their humble efforts. The message went with power in the East, and extended westward, until centers of influence had been established in many places. The laborers of to-day may not have to endure all the hardships of those early days. The changed conditions, however, should not lead to any slackening of effort. Now, when the Lord bids us proclaim the message once more with power in the East; when He bids us enter the cities of the East, and of the South, and of the West, and of the North, shall we not respond as one man and do His bidding? Shall we not plan to send our messengers all through these fields, and support them liberally? . . .

"What are our conferences for, if not for the carrying forward of this very work? At such a time as this, every hand is to be employed. The Lord is coming. The end is near; yea, it hasteth greatly!

In a little while from this we shall be unable to work with the freedom that we now enjoy. Terrible scenes are before us, and what we do, we must do quickly. We must now build up the work in every place possible. And for the accomplishment of this work we greatly need in the field the help that can be given by our ministers of experience who are able to hold the attention of large congregations. . . .

"Before leaving home I promised the Lord that if He would spare my life, and enable me to come to this Conference, I would deliver the message He had repeatedly given me in behalf of the cities, in which thousands upon thousands are perishing without a knowledge of the truth. As I have borne this message to the people, the blessing of God has rested on me richly. And now, my brethren, I appeal to you in the name of the Lord to do your best, and to plan for the advancement of the work in God's appointed way. . . .

"As we do this work, we shall find that means will flow into our treasuries, and we shall have means with which to carry on a still broader and more far-reaching work. Shall we not advance in faith, just as if we had thousands of dollars? We do not have half faith enough. Let us do our part in warning these cities. The warning message must come to the people who are ready to perish, unwarned, unsaved. How can we delay? As we advance, the means will come. But we must advance by faith, trusting in the Lord God of Israel."[10]

---

[10] From a manuscript, portions of which have been published in "Testimonies for the Church," Vol. 9. See pp. 98, 99.

LVII

CLOSING LABORS

To the brethren assembled in General Conference in 1913, Mrs. White wrote freely of some of her experiences during the four years that had passed since she had had opportunity, at the 1909 Conference, of speaking to them personally.

"For a number of months after the close of that meeting," she wrote, "I bore a heavy burden, and urged upon the attention of the brethren in responsibility those things which the Lord was instructing me to set before them plainly. . . . And while I still feel the deepest anxiety over the attitude that some are taking toward important measures connected with the development of the cause of God in the earth, yet I have strong faith in the workers throughout the field, and believe that as they meet together and humble themselves before the Lord and consecrate themselves anew to His service, they will be enabled to do His will. There are some who do not even now view matters in the right light, but these may learn to see eye to eye with their coworkers, and may avoid making serious mistakes, by earnestly seeking the Lord at this time, and by submitting their will wholly to the will of God.

"I have been deeply impressed by scenes that have recently passed before me in the night season. There seemed to be a great movement — a work of revival — going forward in many places. Our people were moving into line, responding to God's call. My brethren, the Lord is speaking to us. Shall we not heed His voice? Shall we not trim our lamps, and act like men who look for their Lord to come? The time is one that calls for light-bearing, for action.

"'I therefore . . . beseech you,' brethren, 'that ye walk worthy of the vocation wherewith ye are called, with all lowliness and meekness, with long-suffering, forbearing one another in love; endeavoring to keep the unity of the Spirit in the bond of peace.'"[1]

PERSONAL ACTIVITIES

Concerning her activities in public labor and at home, Mrs. White wrote in 1913:

"I long to be personally engaged in earnest work in the field, and I should most assuredly be engaged in more public labor did I not believe that at my age it is not wise to presume on one's physical strength. I have a work to do in communicating to the church and to the world the light that has been entrusted to me from time to time all through the years during which the third angel's message has been proclaimed. My heart is filled with a most earnest desire to place the truth before all who can be reached. And I am still acting a part in preparing matter for publication. But I have to move very carefully, lest I place myself where I cannot write at all. I know not how long I may live, but I am not suffering as much healthwise as I might expect.

"Following the General Conference of 1909, I spent several weeks attending camp meetings and other general gatherings, and visiting various institutions, in New England, the Central States, and the Middle West.

"Upon returning to my home in California, I took up anew the work of preparing matter for the press. During the past four years I have written comparatively few letters. What strength I have had

[1] *General Conference Bulletin,* 1913, p. 34.

has been given mostly to the completion of important book work.

"Occasionally I have attended meetings, and have visited institutions in California, but the greater portion of the time . . . has been spent in manuscript work at my country home, 'Elmshaven,' near St. Helena.

"I am thankful that the Lord is sparing my life to work a little longer on my books. O, that I had strength to do all that I see ought to be done! I pray that He may impart to me wisdom, that the truths our people so much need may be presented clearly and acceptably. I am encouraged to believe that God will enable us to do this.

"My interest in the general work is still as deep as ever, and I greatly desire that the cause of present truth shall steadily advance in all parts of the world. But I find it advisable not to attempt much public work while my book work demands my supervision. . . .

"I am more thankful than I can express for the uplifting of the Spirit of the Lord, for the comfort and grace that He continues to give me, and that He grants me strength and opportunity to impart courage and help to His people. As long as the Lord spares my life, I will be faithful and true to Him, seeking to do His will and to glorify His name. May the Lord increase my faith, that I may follow on to know Him, and to do His will more perfectly. Good is the Lord, and greatly to be praised."[2]

THE PIONEERS OF THE MESSAGE

In one of her communications to the brethren assembled in General Conference in 1913, Mrs. White referred to the increasing value of the lessons of past

[2] *General Conference Bulletin,* 1913, p. 164.

experience with which the pioneers in the third angel's message are familiar, and concerning which they can bear positive testimony.

"I greatly desire," she wrote, "that the old soldiers of the cross, those grown gray in the Master's service, shall continue to bear their testimony right to the point, in order that those younger in the faith may understand that the messages which the Lord gave us in the past, are very important at this stage of the earth's history. Our past experience has not lost one jot of its force.

"Let all be careful not to discourage the pioneers, or cause them to feel that there is little they can do. Their influence may still be mightily exerted in the work of the Lord. The testimony of the aged ministers will ever be a help and a blessing to the church. God will watch over His tried and faithful standard bearers, night and day, until the time comes for them to lay off the armor. Let them be assured that they are under the protecting care of Him who never slumbers or sleeps; that they are watched over by unwearied sentinels. Knowing this, and realizing that they are abiding in Christ, they may rest trustfully in the providences of God."[3]

GIVING THE TRUMPET A CERTAIN SOUND

Throughout her life work, Mrs. White's faith in the overruling providences connected with the unfolding truths of the three angels' messages, remained unshaken. Often she bore testimony to her conviction that from the beginning God had been the teacher and the leader of His people. And this conviction as regards divine leadership in the past, all through the advent movement, gave her confidence for the

---

[3] *General Conference Bulletin*, 1913, p. 164.

future. Witness the following statement, written by her in 1890 in review of her own experience, and with full knowledge of the fact that controversies and doctrinal differences would arise in days to come:

"I have had precious opportunities to obtain an experience. I have had an experience in the first, second, and third angels' messages. The angels are represented as flying in the midst of heaven, proclaiming to the world a message of warning, and having a direct bearing upon the people living in the last days of this earth's history. No one hears the voice of these angels, for they are a symbol to represent the people of God who are working in harmony with the universe of heaven. Men and women, enlightened by the Spirit of God, and sanctified through the truth, proclaim the three messages in their order.

"I have acted a part in this solemn work. Nearly all my Christian experience is interwoven with it. There are those now living who have an experience similar to my own. They have recognized the truth unfolding for this time; they have kept in step with the great Leader, the Captain of the Lord's host. In the proclamation of the messages, every specification of prophecy has been fulfilled. Those who were privileged to act a part in proclaiming these messages have gained an experience which is of the highest value to them; and now when we are amid the perils of these last days, when voices will be heard on every side saying, 'Here is Christ,' 'Here is truth'; while the burden of many is to unsettle the foundation of our faith which has led us from the churches and from the world to stand as a peculiar people in the world, like John our testimony will be borne:

" 'That which was from the beginning, which we have heard, which we have seen with our eyes, which we have looked upon, and our hands have handled, of the Word of life; . . . that which we have seen and heard declare we unto you, that ye also may have fellowship with us.'

"I testify the things which I have seen, the things which I have heard, the things which my hands have handled, of the Word of life. And this testimony I know to be of the Father and the Son. We have seen and do testify that the power of the Holy Ghost has accompanied the presentation of the truth, warning with pen and voice, and giving the messages in their order. To deny this work would be to deny the Holy Ghost, and would place us in that company who have departed from the faith, giving heed to seducing spirits.

"The enemy will set everything in operation to uproot the confidence of the believers in the pillars of our faith in the messages of the past, which have placed us upon the elevated platform of eternal truth, and which have established and given character to the work. The Lord God of Israel has led out His people, unfolding to them truth of heavenly origin. His voice has been heard, and is still heard, saying, Go forward from strength to strength, from grace to grace, from glory to glory. The work is strengthening and broadening, for the Lord God of Israel is the defense of His people.

"Those who have a hold of the truth theoretically, with their finger tips as it were, who have not brought its principles into the inner sanctuary of the soul, but have kept the vital truth in the outer court, will see nothing sacred in the past history of this people, which has made them what they are, and has established them as earnest, determined missionary workers in the world. The truth for this time is precious; but those whose hearts have not been broken by falling on the rock Christ Jesus, will not see and understand what is truth. They will accept that which pleases their ideas, and will begin to manufacture another foundation than that which is laid. They will flatter their own vanity and esteem, thinking that they are capable of removing the pillars of our faith, and replacing them with pillars they have devised.

"This will continue to be as long as time shall last. Any one who has been a close student of the Bible will see and understand the solemn position of those who are living in the closing scenes of this earth's history. They will feel their own inefficiency and weakness, and will make it their first business to have not merely a form of godliness, but a vital connection with God. They will not dare to rest until Christ is formed within, the hope of glory. Self will die; pride will be expelled from the soul, and they will have the meekness and gentleness of Christ."[4]

BOOK MANUSCRIPT WORK

Mrs. White's personal correspondence is filled with many references to book manuscripts on which she was laboring lovingly and untiringly. While in Europe, she was amplifying "Great Controversy" and "The Life of Christ." Following the issuance of the subscription edition of "Controversy" in 1888, she completed the companion volume, "Patriarchs and Prophets," in 1890. "Steps to Christ" appeared in 1892, "Gospel Workers" in 1893, and "Thoughts from the Mount of Blessing" in 1896. Her largest literary work, "The Desire of Ages," occupied much of her time during the sojourn in Australasia, and appeared in 1898.

---

[4] From an unpublished manuscript.

When "Christ's Object Lessons" and "Testimonies for the Church," Volume 6, appeared in 1900, some of her friends thought that her laborious efforts to prepare manuscripts for publication in book form, had about ended. But not so. The burden to write was still pressing heavily upon her heart. An impelling sense of the needs of a perishing world, and of many also who claimed to be subjects of King Emmanuel, led her to labor on and on, in an earnest endeavor to give to others that which was filling her own soul with joy and peace. Hear her declaring, when in 1902 she was writing to a friend on the high standard to which Christian believers should attain:

"O, what is there that will give them a consciousness of the responsibility resting on them to be Christlike in word and act! I shall try to arouse their slumbering senses by writing, if not by speaking. The awful sense of my responsibility takes such possession of me that I am weighted as a cart beneath sheaves. I do not desire to feel less keenly my obligation to the Higher Power. That Presence is ever with me, asserting supreme authority and taking account of the service that I render or withhold."[5]

"The Lord commands me to speak, and this I shall do," Mrs. White declared further when feeling thus burdened over her responsibility as a chosen messenger. "I have been instructed to bear my testimony with the decision of authority."[6] And in another communication, penned the same month, she wrote:

"I have every reason to praise my heavenly Father for the clearness of thought that He has given me in regard to Bible subjects. I long to bring out these precious things, so that the minds of ministers and

[5] Unpublished letter, Dec. 9, 1902.
[6] *Idem*, Dec. 7, 1902.

people may, if possible, be drawn away from contention and strife to something that is nourishing to the soul,— food that will give health, hopefulness, and courage. . . .

"In the night season many things are passing before me. The Scriptures, full of grace and richness, are presented before me. The word of the Lord to me is: 'Look on these things, and meditate on them. You may claim the rich grace of truth, which nourishes the soul. Have naught to do with controversy and dissension and strife, which bring darkness and discouragement to your soul. Truth is clear, pure, savory. . . . Speak the truth in faith and love, leaving the result with God. The work is not yours, but the Lord's. In all your communications, speak as one to whom the Lord has spoken. He is your authority, and He will give you His sustaining grace.' "[7]

These words were written about the time "Testimonies for the Church," Volume 7, was in the hands of the printers. Shortly after its appearance, she wrote regarding volumes six and seven:

"I have been impressed to call upon the members of our churches to study the last two volumes of 'Testimonies for the Church.' When I was writing these books, I felt the deep moving of the Spirit of God. . . . They are full of precious matter. In the visions of the night the Lord told me that the truth contained in these books must be brought before the members of our churches, because there are many who are indifferent in regard to the salvation of their souls."[8]

But these volumes were not to be the last. There was much yet to be accomplished. "I must prepare books," she wrote in May, 1903, "and thus give to

[7] Unpublished letter, Dec. 2, 1902.
[8] *Idem*, April 15, 1903.

others the light that the Lord gives me. I do not want to leave an unfinished work." And during the same month she wrote further: "I am trying to prepare for publication matter that will guard the work on every side, so that it may not become disproportionate. We have many things in preparation for publication. . . . The truth must appear just as it is."

In August, 1903, Mrs. White wrote to an old-time friend: "My health is good, and I am able to do much writing. I thank the Lord for this. I have decided not to attend so many camp meetings, but to give my time to my writing. . . . I greatly desire to write on the life of Solomon and on the history following his reign, and I desire, too, to write on the life of Paul and his work in connection with the other apostles. At times the thought of this neglected work keeps me awake at night."

Mrs. White lived to see her desires fulfilled with regard to much that she had planned on doing. Her work on "Education" was completed in 1903; "Testimonies for the Church," Volume 8, in 1904; and "Ministry of Healing" in 1905. Many "Special Testimonies" were prepared for circulation in pamphlet and leaflet form; and in 1909 "Testimonies for the Church," Volume 9, the last of the series, was published. By the close of 1910 Mrs. White had given full consideration to all the problems connected with the reset edition of "Great Controversy." That task having been completed, she found time to supervise the revision of "Sketches from the Life of Paul," and to add several chapters on the life work and the writings of the apostles of the early Christian church. This matter was published in 1911, under the title, "The Acts of the Apostles." The next volume to appear was "Counsels to Teachers, Parents, and Students Regarding Christian Education,'' in 1913; and immediately afterward Mrs. White began the reading of manuscripts that were forwarded to the printers in 1914 for the new edition of ''Gospel Workers.''

When publishing ''Facts of Faith,'' in 1864, Mrs. White included in that little volume matter that carried the story of Israel beyond the days of David. In the seventies she wrote quite fully on the restoration of the Israelites from Babylon, dwelling in detail on the experiences of Nehemiah. In articles, and in the bound volumes of ''Testimonies for the Church,'' she often told and retold the story of Solomon, of Elijah and Elisha, of Isaiah and Jeremiah, of Daniel and the Hebrew worthies, and of the return of the exiles under Zerubbabel and Joshua and Ezra.

''Facts of Faith'' has long been out of print, the matter contained therein having been largely incorporated, with many additions, in the later volume, ''Spirit of Prophecy,'' Volume 1 (1870), and finally in ''Patriarchs and Prophets'' (1890). When ''Patriarchs'' was completed, Mrs. White hoped soon to go on with the story from the close of David's reign, and publish in connected form that which she had been enabled to write through the years concerning the experiences of Solomon and divided Israel, and their final restoration to divine favor as one united people,—a type of spiritual Israel, the church of God on earth to-day, to whom will finally be fulfilled all the covenant promises.

It was the hope of preparing, in some form suitable for publication, this story of the prophets and kings of Old Testament history, that led to the grouping of such material into several series of articles, which have been published in the columns of the *Review*, the *Signs*, and the *Watchman*.

Not long after Mrs. White's return from Australia, work was undertaken anew on the Old Testament story, and continued intermittently for more than ten years. Thus consideration was given to the many manuscripts dealing with this period of Bible history not included in the other volumes of the "Controversy" series.

To the completion of this work, Mrs. White gave much thought during 1913 and 1914. At the time of her accident, in February, 1915, all but the last two chapters had been completed for a volume bearing the title, "The Captivity and Restoration of Israel," covering the broken periods; and these final chapters had been sufficiently blocked out to admit of completion by the inclusion of additional matter from her manuscript file.

During the last year spent by Mrs. White in quiet rest and in closing up her manuscript work, one of her copyists wrote to her son, W. C. White, under date of Dec. 23, 1914:

"Even when exceedingly brain-weary, your mother seems to find great comfort in the promises of the Word, and often catches up a quotation and completes it when we begin quoting some familiar scripture. . . . I do not find her discouraged . . . over the general outlook throughout the harvest field where her brethren are laboring. She seems to have strong faith in God's power to overrule, and to bring to pass His eternal purpose through the efforts of those whom He has called to act a part in His great work. She rises above petty criticism, above even the past failures of those who have been reproved, and expresses the conviction, born, apparently, of an innate faith in the church of the living God, that her brethren will remain faithful to the cause they have espoused, and that the Lord will continue with them to the end, and grant them complete victory over every device of the enemy.

"Faith in God's power to sustain her through the many weaknesses attendant on old age; faith in the precious promises of God's word; faith in her brethren who bear the burden of the work; faith in the final triumph of the third angel's message,— this is the full faith your mother seems to enjoy every day and every hour. This is the faith that fills her heart with joy and peace, even when suffering great physical weakness, and unable to make progress in literary lines. A faith such as this would inspire any one who could witness it."

A SOLEMN CHARGE

The spirit that characterized Mrs. White's life and labors during the closing years of her ministry, is reflected in the communication, "Courage in the Lord," addressed to her brethren assembled at the 1913 General Conference. Her words of exhortation were in reality a prayer and a benediction:

"I pray earnestly that the work we do at this time shall impress itself deeply on heart and mind and soul. Perplexities will increase; but let us, as believers in God, encourage one another. Let us not lower the standard, but keep it lifted high, looking to Him who is the author and finisher of our faith. When in the night season I am unable to sleep, I lift my heart in prayer to God, and He strengthens me, and gives me the assurance that He is with His ministering servants in the home field and in distant lands. I am encouraged and blessed as I realize that the God of Israel is still guiding His people, and that He will continue to be with them, even to the end.

"I am instructed to say to our ministering brethren, Let the messages that come from your lips be charged with the power of the Spirit of God. If ever there was a time when we needed the special guidance of the Holy Spirit, it is now. We need a thorough consecration. It is fully time that we gave to the world a demonstration of the power of God in our own lives and in our ministry.

"The Lord desires to see the work of proclaiming the third angel's message carried forward with increasing efficiency. As He has worked in all ages to give victories to His people, so in this age He longs to carry to a triumphant fulfillment His purposes for His church. He bids His believing saints to advance unitedly, going from strength to greater strength, from faith to increased assurance and confidence in the truth and righteousness of His cause.

"We are to stand firm as a rock to the principles of the word of God, remembering that God is with us to give us strength to meet each new experience. Let us ever maintain in our lives the principles of righteousness, that we may go forward from strength to strength in the name of the Lord. We are to hold as very sacred the faith that has been substantiated by the instruction and approval of the Spirit of God from our earliest experience until the present time. We are to cherish as very precious the work that the Lord has been carrying forward through His commandment-keeping people, and which, through the power of His grace, will grow stronger and more efficient as time advances. The enemy is seeking to becloud the discernment of God's people, and to weaken their efficiency; but if they will labor as the Spirit of God shall direct, He will open doors of opportunity before them for the work of building up the old waste places. Their experience will be one of constant growth, until the Lord shall descend from heaven with power and great glory to set His seal of final triumph upon His faithful ones.

"The work that lies before us is one that will put to the stretch every power of the human being. It will call for the exercise of strong faith and constant vigilance. At times the difficulties that we shall meet will be most disheartening. The very greatness of the task will appall us. And yet, with God's help, His servants will finally triumph. 'Wherefore,' my brethren, 'I desire that ye faint not' because of the trying experiences that are before you. Jesus will be with you; He will go before you by His Holy Spirit, preparing the way; and He will be your helper in every emergency.

" 'For this cause I bow my knees unto the Father of our Lord Jesus Christ, of whom the whole family in heaven and earth is named, that He would grant you, according to the riches of His glory, to be strengthened with might by His Spirit in the inner man; that Christ may dwell in your hearts by faith; that ye, being rooted and grounded in love, may be able to comprehend with all saints what is the breadth, and length, and depth, and height; and to know the love of Christ, which passeth knowledge, that ye might be filled with all the fullness of God.

" 'Now unto Him that is able to do exceeding abundantly above all that we ask or think, according to the power that worketh in us, unto Him be glory in the church by Christ Jesus throughout all ages, world without end. Amen.' "[9]

---

[9] *General Conference Bulletin,* 1913, pp. 164, 165.

LVIII

LAST SICKNESS

For over two years prior to the accident that hastened her death, Mrs. White was freer from suffering and from common ailments than during any other like period in her lifetime. Once her strength failed decidedly, but soon she rallied, and was again able to get about with comparative ease. Her attendant usually took her out driving every pleasant day, and this afforded restful change. She was ordinarily able to go from her upper room to her carriage unaided. But her frame was becoming more and more bowed with the weight of years, and her friends could not hope for long continuance of life.

In the spring of 1914, Mrs. White had the pleasure of meeting once more her son, Elder James Edson White, who spent some weeks in her home. Not long after his return, his mother suffered great weakness from a complication of difficulties, and as the result, largely gave up reading. In the months that followed, she often had others read to her.

The cessation of her ordinary activities, however, did not lead to diminished interest in the progress of the cause of God throughout the world. The pages of the *Review and Herald* and of other denominational papers were as precious to her as ever, and she continued to enjoy letters from old-time friends, and often recounted with animation the experiences of former days.

In the course of a conversation held Dec. 2, 1914, she referred to an incident that occurred many years before. A certain brother had expressed discouragement over the prospect of the extended and difficult work that would need to be done before the world could be prepared for the second advent of Christ. Another brother, one of large faith, turned to him, his face white with strong emotion, and said: "My brother, do you permit such a prospect to bring discouragement? Do you not know that God would have us press the battle to the gate? Do you not know He would have us labor on, and on, and on, knowing that victory lies ahead?"

It was early in December, 1914, also, that she testified to hearing voices in the night season, crying out: "Advance! Advance! Advance! Press the battle to the gate!"

While eager to continue her work, and especially desirous of speaking again in public, Mrs. White knew that her strength was gradually failing, and that she must not presume on her waning energies. This was a real trial to her, yet she felt resigned to the Lord's will. Hear her praying around the family altar at set of sun, Sabbath, Dec. 26, 1914, following petitions by Elder E. W. Farnsworth and others:

"Thou wilt answer our petitions; and we ask Thee, Lord, for Christ's sake, if it is Thy will, to give me strength and grace to continue; or, I am perfectly willing to leave my work at any time that Thou seest best. O Lord, I greatly desire to do some things, Thou knowest, and would be willing to do them if Thou wilt give me strength; but we will make no complaint; because Thou hast spared my life so much longer than many anticipated and than I have anticipated myself. . . . Give us light; give us joy; give us the great grace that Thou hast in store for the needy. We ask it in the name of Jesus Christ of Nazareth."

Feebler and still feebler grew the physical frame; but the spirit was courageous ever. In conversation with Dr. David Paulson on Jan. 25, 1915, Mrs. White said: "The Lord has been my helper, the Lord has been my God, and I have not a doubt. If I could not realize that He has been my guide and my stay, do tell me what I could trust in. Why, I have just as firm a trust in God that He will stand my feet on Mount Zion, as that I live and breathe; and I am going to keep that trust till I die."

When, on the 27th of January, 1915, her son, W. C. White, returned home after a four months' absence in the East and the South, she was apparently as strong as when he had left. She was still enjoying a good degree of comfort, healthwise, and was able to be about. Some two weeks later, only the day before she was stricken, she spent a little time walking in the yard with him, and conversing on the general interests of the cause of God.

It was on Sabbath day, Feb. 13, 1915, that Mrs. White met with the accident that confined her to her couch thereafter and hastened her death. As she was entering her study from the hallway, about noon, she apparently tripped, and fell. Her niece, Miss May Walling, who for a time had been acting as her nurse, was close by in the hallway, and hastened to her assistance. As efforts to help her to her feet proved unavailing, Miss Walling raised her into a chair, drew the chair through the hallway into the bedroom, and finally got her onto the bed, and summoned a physician from the St. Helena Sanitarium.

A preliminary examination by Dr. G. E. Klingerman was followed by a more thorough examination by means of the X-ray, and this revealed unmistakably an intracapsular fracture of the left femur. It was of course impossible to determine when the break in the bone had taken place,— whether before the fall, thus causing Mrs. White to drop to the floor, or as the result of the fall.

The restlessness of the next few days and nights was accompanied with very little pain. In fact, from the very first, the Lord mercifully spared His aged servant the severe pain that ordinarily comes with such injuries. The usual symptoms of shock, also, were absent. The respiration, the temperature, and the circulation were nearly normal. Dr. Klingerman, and Dr. B. F. Jones, his associate, did all that medical science could suggest to make their patient comfortable; but at her advanced age they could hold out but little prospect of ultimate recovery.

All through the weeks and months of her last sickness, Mrs. White was buoyed up by the same faith and hope and trust that had characterized her life experience in the days of her vigor. Her personal testimony was uniformly cheerful and her courage strong. She felt that her times were in the hand of God, and that His presence was with her continually. Not long after she was rendered helpless by the accident, she testified of her Saviour, "Jesus is my blessed Redeemer, and I love Him with my whole being." And again: "I see light in His light. I have joy in His joy, and peace in His peace. I see mercy in His mercy, and love in His love." To Miss Sara McEnterfer, for many years her secretary, she said, "If only I can see my Saviour face to face, I shall be fully satisfied."

In an interview with another she said: "My courage is grounded in my Saviour. My work is nearly ended. Looking over the past, I do not feel the least mite of despondency or discouragement. I feel so grateful that the Lord has withheld me from despair and discouragement, and that I can still hold the banner. I know Him whom I love, and in whom my soul trusteth."

Referring to the prospect of death, she declared: "I feel, the sooner the better; all the time that is how I feel — the sooner the better. I have not a discouraging thought, nor sadness. . . . I have nothing to complain of. Let the Lord take His way and do His work with me, so that I am refined and purified; and that is all I desire. I know my work is done; it is of no use to say anything else. I shall rejoice, when my time comes, that I am permitted to lie down to rest in peace. I have no desire that my life shall be prolonged."

Following a prayer by the one who was making these notes of her conversation, she prayed:

"Heavenly Father, I come to Thee, weak, like a broken reed, yet by the Holy Spirit's vindication of righteousness and truth that shall prevail. I thank Thee, Lord, I thank Thee, and I will not draw away from anything that Thou wouldst give me to bear. Let Thy light, let Thy joy and grace, be upon me in my last hours, that I may glorify Thee, is my great desire; and this is all that I shall ask of Thee. Amen."

This humble, trustful prayer by one who long had been a chosen vessel in the Master's service, was fully answered. Hers was the comfort that causes a child of the great Father of light and love to fear no evil, even while passing through the valley of the shadow of death. One Sabbath day, only a few short weeks before she breathed her last, she said to her son:

"I am very weak. I am sure that this is my last sickness. I am not worried at the thought of dying.

I feel comforted all the time, that the Lord is near me. I am not anxious. The preciousness of the Saviour has been so plain to me. He has been a friend. He has kept me in sickness and in health.

"I do not worry about the work I have done. I have done the best I could. I do not think that I shall be lingering long. I do not expect much suffering. I am thankful that we have the comforts of life in time of sickness. Do not worry. I go only a little before the others."

The comfortable office room on the second story of Mrs. White's home was the most favorable place for patient and nurses, and here it was that she lay the most of the time, surrounded by the familiar objects of the more active life to which she had so long been accustomed. The room was light and airy. In one corner a large bay window flooded a portion of the chamber with sunshine. Here stood her old writing chair. This was transformed into a reclining chair, into which she was lifted nearly every day after the first week or two of illness had passed by. The view from this sunny corner was pleasing and varied, and she greatly enjoyed the changing beauties of springtime and early summer.

Close beside her chair, on a table, were kept several of the books she had written. These she would often handle and look over, seeming to delight in having them near. Like an affectionate mother with her children, so was she with these books during her last sickness. Several times, when visited, she was found holding two or three of them in her lap. "I appreciate these books as I never did before," she at one time remarked. "They are truth, and they are righteousness, and they are an everlasting testimony that God is true." She rejoiced in the thought that when she could no longer speak to the people, her books would speak for her.

At times when her strength permitted, she was taken in a wheel chair to a sunny veranda on the upper floor. From this little balcony, embowered with beautiful climbing roses, the panorama of orchard and vineyard, of mountains and valleys, afforded continual pleasure.

Again and again, during the earlier weeks of her illness, her voice was lifted in song. The words oftenest chosen were:

> "We have heard from the bright, the holy land,
> We have heard, and our hearts are glad;
> For we were a lonely pilgrim band,
> And weary, and worn, and sad.
> They tell us the pilgrims have a dwelling there—
> No longer are homeless ones;
> And we know that the goodly land is fair,
> Where life's pure river runs.
>
> . . . .
>
> "We'll be there, we'll be there, in a little while,
> We'll join the pure and the blest;
> We'll have the palm, the robe, the crown,
> And forever be at rest."

About a fortnight after her accident, she was told of the missionary and bookmen's convention in session at Mountain View, where plans were being laid for an increased circulation of denominational publications. This reference to the bookmen led her to express once more the pleasure she had had two years before in greeting many of them personally in her own home. "I am very glad," she added, "for all they are doing for the circulation of our books. The publishing branch of our cause has much to do with our power. I do desire that it shall accomplish all that the Lord designs it should. If our bookmen do their part faithfully, I know, from the light God has given

MRS. WHITE'S "ELMSHAVEN" HOME

"Where she spent much of her time during the last happy, fruitful years of her busy life."

me, that the knowledge of present truth will be doubled and trebled. This is why I have been in so much of a hurry to get my books out, so that they could be placed in the hands of the people and read. And in the foreign languages the Lord designs that the circulation of our books shall be greatly increased. Thus we shall be placing the cause of present truth on vantage ground. But let us remember, in all our endeavors we must seek daily power and individual Christian experience. Only as we keep in close touch with the Source of our strength shall we be enabled to advance rapidly and along even lines."

Many were the visitors — old acquaintances and others — who came to greet Mrs. White during the last few months of her life. Sometimes she was unable to recognize old associates in labor; at other times she knew those who came. Whenever possible, she would converse with them. She never ceased to take delight in testifying of God's goodness and tender mercy. For months prior to her illness, she frequently quoted the scripture, They overcame "by the blood of the Lamb, *and by the word of their testimony";* and she felt strengthened every time she bore witness to the love of God and to His watchful care.

One Sabbath afternoon, when the family of her son, W. C. White, spent some time with her, she was specially blessed, and spoke many words of counsel to her grandchildren. "The Lord is very good to us," she declared; "and if we follow on to know the Lord, we shall know that His going forth is prepared as the morning. If there is any question in your minds in regard to what is right, look to the Lord Jesus, and He will guide you. We should bring every plan to the Lord, to see if He approves it. . . . Remember that the Lord will carry us through. I am guarding every moment, so that nothing may come between me and the Lord. I hope there will not. God grant that we may all prove faithful. There will be a glorious meeting soon. I am glad that you have come to see me. May the Lord bless you. Amen."

Not alone for her granddaughters and grandsons, but for all the youth throughout the denomination, her heart went out in loving solicitude. At times she talked with her nurses and with her office helpers concerning the need of making wise selections of matter for the youth to read.

"We should advise the young," she urged, "to take hold of such reading matter as recommends itself for the upbuilding of Christian character. The most essential points of our faith should be stamped upon the memory of the young. They have had a glimpse of these truths, but not such an acquaintance as would lead them to look upon their study with favor. Our youth should read that which will have a healthful, sanctifying effect upon the mind. This they need in order to be able to discern what is true religion. There is much good reading that is not sanctifying.

"Now is our time and opportunity to labor for the young people. Tell them that we are now in a perilous crisis, and we want to know how to discern true godliness. Our young people need to be helped, uplifted, and encouraged, but in the right manner, not, perhaps, as they would desire it, but in a way that will help them to have sanctified minds. They need good, sanctifying religion more than anything else.

"I do not expect to live long. My work is nearly done. Tell our young people that I want my words to encourage them in that manner of life that will be most attractive to the heavenly intelligences."

The end came on Friday, July 16, 1915, at 3:40 P. M., in the sunny upper chamber of her "Elmshaven" home where she had spent so much of her time during the last happy, fruitful years of her busy life. She fell asleep in Jesus as quietly and peacefully as a weary child goes to rest. Surrounding her bedside were her son, Elder W. C. White, and his wife; her granddaughter, Mrs. Mabel White Workman; her long-time and faithful secretary, Miss Sara McEnterfer; her niece and devoted nurse, Miss May Walling; another of her untiring bedside nurses, Mrs. Carrie Hungerford; her housekeeper, Miss Tessie Woodbury; her old-time companion and helper, Mrs. Mary Chinnock Thorp; and a few friends and helpers who had spent many years in and about her home and in her office.

For several days prior to her death, she had been unconscious much of the time, and toward the end she seemed to have lost the faculty of speech and that of hearing. The last words she spoke to her son were, "I know in whom I have believed."

"God is love." "He giveth His beloved sleep." To them the long night of waiting until the morning of the resurrection is but a moment; and even to those who remain the time of waiting will not be long, for Jesus is coming soon to gather His loved ones home. As our beloved sister herself declared to those about her one Sabbath day during her sickness, "We shall all be home very soon now."

LIX

THE "ELMSHAVEN" FUNERAL SERVICE

At five o'clock on the afternoon of Sunday, July 18, 1915, at "Elmshaven,"

> "A little spot hallowed by grace,
> Out of the world's wide wilderness,"

there assembled nearly five hundred friends and neighbors to pay their last tribute of respect to the memory of Mrs. Ellen G. White, and to comfort by their presence and sympathy those who had been called to suffer the loss of one they had loved dearly.

The service was held on the lawn in front of Mrs. White's quiet country home, which had long been to her a haven of rest,—a veritable "refuge," as she often styled it when returning from public labors. At one end of the lawn had been erected a canopy for the officiating ministers; while chairs and benches conveniently placed beneath the wide-spreading elms, with sofas and rockers for the aged and the infirm, gave seats for all who came.

The familiar strains of the hymn, "It is well with my soul," sung by a double quartette from the Pacific Union College and the St. Helena Sanitarium, marked the opening of the service. Elder R. W. Munson, in his prayer, petitioned that all might profit by the example of the devoted and godly life of the one now sleeping, and that special help and strength might be found by many through reading her published writings. "Grant especially," he prayed, "to bless those writings which she has sent forth to the four corners of the earth, that the world may hear the message in the many languages into which her books have been translated. We thank Thee for those in China, in Korea, in Japan, in India, in Africa, and in the islands of the seas, who have been helped to a saving knowledge of truth by reading the writings of Thy servant. Bless also, we beseech Thee, those who have gone forth into these countries to carry the truth for this time. . . . O God, hasten the proclamation of this message to all the inhabitants of earth, that this generation may hear it and heed it, and the way be prepared for the coming of our blessed Saviour."

The Scripture reading, by Elder George B. Starr, comprised the following passages, some of which were read only in part: Ps. 116:15; Eccl. 7:2, 4; Rom. 8:35, 37-39; John 6:39, 40; Dan. 12:2, 3; Rev. 14:12, 13; Eze. 37:12-14; Isa. 26:19; Rev. 7:9-17; Rev. 21:4. The reading closed with a few verses especially illustrative of Mrs. White's life experience: Ps. 40:9, 10 and Mark 14:8.

Elder J. N. Loughborough, venerable with many years of Christian service, yet wonderfully sustained by God as a living witness of manifold providences in the rise and progress of the advent movement, was the first speaker. He bore a loving tribute to the life work of the one with whom he had so often labored in close association since the year 1852. His discourse, largely reminiscent, served the purpose of a biographical sketch, though it was far more than a mere sketch, revealing, as it did, the special workings of the Holy Spirit in connection with her labors. He emphasized anew the fact that her published works tend to the purest morality, lead to Christ and to the Bible, and bring rest and comfort to weary and sorrowing hearts.

Elder Starr, the next speaker, referred to some personal phases of Mrs. White's life. "I have never heard any other person," he said, "speak of love for

Jesus, as I have heard her speak. Many times have I heard her exclaim, 'I love Him, I *love* Him, I LOVE Him!' Her entire life was devoted to winning others to love Him and serve Him with all the heart. . . .

"I regarded her as one of the strongest characters I ever met. I can compare her life only to the sturdy oak that meets the wind and bears its severest pressure, or to the mountain that laughs at the storm. . . . Her faith in God was invincible. Under trials that might have swept away the faith of many, she maintained firm confidence, and triumphed."

"In bidding her good-by two weeks ago to-day," Elder Starr continued, "I said, 'We are glad to find you so bright this morning.' Sister White replied, 'I am glad you find me thus, and I wish to tell you it is bright inside.' And then she added, 'I have not had many mournful days, have I?' 'No, Sister White,' I said, 'not in all your life, because you have risen above them.' 'Yes,' she responded, 'my heavenly Father has planned it all for me, and He knows when it will end, and I am determined not to murmur.'

"Then I said to her, 'I can only repeat to you, Sister White, what you wrote us in one of your last letters. You said: "The shadows are lengthening, and we are nearing home. We shall soon be at home, and then we will talk it all over together in the kingdom of God."' She replied, 'Yes; it seems almost too good to be true, but it is true.'"

"Passed away from earth forever,
  Free from all its cares and fears,
She again will join us never,
  While we tread this vale of tears,"

the first lines of the second hymn, affected deeply many in the listening congregation. Years ago these lines were penned by one of Mrs. White's associates in the Master's service, the late Elder Uriah Smith. Sad are the partings of this life;

"But a glorious day is nearing,
Earth's long-wished-for jubilee,
When creation's King, appearing,
Shall proclaim His people free;
When, upborne on Love's bright pinion,
They shall shout from land and sea,
'Death, where is thy dark dominion!
Grave, where is thy victory!' "

Elder E. W. Farnsworth, who had charge of the service, spoke as follows:

"It seems, brethren and friends, almost impossible for any one to think of preaching a sermon, a memorial sermon, commemorative of one whose life and labors have been a constant living sermon for nearly fourscore years. Seventy-eight years ago this summer, Sister White gave her heart to God; and during all those years, there has scarcely been any cessation or interruption in most ardent and earnest labor for the Master, and her life and what it represents in literature is the greatest eulogy that could possibly be pronounced on her funeral occasion.

"I have wondered what Sister White herself would say if she were here alive, and one of us were in her place. I am certain of some things that she would say. I think she would read, for the benefit of her friends and relatives and neighbors and others who are congregated here, this passage:

" 'For the grace of God that bringeth salvation hath appeared to all men'— and I venture to say that no living person in this generation has ever held up more insistently the grace of God for the salvation of men than has she —'teaching us that, denying ungodliness and worldly lusts, we should live soberly, righteously, and godly, in this present world.'

"She would speak to her neighbors and friends along that line, but she would not stop there. This afternoon she would add, 'Looking for that blessed hope, and the glorious appearing of the great God and our Saviour Jesus Christ.' She would emphasize that. She would press it home upon all our hearts and all our minds. Not only that, in a general way; but she would emphasize the fact, the great truth, that that blessed hope is soon to be consummated. She would lift our hearts and our minds up to that blessed hope which was her hope, and her joy, and her inspiration. I should like to echo that voice here this afternoon, brethren and friends and neighbors. I am sure that is the message she would give. But she is at rest.

"Somehow I am impressed that there is a present fulfillment of that passage in the fifteenth chapter of 1 Corinthians, where it says, 'The sting of death is sin.' Let me read it to you. It is this: 'For if the dead rise not, then is not Christ raised: and if Christ be not raised, your faith is vain; ye are yet in your sins. Then they also which are fallen asleep in Christ are perished.' And she would read further: 'Then shall be brought to pass the saying that is written, Death is swallowed up in victory. O death, where is thy sting? O grave, where is thy victory?'

"The thought I have in mind is this,—that there is a certain sense in which the sting is taken out of death here and now, brethren. [Hearty amens.] Our natural affections, the love of our hearts, will force the tears from our eyes, and we cannot help it; but back of it all, brethren, there is the consolation that sin has gone from this one, and hence the sting of sin has been extracted, and death cannot hold such a person a great while. [Many amens.]

"We read in one place of Jesus that it was not possible that He should be holden of death. Why? — Because there was no sin there. Where righteousness reigns and sin is gone, death has lost its grip. The subject may sleep in the grave for a little, but death cannot hold him there very long. The day of deliverance draws near. Soon the trumpet will sound, and, thank the Lord, we shall see Sister White again.

"I say to the family and friends, I am a mourner with you to-day; but there is something about a righteous life in Christ which robs death of its terrors, and the grave of all its woe. Jesus has been there, and we may safely walk the path which Jesus trod. So, brethren, let us look up. Let us look beyond this present vale of tears and sorrow to a brighter and an eternal hope and life, for Jesus' sake, amen."

With the singing of one of the hymns best loved by Mrs. White, "We shall meet beyond the river," and the pronouncement of a benediction by Elder S. T. Hare, the service closed.

LX

THE MEMORIAL SERVICE AT RICHMOND

By special request of the officers of the Pacific Union Conference and of the California Conference of Seventh-day Adventists, a memorial service was held at Richmond, Cal., the day following the funeral of Mrs. White at "Elmshaven."

It was not difficult to arrange for such a service, as the annual camp meeting of the California Conference was in progress at Richmond, and this city is on the main line of railway travel from the Pacific coast to the East, where the body was to be taken for interment in the family burial plot. Accordingly, announcements were sent out to the larger churches close by, and on the morning of July 19 fully a thousand friends from the cities surrounding San Francisco Bay and from more distant points, assembled at the Richmond encampment.

Elder E. E. Andross, president of the Pacific Union Conference, was in charge, assisted by Elder E. W. Farnsworth, vice president of the Union; Elder J. N. Loughborough, an honored pioneer of the advent movement; and Elder A. O. Tait, editor of the *Signs of the Times*.[1]

The opening hymn, "Sweet be thy rest," and the Scripture reading by Elder E. W. Farnsworth (1 Cor. 15:12-20, 35-38, 42-45; 2 Cor. 4:6-18; 5:1-10), prepared the minds of the congregation to enter into the spirit of Elder Loughborough's invocation, in the course of which he acknowledged that "while afflic-

---

[1] The pallbearers were Elder **J. L.** McElhany, president of the California Conference; and Elders A. Brorsen, E. J. Hibbard, G. W. Reaser, W. M. Healey, and C. E. Ford. The singers were Brethren D. Lawrence, C. A. Shull, J. H. Paap, and E. Lloyd.

tions come upon us, and while workers in this cause may lay down the armor because of lack of physical strength,'' yet God's purpose will be accomplished. When the Saviour was laid away, it was thought by His disciples that His work on earth was at an end; but His death on the cross was in reality the very life of the cause He had advocated.

A carefully prepared biographical sketch, written by Elder M. C. Wilcox, of the Pacific Press Publishing Association, was read by an associate, Elder A. O. Tait, because of Elder Wilcox's absence in the East. In the introductory paragraphs the principle was set forth that ''God makes much of individuals. All the great movements, awakenings, and crises of the centuries have centered around individuals, so that the story of the lives of these persons must include the history of God's work in the world, or the history of the crises or movements.'' Citing the biographies of Noah, of Abraham and other Hebrew worthies, of Wycliffe and Luther and the Wesleys, the writer continued:

''And in the advent movement, the giving to the world of the last message of reform, there are two persons whose biographies must include the beginning and the establishment of the movement and its worldwide growth. Nay, more, God's hand through them will affect it to the end. I refer to Elder James White and his beloved wife, Mrs. Ellen G. White.''

In this review of Mrs. White's life history, as read at Richmond, her labors on the Pacific coast were outlined thus:

''The work in California had been inaugurated by Elders J. N. Loughborough and D. T. Bourdeau in the summer of 1868. In the autumn of 1872 Elder and

Mrs. White visited San Francisco, Santa Rosa, Woodland, Healdsburg, and Petaluma. Here her messages were received by earnest souls, and her labors were greatly appreciated.

"In February, 1873, Brother and Sister White went to Michigan, returning to California in December of that year to take up new and greater burdens and start new enterprises. In 1874 they assisted in two tent meetings held in Oakland. Here Mrs. White spoke with telling effect on the temperance question, in a local option campaign.

"It was at this time that publishing work was begun in Oakland, the first issue of the *Signs of the Times* being dated June 4, 1874. In 1875 the Pacific Press Publishing Company was organized, with capital stock first at $28,000. This corporation is now continued in the Pacific Press Publishing Association, with a present worth of nearly $250,000, and a yearly output of over a million dollars in religious and educational literature.

"God revealed to Mrs. White that a great work would be done upon the Pacific coast and in the cities around the bay. This began to materialize very early; for church buildings were erected in Oakland and San Francisco in 1875 and 1876. In helping to build these churches, Mr. and Mrs. White sold all they had in the East.

"Mrs. White was intimately connected with the starting of the college at Healdsburg, from which laborers have gone forth to all parts of the world. That school is now continued in Pacific Union College, near St. Helena, which has also received her hearty support.

"Having borne a great burden in the building up of the Battle Creek Sanitarium, Elder and Mrs. White took special pleasure in encouraging a like work in

California, which resulted in the development of the St. Helena Sanitarium — started as the Rural Health Retreat. A lifelong physical sufferer, Mrs. White's sympathies have ever been drawn out to the afflicted. In connection with three other medical missionary enterprises in California,— at Paradise Valley, near San Diego; at Glendale, near Los Angeles; and at Loma Linda,— Mrs. White has borne heroic burdens and rendered great assistance. This is especially true of the College of Medical Evangelists at Loma Linda.

"In 1878 she visited Oregon. Here she attended Oregon's first camp meeting, at Salem. . . .

"Her life was a life of sacrifice. In poverty, in ill health, in sickness herself and with family ill, laboring with her hands in connection with her husband, economizing to barest necessities of existence, ministering to others hope and cheer under greatest discouragement herself, she more than measured the span of her days in arduous self-denial and self-forgetfulness for others' sake. She has given away many times over what would have kept her in ease. Her appeals to others have been to do, do, do, for God and humanity; but in this she has been greatly blessed of God. Coming down to death's door many times, life despaired of by friends, given up to die again and again by physicians, she has been repeatedly and miraculously restored to health.

"Mrs. White ceased her work here as she began — poor in this world's goods. Her income from her books — no inconsiderable sum — has been used freely in giving assistance to needy enterprises and needy people. Her heart has always been sympathetic, and her own hands have often ministered to the sick and suffering. . . .

"The life of Mrs. White lives after her. Enemies she has made by her straightforward teaching and reproof. She has been maligned and slandered. Those who know her best, can best judge her life. She was human, subject to all the infirmities and weaknesses of the race; but she found in Christ a precious Saviour and Helper. He called her to do a most unpopular work, and she responded. He has used her mightily. She has truly been a mother in Israel.

"Our blessed Lord voiced the calmest judgment of the human heart when He said that a tree is known by its fruits. In the light of this, the life of our sister, and its blessed influence upon all whose lives it has touched, are a witness of her character and work. She 'being dead yet speaketh.'"

For the discourse that followed the reading of the biographical sketch, Elder E. E. Andross chose as his text the words: "Blessed are the dead which die in the Lord from henceforth: Yea, saith the Spirit, that they may rest from their labors; and their works do follow them."

"Of no one," the speaker declared, "can it be said more truly than of our dear sister, that this scripture is fulfilled; still, under circumstances such as these, our hearts cry out for the glorious morning of the resurrection. We want to know that death is to be destroyed, that the sleepers are to awake. However blessed the life that has gone out, we want to know that the loved one will rise again to glorious immortality. And the Lord has not left us to mourn as those who have no hope. 'I will ransom them from the power of the grave,' the prophet writes; 'I will redeem them from death: O death, I will be thy plagues; O grave, I will be thy destruction.' Blessed words! . . .

"Again, I read the words of the prophet Isaiah, as recorded in the twenty-sixth chapter: 'Thy dead men shall live, together with My dead body shall they arise. Awake and sing, ye that dwell in dust: for thy dew is as the dew of herbs, and the earth shall cast out the dead.' Death is eventually to be destroyed, and the sleepers are to awake. . . .

"So to-day, my dear brethren, and especially those who mourn most deeply upon this occasion,— members of the family,— I say to you, We are not to sorrow as those who have no hope. Our sister, after seventy years and more of earnest, faithful toil for the Master, has now lain down to rest in the last sleep; but soon she is to rise again. 'The Lord Himself shall descend from heaven with a shout, with the voice of the Archangel, and with the trump of God.' She will hear His voice, and come forth. . . . O, let us, like our beloved sister, 'follow the Lamb whithersoever He goeth.' And when, in a little while, our labors are ended, like the great apostle we may say, We have fought a good fight, we have finished the course, we have kept the faith."

With the singing of a hymn, and with dismissal by Elder E. W. Farnsworth, the Richmond memorial service closed.

LXI

THE FUNERAL SERVICES AT BATTLE CREEK

On Sabbath day, July 24, 1915, Mrs. White was laid to rest by the side of her husband, the late Elder James White, in the Oak Hill Cemetery, Battle Creek, Mich., there to await the summons of the Life-giver.

IN THE TABERNACLE

Many friends had come in from the cities and towns near by, to unite with the members of the Battle Creek church and with the citizens there in paying a tribute of respect and love to the memory of the one who had been called to rest. A considerable number, also, had come in from adjoining states, including the presidents and other executive officers of local conferences, of the Lake Union Conference, of the North American Division Conference, and of the General Conference of Seventh-day Adventists.

The setting for the funeral was fitting and impressive. The service was held in the great Tabernacle, to the building of which a whole people contributed nearly two score of years before, and in which Mrs. White had many times spoken the words of life. The floral tributes were such as to form a garden-like bower of beauty. The friends at the Battle Creek Sanitarium had sent a wealth of potted palms, ferns, lilies, and marguerites, almost covering the rostrum, and extending to left and right up the gallery stairs. Many floral pieces had been contributed, symbolical of the occasion and of the hope beyond. The church at Battle Creek presented a broken wheel, the Review and Herald Publishing Association a broken column, the General Conference and the North American Division Conference a cross and a crown, and the Pacific Press Publishing Association an open Bible, on the pages of which stood forth the Saviour's promise, "Behold, I come quickly; and My reward is with Me."

For two hours preceding the service the body lay in state in front of the rostrum. Guards of honor[1] stood by, while thousands passed to look upon the aged and worn servant of Jesus, sleeping her last sleep. In that long procession of humanity were men and women bowed down with the weight of years, who in their prime had often sat under the ministry of her whose loss from the ranks of workers in the cause of God they now mourned. Tears coursed down the cheeks of many a noble pioneer who for upwards of half a century had kept the faith once for all delivered to the saints, and who is still rejoicing in the hope of the final reward that awaits the faithful.

When the hour appointed for the service came, the Tabernacle, which seats nearly 3,500, was filled, with many standing; and it is estimated that 1,000 or more who could not enter turned away.

Among the members of Mrs. White's family present were both of her surviving sons — Elder James Edson White, of Marshall, Mich., and Elder W. C. White, of St. Helena, Cal.; Miss Sara McEnterfer, of St. Helena, Cal.; Mrs. Addie Walling MacPherson, a niece living in Suffern, N. Y.; Mrs. L. M. Hall, at one time a member of Mrs. White's household; and several others who in former years had been associated more or less closely with the deceased. Many hearts went out in deep

---

[1] There were six guards of honor, two serving at a time,— Elders C. S. Longacre, of Washington, D. C.; M. L. Andreasen, of Hutchinson, Minn.; W. A. Westworth, of Chicago, Ill.; E. A. Bristol, of Indianapolis, Ind.; L. H. Christian, of Chicago, Ill.; C. F. McVagh, of Grand Rapids, Mich.

sympathy for Mrs. Emma White, wife of Elder J. E. White, absent because of a rheumatic affliction which for the past two years has rendered her unable to leave home.

The service was impressive throughout. Singers,[2] pallbearers,[3] and ministers[4] ascended to the rostrum, kneeling for a few moments in silent prayer. Then the choir sang:

"Asleep in Jesus! Blessed sleep,
From which none ever wake to weep!
A calm and undisturbed repose,
Unbroken by the last of foes!

. . . .

"Asleep in Jesus! Soon to rise,
When the last trump shall rend the skies!
Then burst the fetters of the tomb,
And wake in full, immortal bloom!"

SCRIPTURE READING

"And I saw a new heaven and a new earth," read Elder F. M. Wilcox, of Washington, D. C. "Behold, the tabernacle of God is with men, and He will dwell with them, and they shall be His people, and God

---

[2] The singers were Mrs. H. M. Dunlap, Miss Florence Howell, Mrs. George R. Israel, Miss Nenna Dunlap, Prof. Frederick Griggs, Mr. M. H. Minier, Dr. M. A. Farnsworth, and Mr. Frank W. Hubbard.

[3] The pallbearers were Elders I. H. Evans, president of the North American Division Conference; W. T. Knox, treasurer of the General Conference; G. B. Thompson, secretary of the North American Division Conference; Prof. Frederick Griggs, educational secretary of the General Conference; F. M. Wilcox, editor of the *Advent Review and Sabbath Herald;* and G. E. Langdon, pastor of the Battle Creek Tabernacle church.

[4] The ministers were Elders A. G. Daniells, president of the General Conference of Seventh-day Adventists (in charge of the service); S. N. Haskell, of South Lancaster, Mass.; M. C. Wilcox, of Mountain View, Cal.; C. B. Stephenson, of Atlanta, Ga.; William Covert, of Aurora, Ill.; L. H. Christian, of Chicago, Ill. Elder George I. Butler, of Bowling Green, Fla., long a close associate of Elder and Mrs. James White in administrative affairs, had been invited by the General Conference to assist in the service, but was unable to be present.

Himself shall be with them, and be their God. And God shall wipe away all tears from their eyes; and there shall be no more death, neither sorrow, nor crying, neither shall there be any more pain: for the former things are passed away.'' The passages read from the visions of John on the isle of Patmos were Rev. 21:1-7; 22:1-5; and with these were linked the precious promises recorded in the thirty-fifth chapter of Isaiah's prophecy. ''The ransomed of the Lord shall return, and come to Zion with songs and everlasting joy upon their heads: they shall obtain joy and gladness, and sorrow and sighing shall flee away.''

THE PRAYER

Elder M. C. Wilcox, of Mountain View, Cal., petitioned the throne of grace:

''Gracious God, our heavenly Father, we are glad that there is no trial of earth so great but that Thou hast comfort and strength for Thy children. We are glad that we can come to Thee this morning and know that Thou art our Father; glad for the great love wherewith Thou dost love us even in our sinful, mortal condition, not because we are lovable, but because Thou art love.

''We thank Thee for the gift of Thine only-begotten Son; that He died in our behalf, and that in Him Thou canst take such unworthy mortals as we are, and fit them for the glorious inheritance of which we have been hearing.

''We thank Thee that Thy power is so great that Thou canst subdue and conquer all in us that is unlovely; that Thou canst take the poor, base alloys of our human nature, and make them the genuine gold of God.

"We thank Thee for all the precious promises and assurances of Thy word; for all its faithful warnings; for all its holy precepts; for the blessed hope of our Lord's coming which lies just before us, when He shall take this earth and change it by His own power for an everlasting home for all His children.

"We thank Thee, our Father, for what Thou hast done for us in this last great gospel movement. We thank Thee for the work Thou hast wrought through Thy handmaid, our sister, who lies before us this morning; for all the counsel and instruction Thou hast given by her; for all the work Thou hast wrought through her; for the institutions she has helped to establish; for the mighty message she has borne.

"And while our hearts are inexpressibly sad this morning, our Father, still we praise Thee for what Thou hast done in taking poor, feeble humanity and making such an instrument for the building up of Thy work.

"Come near to the hearts that are torn this morning. Pour into them the balm of Thy Spirit, of Thy healing goodness. Fill all the vacancies that are made by death, with Thine own precious presence. Help them that mourn, to look beyond this time to the glorious morning which lies just before us, when the Lord Jesus Christ shall heal every wound that sin has made, shall comfort every heart that trusts in Him, and shall make all things eternally new.

"We pray that Thou wouldst help us to learn the lesson of the brevity of human life; of the necessity of giving ourselves to Thee; of the great encouragement Thou dost give us, in this life that has just closed, as to what Thou wilt do for those who lend themselves to Thy service.

"We know that our sister is safe. We can leave her with Thee. Thou wilt speak in a little while, and the dead will come forth to immortality. But we pray for the living. We pray for those who are left to meet the struggles and the trials and the conflicts of these last days. How weak we are—how utterly incapable of meeting any of these things! Our hope this hour is in Thee. And we pray that the great God who has called us will fit us for His service; will nerve us for stronger effort; will give us firmer faith, more diligence, and greater grace to meet the trials and the conflicts; that He will save us from all the deceptions and allurements and snares of the enemy; that He will give us a clearer vision to see what God would have each and all to be and to do; and that He will give us speedy triumph at last at the coming of our Lord.

"And so, Father, on this sad day, we leave these things in Thy hands, and pray that the great God who has guided, who has been with us, will guide every step of the way; guide us out of all the wilderness of doubt and trial; guide us to the land of perfect day, where there will be no more sin, no more sorrow, and where we shall bask in the smiles of our blessed Redeemer, who has conquered sin and therefore is victor over death. And grant, O our Father, that in that great day, those assembled here may be among the number who shall live forever with the good who have gone and those who shall remain until Thy coming. We ask it all in Jesus' name. Amen."

ADDRESS BY ELDER DANIELLS

A solo, "Rest for the Toiling Hand," rendered by Professor Griggs, was followed by an address from the president of the General Conference, Elder A. G. Daniells. The speaker traced briefly yet clearly the early life and Christian experience of Mrs. White, and also her late labors. The first portion of his address served the purpose of a biographical sketch, and also formed a basis for the main line of thought running throughout; namely, that in very truth God has been bestowing upon the remnant church the precious gift of the spirit of prophecy.

Regarding Mrs. White's call early in life to special ministry for God, and the fruits that have characterized this ministry, Elder Daniells said:

"Taking the Bible as the supreme guide of her life, she became fully convinced, by its teaching, that the second coming of Christ was near at hand. On this point she never wavered, and, believing it with her whole soul, she felt that the one supreme purpose of every individual at this time should be to live a blameless life in Christ, and to devote every resource at command to the salvation of the lost.

"This view led her to unceasing prayer for the indwelling presence of the Holy Spirit. Her yearning for this divine presence was answered beyond all that she had conceived. . . . Her life of full surrender, obedience, and prayer for divine help was rewarded by the bestowal of the gift of prophecy, one of the choicest of all the gifts of the Spirit.

"In December, 1844, the Holy Spirit gave her a revelation of the second coming of Christ. In this vision of the future there was given a view of the glorious reward that awaits the redeemed and the terrible fate that will come to all who refuse to serve their Lord and Master. This view of the destiny of the human family made a profound impression upon her heart. Here she received her appointment as a messenger of God. She felt that God was commanding her to give this message of light and salvation to others.

"This was a great trial to her. She was but seventeen years old, small, frail, and retiring; but after a long, severe struggle, she surrendered to the call of her Lord, and then courage and strength were given her to enter upon her life work.

"Following this surrender and victory there came to her a series of remarkable spiritual experiences, unmistakably genuine, and regarded by her associate workers of that day as a manifestation of the gift of prophecy promised by Christ to the remnant church. Those who have been associated with her through all the years that have passed since that time have never had occasion to alter their conviction that the revelations which have come to her through the years have come from God.

"The late Uriah Smith, a lifelong associate in this work with both Elder and Mrs. White, left the following testimony to this gift as manifested in her teachings:

" 'Every test which can be brought to bear upon such manifestations, proves them genuine. The evidence which supports them, internal and external, is conclusive. They agree with the word of God, and with themselves. They are given, unless those best qualified to judge are invariably deceived, when the Spirit of God is especially present. Calm, dignified, impressive, they commend themselves to every beholder, as the very opposite of that which is false or fanatical.

" 'Their fruit is such as to show that the source from which they spring is the opposite of evil.

" '1. They tend to the purest morality. They discountenance every vice, and exhort to the practice of every virtue. They point out the perils through which we are to pass to the kingdom. They reveal the devices of Satan. They warn us against his snares. They have nipped in the bud scheme after scheme of fanaticism which the enemy has tried to foist into our midst. They have exposed hidden iniquity, brought to light concealed wrongs, and laid bare the evil motives of the false-hearted. They have warded off dangers from the cause of truth upon every hand. They have aroused and re-aroused us to greater consecration to God, more zealous efforts for holiness of heart, and greater diligence in the cause and service of our Master.

" '2. They lead us to Christ. Like the Bible, they set Him forth as the only hope and only Saviour of mankind. They portray before us in living characters His holy life and His godly example, and with irresistible appeals they urge us to follow in His steps.

" '3. They lead us to the Bible. They set forth that book as the inspired and unalterable word of God. They exhort us to take that Word as the man of our counsel, and the rule of our faith and practice. And with a compelling power, they entreat us to study long and diligently its pages, and become familiar with its teaching, for it is to judge us in the last day.

" '4. They have brought comfort and consolation to many hearts. They have strengthened the weak, encouraged the feeble, raised up the despondent. They have brought order out of confusion, made crooked places straight, and thrown light on what was dark and obscure.'

"August 30, 1846, Miss Harmon was married to James White, a native of Palmyra, Somerset County, Maine. From the time of their marriage, Mrs. White's life was closely linked with that of her husband in strenuous gospel work until his death, August 6, 1881. They traveled extensively over the United States, preaching and writing, planting and building, organizing and administering. Time and test have proved how broad and firm were the foundations they laid, and how wisely and well they built.

"The views held and widely promulgated by Mrs. White regarding vital fundamental questions — the sovereignty of God, the divinity of Christ, the efficacy of the gospel, the inspiration of the Scriptures, the majesty of the law, the character of sin and deliverance from its power, the brotherhood of man and the relationships and responsibilities in that brotherhood — her teaching regarding these great questions, and her life of devotion to her Lord and of service to her fellow men, were made impressive through the revelations given her by the divine Spirit. They are the fruits of that Spirit — the fruits by which her life work is to be judged. They must determine the source and the character of the Spirit that has dominated her whole life. 'By their fruits ye shall know them.' 'To the law and to the testimony: if they speak not according to this word, it is because there is no light in them.'

"This question is not involved in any uncertainty whatever. Her teaching is clear, and the influence of her life has been positive.

"No Christian teacher in this generation, no religious reformer in any preceding age, has placed a higher value upon the Bible. In all her writings it is represented as the book of all books, the supreme and all-sufficient guide for the whole human family. Not a trace of 'higher criticism,' 'new thought,' nor skeptical, destructive philosophy can be found in any of her writings. Those who still believe that the Bible is the inspired, infallible word of the living God will value most highly the positive, uncompromising support given this view in the writings of Mrs. White.

"In her teaching, Christ is recognized and exalted as the only Saviour of sinners. Emphasis is placed upon the bold and unqualified announcement of the disciples that 'there is none other name under heaven given among men, whereby we must be saved.' The power to redeem from sin and its effect is in Him alone, and to Him all men are directed.

"Her writings hold firmly to the doctrine that the gospel, as revealed in the sacred Scriptures, presents the only means of salvation. No recognition whatever is given to any of the philosophies of India or the ethical codes of Burma and China as compared with the gospel of the Son of God. This alone is the hope of a lost world.

"The Holy Spirit, Christ's representative on earth, is set forth and exalted as the heavenly teacher and guide sent to this world by our Lord at His ascension, to make *real* in the hearts and lives of men all that He had made *possible* by His death on the cross. The gifts of this divine Spirit, as enumerated in the Gospels and Epistles of the New Testament, are acknowledged, prayed for, and received as fully as the Spirit sees fit to impart them.

"The church instituted by our Lord and built up by His disciples in the first century is set forth as the divine model. Its prerogatives and authority are fully acknowledged, and all its ordinances and memorials are observed. Strong emphasis is placed upon the value of gospel order and organization, as revealed in the Scriptures, for the efficiency of the church in all its world-wide operations.

"Through the light and counsel given her, Mrs. White held and advocated broad, progressive views regarding vital questions that affect the betterment and uplift of the human family, from the moral, intellectual, physical, and social standpoint as well as the spiritual. Her writings are full of instruction, clear and positive, in behalf of a broad, practical, Christian education for every young man and young woman. In response to her earnest counsels, the denomination with which she was associated now maintains a system of education for all its children and young people.

"Her writings present most comprehensive views regarding temperance reform, the laws of life and health, and the use of rational, effective remedies for the treatment of disease. The adoption of these principles has placed the people with whom she worked, in the front ranks with others who are advocating sane temperance reforms and working for the physical improvement of mankind.

"Nor is the social status of the human family lost sight of. Slavery, the caste system, unjust racial prejudices, the oppression of the poor, the neglect of the unfortunate,— these all are set forth as unchristian and a serious menace to the well-being of the human race, and as evils which the church of Christ is appointed by her Lord to overthrow.

"In the writings of Mrs. White prominence is given to the responsibilities of the church in both home and foreign mission service. Every member of the body is admonished to be a light in the world, a blessing to those with whom he may associate. All must live the unselfish life of the Master for others. And the church in Christian lands must put forth their highest endeavors to evangelize those who are groping in the darkness and superstition of heathen lands. Go to all the world, give to all the world, work for all the world, is the exhortation running through all the writings of Mrs. White, as the following quotation will illustrate:

" 'Let the members of the church have increased faith, gaining zeal from their unseen, heavenly allies, from a knowledge of their exhaustless resources, from the greatness of the enterprise in which they are engaged, and from the power of their Leader. Those who place themselves under God's control, to be led and guided by Him, will catch the steady tread of the events ordained by Him to take place. Inspired by the Spirit of Him who gave His life for the life of the world, they will no longer stand still in impotency, pointing to what they cannot do. Putting on the armor of heaven, they will go forth to the warfare, willing to do and dare for God, knowing that His omnipotence will supply their need.'

"Thus for fully seventy years she gave her life in active service to the cause of God in behalf of sinful, suffering, sorrowing humanity. After traveling extensively through the United States from 1846 to 1885, she visited Europe, where she devoted two years to the work there, which was then in a formative period. In 1891 she went to Australia, where she remained nine years, traveling about the colonies, and devoting all her energies to the upbuilding of the work.

"On returning to the United States in 1900, at the age of seventy-three, she seemed to feel that her duty to travel was about done, and that she should devote the rest of her life to writing. Thus she toiled on until within a short time of her death, at the ripe age of almost eighty-eight years.

"Perhaps we are not wise enough to say definitely just what part of Mrs. White's life work has been of the greatest value to the world, but it would seem that the large volume of Biblical literature she has left would prove to be of the greatest service to mankind. Her books number upwards of twenty volumes. Some of these have been translated into many languages in different parts of the world. They have now reached a circulation of more than two million copies, and are still going to the public by thousands.

"As we survey the whole field of gospel truth — of man's relation to his Lord and his fellow men — it must be seen that Mrs. White, in all her teaching, has given these great fundamentals positive, constructive support. She has touched humanity at every vital point of need, and lifted it to a higher level.

"Now she is at rest. Her voice is silent; her pen is laid aside. But the mighty influence of that active, forceful, Spirit-filled life will continue. That life was linked with the Eternal; it was wrought in God. The message proclaimed and the work done constitute a monument that will never crumble nor perish. The many volumes she has left, dealing with every phase of human life, urging every reform necessary to the betterment of society as represented by the family, city, state, and nation, will continue to mould public sentiment and individual character. Their messages will be cherished more than they have been in the past. The cause to which her life was devoted, and which that life influenced and advanced to so great a degree, will press forward with increasing force and rapidity as the years go by. We who are connected with it need entertain no fear except the fear of our own failure to do our part as faithfully and loyally as we should."

DISCOURSE BY ELDER HASKELL

In his discourse following Elder Daniells's address, Elder S. N. Haskell called attention to the words of the psalmist, "Precious in the sight of the Lord is the death of His saints." Ps. 116:15. Some may regard this as a strange statement; it is nevertheless true. The servants of God who are now sleeping, are to Him exceeding precious. So long as time shall last, the influence of their godly life will continue to yield rich fruitage. No longer can the enemy of the human race imperil their welfare; they are safe from his power. Jesus claims them as His own, and on the morning of the resurrection He will bestow upon them fullness of joy.

In one of the glorious visions given John the beloved on the isle of Patmos, the prophet's attention was arrested by "a voice from heaven" bidding him write: "Blessed are the dead which die in the Lord from henceforth: Yea, saith the Spirit, that they may rest from their labors; and their works do follow them." Rev. 14:13. Wonderful words these, and especially when considered in the light of their setting at the close of the prophecy concerning a threefold message to be sounded preparatory to the end of the world and the second advent of Christ.

Heaven seemed desirous of helping us to understand that at the time of the end, when these messages are proclaimed in the power of the Holy Spirit, some of those engaged in this work will be permitted to rest from their labors. All such, we are assured, are accounted blessed of God. Nor are their unceasing efforts to bear aloft the banner of truth, without result; "their works do follow them." To-day, in the light of this assurance direct from heaven to the children of men, we can say of our dear sister who now sleeps, that she "being dead yet speaketh." Heb. 11:4.

Elder Haskell reviewed the experience of the believers at Thessalonica who were early called upon to suffer cruel persecutions, even unto death. The apostle Paul, in his first epistle to the sorrowing ones there, comforts them with the certainty of the Christian's hope. "Sorrow not, even as others which have no hope," he exhorts; "for if we believe that Jesus died and rose again, even so them also which sleep in Jesus will God bring with Him. For this we say unto you by the word of the Lord, that we which are alive and remain unto the coming of the Lord shall not prevent [go before] them which are asleep. For the Lord Himself shall descend from heaven with a shout, with the voice of the Archangel, and with the trump of God: and the dead in Christ shall rise first: then we which are alive and remain shall be caught up together with them in the clouds, to meet the Lord in the air: and so shall we ever be with the Lord. Wherefore comfort one another with these words." 1 Thess. 4:13-18.

The speaker invited attention to the expression, "For if we believe that Jesus died and rose again, even so"— even as Christ was raised from the dead — "them also which sleep in Jesus will God bring with Him," and he illustrated this by the experience of Mary at the rent sepulcher. Bitterly disappointed in not finding her Lord, "Mary stood without at the sepulcher weeping: and as she wept, she stooped down, and looked into the sepulcher, and seeth two angels in white sitting, the one at the head, and the other at the feet, where the body of Jesus had lain. And they say unto her, Woman, why weepest thou? She saith unto them, Because they have taken away my Lord, and I know not where they have laid Him." Her heart cried out after her Saviour, and at that very moment He was by her side, though she recognized Him not. "Jesus saith unto her, Woman, why weepest thou? whom seekest thou? She, supposing Him to be the gardener, saith unto Him, Sir, if Thou have borne Him hence, tell me where Thou hast laid Him, and I will take Him away.

"Jesus saith unto her, Mary." That is all He said—"Mary." Many a time she had heard that familiar voice, and she must have recognized Jesus by His tone or expression, for immediately she acknowledged Him as her Master and Lord. "Touch Me not," He said to her; "for I am not yet ascended to My Father: but go to My brethren, and say unto them, I ascend unto My Father, and your Father; and to My God, and your God." John 20:11-17. Then it was that Mary hastened to the disciples with the glad tidings of a risen Saviour.

"It was her love for the Master," the speaker continued, "because of what He had done for her in forgiving her sins and in connecting her soul with heaven, that kept the Saviour on earth after His resurrection until He had made Himself known to her. There is something very touching in this narrative. It shows that the Saviour is willing to reveal Himself to those who are devoted to Him and to His service,—those who desire above all things else to maintain a living connection with heaven. As Mary recognized her Lord after His resurrection by His voice and His general demeanor, so I believe we shall be able to recognize again our sister who now sleeps. While we cannot hear her voice in this world any more, yet her influence lives; and in the resurrection morning, if we remain faithful, and have a part with the people of God in that glad hour, we shall hear her voice once more, and we shall recognize her. My dear friends, there is a living connection between heaven and this earth still, and the promises the Lord has made to His people will be verified. Not one word will fail of fulfillment. May the Lord help us all to be among those who shall meet their Lord in peace, and who shall have the privilege of greeting our sister in the kingdom of heaven. May God grant it for His name's sake."

The hymn, "We shall meet beyond the river," and benediction by Elder W. T. Knox, closed the Tabernacle service. Carriages and cars were in waiting, and these conveyed many hundreds to the burial place in Oak Hill Cemetery.

AT THE GRAVE

Half a century had passed since Mrs. White and her husband buried their youngest child and soon afterward their first-born in the beautiful spot where now she herself was to rest. When in 1881 Elder James White was laid beside the children, little did his bereaved companion think that the Lord would strengthen her to continue in ministry for a full third of a century. Yet such had been the case; and now, her labors ended, she was to rest by the side of her loved ones.

Elder I. H. Evans read the story of the raising of Lazarus from the dead, as recorded in the eleventh chapter of John. Jesus has declared: "I am the resurrection, and the life: he that believeth in Me, though he were dead, yet shall he live: and whosoever liveth and believeth in Me shall never die." Elder Evans also read, from the apostle Paul's inspired testimony in 1 Corinthians 15, many positive and comforting assurances concerning the resurrection of the righteous. "If there be no resurrection of the dead, then is Christ not risen: and if Christ be not risen, then is our preaching vain, and your faith is also vain." "If in this life only we have hope in Christ, we are of all men most miserable. But now is Christ risen from the dead, and become the first fruits of them that slept." "In Christ shall all be made alive." "Death is swallowed up in victory. O death, where is thy sting? O grave, where is thy victory?" "Thanks be to God, which giveth us the victory through our Lord Jesus Christ. Therefore, my beloved brethren, be ye steadfast, unmovable, always abounding in the work of the Lord, forasmuch as ye know that your labor is not in vain in the Lord."

"We may sleep, but not forever;
There will be a glorious dawn;
We shall meet to part, no, never,
On the resurrection morn.
From the deepest caves of ocean,
From the desert and the plain,
From the valley and the mountain,
Countless throngs shall rise again."